Minding Justice

Minding Justice

*Laws That Deprive People
with Mental Disability
of Life and Liberty*

Christopher Slobogin

Harvard University Press
Cambridge, Massachusetts
London, England
2006

Library of Congress Cataloging-in-Publication Data

Slobogin, Christoper, 1951–
Minding justice : laws that deprive people with mental disability of life and liberty /
Christopher Slobogin.
p.   cm.
Includes bibliographical references and index.
ISBN 0-674-02204-1 (alk. paper)
1. People with mental disabilities—Legal status, laws, etc.—United States.   2. Mentally ill
offenders—Legal status, laws, etc.—United States.   3. Insanity—Jurisprudence—United States.
4. Insane—Commitment and detention—United States.   I. Title.

KF480.S545 2006
346.7301'38—dc22   2005052800

To Alice and John,
my first clients

Contents

Preface

The title *Minding Justice* is meant to be a triple entendre. The first meaning is descriptive. As the subtitle makes clear, this book is about the state's legal authority to deprive of life or liberty those people whose problems we normally attribute to a malfunctioning mind. Thus, one goal of *Minding Justice* is to describe the wide array of statutes and judicial decisions that determine when government may incapacitate people with mental disability. These include laws dealing with the insanity defense, the death penalty, commitment of so-called sexual predators and others thought to be dangerous to others, and hospitalization of people considered unable to make rational decisions. In the course of discussing these legal doctrines and rules, the book also examines a number of well-known cases that illustrate how they work, including the cases of John Hinckley (the man who tried to assassinate President Ronald Reagan), Andrea Yates (the woman who drowned her five children), Leroy Hendricks (the child molester whose case revolutionized the law of civil commitment), Theodore Kaczynski (also known as the Unabomber), and Colin Ferguson (the man who was allowed, despite flagrant psychosis, to represent himself in his trial on charges of killing six people on the Long Island Railway).

The second meaning of *Minding Justice* is prescriptive: we should care about and analyze carefully the manner in which we deprive people with mental disability of life and liberty. The primary goal of this book is to advance new ways of thinking about this subject. The book argues for a complete revamping of the insanity defense, the abolition of the guilty but mentally ill verdict, and a prohibition on executing people with mental disability. It also proposes a revised "jurisprudence of dangerousness" that would have significant implications for sex offenders and all other individuals subject to police power commitment, including terrorists. Finally, it contends that the notion of "incompetency" needs rethinking, and suggests reforms that would change the law concerning the right to refuse treatment, competency to stand trial, and how courts deal with criminal defendants who disagree with their attorneys. As this brief listing indicates, the principles developed in this book apply not just to people with mental disability but to anyone subject to the criminal law, preventive detention, and involuntary treatment.

That leads to the third meaning of *Minding Justice*, the ironic meaning. More so than in any other area of legal regulation, including matters having to do with race and gender, modern society has been unwilling to treat people with mental illness in a just manner; it has truly "minded" even thinking about their problems. In describing laws that deprive them of life and liberty, and in prescribing reforms of those laws, this book always tries to keep in the foreground the repugnance our society feels toward people who suffer from mental disability and how it has affected the legal regime that governs them. It uses the somewhat cumbersome phrase "people with mental disability" (rather than "the mentally disabled") to emphasize that these are people first, people who happen to have as one of their characteristics a problem associated with the mind. Ultimately, it concludes that, at least in connection with deprivations of life and liberty, people with mental disability should generally be treated no differently than people who are not so labeled, a conclusion that stems in no small part from a desire to destigmatize this maltreated segment of society.

Numerous individuals gave me useful feedback on the ideas expressed in this book, including Richard Bonnie, James Ellis, Mark Fondacaro, John Monahan, Stephen Morse, Michael Perlin, Elyn Saks, and Robert Schopp. The following articles of mine are adapted with permission, in the rough order in which they influence the book: "Rethinking Deprivations of Liberty: Possible Contributions from Therapeutic and Ecological Jurisprudence," 48 *Behavioral Science & the Law* 499 (2000) (with Mark Fondacaro); "An End to Insanity," 86 *Virginia Law Review* 1199 (2000); "The Integrationist Alternative to the Insanity Defense: Reflections on the Exculpatory Scope of Mental Illness in the Wake of the Andrea Yates Trial," 30 *American Criminal Law Review* 315 (2003); "What Atkins Could Mean for People with Mental Illness," 33 *New Mexico Law Review* 293 (2003); "Is Atkins the Antithesis or Apotheosis of Anti-Discrimination Principles? Sorting out the Group-wide Effects of Exempting People with Mental Retardation from the Death

Penalty," 55 *Alabama Law Review* 1101 (2004); "Mental Illness and the Death Penalty," 24 *Mental & Physical Disability Law Reporter* 667 (2000); "The Guilty but Mentally Ill Verdict: An Idea Whose Time Should Not Have Come," 53 *George Washington Law Review* 494 (1985); "A Jurisprudence of Dangerousness," 98 *Northwestern University Law Review* 1 (2003); "The Civilization of Criminal Law," 58 *Vanderbilt Law Review* 121 (2005); "The Criminal Defense Lawyer's Fiduciary Duty to Clients with Mental Disability," 68 *Fordham Law Review* 1581 (2000) (with Amy Mashburn); "'Appreciation' as a Measure of Competency: Some Thoughts about the MacArthur Group's Approach," 2 *Psychology, Public Policy, & Law* 18 (1996); "Rethinking Legally Relevant Mental Disorder," 29 *Ohio Northern University Law Review* 497 (2003).

Two stylistic points. First, although the text speaks for itself, many of the points it makes are supplemented by material found in the notes at the end of the book. Those wishing to explore a particular issue further should be aware that the notes contain more than mere citations. Second, an apology: although I have endeavored to use gender neutral language throughout the book, frequently the usual methods of accomplishing that aim became too cumbersome. Please excuse the lapses.

Minding Justice

—1—

The Clinical and Legal Landscape

This book is an analysis of laws that society uses to deprive people with mental disability of life and liberty. The "life and liberty" language comes, of course, from the Fifth and Fourteenth Amendments to the U.S. Constitution, which together tell the federal and state governments that they may not "deprive any person of life, liberty or property, without due process of law." This book, then, is an exploration of the "process" that people with mental disability are "due" when the state intervenes in their life, with a particular emphasis on what lawyers call "substantive due process"—the rules that tell the state when it may confine or execute someone.

The title's reliance on Fifth and Fourteenth Amendment language should not lead the reader to conclude that this book's analysis is confined to constitutional doctrine and precedent, however. Rather, the book draws from a wide array of legal, philosophical, historical, and empirical materials in attempting to discern the most just methods of sanctioning, controlling, and protecting individuals with mental disorder. In other words, this effort is "pragmatic," a term legal scholars have recently begun using to refer to eclectic approaches to policy formation.

Before embarking on this pragmatic exploration, the focus of this book demands that two questions be addressed. First, what is meant by the term "mental disability" and similar labels? Definitional conundrums associated with the concept of mental disability are addressed throughout the book, but the first part of this chapter lays the groundwork by parsing various clinical approaches to the issue. Second, what are the laws that deprive people so labeled of life and liberty? The answer to this question requires an exposition of the analytical framework for this book, which is described in the second part of this chapter. The final part of the chapter follows up

1

with a more detailed description of the book's organization and thematic structure.

I. Mental Disability: A Socially Constructed Reality

It is a commonplace that "mental disability" and its semantic brethren, "mental illness" and "mental disorder," are not easily defined. The only thing we can say for sure about the concept is that it has continually expanded in scope. Stretched by new discoveries about the causes of human behavior, our society's willingness to call all sorts of quirky behavior and criminal conduct "sick," and—if one believes the cynics—the desire on the part of mental health professionals to be compensated by insurance companies for all their patients' problems, the term "mental disability" applies to a far wider array of phenomena than it did a century ago.

Consider the approach taken in the American Psychiatric Association's Diagnostic and Statistical Manual, the bible of psychiatric nosology known simply as the DSM (now in its fourth edition in a text-revised version, and thus known as DSM-IV-TR). The DSM states that a "mental disorder" is "a clinically significant behavioral or psychological syndrome or pattern that occurs in an individual and that is associated with present distress (e.g., a painful symptom) or disability (i.e., impairment in one or more important areas of functioning) or with a significantly increased risk of suffering death, pain, disability, or an important loss of freedom."[1] Although the DSM also states that the syndrome or pattern cannot be "an expectable and culturally sanctioned response to a particular event" (such as death of a loved one),[2] its definition of mental disorder ultimately imposes few limitations. Many have noted that terms such as "distress," "disability," "loss of freedom," and "expectable and culturally sanctioned" are hugely value-laden and still permit considerable leeway in defining specific disorders.[3] The drafters of the DSM admit as much, stating "that no definition adequately specifies precise boundaries for the concept of 'mental disorder.'"[4]

Undeterred by this admission, the drafters of the DSM have included in their listing of "mental disorders" an enormous number of syndromes and psychological patterns (more than three hundred in the fourth edition). In the approximate hierarchy likely to occur to a layperson asked to define "craziness," the major DSM categories might be organized as follows:

- Psychoses (for example, schizophrenia, manifested by hallucinations, delusions, or other evidence of very disorganized thinking).

- Dementias (involving a significant loss of consciousness and memory).
- Mood disorders (for example, the bipolar disorders, manifested by swings between severe depression and mania).
- Dissociative disorders (including dissociative identity disorder, formerly known as multiple personality disorder).
- Mental retardation (generally requiring an IQ of 70 or lower).
- Anxiety disorders (including post-traumatic stress disorder).
- Personality disorders, a large category that is meant to encompass "an enduring pattern of inner experience and behavior that deviates markedly from the expectations of the individual's culture," and that includes paranoid personality disorder; schizoid personality disorder (detachment from social relationships and a restricted range of emotional expression); schizotypal personality disorder (odd beliefs or magical thinking, unusual perceptual experiences including bodily illusions, and excessive social anxiety); antisocial personality disorder (disregard for, and violation of, the rights of others); borderline personality disorder (impulsivity and inappropriate, intense anger and transient paranoia or dissociation); histrionic personality disorder (excessive emotionality and attention seeking); narcissistic personality disorder (grandiosity, need for admiration, and lack of empathy); avoidant personality disorder (feelings of inadequacy and hypersensitivity to negative evaluation); dependent personality disorder (submissive and clinging behavior related to an excessive need to be taken care of); and obsessive-compulsive personality disorder (preoccupation with orderliness, perfectionism, and control).
- Sexual disorders (including pedophilia) and impulse disorders (including pyromania and kleptomania).
- Eating and sleeping disorders and disorders that feature exaggerated symptoms (somatoform and factitious disorders).
- Substance abuse disorders that do not result in dementia, including not just alcohol- and drug-related disorders, but also caffeine- and nicotine-related disorders.[5]

One can certainly dispute the ordering of this list. But its expansive scope, which overlaps with behaviors many of us experience at least to some degree,[6] cannot be denied.

Uncomfortable with that fact, some have tried to cabin the concept of mental disability in various ways. In doing so, they have focused on either the *effects*, the *process*, or the *cause* of the phenomenon to be labeled. One example of the effects approach is a proposal that would narrow the DSM's emphasis on distress and disability to conditions that impose a serious "biological disadvantage"—more specifically, death or reduced fertility.[7] As envisioned by R. E. Kendell in the 1970s, this threshold is said to encompass only the first three categories listed above, plus severe drug dependence and sexual disorders such as homosexuality.[8] A prominent illustration of the process approach is the equation of mental illness with "irrational" thought content.[9] Advocates of this approach contend that irrationality is most likely to be a feature of the first few symptom complexes listed above, although it could occasionally occur in connection with some of the other symptom patterns as well.[10] Finally, as an example of the etiological move, some mental health professionals believe that the term "mental illness" should be reserved for those problems that are biological in origin, leaving the term "mental disorder" to cover the rest.[11] The theory here is that organically caused disabilities, among which the psychoses are thought to be good examples, are more deserving of the (more serious?) illness rubric.

There are obvious problems with all these definitions. Using an increased chance of death and reduced fertility as markers of illness seems both under- and overinclusive: for instance, eating disorders and routine substance abuse (neither of which are considered illnesses under this approach) often hasten death and diminish sexual drive, while the psychoses (which are supposed to be illnesses on this view) do not necessarily shorten life or decrease procreative powers.[12] Perhaps, however, a critique of this definition need note nothing more than it classifies homosexuality as a mental illness. Irrationality probably comes closest to capturing the lay sense of "craziness." But it can be almost as difficult to operationalize as mental disorder itself, a claim explored more fully in several of the following chapters. And biology may well play a major role in causing *all* mental problems. As the drafters of the DSM state, "[a] compelling literature documents that there is much 'physical' in 'mental' disorders and much 'mental' in 'physical' disorders."[13] Eric Kandel summarizes the literature in this way: "[B]ehavioral disorders that characterize psychiatric illness are disturbances of the brain function, even in those cases where the causes of the disturbances are clearly environmental in origin."[14]

At the same time, as these last statements suggest, the image of mental disorder as simply the product of defective organs is wrong, a fact that further complicates matters. Kandel writes:

Social or developmental factors also contribute very importantly to behavior, including social behavior, so behavior and social factors can exert
actions on the brain by feeding back upon it to modify the expression of
genes and thus the function of nerve cells. Learning, including learning
that results in dysfunctional behavior, produces alterations in gene expression. Thus, all of "nurture" is ultimately expressed as "nature."[15]

The so-called medical (or biological) model of mental illness appears to be
ascendant at the present time, but developmental, learning/behavioral, and
social factors also significantly influence behavior and mental processes,
"disordered" or not.[16] Mental disorder may be, as the DSM definition cited
above asserts, "in an individual," but it is virtually always a product of interaction with the rest of the world.

In part for this reason, Thomas Szasz has famously argued that mental
illness is a "myth."[17] To Szasz, either a person has a brain disease, in which
case the appropriate intervention is neurological, or he or she has a "problem in living," which is not an illness but a social condition.[18] For most of
what we call mental disorder, Szasz asserts, "the norm from which deviation
is measured is a *psychosocial and ethical* standard," not a physical one.[19]
Although there is much to be said against Szasz's ultimate position that
mental illness does not "exist,"[20] his insight about the strong influence social norms exert on the definition of mental illness is worthy of emphasis.
Indeed, in a sense Szasz does not go far enough in his critique. Regardless of
our ability to correlate certain brain structures and bodily chemicals with
certain symptoms, the definition of mental illness, like the definition of illness generally, is as much cultural as it is scientific.[21] As Ralph Slovenko has
said, "mental disorders are exaggerations of normal psychodynamics,"[22]
with society in general and mental health professionals in particular determining what is "exaggerated" and what is "normal."

The foregoing discussion is important background to this book because it
establishes that mental disorder is an elusive and potentially boundless concept. Fortunately, further inquiry into the clinical or lay meaning of this
amorphous construct is unnecessary, because this book is ultimately about
law, not human psychology. Just as societal norms drive the definition of
mental illness in society at large, legal norms determine the parameters of
mental illness in legal contexts. The DSM itself cautions against use of its con-
tents for legal purposes,[23] and the U.S. Supreme Court has stated that "[l]egal
definitions . . . which must take into account such issues as individual re-

sponsibility . . . and competency, need not mirror those advanced by the medical profession."[24] Thus, the normative concerns of the law—not clinical categories meant for treatment and research purposes and not the unanalyzed intuitions of the public—should govern in deciding when government can deprive someone of life or liberty on the basis of mental condition.

Consistent with the observations of the DSM's drafters and the Supreme Court, this book argues that there is no direct correlation between any particular diagnosis and legally relevant mental states. Given that position, it would be preferable to avoid diagnostic labels, as well as phrases such as "mental disability" and "mental illness," in favor of the functional descriptions that are normatively pertinent. Doing so, however, would be cumbersome and, at least initially, confusing; as will be seen, the relevant (dys)functions are not easily described or explained in a word or two. Some commentators have suggested using the word "crazy" as a stand-in for legally relevant states, because it better describes those states than terms such as "mental disability" and because it is less likely to connote a medical condition.[25] But that word is very offensive to some; more important, it does *not* capture the mental states that I consider legally relevant. Thus, until it develops the appropriate terminology, this book will continue to use the phrases "mental disability," "mental disorder," and "mental illness" interchangeably and in a relatively broad sense (meant to encompass all the DSM disorders listed earlier), with the understanding that these terms are socially contingent and should mean different things in different legal contexts. As the DSM recommends,[26] this book will also use terms such as "people with mental disability" and "a person with schizophrenia," rather than "the mentally disabled" or "a schizophrenic," to emphasize the fact that clinical phrases classify disorders, not people.

II. Laws That Affect Life and Liberty: Three Models

This brief discourse on the meaning of "mental disability" and like terms deals in a preliminary fashion with the first matter of scope important to this book. The second conceptual issue that needs to be addressed before proceeding concerns the nature of the laws that affect life and liberty. The four specific legal regimes that fall in this category can be listed simply enough. The criminal justice system, which determines who may be punished for crime, is the most obvious example. Every state also has a separate, ostensibly more rehabilitation-oriented, system for dealing with crimes committed by juveniles. Civil commitment laws authorize involuntary hospitalization of people considered dangerous to self or dangerous to others because of mental disorder. And a criminal defendant who is found incompetent to proceed with trial can be involuntarily hospitalized for the purpose of restoring him or her to competency.

Much more difficult than listing these liberty-deprivation mechanisms is discovering their rationales. Traditional legal doctrine has justified government-sponsored deprivations of life and liberty on one of two grounds. The *police power* authorizes government intervention for the welfare of society, while the *parens patriae* power—the state's power to act as parent or guardian—authorizes intervention for the welfare of the individuals subject to it.[27] The criminal justice system (including hospitalization to restore fitness for trial) and involuntary commitment of those who are dangerous to others are typically lumped together as exercises of the police power,[28] whereas juvenile justice and involuntary commitment of those who are dangerous to self are usually said to be exercises of the parens patriae authority of the state to care for those who cannot take care of themselves.[29]

In fact, however, none of these liberty-deprivation systems can be so simply explained. As subsequent chapters make clear, the goals of criminal punishment, which include retribution and rehabilitation as well as deterrence and incapacitation, can have as much to do with affirming the dignity and worth of the individual offender as with protecting society. More generally, the fact that criminal justice and involuntary commitment of those who are dangerous to others both fit under the police power umbrella suggests that the rationale adequately explains neither, since the two systems differ drastically, both dispositionally and in terms of the showing the state must make before intervention may occur. Conversely, juvenile justice, especially as practiced today, is closer to a "get tough" police power regime than one interested in children's welfare. Casting further doubt on the usefulness of current descriptions of the parens patriae power is that commitment on danger to self grounds often does not require a finding of incapacity[30]—even though the parens patriae authority is conceptualized as the state acting as a guardian—while involuntary hospitalization of those found incompetent to stand trial clearly does require an incapacity showing, even though it occurs in connection with the criminal process.

In an attempt to clarify thinking about the topic, this book uses a new typology for government-sponsored deprivations of life and liberty. Specifically, it advances three justificatory models of liberty deprivation: the punishment model, the prevention model, and the protection model. Under a *punishment* system, the goal of government is to punish people for the harm they have caused. This type of liberty deprivation is based solely on an assessment of culpability. Under a *prevention* system, the goal of government is to prevent harm to self or others, through either deterrence or restraint. Past conduct may be relevant as a means of establishing whom to use as a deterrent or who requires restraint, but the goal is minimization of future harm. Under a *protection* system, the goal of government is to ensure that rights and privileges are exercised autonomously. The inquiry here is on restoring one's decision-making capacity. Functionally, a punishment system is interested in retrospective assessments (of antisocial conduct), a prevention system requires prospective assessments (of the efficacy of deterrence or of the need for restraint), and a protective system is concerned with assessments of present status (in terms of autonomy).

These models seldom exist in their pure form. The criminal justice system is the closest manifestation of the punishment model, but as noted above it usually also incorporates aspects of the deterrent and incapacitative agendas. The juvenile justice system is even more conflicted in this regard, at times seeming to endorse all three models. Involuntary commitment of those thought to be dangerous to self or others best exemplifies the prevention model, but it also implements the protection model to the extent that incompetency to make treatment decisions is a necessary predicate for commitment. The process that ensures criminal defendants' competency to participate at their trials is an example of the protection model at work, but prevention objectives are sometimes involved here as well.

Although these models do not map onto existing systems of liberty deprivation any more precisely than traditional justifications, this book will demonstrate that they are useful heuristics for making important distinctions that the police power–parens patriae dyad and other means of differentiating liberty deprivations do not recognize. To begin that demonstration, the following discussion briefly answers three questions with respect to each of the three models: (1) What is the goal of the model? (2) What are the traditional justifications for the goal? (3) How is the goal currently operationalized, conceptually and practically?

A. The Punishment Model

Goal
A punishment model of liberty deprivation focuses solely on sanctioning past acts. It is not concerned with prevention or protection, but rather seeks

to ensure that people who commit antisocial acts receive their just deserts. Put in traditional philosophical terms, the punishment model aims to exact retribution.

Justifications

The retributive stance is often defended on purely deontological grounds. Put most simply, the argument is that a just society is morally obligated to punish the blameworthy and, conversely, may not condone punishment of the blameless. As Immanuel Kant put it, "punishment is a categorical imperative."[31] In similar fashion, Georg Hegel argued that punishment is necessary to cancel the Wrong and restore the Right,[32] while Michel Foucault saw it as the means of expunging the evil represented by crime.[33] Stated in these types of terms, the retributive rationale resembles a religious assertion, and is at least a transcendental one.

Paul Robinson provides a more instrumental rationale for retributivism. He notes the universal urge to maintain a separate criminal justice system based on moral condemnation and argues that, even if such condemnation is not dictated as a matter of theory, "[c]riminal policy must take account of the fact that the world is made up of people who see blame, condemnation, and punishment as natural and necessary aspects of human interaction."[34] Robinson also asserts that people are more likely to abide by the commands of the criminal law if they believe it has "moral credibility," which it will lack if it imposes blame where there is none.[35] Related to this rationale for punishment is the idea that punishment fulfils an expressive function that allows us to vent our feelings about the act in question.[36]

All these justifications for the punishment model assume that people can freely choose their conduct or that society should at least act as if they do. The so-called free will postulate is an essential premise of the model. If behavior is determined by forces over which the person has little or no control, then punishment would not be just, because it would not be deserved.

Implementation

Given the free will postulate, virtually all retributive theorists require proof that the actor "voluntarily" chose to engage in antisocial conduct before it may serve as the basis for government intervention. If the antisocial act is perceived as involuntary or accidental, punishment is generally thought to be undeserved.[37] Even intentional conduct should not be punished if it was justified by circumstances, or if it was excused by mental abnormality. In short, the punishment model of liberty deprivation is concerned with the culpability of offenders.

Culpability can be defined along a spectrum ranging from complete objectivity to complete subjectivity. An objective approach, for instance, might permit punishment for any killing under circumstances that would lead the reasonable observer to believe the killing was likely to occur or could have been avoided. A predominantly subjective approach would permit punishment only if the actor *actually* intended the killing or was at least aware it was a likely result of the actor's conduct, and even then would refuse to punish if the actor harbored an honest belief that the killing was justified or was afflicted by a significant mental abnormality.[38] As Chapter 2 elaborates, the general trend in U.S. criminal law has been in the direction of a more subjective approach to culpability assessments.

B. The Prevention Model

Goal

The goal of a prevention regime is reduction of harm to others. Of course, a punishment regime may, as a side effect, prevent harm as well. But the sole goal of the punishment model is sanctioning based on blame, whereas a prevention regime authorizes intervention solely for the sake of reducing crime.

Justifications

The rationale for a prevention regime is explicitly utilitarian. Prevention of harm, at least of serious harm, is an obvious and compelling objective of any government. But not every type of preventive measure can be justified. Rather, as Jeremy Bentham, the father of this type of analysis, insisted, cost-benefit analysis is essential.[39] For instance, maximum harm prevention might be achieved by executing anyone who commits antisocial conduct. But the social cost of such executions would be tremendous. Potentially productive members of society would be lost; behavior that is objectively legitimate but that might be construed as antisocial would be chilled; fear of government and its agents might produce significant inefficiencies; and the harms perpetrated in such an environment might well be more serious (for instance, a pickpocket might murder the person from whom he steals because an eyewitness will ensure an execution). Thus, a prevention regime is subject to significant limitations based on an assessment of the relevant costs of harm prevention.

Implementation

The principal means of achieving prevention of harm to others are deterrence, incapacitation, and rehabilitation.[40] Thus there are, in theory, three separate types of prevention regimes that might result in deprivations of liberty. The first permits government actions that would deter others from committing antisocial acts.[41] The second authorizes deprivations of liberty to prevent a particular person from reoffending. The third permits interventions against a particular person to ensure treatment designed to prevent recidivism. Analyzed more closely, however, the second and third types of prevention regimes collapse into each other. Unless treatment is designed to prevent harmful conduct, it does not promote the goal of a prevention system. Thus, the predicate for a rehabilitation-oriented regime, like the predicate for an incapacitative one, is a finding of dangerousness, albeit dangerousness that is treatable.

This leaves two types of prevention regimes, which can be referred to as *deterrence based* (designed to prevent harm by others) and *control based* (designed to prevent harm by the individuals subject to government intervention). A deterrence-type regime, although very different in goal and justification from a punishment system, probably produces gradations of liberty deprivation quite similar to those required by retributive analysis. For instance, under deterrence theory, offenses with a perceived low probability of apprehension should be sanctioned severely, whereas those with a high likelihood of apprehension should be treated in opposite fashion. Because accidental, negligent, and irrational actions are more likely to result in apprehension than intentional ones (precisely because they are not anticipated and thus are more likely to be observed by others), deterrence theory suggests that they should receive lesser sanctions, the same result produced by the culpability-driven rules in a punishment regime.[42] Because of this close relationship between the punishment model and the prevention-deterrence model, this book generally will not differentiate between the two.

A prevention system based on dangerousness (henceforth simply called the prevention model) stands in much sharper contrast to the punishment model. Requiring proof of culpability, as the punishment model does, could often prevent intervention against a clearly dangerous person (say, for instance, an insane individual); conversely, it would be inefficient from a prevention perspective to intervene against a nondangerous person simply because he or she is culpable. Perhaps the foregoing discussion of the differences between the deterrence and control versions of the prevention model explains why there are no obvious examples of liberty-deprivation regimes based solely on deterrence (the criminal justice system, for instance, is generally thought to be based on a mixed retributive and prevention rationale),[43] while there are many distinct examples of a dangerousness-driven prevention regime (most notably, civil commitment laws and the recently popular sexual predator statutes).

C. The Protection Model

Goal

The punishment model of intervention aims to sanction blameworthy conduct, and the prevention model of intervention seeks to reduce harmful conduct. The goal of the protection model is to assure autonomous conduct, through a deprivation of liberty if necessary. More specifically, its goal is to assure autonomous decision making in any context where we believe such decision making should be left to the individual.

Justifications

The justification for intervention on protection grounds is that autonomy is a good that must be promoted. Kant, from a deontological perspective, and John Stuart Mill, using utilitarian analysis, provided some of the earliest arguments in favor of honoring individual choices, even those that are imprudent. According to Kant, every person possesses an inalienable right to be treated as a rational actor and to avoid being treated as a means to achieve the ends of others; thus the state may not substitute its judgment for the individual's.[44] Mill felt that decision-making rights should be maintained as a means of assuring development of decision-making capacities, which he viewed as necessary to human dignity and self-fulfillment.[45] He also believed that competent adults know their own abilities and preferences better than anyone else, including the government, and are thus better able to direct their own affairs. According to Mill, an individual's "voluntary choice is evidence that what he so chooses is desirable, or at least endurable, to him, and his good is on the whole best provided for by allowing him to take his own means of pursuing it."[46] A number of Supreme Court decisions, in a number of contexts, have affirmed this basic proposition.[47]

The negative implication of this preference for autonomy, which Mill, if not Kant, recognized, is that decision making by a nonautonomous actor should not be permitted.[48] Persons who do not understand their abilities, cannot access their preferences, and do not understand the choices to be made cannot achieve self-fulfillment, and represent the antithesis of human dignity. In this situation, the state is justified in attempting to enable the person to respond in a meaningful fashion and, if that fails, may also be justified in making the decision for him or her. Allowing the nonautonomous individual to make the decision would not only be insulting to the individual; it would also make a mockery of the concept of autonomy itself. It would suggest that society sanctions random decision making. Thus, the traditional justification for the protection model posits, ensuring autonomy protects not only the individual's interests but those of society at large.

Implementation

The law's word for legally sufficient autonomy is "competency"—the capacity to decide or to perform certain functions. The competency notion permeates both the civil and criminal justice systems, although the precise decisions to be made and functions to be carried out vary from context to context. In civil cases, for instance, competency may refer to a capacity to understand and approve the terms of a contract or a will, manage financial affairs, or make treatment decisions. In criminal cases, it may designate the capacity to comprehend legal proceedings and communicate with an attorney, or to understand and waive certain rights, such as the right to remain silent.

In all of these situations, the state may intervene to ensure that a person is capable of performing the required tasks. Most significantly for purposes of this book, this intervention can sometimes result in a deprivation of liberty. For instance, the person found incompetent to stand trial may be forcibly treated, in a hospital or elsewhere, for the purpose of "restoring" competency to undergo legal proceedings and make waiver decisions; in the meantime he or she will be prevented from obtaining adjudication of the pending charges.[49] A person found incompetent to make treatment decisions might be involuntarily hospitalized as well, in the hopes treatment will restore competency and, in any event, to ensure the individual is cared for. In the meantime, a guardian or doctor may make treatment decisions for the individual.[50]

D. Summary

The various aspects of the three models of liberty deprivation discussed above are summarized in the table below.

Intervention model	Purpose of intervention	Animating legal construct
Punishment model	Punishing harmful acts	Culpability
Prevention model	Preventing harmful acts:	
Deterrence-type	by others	Deterrence
Control-type	by subjects of intervention	Dangerousness
Protection model	Promoting autonomous acts	Competency

Each of these models, as implemented in today's legal system, reserves a central role for mental disability, albeit often without clearly defining that term. Under the punishment model as it operates in the criminal justice system, people with severe mental disability are considered blameless and excused from crime on insanity grounds, while those with lesser impairments, although convicted, might still be perceived as less than fully culpable and receive a reduced sentence. (As suggested earlier, the prevention-deterrence model probably arrives at the same results, although for different reasons.) Under the prevention-control model as implemented in general commitment and sexual offender laws, some type of "mental abnormality" is almost always an explicit predicate because of its perceived association with particularly virulent or treatable dangerousness. Similarly, protection regimes focus on mental disorder, because mental disorder is usually thought to be the primary cause of the relevant incapacity, whether it is incompetency to stand trial, plead guilty, or make treatment decisions.

III. Organization and Preview of the Book

This book is dedicated to figuring out whether these various roles for mental disability make sense and, if not, how the roles should be reconfigured. Part 1 of the book, consisting of Chapters 2 and 3, examines mental disability and the punishment model; Part 2, composed of Chapters 4 and 5, explores the prevention model; and Part 3, made up of Chapters 6 and 7, analyzes the protection model. Chapter 8 revisits a number of the issues discussed in the foregoing pages, and reaches some overarching conclusions about mental disability and deprivations of liberty.

A bit more detail about the thesis of each chapter will help the reader understand the overall project. Chapter 2, the first chapter on the punishment model, takes on the insanity defense. In a retributive system, the cognitive and volitional impairments associated with mental disability are highly relevant, because they clearly can diminish culpability. This chapter argues, however, that current formulations of the insanity defense—whether they focus on appreciation of wrongfulness, rationality, or volitional impairment—do not capture the type of mentally disabled person who should be considered completely blameless. In place of the insanity defense, the chapter advances an "integrationist" approach to the role of mental disorder in determining criminal liability. An integrationist regime would excuse people with mental disability only on grounds available to *all* offenders, assuming those defenses are subjectively defined. In other words, people with mental disability would be excused for crime if, and only if, they did not intend to commit the crime or intended to commit it in the belief that circumstances amounting to a valid justification or duress defense existed. Integrationism avoids the arbitrariness of current exculpatory formulations, which must invent crabbed and ultimately rootless interpretations of "lack of appreciation," "irrationality," and "impulsive behavior" to avoid opening the floodgates to psychiatrically based claims. Instead, it places a normatively sensible limitation on the exculpatory effect of mental disability, one that is coherent regardless of what science ends up telling us about the extent to which we can control our behavior, feelings, and thoughts. A side benefit of integrationism is that it would help destigmatize mental disorder, because it would eliminate that much maligned category of people known as the "criminally insane."

The death penalty is the subject of Chapter 3, the book's second chapter concerning the punishment perspective on deprivations of liberty (and life). Although this chapter does not directly challenge the legitimacy of the death penalty, it takes a very hostile view toward the ultimate punishment when it is imposed on those who suffer from serious mental disability. It makes three arguments in this vein. First, now that the Supreme Court has exempted people with mental retardation from execution, there is no rational basis for continuing to execute people who are severely mentally ill. Second, given the substantial research indicating that capital sentencing juries typically treat mental disability as an *aggravator* despite being instructed to the contrary, any death sentence imposed on a seriously mentally disabled person is highly suspect and perhaps even a violation of due process. Third, forcibly treating a person who is incompetent to be executed in order to restore competency and ensure execution is cruel and unusual punishment, primarily because of the ethically untenable position in which such treatment places mental health professionals.

The chapter also briefly explores the implications of these arguments for noncapital sentencing. Whereas only people who meet the integrationist test described in Chapter 2 should be excused from punishment, any offender who meets the broadest version of the cognitive insanity test should receive a reduction in sentence. Because it fails to implement that goal, I also argue that the popular "guilty but mentally ill" verdict, periodically proffered as an alternative disposition for people with mental disability who are not insane, is conceptually bankrupt and should not be adopted.

Chapter 4 begins the book's discussion of the prevention model of liberty deprivation, which, it will be remembered, is designed to control those who might cause harm, rather than punish those who have already caused it. The chapter attempts something that has yet to appear in the literature: the development of a comprehensive jurisprudence of preventive detention. It proceeds by first attending to the major objections lodged against this form of liberty deprivation, which include the complaints that dangerousness cannot be assessed reliably and, indeed, cannot even be defined succinctly, and that preventive detention is merely criminal punishment in disguise and even more dehumanizing. The chapter concludes that, while all these objections suggest limitations on preventive detention, none invalidates it as a mechanism for government liberty deprivation. The chapter also concludes, however, that to the extent the punishment model continues to be our primary response to criminal conduct, preventive detention should be reserved for those who are undeterrable, in the sense of being impervious to criminal punishment. This type of undeterrability will often be linked to severe mental disability, which can prevent offenders from realizing they are committing a crime (the subject of Chapter 2). But it might also be associated with less disorienting, characteriological conditions, such as the extreme impulsiveness experienced by the sex offender who literally commits a crime with a police officer at the elbow. It might also be correlated with political agendas, as in the case of the terrorist who will commit a crime despite a high likelihood of death or capture. This chapter also develops two new principles for dealing with the age-old problem of figuring out who is "dangerous" enough to warrant preventive detention. The proportionality principle requires that any preventive liberty deprivation that takes place be roughly proportionate to the risk associated with the detainee. The consistency principle requires that the threshold of danger mandated for preventive detention be consistent with the criminal law's use of dangerousness as a ground for punishment (a principle that has interesting implications for both preventive detention and criminal law).

Chapter 5 continues the discussion of preventive detention, but from an entirely different perspective. While Chapter 4 assumes that criminal punishment should be the preferred method of dealing with antisocial behavior, Chapter 5 attacks that venerable principle head-on. In essence, the chapter reinvigorates the arguments of Barbara Wooton and other commentators of the 1950s who believed that prevention—relying on treatment and, when necessary, incapacitation—should be the sole goal of government-sponsored limitations on liberty. The chapter debunks the rationales for the punishment model described earlier in this introduction, as well as several others derived from deontological, utilitarian, and ethical philosophy. It then suggests that a prevention regime can be just as accurate and perhaps even more cost-effective and conducive to human dignity than a retribution- or deterrence-based system of justice. The implications of this position range far beyond control and rehabilitation of those with mental disability, of course. And even if the argument does not convince anyone that radical change is needed in the adult criminal system, it strongly reinforces the case for a separate, prevention-oriented juvenile justice system, which has been under furious attack in recent years.[51]

Chapter 6 is the first of two chapters on the protection model of liberty deprivation. It addresses competency in criminal cases, specifically competency to stand trial and to make decisions about waiving the rights to trial, counsel, and the like. The chapter first develops the "basic rationality and self-regard" test for competency, which holds that a person is incompetent for these purposes only when he or she does not understand the relevant information or holds a fixed, false belief about relevant facts. It then argues, contrary to a number of commentators, that this competency test should apply in every criminal decision-making context, whether the decision involves serious or minor charges, and whether the attorney agrees with the defendant's decision or not. The chapter also confronts a number of hotly contested issues that face attorneys representing a client with mental disability: whether there is an obligation to raise the competency issue (and risk potentially long-term hospitalization) when competency is in doubt (yes); whether the attorney can ever override a competent client's decision (yes, under very limited circumstances); and whether a defendant may be tried once attempts to restore his or her competency have failed (no, unless only decision-making capacity, as opposed to the capacity to understand the criminal process and communicate with the attorney, remains compromised). This chapter makes clear that the answers to these questions depend heavily on practical as well as theoretical considerations, concerning not only the autonomy of the client but also the autonomy of the attorney.

Chapter 7 takes on the even more hotly disputed issues connected with the right to refuse psychiatric treatment. It begins by parsing the relevant case law concerning treatment refusals by those who are incompetent to stand trial, those who are considered dangerous to self, and those thought to be dangerous to others. It concludes that the Supreme Court's decisions on this topic are seriously flawed, in particular because they slight incompetency as a threshold requirement for overriding treatment refusals. The chapter then revisits that elusive concept, using as a stalking horse the highly sophisticated conceptual and empirical work of the MacArthur Treatment Competence Study, conducted in the 1990s. While the chapter lauds the study's efforts, it parts company with its authors on the most important aspect of competency assessment—the definition of "rationality" in decision-making settings. The study's research instruments implicitly assume that strongly held disagreement with medical opinion is indicative of irrationality and thus incompetency. Chapter 7 contends, in contrast, that only an inability to understand, or demonstrably false beliefs about, treatment risks and benefits renders a person legally incompetent to make treatment decisions. This definition, which is identical to that proposed in Chapter 6 in the criminal context, is meant to endorse an expansive view of autonomy without making a mockery of the concept.

Chapter 8, the final segment of the book, is in part a review of all the preceding chapters. In particular, it summarizes the basic tenets of the book's major proposals concerning mental disability and liberty deprivations—integrationism in the punishment context, the undeterrability predicate in the prevention context, and the basic rationality and self-regard test in the protection setting. But it also develops a common theme found in each of these proposals. Despite the differences among them (and there are significant differences), each proposal focuses on the *content* of the person's thoughts, rather than on the person's thought process, predispositions, or behavior. A person is excused from crime only if intent is absent or a belief in justifying events is present (under the punishment model), may be subjected to preventive intervention only when there is a characteristic obliviousness to punishment (under the prevention model), and is declared incompetent only if his or her beliefs about the relevant facts are demonstrably false (under the protection model). The Chapter 8 argues that this focus on belief content is preferable as a normative matter because it reinforces the notion that choices—whether they have to do with committing crime or waiving a right—should not be dismissed as "sick" and therefore unworthy of respect merely because they stem from "pathology" or "character flaws," or because they produce a disagreeable result. A content-based definition of legally relevant mental states is probably also less likely than competing approaches to produce errors. Finally, a content-based approach is less stigmatizing, because it judges a person's culpability, dangerousness, and competency without reference to whether a person is "mentally disabled."

One is unlikely to agree with all the points made in subsequent pages. But, at the least, the reader should come away with a new appreciation of the many theoretical and practical nuances in this area of the law. That is a primary goal of this book.

A second goal is to sensitize readers to the plight of people with mental disability involved in the criminal and quasi-criminal justice systems. The doctrines and practices considered here are extremely important in human terms. Although only a very small number of defendants are found insane,[52] ferment over the scope of the insanity defense has had major repercussions on the criminal justice system, as the "guilty but mentally ill" craze and other reforms demonstrate. The proportion of the 1.5 million adult and juvenile offenders currently in our jails and prisons who have mental disorder is variously estimated at between 6 and 50 percent (depending on whether "moderate" disorder is included), and the proportion of mentally disordered offenders on death row may be just as high.[53] With the advent of sexual predator laws in recent years, the number of "sex offenders" who are committed under special dispositional statutes is increasing daily,[54] and the number of those subjected to general civil commitment each year reaches into the hundreds of thousands.[55] More than 60,000 criminal defendants are evaluated for competency each year, roughly 25 percent of whom are hospitalized or otherwise subjected to restrictions on liberty after a finding of incompetency.[56]

Despite these numbers, mental health law is a legal backwater. Many, and perhaps most, of the judges, lawyers, and mental health professionals who apply these laws do not fully understand either their letter or their purpose, or consciously abuse them, problems that neither law schools nor bar associations do much to combat. Despite the fact that they can lead to significant losses of liberty, commitment and competency cases continue to be handled by "special," lower-level courts that are often not even courts "of record" because their proceedings are not transcribed. Although treatment facilities and modalities have improved immensely from fifty years ago, the quality and quantity of mental health treatment programs for people in institutions or otherwise subject to legal constraint are still scandalous in many jurisdictions. In other words, from the legal perspective, this area of the law occupies a very low status. Similarly, from the clinical perspective, it is probably fair to say that forensic practice sits at or near the bottom of the mental health profession hierarchy. And, with the exception of the insanity defense, this entire area of law is off the typical citizen's radar screen.

The primary reason for this state of affairs is society's general disregard for and ignorance about people with mental disability, in particular those who violate norms or are significantly dysfunctional. This book is meant to act as a partial corrective for that willful blindness. It is aimed at getting society and the legal system to mind—care about—justice for people with mental disability, rather than see it as a nuisance that is someone else's responsibility.

—I—

The Punishment Model

— 2 —

The Insanity Defense

Insanity defense jurisprudence has long been in a state of disarray. As long ago as 1925, Sheldon Glueck stated:

> Perhaps in no other field of American law is there so much disagreement as to fundamentals and so many contradictory decisions in the same jurisdictions. Not a modern text or compilation begins the discussion of the subject of insanity and its relation to the criminal law without a doleful reference to chaos in this field.[1]

Almost seventy years later Michael Perlin began his book length treatment of the insanity defense with the assertion that "[o]ur insanity defense jurisprudence is incoherent."[2]

Some have responded to this unfortunate situation by calling for abolition of the defense,[3] while others have tinkered further with its scope.[4] In this chapter, I propose what amounts to an intermediate position. I argue that insanity should be eliminated as a separate defense, but that the effects of mental disorder should still carry significant moral weight. More specifically, mental illness should be relevant in assessing culpability only as warranted by general criminal law doctrines concerning *mens rea,* self-defense, and duress. I call this approach the "integration" position, because it integrates claims of mental disability into the preexisting framework on the criminal law.

While a few scholars and courts have toyed with the integration idea,[5] it has yet to be fully endorsed or coherently defended by any of them. This chapter provides such a defense. It contends that, both morally and practically, the most appropriate manner of recognizing mental illness's mitigating impact in criminal cases is to recast mental disorder as a factor relevant to the general defenses, not treat it as a predicate for a special defense.

23

The starting point for this claim is the retributive principle that blameworthiness should be the predominating guidepost of the criminal law's attempt to define the scope of liability; in the language adopted in this book, the punishment model should be the governing concept in this context. One can imagine, as Chapter 5 does, a system of liberty deprivation that is agnostic about culpability and focused on prevention and treatment. But it is clear that the preventive model has not yet gained significant ground as the primary means of dealing with antisocial behavior, and that in the foreseeable future the disposition of those with mental illness who commit crimes will depend on the extent to which the mental impairment diminished blameworthiness at the time of the offense. That is where the kind of inquiry the insanity defense mandates comes into play. It is meant to help us decide whom among those who commit criminal acts deserve to be the subject of criminal punishment.

The central assertion made here, however, is that the insanity defense does not adequately carry out this definitional task. At least in its modern guises, the insanity defense is overbroad. Instead, mental disorder should be relevant to criminal culpability only if it supports an excusing condition at the time of the offense that, under the subjective approach to criminal liability increasingly accepted today, would be available to a person who is *not* mentally ill. The three most prominent such conditions would be: (1) A mistaken belief about circumstances that, had they occurred as the person believed, would amount to a legal justification. (2) A mistaken belief that conditions exist that amount to legally recognized duress. (3) The absence of intent to commit crime (that is, the lack of mens rea defined subjectively, in terms of what the defendant actually knew or was aware of). Again, I call this approach integrationist, because it eliminates the special defense of insanity while providing people with mental disability the same defenses available to everyone else.

Before justifying this position, I will provide some examples of how it would apply in well-known actual and hypothetical cases. Take first the famous *M'Naghten* case, from whence much of current insanity defense jurisprudence derives.[6] In 1843, Daniel M'Naghten killed the secretary of Prime Minister Peel, apparently believing the secretary was Peel and that killing Peel would bring an end to a campaign of harassment against him. He was found insane by the trial court judges. Whether M'Naghten would have been acquitted under the proposed approach would depend on whether he believed the harassment would soon lead to his death or serious bodily harm, and whether he thought there was any other way to prevent that occurrence. Because in his paranoid state he feared he would be assassinated by his enemies and had on several occasions unsuccessfully applied to the police for protection, he may have had such a defense. If, however, the circumstances in which he thought he was involved would not amount to self-defense, no acquittal would result, although a conviction of manslaughter rather than murder might have been appropriate, analogous to the result under the modern theory of "imperfect" self-defense.

Andrea Yates, the Texas woman who was convicted of drowning her five children, would probably have been excused under the integrationist test as well. Apparently she believed that the killings prevented her children from going to hell, a belief that, had it been true, presumably would have been found to justify her criminal conduct.[7] Because her case raises a number of interesting issues, full discussion of it is delayed until later in this chapter.

Now consider the case of John Hinckley, who convinced a jury he was insane when he tried to kill President Ronald Reagan. If, as even his defense attorneys admitted, Hinckley shot Reagan simply because he believed Reagan's death would somehow unite him with actress Jodi Foster,[8] he would be convicted under the integrationist approach. Regardless of how psychotic Hinckley may have been at the time of the offense, he would not have an excuse under the proposed regime, because killing someone to consummate a love affair is never justified, nor is it deserving even of a reduction in charge. A similar result would be reached in the highly publicized case of Jeffrey Dahmer, who killed and cannibalized thirteen individuals. The jury was right to convict him. As "sick" as his actions were, even he never thought they were justified, and he would not be excused in an integrated regime.[9]

In these cases, then, whether a defense existed under the proposed approach would depend on *self-defense* principles applied to the circumstances as the defendant believed them to be. A second variety of cases can be analyzed in terms of a similarly subjectified version of *duress*, which traditionally has excused crimes that are coerced by serious threats to harm the perpetrator. For instance, some people with mental illness who commit crime claim they were commanded by God to do so.[10] If the perceived consequences of disobeying the deity were lethal or similarly significant, such a person would deserve acquittal, perhaps even if the crime charged were homicide. Contrary to Justice Benjamin Cardozo's famous hypothetical suggestion,[11] however, the mere fact that the defendant honestly believed

God ordained a crime would not automatically be an excuse. This would be true even if the person believed God's commands abrogated human laws and made the act legal, an ignorance of the law scenario discussed below.

The third type of excuse that might apply when people with mental illness commit crime—*lack of mens rea*—is extremely rare. M'Naghten, Hinckley, Yates, Dahmer, and Cardozo's hypothetical defendant all intended to carry out criminal acts. Indeed, most crimes in which mental illness plays a role are intentional; people who are so disordered that they cannot form intent are often also so disorganized behaviorally that they are unlikely to be able to carry out a criminal act. Nonetheless, when mens rea is defined subjectively, there are at least four possible lack-of-mens rea scenarios: involuntary action, mistake as to results, mistake as to circumstances, and ignorance of the law.

First, a person may engage in motor activity without intending it to occur (for example, a reflex action that results in a gun firing and killing someone). The criminal law typically classifies such events as involuntary acts.[12] Although mental disorder usually does not eliminate conscious control over bodily movements associated with crime, when it does (for example, in connection with epileptic seizures or serious frontal lobe dysfunction), a defense would exist on the premise that culpability requires actual intent.[13]

Second, a person may intentionally engage in conduct but intend a different result than that which occurs (such as when firing a gun at a tree kills a person due to a ricochet). Distortions of perception caused by mental illness might occasionally lead to such accidental consequences; for instance, a mentally ill person driving a car may accidentally hit someone because "voices" and hallucinations prevent him from perceiving relevant sounds and visual cues. In such situations a subjectively defined mens rea doctrine would absolve him of criminal liability for any harm caused.

Closely related is the situation in which a person intentionally engages in conduct and intends the physical result that occurs, but is under a misapprehension as to the attendant circumstances (such as when a person intentionally shoots a gun at what he thinks is a dummy but what in fact is a real person). Of the various mens rea defenses, mental illness is most likely to play a role here, in what has sometimes been labeled the "mistake of fact" defense. Consider two actual cases. In one, the person believed she was shooting the devil when in fact she was killing a person.[14] In the other, the defendant exerted control over property in an apartment he delusionally believed to be his.[15] The first offender would be acquitted of homicide and the second of theft, if mens rea is subjectively defined. Another, more subtle example of this type of mens rea defense is most likely to arise in connection with a person who is mentally retarded rather than mentally ill. Like a young child, such a person may kill not realizing that a life has been ended, because of an incomplete conception of what life is; for instance, the offender may believe the victim will rejuvenate like a cartoon character.[16] Mens rea, subjectively defined, would be absent in such cases because murder requires not only an intentional killing, but also that the offender understands that the victim is a human being who is capable of dying.

Finally, a person may intentionally engage in conduct and intend the result, under no misapprehension as to the attendant circumstances, but still not intend to commit a crime because of an inadequate understanding of what crime is. There are actually two versions of this type of mens rea requirement. First, the person may not be aware of the *concept* of crime (as might be true of a three-year-old). Second, the person may understand that criminal prohibitions exist but believe that his or her specific act is legally permissible (such as might occur when a person from a different country commits an act that would be perfectly legal in his culture, although illegal in another). The first situation might be called "general" ignorance of the law, while the second might be called "specific" ignorance of the law. Outside of the insanity and infancy contexts, neither type of ignorance has been recognized as an excuse for *mala in se* crimes.[17] However, for reasons discussed in more detail later in this chapter, a subjectively defined mens rea doctrine should excuse general ignorance of the law whether or not it is due to mental disability, a position that would excuse those rare individuals who intentionally carry out criminal acts without understanding the concept of good and evil. In contrast, the mere fact that one believes one's specific act is legal, without a showing it sounds in justification or duress, should not support a defense for anyone (whether it is a person from a different culture or the person who receives a nonthreatening command from God).

In short, the integration approach would treat people with mental disorder no differently from people who are not mentally ill, assuming (and this is admittedly a big assumption) a modern criminal justice system that adopts a subjective approach to culpability. The rest of this chapter will try to justify this proposal. It will do so from three perspectives: historical, moral, and instrumental. First, as a historical matter, the insanity defense was the only method of mitigating culpability for unreasonable actions; now that other aspects of criminal law doctrine have taken on this role, the defense has lost much of its raison d'être. Ironically, the scope of the insanity defense began expanding at roughly the same time developments in other parts of the criminal law rendered the original defense redundant in many respects. Second, and most important, the integrationist approach captures the universe of mentally disordered individuals who should be excused. The expansion of the defense that has occurred in modern times, whether it encompasses anyone with an "abnormal" condition or is limited to those who are viewed as "irrational," does not adequately distinguish those we excuse from those we do not. Third, the proposal has several practical advantages, including enhancing respect for people with mental illness, facilitating treatment, and promoting the legitimacy of the criminal justice system.

I. The Lessons of History

The insanity defense has been through several well-known permutations, generally in the direction of expansion, although in very modern times some retrenchment has occurred. Less acknowledged, at least by those commentators who have focused primarily on the insanity defense, is the trend toward subjectification of the rest of the criminal law. The intersection of these two trends suggests that the insanity defense, in its current form, has outlived its usefulness.

A. The Insanity Defense

For most of its existence in Anglo-American law, the insanity defense or its functional equivalent has required gross impairment. Although we have virtually no direct evidence about the facts of individual cases in medieval and renaissance times,[18] commentators of the period consistently spoke of a requirement that the defendant lack understanding of good and evil or be devoid of all reason, and often equated the insane with animals or infants.[19] Thus, using the terminology introduced above, it appears that for several centuries of English law only mentally ill defendants who lacked mens rea in the involuntary act, mistake, or general ignorance senses were entitled to royal pardon or acquittal.

Beginning no later than the early 1800s, courts in both England and the

United States increasingly referred to insanity as an inability to distinguish "right and wrong."[20] The latter language could be construed to mean that a person who intentionally harmed another and was generally aware of the concept of crime might still be acquitted if, because of mental disorder, he either did not believe the law proscribed his particular act (that is, the specific ignorance mens rea test described above) or delusionally perceived facts that amounted to a justification. In practice, most people who were tried under these tests were convicted, irrespective of whether they felt the act was legally permissible, so long as they intended harm. Illustrative are the *Arnold*, *Ferrers, Bellingham,* and *Oxford* cases in eighteenth- and nineteenth-century England, each of which involved defendants with serious mental problems who apparently felt justified in killing their victims but nonetheless intended to kill them; all except Oxford were convicted.[21] Similarly in the United States, in the ten early–nineteenth-century American insanity cases with a known disposition that are described by Anthony Platt and Bernard L. Diamond, eight resulted in guilty verdicts despite evidence of derangement (and one of the acquittals, Platt and Diamond aver, had more to do with the elevated social status of the defendant than mental state).[22]

At the same time, it is clear that at least *some* judges and juries prior to the mid-nineteenth century were willing to relax the legal threshold for insanity below the medieval devoid-of-reason test. Although the precise grounds for these results are unclear, these cases were not inconsistent with the notion that a person who, for instance, knew that he was killing someone might still obtain an insanity verdict if delusions convinced him he needed to act to defend himself or others. The two most prominent examples are *M'Naghten* itself, the facts of which were described earlier, and Rex v. Hadfield, where the jury acquitted a defendant who believed God had told him to sacrifice himself to save the world and who chose assassination of the king as the best way to assure his demise.[23]

In any event, the *M'Naghten* test, promulgated by the House of Lords in 1843, appeared to recognize both versions of insanity by excusing those who, by virtue of mental disorder, either did not know the nature and quality of the act or that it was wrong.[24] The House of Lords also refined the latter test for those defendants who were not "totally" insane but rather experienced their delusions primarily in connection with the offense:

As to a person who labours under such partial delusion only, and is not in other respects insane, we think he must be considered in the same situation as to responsibility as if the facts with respect to which the delusion exists were real. For example, if under the influence of his delusion he supposes another man to be in the act of attempting to take away his life, and he kills that man, as he supposes, in self-defence, he would be exempt from punishment. If his delusion was that the deceased had inflicted injury to his character and fortune, and he killed him in revenge for such supposed injury, he would be liable to punishment.[25]

This language explicitly allows a defense for offenders who, regardless of their knowledge about the law, erroneously believe they are confronted by facts that, if true, made their act justifiable (and thus presages to some extent the integration position).

The next steps in insanity defense jurisprudence responded to two criticisms leveled at M'Naghten. First, M'Naghten was faulted because it focused solely on cognitive impairment, thus failing to recognize volitional impairment.[26] A person who knew what he was doing was wrong, but who felt "compelled" to commit the criminal act—say, a person suffering from kleptomania or manic-depressive psychosis—would be criminally punished in a M'Naghten jurisdiction. The second criticism was that, even if restricting the insanity defense to those who are cognitively impaired is legitimate, the M'Naghten test did not give the excuse broad enough scope.[27] Even many severely crazy people know in some sense the nature of their act and that it is legally wrong, but either do not emotionally relate to the consequences of their act (as might have occurred in Hinckley's case), or believe, as in the command-from-God scenario, that their act is *morally* justified despite its "illegality" under the criminal law.

The law eventually responded to both these criticisms. A number of U.S. jurisdictions added the so-called irresistible impulse test to the M'Naghten test, thereby recognizing volitional impairment as a defense.[28] Many jurisdictions also interpreted the M'Naghten language loosely. Total cognitive impairment was not required, nor was mere awareness that the act was prohibited by statute a bar to acquittal; the focus was on whether the accused's mental disease deprived him of the capacity to recognize the wrongfulness of the offense in some larger sense.[29]

These developments culminated in the test found in the American Law Institute's Model Penal Code. This test reads as follows: "A person is not responsible for criminal conduct if at the time of such conduct as a result of mental disease or defect he lacks substantial capacity either to appreciate the criminality [wrongfulness] of his conduct or to conform his conduct to the requirements of the law."[30] Note that this language recognizes both cognitive and volitional impairment as an excuse, and requires only substantial, not total, incapacity.[31] It also uses the broader term "appreciate," rather than "know," in defining the type of cognitive impairment that leads to insanity, in an effort to recognize lack of affective, or emotional, understanding as a defense.[32] Finally, it provides the "wrongfulness" option, meant to allow an insanity finding not only if the person did not know the act was illegal under the law, but also under circumstances where mental illness led to a belief that the act was morally permissible according to community standards.[33]

Since the early 1950s, when the American Law Institute (ALI) test was first promulgated, several other insanity defense formulations have been advanced. The two most expansive were both proposed in their modern American form by Judge David Bazelon, one of the giants of mental health law. In Durham v. United States,[34] he rejuvenated the so-called product test. Derived from the writings of the nineteenth-century medical scholar Isaac Ray,[35] this test excuses crime simply if it is caused by mental illness, with no particular proof of cognitive or volitional impairment required. Several years later, disenchanted with the medical model underlying the insanity defense and with the conclusory expert testimony the product test produced, Bazelon called for acquittal whenever the person cannot be held "justly responsible" for the criminal act.[36] This test is the broadest of any of those discussed here, because it entirely delinks the "insanity" test from any mental disorder predicate and thus gives the fact finder free rein to decide who should be held accountable for criminal acts. Alternatively, academics from the clinical and legal disciplines such as Herbert Fingarette,[37] Michael Moore,[38] Stephen Morse,[39] Benjamin Sendor,[40] and Robert Schopp[41] have proposed tests that focus on the rationality of the defendant, a construct that is cognitively oriented but that, its proponents claim, also captures those with volitional impairment who ought to be excused.[42] Although the rationality tests vary in form, they all look at the extent to which the thought content of the criminal defendant reflects reality and the manner in which the defendant processes information.

None of these latter tests has been adopted by any state, and the product test exists in only one state.[43] The ALI test, in contrast, proved quite popular, at one time holding sway in virtually all the federal circuits and more than half the states (with the rest using M'Naghten alone or combined with an irresistible impulse defense).[44] After Hinckley's acquittal on charges of attempting to assassinate Reagan, however, the federal government, as well as several states that had adopted the ALI test, eliminated the volitional prong and tried to narrow the scope of the defense in other ways.[45] Furthermore, at least five states have now eliminated the insanity defense altogether, while maintaining the so-called mens rea alternative, which permits psychiatric evidence only on the issue of whether the defendant intended the criminal conduct.[46] That alternative reduces the exculpatory scope of mental illness considerably because, as noted earlier, even significantly impaired offenders usually intend their actions at the time of the crime.

B. Other Defenses

Running parallel to the expansionary developments in insanity defense jurisprudence through the 1970s were much more significant developments, in terms of the number of cases affected, concerning the mens rea required for specific offenses and the scope of affirmative defense doctrines such as self-defense, provocation, and duress. These other legal defenses have also, over time, generally expanded. What is especially important for purposes of this discussion is a particular sense in which they have expanded: They have all moved toward a more subjective definition of culpability that makes evidence of mental disorder relevant independent of the insanity defense.

In early medieval times, proof of the act alone may have been sufficient to convict;[47] neither mens rea nor affirmative defense doctrine existed in the formal substantive criminal law. Even accidental harm or harm perpetrated in self-defense appears to have been punished criminally, although perhaps not as severely as intentional unjustified conduct.[48] By the twelfth or thirteenth century, the courts, under the influence of the church, did begin to speak of an evil or vicious mindset as a predicate for guilt,[49] but this requirement was not particularly significant. It appeared to bar conviction for pure accident and objectively reasonable self-defense and perhaps for involuntary acts as well. Other than that, as already noted, noninsane individuals who committed crime—people who knew their acts were causing harm—were considered culpable regardless of the degree of purposefulness behind their conduct or the precise goal of that conduct.[50]

By the fifteenth century, the law regarding mens rea showed signs of progression toward a more refined subjective approach. Courts began to differentiate between mental states, so that in the law of homicide, for instance, those whose acts were "wanton and willful" were viewed as more culpable than those who acted less deliberately.[51] Many crimes were said to require what came to be called "specific intent,"[52] that is, an intent to cause a result beyond that associated with knowingly engaging in particular conduct. Thus, burglary (defined as entering a dwelling with an intent to commit theft) was said to require the specific intent to commit theft.

In theory, a person who, because of mental disorder, did not kill "willfully," or otherwise did not possess the required specific intent, should be acquitted of these types of offenses. In practice, however, the subjectification of mens rea went only so far. Prior to the mid-twentieth century, evidence of impaired mental state was rarely considered relevant, outside of the insanity context, even in the relatively more liberal United States.[53] Moreover, even the formal law of mens rea remained predominately objectively defined with respect to mistakes of fact (for example, mistakes about ownership of property, consent, identity of the victim).[54] This objective approach significantly curbed the usefulness of psychiatric testimony because, as noted earlier, mental illness is much more likely to lead to such mistakes than to an inability to form an intent to carry out the conduct or cause the particular result associated with the crime.

Other defensive doctrines were even more clearly defined in objective terms until well into the twentieth century. A person was acquitted on self-defense grounds only if, as an objective matter, the harm committed was no greater than the harm prevented.[55] A person who asserted provocation (a defense that reduces murder to manslaughter) could prevail on that claim only if certain types of provoking events, derived from assumptions about how reasonable people react to such events, were proven.[56] Duress was available only in a very limited number of objectively defined circumstances.[57] Under these defenses, the defendant's assertions about his or her feelings at the time of the offense, even if believed, were hardly dispositive, and often not even deemed relevant. In particular, evidence of mental illness was not considered pertinent.[58]

Probably the single most important trend in U.S. criminal law during the twentieth century has been the erosion of this objective approach to mens rea and the defenses. The leader in this trend toward subjectively defined culpability, as with the insanity defense, was again the ALI's Model Penal Code.

With respect, first, to mens rea, the Code expresses a strong preference for criminal liability based on proof of actual awareness that one is causing the result under the circumstances required for the crime,[59] a position that, as discussed above, the common law never fully embraced. Following logically from this proposition, the Code permits evidence of mental abnormality to be introduced not only on the insanity issue, but also on the issue of whether the accused had the mens rea associated with the crime.[60] For instance, to repeat previous examples, if a person's mental disorder leads to an accidental killing, or to a belief that he is shooting the devil rather than a person, he should be acquitted of both murder and manslaughter under the Model Penal Code,[61] regardless of his likely success with the insanity defense, because he did not intend to end the life of a human being, nor was he even aware of the risk of doing so. (Whether such a person would be convicted of negligent homicide is discussed later in this chapter.) This idea is often referred to as the "diminished capacity" defense, but that is a misleading phrase to the extent it suggests a special defense for those with mental illness.[62] In fact, this provision of the Code is nothing more than a recognition that mental illness, like inadvertence and incompetence, can negate the requisite mens rea for the crime.

Even more significant is the Model Penal Code's approach to defensive doctrines such as self-defense, provocation and duress. In contrast to the common law, the Code permits the defendant asserting these defenses to submit evidence about his or her own feelings and thoughts at the time of the offense. For instance, in the justification domain the Code permits the use of deadly force whenever "*the actor believes* such force is necessary to protect himself against death, serious bodily harm, kidnapping or sexual intercourse compelled by force or threat."[63] This formulation makes the actor's beliefs, relevant to, although not dispositive of, a self-defense claim. As such, the defense is not a justification, in the sense of acquitting a person whose acts we condone or perhaps even encourage, but rather is an excuse, because it permits acquittal given the kind of person the defendant is. One might call the Model Penal Code's approach "subjective justification" because, although the ultimate judgment as to whether the person's actions were justified depends on an objective balancing of the harm caused against the harm prevented, the harms to be balanced are determined by the subjective perceptions of the actor, not those of the outside world.

The provision of the Code that is analogous to the common law provocation doctrine is somewhat more objectively defined but still incorporates subjective elements. It states that a homicide that would otherwise be murder is manslaughter if it is "committed under the influence of extreme mental or emotional disturbance for which there is reasonable explanation or excuse, . . . the reasonableness of such explanation or excuse to be determined *from the viewpoint of a person in the actor's situation under the circumstances as he believes them to be.*"[64] Similarly, with respect to duress, the Code provides for an affirmative defense when a person commits a crime "because he was coerced to do so by the use of, or a threat to use, unlawful force against his person or the person of another, which a person of reasonable firmness *in his situation* would have been unable to resist."[65] The commentary to the Code makes clear that the intent of the latter italicized language "is to give effect to the defense when an actor mistakenly believes that a threat to use unlawful force has been made."[66]

Theoretically, therefore, evidence of mental abnormality could be relevant under any of these affirmative defenses.[67] As with the insanity defense, many states have refused to follow the Model Penal Code's lead in defining the mens rea and affirmative defenses subjectively.[68] But, in large part due to the impetus provided by the Code, the subjective approach to criminal culpability is now well entrenched in criminal justice jurisprudence.

C. Implications

From this brief overview, two facts should be clear. First, the insanity defense developed at a time when no other culpability doctrine mitigated punishment for nonaccidental crime. Even in relatively recent times, insanity was the only possible defense for a person with mental illness who acted "unreasonably" in committing an offense. For such persons, there was no mens rea, provocation, or subjective justification plea.

In a sizeable number of jurisdictions today, however, anyone—mentally ill or not—who makes a mistake as to result or fact or who believes he or she is confronted by circumstances that would lead to justification, provocation, or duress, may have a defense. Thus, the universe of excuses has expanded to the point where many of those who would be acquitted under an insanity defense could also succeed under another doctrine. For example, a criminal defendant who did not know the nature and quality of a criminal act will usually lack mens rea if the latter is subjectively defined, while a person who did not think the act was wrong will often have a subjective justification. Although the subjectification trend pioneered by the Model Penal Code has its detractors,[69] it has also been vigorously defended,[70] and the rest of this analysis will be premised on the assumption, without further discussion, that it represents the morally appropriate view.

One could conclude from all of this that the insanity defense is no longer needed. If, as I eventually propose, general ignorance of the law is added to the list of excuses recognized in the Model Penal Code, the subjectively defined defensive doctrines provide a broader basis for exculpation than both the pre-*M'Naghten* formulations of the defense and the *M'Naghten* test itself (at least if literally interpreted). Thus, if the latter formulation is morally sufficient for purposes of recognizing the exculpatory effect of mental disorder, the integration approach should be as well.

Some defendants who might be acquitted under more modern versions of the insanity defense, however, would not be entitled to a defense under these other subjectively defined doctrines. As illustrated at the beginning of this chapter, for instance, those whose beliefs, if true, would not amount to justification (Hinckley, for instance) would not be acquitted under any of the subjectified defenses; an insanity defense under the ALI or Bazelon tests would be their only hope of avoiding conviction. Similarly, those who exhibit only volitional impairment would generally have a defense only under the volitional prong of the insanity test still recognized in some jurisdictions. The question thus becomes whether there are normative reasons for recognizing a separate, special defense in such situations.

II. Moral Considerations

Current insanity tests are overbroad because, if taken literally, they move too far toward the deterministic *reductio ad absurdum* that no one is responsible. The rationality test favored by a number of scholars begins to deal with the problem, because only a small percentage of offenders are truly irrational. But it too is overinclusive, because it fails to explain why irrational reasons are necessarily exculpatory. Allowing subjectively defined defensive doctrines to do the work better captures the universe of people who should be excused.

A. The Assault of Determinism

The development of the modern behavioral sciences has made the criminal law's attempt to draw a coherent line between responsibility and nonresponsibility ever more difficult. The claim embodied in the insanity defense, regardless of the specific language used, is that symptoms of mental illness over which the defendant had little or no control caused the crime. As long as mental disorder is kept narrowly defined, as was the case before the advent of modern psychiatry, this type of claim is not particularly threatening to the legal system and a culture that treasures a belief in autonomy. But when behavioral scientists tell us that we have as little control over aspects of "character" as we do over mental illness, when science begins establishing clear correlates between physiology and aggression, and when the medical model of mental disease is supplemented with other, more exogenous models of disorder, determinism's assault on the citadel of free will begins to carry the day.

Consider first the number of mental impairments that fall under the rubric of character deficiencies, as distinguished from the psychotic dysfunctions such as schizophrenia (characterized by delusions and hallucinations) and the bipolar disorders (characterized by mania) that have traditionally formed the basis for the insanity defense. The DSM includes a plethora of disorders that fit in this category, including mental retardation, many types of impulse disorders (such as pedophilia), and an even larger number of so-called personality disorders (such as schizoid personality, borderline personality, dependent personality, paranoid personality, and antisocial personality).[71] All these disorders are thought to be congenital or at least produced by early childhood influences, and many of them are even more immune to change than the psychoses.[72] At any given time in the United States, perhaps 15 percent of the general population,[73] and well over 40 percent of the prison population, suffers from one of these nonpsychotic disorders.[74] All by themselves, people diagnosed as psychopaths, a well-studied subcategory of antisocial personality disorder, comprise perhaps 20 percent of those in prison.[75]

Then there are numerous studies showing correlations between antisocial behavior and genetic makeup (for example, an extra Y chromosome), hormonal imbalances, abnormal EEGs, certain deficiencies in intellectual capacities, and various types of brain dysfunctions.[76] Although many of these studies are inconclusive, or are contradicted by other studies,[77] it is clear that some biological factors do strongly predispose people to commit crime.[78] The number of people afflicted by such physiological problems is substantial.[79]

Finally, there are mental impairments that are more clearly caused by external factors, such as bad relationships, trauma, and general stress. The "battered women syndrome" and "Vietnam veteran syndrome" (both based on the official diagnosis of post-traumatic stress disorder),[80] "black rage," and the "abuse excuse" are among the many legal creations meant to capture this notion.[81] Given their vague contours, the prevalence of such phenomena is hard to estimate, but it is not insubstantial.[82]

These various psychological insights pose a potentially significant problem for the law of insanity, because a vast number of people who commit crime can now make a plausible claim that they were significantly impaired by a mental disorder at the time of the offense. Although courts for the most part have rejected exculpatory claims based on nonpsychotic disorders,[83] the justification for doing so is often weak. The best way to see why is to look at insanity doctrine through the prism of its three most prevalent manifestations, what I will call the Volitional Test, the Appreciation Test, and the Rationality Test. After demonstrating the unsatisfactory nature of these tests, the Integrationist Test that I advocate will be revisited and refined, and the case for it reinforced.

B. The Volitional Test

At least three insanity formulations focus on lack of volition: the "irresistible impulse" test, the ALI's prong excusing substantial inability to conform behavior, and the *Durham* case's product test. Applied literally, the first test is the narrowest and the last test the broadest. But for present purposes the differences between these formulations are not important. The key point is that, given the wide array of mental disorders that can be said to affect volition, these tests open the door to excusing so many people that the punishment model of liberty deprivation becomes hard to sustain as a meaningful enterprise.

The usual volitional impairment claim consists of an assertion that the offender "felt compelled" to carry out the offense. For instance, psychotic individuals who hear voices telling them to kill may experience powerful urges to commit crime. Unfortunately, however, that compulsion claim does not distinguish them from a large number of other, less "ill" individuals. From what we can ascertain, the subjectively felt urges of pedophiles, repeat rapists, and thieves who steal to feed an addiction are at least equal to the impulses experienced by people with manic-depressive and other psychoses.[84] The same can probably be said of people with other types of nonpsychotic disorders, such as borderline personality disorder and attention deficit disorder.[85] Psychiatrists tell us that kleptomania, fire setting, and even some homicides are the result of strong urges spurred by an unconscious desire to resolve profound emotional conflicts.[86] And commonplace temper tantrums and other violent outbursts are also often experienced as "uncontrollable," perhaps as a result of chemical imbalances. As one researcher put it, in such cases "the so-called irresistible impulse is perhaps less psychological than physiological."[87] Even the greedy corporate executive who manipulates accounts, or the teenage boy on a Friday night who wants to have intercourse with an underage girlfriend, may feel as compelled as the psychotic offender. A punishment model of liberty deprivation that recognized an excuse in all, or even just in many, of these situations would begin to look whimsical.

The Volitional Test is even more insidious, however, because it countenances not only the subjective urge claim, but also the predisposition claim. The latter type of assertion goes something like this: "I have characteristics or have experienced events that are highly correlated with criminal behavior; therefore I am compelled (or strongly predisposed) to commit crime." Defendants who assert the "extra male chromosome" defense,[88] an abnormal brain pattern,[89] or the rotten social background defense[90] are making this type of claim. Note that these people do not say they did not intend the criminal act, or that they committed it for "crazy" reasons. They are stating instead that their criminal behavior is driven by factors outside their control.

Recognition of an excuse here would not just disrupt a culpability-based system, but spell the end of it. As a dramatic illustration of this point, consider a report in the journal *Science* of a study finding that 85 percent of those individuals who had been abused as children and registered low MAOA neurotransmitter levels commit crimes against persons by age twenty-six.[91] It is rare to find such a high correlation between just two variables and crime, on the surface making these individuals particularly strong candidates for a volitional defense. But recognizing an excuse for these people would, in principle, require that we excuse *all* crime. For, as the scientific literature described above suggests, the only difference between the sample described in *Science* and any other group of criminals is that with other groups we need more than two variables to explain the criminal behavior. If identification of the correlates of crime is an excuse, it should, in principle, be an excuse whether the correlates are two or a dozen in number.

A proponent of the Volitional Test might object to all this by reminding us that, as a historical matter, the test was meant to excuse only offenders with a "severe" mental disease or defect. That is true, as a historical matter. But no logical basis for that limitation exists. While people with psychosis may be more likely to commit violent crime than people in the general population, they are *less* likely to do so than people with psychopathy, an impulse disorder, or a substance abuse problem,[92] reinforcing the notion that the urges of a person with mental illness are not provably greater than the urges of people we would never think of excusing. And if an offender truly does have serious difficulty avoiding commission of crime, he should not be barred from exculpation simply because psychosis is absent. A psychosis-only limitation, or anything similar, is justified at best by a bare desire to cabin the insanity defense.

In sum, the Volitional Test, assuming it is not arbitrarily limited, creates a huge potential for chaos in a culpability-based criminal justice system. If we conclude that some psychotic individuals are so compelled that they should be found nonresponsible, then we probably have to excuse pedophiles and many other garden-variety criminals as well, because they also plausibly claim to experience very strong urges. If we excuse those who were abused as children and have low serotonin levels because 85 percent of them commit crimes, then we probably also must excuse every criminal with an antisocial personality disorder—which would empty quite a few cells in today's prisons—because at least 85 percent of people with this disorder commit crime.[93] Those conclusions would significantly compromise our present system of criminal justice.

There are two solutions to this problem. One is to reject the culpability orientation of the criminal justice system, a proposition that Chapter 5 explores. The other is to retain the punishment model and reject volitional-based insanity claims entirely. But the latter stance may strike some as unfair. If we are willing to recognize an excuse for those coerced by external sources (the duress defense), how can we fail to recognize a defense based on internal compulsions? In other words, how can a culpability-oriented system legitimately ignore credible claims that crime was caused by factors outside the criminal's control?

The best attempt at reconciling this tension comes from Michael Moore, one of the first proponents of the irrationality formulation that will be discussed below. To the determinist claim that all of us are volitionally impaired and thus cannot be held responsible, Moore responds, "causation is not compulsion."[94] Moore *assumes* that all behavior is caused by biological, characterological, unconscious, or environmental factors.[95] But, he argues, none of those causes necessarily disrupt one's ability to generate reasons for one's actions, based on one's desires and beliefs. These reasons, Moore demonstrates, are also causes of behavior, even if they themselves are caused by biological or other factors. Thus, when a person acts for reasons he is, so to speak, the "proximate" cause of his actions and generally should be held responsible for them (unless the reasons are irrational).[96]

Stephen Morse, another rationality theorist, bolsters these arguments with observations about the incoherence of the traditional volitional impairment inquiry.[97] Aside from reflex events, Morse argues, everyone, no matter how compelled they feel, has choices at the time they act. When the pressure to act is external, as when someone puts a gun to one's head and orders a crime be committed, an excuse may make normative sense.[98] But Morse suggests that when the pressure to act is internal, as might be the case with a drug addict or pedophile, a separate volitional excuse generally cannot be sustained for practical and conceptual reasons. First, "it will often be too difficult to assess the degree of threatened dysphoria that creates the hard choice."[99] As Morse noted twenty-five years ago, in a statement that still holds true, "[t]here is no scientific measure of the strength of urges"[100] (a conclusion that Chapter Four demonstrates in more detail). Second, "it is simply not clear that the fear of dysphoria would ever be sufficient to excuse the breach of important expectations, except in precisely those cases in which we would assume naturally that the agent's rational capacity was essentially disabled."[101] For example, Morse says, the "police officer at the elbow" test, which limits the volitional prong of the insanity defense to situations in which the urge to commit crime is so strong that not even the presence of a law enforcement official disinhibits the person, "is . . . better interpreted as a rationality test."[102]

Moore and Morse make a solid argument against the contention that determinism defeats the law's effort to attribute culpability, as well as a convincing case for looking at a person's desires and beliefs at the time of the crime in deciding when culpability should be imposed. If one accepts their arguments, the Volitional Test can legitimately be discarded as a contender for the insanity defense, meaning that only the Appreciation, Rationality, and Integrationist tests are left standing. Moore and Morse endorse the Rationality Test. Before discussing that approach to the insanity defense and revisiting the Integrationist Test that I propose, it will be useful to examine the Appreciation Test, because an understanding of its flaws helps to explain why the Rationality Test is superior, and why the Integrationist Test is even better.

C. The Appreciation Test

The ALI's appreciation of wrongfulness formulation is the most popular insanity test today, grudgingly endorsed even by a Congress intent on limiting insanity doctrine after the Hinckley verdict (although the federal test does remove the word "substantial" from in front of the words "incapacity to appreciate," which suggests a tougher stance).[103] Thus, it is particularly unfortunate that, if applied honestly, the Appreciation Test, like the Volitional Test, would excuse numerous people whom most members of Congress, as well as many others, would not want excused. Modern knowledge about behavior leads irrevocably to the conclusion that the Appreciation Test, like its volitional counterpart, would upend the criminal justice system, if it is taken seriously. The same is true of the *M'Naghten* test, to the extent the word "know" in that test is applied in the deeper, affective sense, as some research suggests it normally is.[104] In the following discussion, however, I will assume there is a distinction between the Appreciation Test and the "literal" *M'Naghten* test (as well as the Integrationist Test), and highlight that distinction, so the differences can be better understood.

Exhibit A in the case against the Appreciation Test is the psychopathic personality, virtually everyone's paradigm of the "evil" person who should be punished if he or she commits crime. Dr. Robert Hare, the leading researcher on this particular phenomenon, summarizes it as follows: "[Psychopaths] seem unable to 'get under into the skin' or to 'walk in the shoes' of others, except in a truly intellectual sense. . . . [They] are glib and superficial, lack remorse or guilt, lack empathy, have shallow emotions and lack responsibility."[105] This type of person, if he commits crime, clearly does not meet a literal *M'Naghten* test, because he knows his act is criminal and not justified. For the same reason, he would not be excused under the Integrationist Test. But he would meet the Appreciation Test, if honestly applied. People with psychopathic personalities do not internalize the enormity of the criminal act. *By definition*, they do not emotionally appreciate its wrongfulness.

Probably for that reason, the drafters of the ALI test declared, in a supplementary paragraph to their insanity formulation, that a mental disease or defect that is "manifested solely by repeated antisocial behavior" may not form the predicate for the insanity defense.[106] On its face, this language does not accomplish its apparent goal, since the diagnosis of psychopathy and its close relative, antisocial personality disorder, require other symptoms besides repeated crime.[107] But assuming psychopathy is meant to be subsumed by this provision, an insanity test that has to exclude by fiat a mental disorder that clearly falls within its terms has not done a good job of identifying the relevant excusing condition.

Another class of people who commit a large amount of crime is comprised of people with mild retardation, defined as those with an intelligence quotient of between 50 and 70.[108] Consider this observation about their cognitive capacities: "Mildly retarded persons may be able to distinguish right from wrong in the abstract, but they have difficulty applying abstract concepts in specific actual settings and are unable to appreciate the wrongfulness of what they do."[109] If this statement is accurate, people with mild retardation, while generally sane under a literal *M'Naghten* test and the Integrationist Test, should be found insane under the Appreciation Test. Yet the latter result would be repugnant to many people, including some advocates for people with mental retardation.[110] Criminals with mild mental retardation should escape execution, as the Supreme Court recently held,[111] but few should escape conviction.

The Appreciation Test, honestly applied, also excuses many people whose principal dysfunction appears to be volitional rather than cognitive. Here, for example, is an excerpt from testimony in State v. Companaro,[112] involving a person who was found insane under the Appreciation Test for embezzling money to support his pathological gambling habit:

> Well, here's a man who is a law enforcement officer, who knows the law well, who knows about right and wrong [and therefore would not meet the literal *M'Naghten* test or the Integrationist Test], but who is in a desperate strait. He's under a tremendous amount of stress at that point, does not consider right and wrong. I don't think that becomes part of the thinking process. His process then is to survive. He's losing his job, his family, his children, his reputation, everything is going down.[113]

Companaro's case illustrates how the Appreciation Test permits volitional impairment to be described, and excused, in terms of cognitive impairment. People under stress, the argument goes, do not think through the consequences of their actions, and thus do not appreciate the wrongfulness of what they're doing. If that argument is allowed, prohibition of volitional-based insanity claims will accomplish very little, because many volitional impairment cases can be recharacterized as cognitive impairment cases. Indeed, even many people who do not have mental disorders as we normally define them (for instance, those who offend in a "blind rage") might not "consider right and wrong" at the time they commit crime.

Again, as with the Volitional Test, one could try to solve these problems by limiting application of the Appreciation Test to cases of psychosis and like disorders. Richard Bonnie, a proponent of this view, would tie the insanity defense to "severe" disorders, by which he means "a pathological process within the brain, over which the person has no control, leading to mental experience that is qualitatively different from ordinary experience."[114] Although this type of move may conform with the intuitions of most people, the rationale for privileging "severe" mental illness over other forms of mental disorder is no more obvious in this context than it is when looking at volitional claims. Already noted is the research indicating that people with psychosis are less influenced by their delusions than intuition suggests, as well as less dangerous than is commonly believed.[115] We've also learned much more about other kinds of mental disorders, and much of that knowledge suggests that making meaningful distinctions between severe and not-so-severe disorders is an elusive goal.

Consider, for instance, whether psychopathy fits Bonnie's definition of "severe" disorder. Psychopathy is also "pathological," possibly "congenital" and probably "neurological."[116] Further, it is a condition that is not easily within the person's "control," and indeed is much less so than the condition of a severely mentally ill person for whom there is at least some meaningful treatment.[117]

Finally, psychopaths are—again using Bonnie's words explaining why psychosis should be the focus of insanity—out of touch "with ordinary experience." The results of one simple study graphically makes this latter point. A group of people with psychopathy and a control group were hooked up to a device that measures physiological responses, and both groups were read five words: chair, table, apple, house, murder. The controls—the nonpsychopathic group—registered a significant blip on the screen when the word "murder" was announced. But that word occasioned no reaction from the psychopaths. Their emotional response was nonexistent.[118] The inner experiences of the person with psychopathy are as alienated from normal experience as delusions are, albeit in a different way.

Even if the Appreciation Test is arbitrarily limited to cases of gross mental disorder, however, it may excuse people who should not be excused. Charles Manson's gang executed a complicated plan to kill several rich white people, including the actress Sharon Tate.[119] Why? Manson, who has been diagnosed with schizophrenia,[120] apparently believed that the world would eventually be taken over by African-Americans, who would then kill off most of the white race in a bloodbath. Manson meant to prevent that debacle by slaughtering white people and then, by planting various pieces of evidence obtained at the murder scene, framing African-Americans for the crimes, thereby alerting the white world to the dangers presented by the black race.[121]

Manson knew it was wrong to order Tate and the others killed. He would not meet the literal *M'Naghten* test. However, a plausible argument could have been made (although it was not, because he refused to allow evidence of insanity to be introduced)[122] that Manson did not "appreciate the wrongfulness of his conduct." Rather, he felt he was in the right when he ordered the killings, because doing so would stop the impending massacre by African-Americans.

Note that this sense of justification would not excuse Manson under the Integrationist Test. That test uses societal views as a benchmark against which to judge the exculpatory nature of the defendant's motivations, and Manson's beliefs, even if true, would not justify his behavior. In contrast, the Appreciation Test asks the fact finder to base its decision solely on the nature of the offender's beliefs about the propriety of his actions, an essentially standardless inquiry.

The same conundrum is illustrated by the case of Ted Kaczynski, also known as the Unabomber. The people to whom he mailed letter bombs all were somehow involved with technology.[123] From what we know from public documents, Kaczynski, who was clearly suffering from schizophrenia,[124] picked these victims because he wanted to send a message that if his victims and people like them failed to curb society's reliance on sophisticated machinery, computers and the like, the world as we know it would come to an end.[125] His crimes, to which he ended up pleading guilty so that his motivations would not be labeled crazy,[126] were his way of preventing this destruction of the world by technology. He knew that it was wrong to kill people and he knew that sending the letter bombs would result in other people's deaths, so he did not meet the literal *M'Naghten* test. Nor would any jury likely find his motives justificatory, and thus he would not be excused under the Integrationist approach. But there is a strong argument that he did not appreciate the wrongfulness of his actions, because in his confused state he felt they were necessary.

Perhaps the reader believes that both Manson and Kaczynski *should* have been excused for their crimes. The problem then becomes how to distinguish them from other less "crazy" offenders who convinced themselves their crimes were justified, such as John Wayne Gacy, who believed he was doing the world a service when he killed more than twenty men he thought were homosexual prostitutes.[127] Similarly, many pedophiles rationalize their molestations on the ground that the children somehow benefit.[128] The only basis for refusing to excuse these latter type of offenders while excusing people like Manson and Kaczynski is that the latter two defendants somehow held their self-justificatory beliefs more intensely. That distinction is footless, for reasons best developed in connection with the Rationality Test, which more squarely raises the issue.

D. The Rationality Test

At first glance, an insanity test based on irrationality would seem even more likely to open the floodgates of exculpation than either the Volitional Test or the Appreciation Test, because virtually all criminal behavior could be labeled "irrational." But, as Michael Moore defines the term, irrationality should not be equated with inaccurate, abnormal, or bad judgments. Rather, it exists only when a person exhibits unintelligible desires, strongly held but inconsistent beliefs, and incoherent thought process.[129] This, of course, comes close to the traditional definition of psychosis. So defined, it is not surprising that the Rationality Test justifies, better than either the Volitional or Appreciation tests, a threshold for insanity that puts the psychoses on one side and most other disorders and mental phenomena on the other. As a result, the Rationality Test is preferable to either of these other two tests as a legal response to the challenges of modern behavioral science.

Yet the same type of question asked in connection with the Volitional and Appreciation tests is germane here as well. Why is irrationality (qua psychotic-like symptoms) singled out? What is it about irrationality that makes it the excusing condition? The proponents of the Rationality Test do not give a sufficient answer to this question. Moore's entire case for an insanity test that focuses on irrationality is as follows:

> Only if we can see another being as one who acts to achieve some rational end in light of some rational beliefs will we understand him in the same fundamental way that we understand ourselves and our fellow persons in everyday life. We regard as moral agents only those beings we can understand in this way.[130]

Morse—who, it will be remembered, is another Rationality Test advocate—offers a somewhat different rationale, one suggested at the end of the last section: irrationality is the preeminent excusing condition because, in Morse's words, it "make[s] it too hard" for a person "to grasp or be guided by good reasons not to offend."[131]

One can concede Moore's point that we view irrational people differently without being forced to reach the conclusion that they thereby deserve exculpation from criminal offenses they commit. In fact, his explanation is tautological on the question of who should be considered responsible; it simply declares that irrational persons are not "moral agents."[132] To bolster his point, he notes the medieval tendency to equate mentally disordered persons with beasts and infants, whom he says we do not regard as moral beings.[133] But that equation applies only in those cases in which the medieval cases applied it: when the offender did not know the nature and quality of the act, and thus lacked the capacity to form intent, or at least was ignorant of the law in the general sense. People who know they are harming another cannot so easily be consigned to the "nonmoral being" category, assuming such a category should exist in the first place (an issue taken up in more detail in Chapter Four).

Morse provides a more cogent reason for using irrationality as the test, but in doing so engages in the same reasoning he criticizes in those who support the volitionality inquiry. How do we know when, to use Morse's language, it is *"too hard . . . to grasp or be guided by good reasons not to offend"*? The assumption that irrational individuals find it more difficult to obtain or process information than do other people sounds remarkably like the proposition that mentally ill people find it more difficult to control their behavior than do other people.[134] As noted earlier, the latter proposition is roundly rejected by Morse, in large part because it is empirically unverifiable.

Although Morse does not go into detail as to why irrationality makes access to good reasons difficult, Robert Schopp, another advocate of a rationality-type test, provides a good description of the effects of psychopathology on one's practical reasoning abilities.[135] He notes that people with a major mental disorder, such as schizophrenia, can experience disturbances in three areas: cognitive focus, reasoning, and concept formation. With respect to cognitive focus, people with schizophrenia often have difficulty attending to essential information and become distracted by irrelevant stimuli; for instance, they may engage in "perseveration" (repeating references that are no longer relevant) or experience "thought blocking," which involves a complete halt to thinking. Their reasoning ability is disturbed by the tendency to overgeneralize (by drawing conclusions without evidence or attributing elaborate meaning to something) and to engage in combinative thinking (for example, condensation of impressions into beliefs that are completely unrealistic). Finally, they have difficulty forming abstract concepts correctly, often by including information in categories to which they bear virtually no relationship.

Schopp illustrates many of these various disturbances in thought process with the story of Mary, based on a real case.[136] Mary stabbed to death a woman she had never met, as the woman came out of a church. Mary explained that she "had to" commit the crime because some "bad criminals" were going to kill her unless she convinced them that she, too, was bad. She knew of this threat because she had heard "them" talking about her on the phone (as she walked under the telephone wires), and because some people, whom she took to be the bad people, had been watching her on the subway. She chose the woman as her victim because a man she had thought about killing earlier "was too strong"; because she realized she was "supposed to" pick someone from a church after she found a dollar bill with "In God We Trust" on it; and because the woman had come out of the church just when Mary got there, "so I knew God wanted me to pick her." Asked whether she was still being watched at the time of the interview, she answered: "Yes, but now they think I'm bad like them—but I'm good—I fooled them." She blamed the act on her "delusions" and insisted the crime "wasn't my fault."

To Schopp, Mary demonstrated overgeneralized thinking when she concluded that people looking at her in the subway were "watching" her, and poor abstraction ability when she interpreted the words "In God We Trust" as a symbolic message.[137] Her reasons for stabbing the victim—in particular, the glances of the subway passengers, the dollar bill motto, and the fact that the woman was leaving the church when Mary arrived—illustrated attention to irrelevant details and unwarranted interpretations. She also held flatly inconsistent beliefs, according to Schopp; for instance, she believed that criminals are bad but did not wonder how she could stab someone and remain good. (Of course, these mental states are not inconsistent if she believed the stabbing was justified.) Schopp goes on to note that these types of perceptions and thoughts "are not mere mistakes about the environment. They occur as part of a pattern of pathological cognitive functioning in which the person's distorted cognitive processes allow him to accept these perceptual and cognitive distortions as accurate representations of the world and to interpret his other experiences in light of them." Thus, Schopp concludes, people like Mary "lack the capacity to generate action-plans through the normal process of practical inference."[138]

Clearly, Mary's cognitive focus, reasoning, and concept formation capacities are severely disturbed, much more so than those of someone who is not mentally ill. The key question, however, is whether this disturbance prevented her from assessing the good reasons for not killing, or at least made it relatively more difficult for her to access them. In this case, the principal reason for not committing the criminal act is that it is wrong to kill an innocent person.

Although we have no direct information on this point, it is improbable that this thought never occurred to Mary. Despite her many inaccurate perceptions about the world, she knew the victim had not tried to harm her and insisted that the crime was not her "fault" after it occurred, suggesting a sense of guilt. To protest that she may not have accessed this sense at the precise moment of the crime, but only afterward, is fruitless; many criminals—ranging from those who act in a fit of temper to those who rob banks for a living—do not consider the wrongfulness of their crimes while they are committing them.

Let us assume, however, that Mary did not, at any point at or near the time of the act, consider the possible reasons the killing was the wrong thing to do, perhaps because, given the dollar motto and the serendipity of the woman's egress from the church, she felt God was directing her. The crucial empirical question that must be answered is whether, to paraphrase a well-known query in the volitional impairment context, this lack of consideration was because she *could not* engage in such consideration at the time of the act or just *did not* do so. Just as we cannot know whether an impulse was irresistible or merely not resisted, this question about whether a certain reasoning process could not occur or just did not occur is not answerable. And if we pretend that we can answer it, disturbing implications would follow. As H. L. A. Hart stated:

[A] theory that mental operations like . . . thinking about . . . a situation are somehow "either there or not there," and so utterly outside our control, can lead to the theory that we are *never* responsible . . . For just as [someone] might say "My mind was a blank" or "I just forgot" or "I just didn't think, I could not help not thinking," so the cold-blooded murderer might say "I just decided to kill, I couldn't help deciding."[139]

It is also worth comparing Mary to people in similar situations who are not severely disordered. For instance, how is Mary different, in terms of coming up with reasons for not killing and giving those reasons their due, from a would-be gang member who is told his life will end unless he kills someone as part of a gang initiation? Or from a woman with a dependent personality who kills at the direction of a dominant other?[140] The youth and the dependent woman are presumably more adept than Mary at assessing relevant information (including the possibility of jail time) and formulating a coherent action plan. But, as Morse himself might say, we simply cannot know whether Mary, in formulating her action plan, found it any harder to think about or follow reasons not to kill. Mary said, "I thought I had to do it," but the other two might (honestly) say the same thing. Indeed, the juvenile could also plausibly argue that killing an innocent is excused when necessary to prevent one's own death (an argument that is cognizable under the Model Penal Code, although not under the common law).[141] If Mary is to be excused it should be under this type of duress theory (which the Integrationist Test would recognize),[142] not on the unprovable judgment that it was harder for her than for a nonmentally ill person to act for, or be guided by, good reasons. That conclusion is bolstered by the intuition that had Mary killed the woman from the church simply to prevent people from laughing at her, the urge to exculpate would not be nearly as strong, regardless of her cognitive distortions.

Other attempts to differentiate these three individuals do not work either. Schopp might say, for instance, that Mary should be excused because her psychopathology causes disorganized, inconsistent thinking; for example, she believes that killing is wrong one minute and not wrong the next. The juvenile (who is likely to be very conflicted over what he should do) is likely to experience similar contradictory feelings, and the dependent woman may never even consider that killing at the behest of her lover is wrong. It might also be argued that, at the time of the crime, Mary is not "herself" and that, once medicated, she would never dream of killing. The same can be said of the juvenile once removed from his gang-dominated environment and of the dependent woman once her lover is gone.

Consider another real case, involving a man we shall call Ralph.[143] Ralph killed his father because he believed the father was sleeping with Ralph's wife and daughter. This information, which was clearly wrong, had been communicated to Ralph through "voices" that let him know everything his father did. On the day of the murder, Ralph woke up and, in his words, "found a knife by the side of my bed." He drove to his father's house, met his father outside the house, and stabbed him twelve times. During a post-offense interview, Ralph stated that he knew it was not "right" to kill his father for sleeping with his wife, but mentioned that his father had abused him as a child and that the voices continually harped on his father's indiscretions with Ralph's wife and daughter. Again, it is impossible to know whether this person's ability to be guided by good reasons was any more diminished than either that of a mentally ill person with similar beliefs who does not kill his "tormentor" or that of a nonmentally person who kills when he discovers that his father *is* sleeping with his wife and daughter. As Dr. Drew Ross, a psychiatrist who has spent years evaluating murderers, notes "psychosis may enhance and enact the drama already present, and the drama is not necessarily an innocent one."[144]

Examples can easily be multiplied that lead one to question whether rationality makes sense as the culpability threshold. Some people with paranoid schizophrenia harm those whom they inaccurately perceive are harassing them, while other paranoid individuals, also irrationally fearful, do not.[145] At the same time, those who are generally not irrational may be just as likely as people with paranoid schizophrenia to react disproportionately to perceived threats. The law books are full of cases in which sensitive but otherwise normal people are convicted, albeit sometimes only of manslaughter, when they kill a person who has slighted them.[146] Among irrationality theorists, Morse at least is candid in noting that irrationality might even describe some offenders with pedophilia and psychopathy, results that make the Rationality Test as problematic as the Volitional and Appreciation tests.[147] In short, just as the existence of a disorder cannot tell us how hard it is to *do* what is right, the existence or nonexistence of irrationality usually cannot tell us how hard it is to *perceive* what is right.

E. Integrationism Reprised

Any test for insanity, whether it focuses on volitionality, appreciation, or irrationality, is a futile attempt to define a particular type of blamelessness: "controllessness." The question sought to be answered is the extent to which behavioral control is compromised due to a physiological/psychological inability to constrain behavior, an emotional inability to appreciate consequences, or a cognitive inability to perceive reality and process information. Perhaps if it could be demonstrated that such people really could not control their behavior, but rather acted as if some giant hand propelled them into their criminal conduct against their will, then they would be blameless.[148] But as Morse and others have shown, even the most severely crazy people usually intend their acts and therefore have some control of them.[149] And while some people do seem to have more difficulty choosing the right behavior than others, determining who has the most difficulty is probably impossible. Even if some day we are able to determine whose choices are the most difficult, it is unlikely that serious mental illness or irrationality would provide the right dividing line.

For all of these reasons, the linchpin of culpability analysis should not be volitionality, appreciation, or rationality, but rather the mens rea and subjective justification inquiries that form the basis for determining criminal culpability when mental disability is not involved. Sound reasons exist for these exculpatory doctrines. And if the exculpatory threshold is so defined, there would be no need to draw the lines made so difficult, so unfair, and, ultimately, so meaningless by our inability to decipher the deterministic influence. Hard decisions about the presence or absence of intent, the reasons for acting, and whether those reasons sound in justification, duress, and so on would still have to be made. But none of this would require explicit or implicit determinations about whether the person was capable of conforming behavior to the law.

In sum, then, mental disorder should have exculpatory effect when, and only when, its effects lead to a lack of the required mens rea or to reasons for committing the crime that sound in justification or duress. Two ambiguities about this rule left unresolved earlier can now be taken up: (1) What role should mental illness play when negligence is the mens rea? and (2) When, if ever, should ignorance of the criminal law due to mental disorder be an excuse? Answering these questions involves not only consideration of retributive issues, but also contemplation of the type of message the criminal law should send to people with mental illness and whether they will hear it. These considerations suggest that mental disorder can be exculpatory even when negligence is the mens rea, as well as when it causes an incapacity to grasp the concept of criminal law, but that exculpation should not be based on avoidable mental disorder or on a mistake of criminal law, even when it is attributable to mental disorder.

Liability based on negligence, as defined at common law, can be imposed even on a person whose mental disability caused a mistake as to result or fact, if a reasonable person would not have made such a mistake[150]—in other words, most of the time. Persuasive arguments have been made against negligence as a basis for criminal liability.[151] Even the generally subjectively oriented Model Penal Code, however, retains negligence as grounds for conviction in a number of situations, including homicide,[152] so that a person who should have known of the risks attendant to his behavior will be found liable, albeit for a lesser grade of crime. At the same time, in line with its general orientation, the Code's definition of negligence is decidedly more "subjective" than the common law's, because it looks at whether the actor should have been aware of the mistake, "considering the nature and purpose of his conduct and the circumstances known to him."[153] Under this definition, a person whose mental illness leads, erroneously yet firmly, to a belief that he or she is about to be killed would not be acting negligently in killing the perceived assailant; in essence, under the Code as it would apply in the situations we are addressing, negligence analysis would normally collapse into subjective justification analysis.

There may be one situation, however, where a person with mental disorder may be liable even if the criminal act was reasonable under the circumstances known to him at the time of the crime. Both the case law and modern statutes such as the Model Penal Code refuse to recognize an affirmative defense when the actor is responsible for the extenuating circumstances in which he finds himself. For instance, in defining its general choice of evils defense (the predicate for all the justification defenses), the Model Penal Code states that "[w]hen the actor was reckless or negligent in bringing about the situation requiring a choice of harms or evils . . . the justification afforded by this Section is unavailable in a prosecution for any offense for which recklessness or negligence, as the case may be, suffices to establish culpability."[154] Under this provision, a person with mental disability who knows that, while unmedicated, he is prone to engage in violent behavior may be liable for negligent or even reckless homicide if he fails to remain on medication and then kills. This would be so even if, at the time of the crime, his delusions otherwise satisfy the elements for subjective self-defense. The rationale for such a position is in the first instance retributive,[155] but also can be seen as utilitarian, to the extent a person with mental illness can be cajoled by the commands of the criminal law into taking his responsibility toward others seriously. It is also worth noting that laypeople consider one's culpability for bringing about one's mental condition highly relevant to criminal responsibility.[156]

The case of Andrea Yates, the woman who drowned her five children, is illustrative. As noted earlier, if one subscribes to the defense theory of the case, Yates had a strong subjective justification defense to the homicide charges brought against her. For instance, Dr. Phillip Resnick, a defense witness, believed Yates killed her children because she thought that if she did not do so they would go to hell, whereas killing them would send them to heaven.[157] Assuming that those delusions existed and that they represent reality, Yates would seem justified in her actions. She might still be convicted in an integrationist regime, however, if she were responsible for the delusions that she experienced and knew that they might lead to hostility toward the children. The evidence presented at trial indicated that she twice refused electric shock treatments. She often did not take her medication, against medical advice. She hid her symptoms from the doctor, knowing that when she did not take her medication she became very irritable with her children.[158] These kinds of facts should reduce the possibility of a complete defense, even if we assume a justificatory mental state at the time of the crime, because they suggest recklessness (an awareness of the risk that the offense would occur if the illness was not treated and a conscious decision to do nothing about it).[159] However, if Yates did not believe she was ill, or was not aware that failure to take treatment would exacerbate her violent delusions, then she would still be fully excused under this analysis.

Similar reasoning suggests a nuanced approach toward the exculpatory scope of ignorance about the criminal law. As noted earlier, some people who intentionally commit criminal acts are either unfamiliar with the concept of crime (earlier referred to as general ignorance of the law) or believe that their particular act is permitted by the criminal law (specific ignorance of the law). An example of the first type of person would be an infant or someone who, from birth, has been so retarded or mentally ill that no socialization has taken place. An example of the second type of person would be an individual from a culture that does not criminalize the particular behavior in question, or a person who, as a result of retardation or illness, believes that the criminal law authorizes something it clearly does not, such as killing in response to insults.[160]

Although American criminal law has generally not recognized ignorance about the criminal law as an excuse, a person who is not cognizant of *any* of society's constraints cannot justly be held liable for violating those constraints. Even the medieval tests of insanity would excuse a person who is generally ignorant of the criminal law. Such a person is likely to lack mens rea in either the mistake-as-to-result or mistake-of-fact sense in any event.

Thus, general ignorance of the law, whether caused by mental disability or some other factor, ought to be an excuse.

The same cannot be said when the mentally disordered person misperceives the criminal law's application in a particular instance, however. Such a person is generally aware of societal prohibitions and intends to commit the crime under actual or imagined circumstances that do not amount to self-defense or duress, but argues that he thought the law recognized a justification or duress defense under those circumstances. Outside of the insanity context, the law has been resistant to ignorance of specific legal rules as an excuse for two reasons: evidentiary concerns (How do we know that the person was ignorant of the law and whether the ignorance was his fault?),[161] and a desire to maintain the rule of law by ensuring that legislatures, not criminal actors, define the prohibitions of the criminal law, thus enhancing deterrence and fairness.[162] Both concerns might be thought to be mitigated in the insanity context, the first on the ground that mental illness is its own excuse for being ignorant, and the second on the ground that the integrity of the law is not threatened when people known to be mentally ill define its scope. But neither distinction is persuasive.

First, even when a claim of specific ignorance is from a person with mental disability it will normally be incredible in the type of *mala in se* crimes that trigger the insanity defense. For instance, a defendant's claim that he thought killing a taunter is justifiable homicide (as hypothesized above) is unlikely ever to be true,[163] except perhaps when the claimant is so disordered he is generally ignorant of the law. Even if that is not the case, notions underlying the rule of law counsel against recognizing such a claim. Carried to its logical end, the specific ignorance excuse allows the defendant to define the scope of self-defense and other justificatory doctrines, disregarding completely society's views on the matter. The consequent insult to the principle of legality and the criminal law's deterrent effect might not be significant, but it is nonetheless real. Similar reasoning has usually led courts to reject the analogous cultural defense.[164]

Limiting the exculpatory significance of ignorance of the law to the general ignorance category avoids these problems except in cases of the grossest disability, where the proof and legality dangers are not significant. In all other respects, the integration approach reinforces the rule of law, because an excuse would be available only when the reasons given by the defendant sound in justification or duress. If so, the defendant prevails, but only after society, through the vehicle of a judge or jury, has assessed the circumstances as the defendant believed them to be from *society's* standpoint, thus signaling that the verdict depends ultimately upon communal, not individual, preferences.

Putting all the conclusions reached in the foregoing discussion together and applying it to people with mental disorder, the Integrationist Alternative might read something like this:

> A person shall be excused from an offense if at the time of the offense [by reason of mental disease or defect] he (a) lacked the subjective mental state for the conduct, circumstance, or result element of the crime; (b) believed circumstances existed that, if true, would have justified the offense; (c) believed circumstances existed that, if true, would have amounted to duress; or (d) was unaware of the general prohibitions of the criminal law, provided that he or she did not cause any of these mental states by purposely avoiding treatment, aware that such states would occur without such treatment.

Although different people might apply integrationist analysis differently, the common theme under this approach is that insanity would no longer be a defense. Instead, judges and juries would apply the same defenses to people with mental illness that are applied to people who are not mentally ill (which is why the bracketed language need not be part of the test). Bonnie has suggested that the Integrationist Test is "arbitrary" because it relies on the Model Penal Code's choice-of-evils assessment of what is right and wrong.[165] But in fact that reliance makes integrationism *less* arbitrary, because the Code is bottomed on the normative judgments of society. Most people with mental illness are not ignorant of or oblivious to those judgments. Indeed, recent research confirms that, when people with serious mental illness do commit violence, it is almost always because they perceive they are being attacked or harmed in some other way by their victim.[166] If we were to assume their perceptions are accurate, their actions would often be considered quite reasonable, which happens to be precisely the situation in which the Integrationist Test is most likely to provide a defense.

In contrast, current cognitive formulations of insanity are exceedingly whimsical, because they allow the individual, rather than society, to define the scope of excuse. As Bonnie notes, the cognitive tests focus on the "intensity of the psychotic experience," the degree to which the person is "detached" from reality, and the extent to which he or she could have been more "restrained."[167] The only distinguishing feature in all these inquiries is the degree of psychosis, a condition that, as much of this chapter has demonstrated, bears only a tenuous relationship to culpability. If the individual's psychosis is so flagrant that he is not aware of the nature of his actions, he is excused under any of the formulations discussed in this chapter, including the Integrationist Test. But for those mental states that fall short of this sort of unawareness, Bonnie's "degree of psychosis" test does not offer any identifiable rationale for separating those who should be exculpated from those who are not. As a result, the insanity inquiry under modern cognitive formulations—whether it is the Appreciation or Rationality test—is much more prone to random outcomes than the inquiry required by the integrationist approach.

As a final matter of refinement, the Integrationist Test must be distinguished from both the *M'Naghten* test and the recently popular reform of the insanity defense, the so-called mens rea alternative. Although the Integrationist Test may well be narrower than the *M'Naghten* test to the extent the latter formulation is interpreted to be congruent with the Appreciation Test, it bears a very strong resemblance to the "literal" *M'Naghten* rule and in significant ways is more expansive than that rule. The Integrationist Test's lack of mens rea and general ignorance of the law components are consistent with *M'Naghten*'s willingness to excuse those who do not know the nature and quality of their acts. And its subjective justification component is identical to *M'Naghten*'s "partial delusion" test. At the same time, the Integrationist Test adds a subjective duress component and, most important, does away with the "mental disease or defect" predicate, ultimately making it broader than the original *M'Naghten* standard.

These comments also ought to make clear why the Integrationist Test is very different from, and much broader than, the mens rea alternative, which recognizes only lack of mens rea as a defense.[168] As noted earlier, five states have replaced the insanity defense with this approach. It is very possible that, despite the contrary decisions by courts in some of these states,[169] the mens rea alternative is unconstitutional. Early cases from the U.S. Supreme Court could lead one to predict that the insanity defense is not a crucial aspect of due process, and thus that such attempts to significantly reduce the role of mental disorder in criminal cases would be upheld.[170] But in 1996 the Court decided Egelhoff v. Montana,[171] which involved a challenge to a Montana statute that abolished the intoxication defense. The Court did not consider that particular law an infringement of due process.[172] But the primary reason it gave for its holding was that the intoxication defense is of "recent vintage" and thus not a fundamental aspect of criminal justice.[173] In contrast, of course, the insanity defense is *not* of recent vintage; it is ancient. Perhaps, therefore, when the Supreme Court hears a case challenging the mens rea alternative it will hold that the mental disorder must be allowed to play a greater role in blameworthiness assessments.[174]

That holding would not threaten the Integrationist Test, however. If *M'Naghten* is a constitutionally adequate formulation of insanity, then the Integrationist Alternative should be as well. Because the latter approach is better than *M'Naghten* at giving mental illness its proper exculpatory scope, at the same time it avoids the pitfalls of the Volitional, Appreciation, and Rationality tests, it should be seriously considered as a replacement for the insanity defense.

III. Instrumental Benefits

The case for abolishing the insanity defense and substituting the subjective justification and excuse defenses is strengthened by three potential practical benefits, briefly noted here. First, such a reform of the criminal law's approach to mental disorder should improve the public's image of the criminal justice system. Second, it may well reduce the stigma associated with mental illness. Third, it should facilitate treatment of those with mental problems.

Frustration with the outcome in insanity cases has occasioned enmity not only toward the defense itself, but also toward criminal law as a whole. As Judge Bazelon stated, the insanity defense is a "a scapegoat for the entire criminal justice system."[175] To some extent this reaction may stem simply from the fact that a "factually guilty" person has escaped punishment. But it is also due to irritation that, regardless of the truth of the matter, "insanity" *seems* to be an unbounded condition that could apply to any number of people who commit serious crime; thus we have the statement by William French Smith when he was U.S. attorney general that "[t]here must be an end to the doctrine that allows so many persons to commit crimes of violence."[176] Although people with mental disorder would still be acquitted under the integration approach, the rationale for the verdict would be more palatable to a citizenry that is often outraged by insanity verdicts. Acquitting a person because he thought, albeit mistakenly, that he acted in self-defense is likely to make much more sense to the public than acquittal based on "insanity."

More broadly, abolition of the insanity defense may well have a beneficial impact on society's view of people with mental illness. Michael Perlin has written about the "sanist" attitudes of society toward those with mental disorder.[177] One particularly insidious sanist notion, clearly belied by the data noted in this chapter, is that offenders with mental illness are abnormally dangerous, and a second notion, also incorrect (if one agrees with the assertions in this chapter), is that they have significantly less control over their behavior than do all those offenders who are not "mentally ill." Some have plausibly argued that the insanity defense, by drawing a direct connection between mental illness on the one hand and crime and nonresponsibility on the other, bears some of the blame for these discriminatory attitudes.[178] The elimination of a special defense of insanity, and the integration of mental illness claims into the same defensive framework used by those who are not mentally ill, would be at least a small step toward eradicating sanism. Of course, more people with mental illness would be called "criminal" under an integration approach. But the argument here is not that the criminal moniker is less stigmatizing than the insanity label (although research indicates it probably is,[179] and it is certainly less stigmatizing than the double whammy inflicted by the phrase "criminally insane").[180] Rather the argument is that the insanity defense unfairly perpetuates myths about mentally ill people *as a class,* whereas a guilty verdict can have no analogous effect on criminals as a class.

The third possible benefit of abolition is an improvement in the efficacy of mental health treatment for those charged with criminal offenses. For instance, one complaint sometimes heard from mental health professionals who work in forensic institutions is that those found "not guilty" by reason of insanity, influenced by the semantics of their verdict, refuse to admit they have done anything wrong; this refusal is said to inhibit treatment, which is usually premised on an acceptance of responsibility.[181] A separate, but somewhat overlapping, impact of the insanity verdict is that, just as it links mental disorder with violence in the public mind, it may exacerbate the perceptions of those found insane that they are dangerous outcasts with no prospects for change.[182] In contrast, to the extent the proposal advanced here leads to conviction of such individuals, it should impress upon them the seriousness of the crime and thus facilitate their rehabilitation (a process that could well receive more attention from the correctional authorities if it is no longer seen as the special preserve of the "insane" mentally ill).[183] Even those who are acquitted may have a more contrite and less fatalistic attitude toward change, because they will know their acquittal resulted from the precise reasons for the offense, not because of some general trait of mental disorder they are said to be unable to control. If so, they too may respond better to treatment efforts, assuming they meet the relevant commitment criteria.

Our society has too long been unjustly leery of people who are mentally ill. Perhaps if the criminal justice system treats them more like others, significant changes in the attitudes of both society and those with mental illness will occur, along the lines suggested in the foregoing paragraphs. Although my justification for abolition of the insanity defense is primarily retribution-based, such attitudinal change would be a welcome by-product.

Conclusion

I have argued that the insanity defense should be abolished and that people with mental disorder should have a complete defensive claim only when they lack mens rea or act for reasons that sound in justification or duress. This position may strike some as unduly harsh. Responding to *M'Naghten*'s (narrower) version of this approach, one court, writing more than one hundred years ago, stated, "It is probable no ingenuous student of the law ever read it for the first time without being shocked by its exquisite inhumanity."[184]

There is no doubt that, compared to the broadest modern formulations of the insanity defense, the integration approach would result in fewer acquittals of those with mental illness. That result is not "inhumane," however. As outlined in the next chapter, offenders who are not excused from crime but who are significantly impaired in terms of appreciation of wrongfulness or rationality should still receive mitigation at sentencing. And if the concern is that people with mental illness should not be sent to prison or languish there without help for their suffering, the proper response is better rehabilitative programs for all those who need treatment. Reliance on the insanity defense as a means to achieve that goal is seriously misguided, given the small proportion of treatable mentally disordered offenders who are acquitted under any version of the defense.[185] Moreover, this rationale for the insanity defense wrongly suggests that those who are "sane" do not deserve treatment.[186]

Putting concerns about inhumaneness to one side, then, one can focus on the true reasons mental illness should be exculpatory. The belief that some persons with mental illness do not deserve punishment even when they intentionally cause harm in the absence of delusion-based justification or duress reflects misguided intuitions about mental illness, intuitions that should not be fed by a special defense for the "criminally insane." People who are mentally disordered are not any less able to control their behavior than many other people who commit criminal acts. Accordingly, for purposes of the criminal law, they should be treated the same as those who are not mentally ill.

Of course, on the latter premise, we could opt for acquittal of many non-mentally ill people whom we currently convict. Or, because so many would thereby be excused, we might give up entirely on culpability assessments (an option explored in Chapter 5). Adhering for now, however, to the twin assumptions that the blameworthiness inquiry is essential and that this inquiry should be based on something other than lack of control, the better approach is to convict all those who act intentionally and in the absence of subjective justification or duress.

— 3 —

Mental Disability and the Death Penalty

The previous chapter focused on the relevance of mental disability to adjudications of guilt. At least as significant in practical terms is the role of mental disability in determining the degree of punishment once conviction occurs. A defendant who has been found insane or excused under the mens rea or integrationist alternatives would, of course, not be subject to sentencing. But, as the first two chapters have made clear, a vast number of convicted offenders could also plausibly be labeled "mentally ill" or "mentally disabled." A central task of this chapter is to identify who, among those with a psychiatric diagnosis or syndrome, is entitled to dispositional mitigation under the punishment model.

Traditionally courts and legislatures have paid virtually no attention to this issue. Until the last quarter of the twentieth century, most jurisdictions imposed minimal structure on sentencing; rather, they permitted a judge to choose a sentence within a wide range, relying on virtually any criteria the judge considered important. As a result, there was very little law on the extent, if any, to which mental disability ought to affect punishment.[1]

More attuned to the culpability assessments required under a punishment model are the increasingly popular determinate sentencing schemes that explicitly permit a "downward departure" from the presumptive sentence if there is proof of a mental disability that mitigates blameworthiness for the crime.[2] From a punishment perspective these schemes represent a significant improvement on the older indeterminate sentencing regimes, because they at least provide some direction on the matter. Even so, determinate sentencing judges are not particularly generous in granting sentence reductions based on mental dysfunction,[3] and the law in this area remains vague (vagueness that may only be exacerbated by recent U.S.

Supreme Court cases finding unconstitutional certain types of determinate sentencing).[4]

In an effort to explore further the nuances of the role mental disability might and should play at sentencing, this chapter focuses on the most highly charged context the punishment model presents: the death penalty. Nowhere is our society's ambivalence toward mental disability more dramatically highlighted than in capital cases. Mental illness is expressly recognized as a mitigating factor in most death penalty statutes,[5] and the U.S. Supreme Court has held, in Ford v. Wainwright,[6] that it is cruel and unusual punishment under the Eighth Amendment to execute a person whose mental state renders understanding of capital punishment impossible. Yet a significant proportion of death row inmates are mentally ill,[7] and the research evidence described in this chapter strongly suggests that mental illness is often, in fact if not in law, an *aggravating* factor as far as capital sentencing bodies are concerned.

In this chapter, I advance three reasons why the death penalty, even if generally a valid exercise of state authority, should never or rarely be imposed on those who are mentally ill. First, execution of those who have a mental illness violates equal protection of the laws, now that the Supreme Court has prohibited execution of people with mental retardation. Second, even if the execution of people with mental illness is constitutional as a general proposition, the bulk of death sentences imposed on mentally ill people are deprivations of life without due process of law, because, as noted above, capital sentencing juries usually treat mental illness as an aggravating circumstance rather than a mitigating factor. Third, even if most death sentences imposed on people with mental illness are valid, the Eighth Amendment should usually prohibit carrying out the sentence, because many people with mental illness who are on death row either are incompetent under the *Ford* standard, properly construed, or are competent only because of an unconstitutional imposition of medication. Although these arguments focus on the death penalty, they also have implications for regular sentencing, implications that are made explicit at the end of the chapter.

The arguments in this chapter are framed in constitutional terms because, in my view, fundamental rights are involved. But the technicalities of constitutional doctrine should not mask the underlying policy choices. Even if the equal protection, due process and Eighth Amendment guarantees cannot be stretched in the manner suggested here, the normative principles on which they rest should control the treatment of mental disability at sentencing.

I. The Equal Protection Argument

In Atkins v. Virginia,[8] the Supreme Court held that execution of people with mental retardation violates the Eighth Amendment ban on cruel and unusual punishment. The equal protection argument against execution of those with mental illness is simply that people with mental illness must benefit from the same exemption. This argument is strengthened by the Supreme Court's even more recent decision in Roper v. Simmons,[9] which prohibited execution of juveniles younger than age eighteen; certainly if "mentally healthy" juveniles under eighteen cannot be executed, people with serious mental illness at the time of the offense should not be. The equal protection argument made here will focus on Atkins, however, because people with mental retardation are, as a psychological matter, more comparable to people with mental illness than juveniles.

One obvious hurdle for this argument is the Supreme Court's consistent holding that laws that differentiate based on mental disability need only meet the "rational basis" test, which is generally an extremely easy test to meet. But that hurdle might not be as significant as many think. First, the Supreme Court's equal protection case law can be said to require a good reason, not just a plausible one, for discrimination based on disability. Second, if—as Atkins seems to indicate—the most important factors in determining which murderers may be put to death are relative culpability and deterrability, there may not even be any plausible reasons for differentiating between execution of people with mental illness and execution of people with mental retardation. Finally, it is worth noting that the death penalty is a special context that often produces surprising results; after all, as recently as 2000, very few people would have predicted Atkins would be decided the way it was. Already, several powerful organizations, among them the American Bar Association (ABA), the American Psychiatric Association, and the American Psychological Association, have, or soon will, put their weight behind a resolution calling for a prohibition on execution of people with serious mental illness at the time of the offense, a development (described in more detail below) that could eventually lend impetus to judicial or legislative recognition of the argument made here.

I first examine the Court's Eighth Amendment analysis in Atkins. The best explanation for this decision is the Court's recognition that murderers with developmental disability are less culpable and less deterrable than the average murderer. On the assumption that the same can be said for people with significant mental illness who commit murder, I then look at the Court's equal protection case law to determine how persuasive the evidence of similarity must be in order to enforce a ban on execution of people with mental illness. The decisions are ambiguous, leaving room for the argument, suggested above, that government needs more than a rational basis for discriminating against people with mental disability.

Next, I investigate more thoroughly how similar people with retardation and people with mental illness are, not just in terms of relative culpability and deterrability, but also with respect to other possibly relevant variables, such as ease of identification and dangerousness. This investigation focuses on comparing people with *psychosis* to people with retardation, but in a separate section I also conclude that a wide array of other individuals with significant impairments ought to be exempted from capital punishment. Finally, I address a concern, raised by disability rights advocates, that exempting people with disability from the death penalty stigmatizes them. Although this argument is similar to my contention in Chapter 2 that the special defense of insanity is stigmatizing, in this context I think special treatment is *de*stigmatizing. The ultimate conclusion is that the punishment model of life and liberty deprivation requires recognition of the diminished responsibility of offenders affected by significant mental disorder, and that this position reaffirms, rather than denigrates, the dignity of people with mental disability.

A. *Atkins* and the Eighth Amendment

Ever since Trop v. Dulles,[10] the Court has adhered to the principle that the Eighth Amendment's ban on "cruel and unusual" punishment "must draw its meaning from the evolving standards of decency that mark the progress of a maturing society."[11] When the Court has gone looking for these "evolving standards," it has generally focused on the judgments of state legislatures as the most "objective" measure of American values.[12] It did so in *Atkins* as well and relied heavily on the fact that eighteen of the thirty-eight states that have the death penalty have outlawed execution of people with mental retardation in the past fourteen years.[13] The majority also found evidence of consensus in the low number of people with retardation who were actually executed and in the opinions of a wide array of organizations and of people surveyed in polls.[14]

As Justice Antonin Scalia's dissenting opinion pointed out, however, this evidence is not very impressive when compared to the level of consensus that had been required in other cases finding an Eighth Amendment violation (dealing with provisions rejected by anywhere from 78 to 97 percent of death penalty states).[15] In Scalia's words, "[w]hat the Court calls evidence of 'consensus' in the present case (a fudged forty-seven percent) more closely resembles evidence that we found inadequate to establish consensus in earlier cases."[16] Scalia was equally dismissive of the majority's other evidence of consensus. He disputed the majority's assumption that executions of people with mental retardation are rare,[17] and noted that, even if this were so, it likely resulted from the fact that mental retardation is a constitutionally mandated mitigating factor,[18] not from a belief that people with retardation should be immune from execution under all circumstances.[19] To the majority's reliance on nonlegal sources of support for such a ban he awarded "the Prize for the Court's most Feeble Effort to fabricate 'national consensus'"[20] and cross-referenced to Chief Justice William Rehnquist's opinion questioning the methodology of the polls and the representativeness of professional and religious organizations.[21]

In the context of these rebuttals, which have some bite to them, the most crucial statement in Justice John Stevens's majority opinion might be the following: "[O]bjective evidence, though of great importance, [does] not 'wholly determine' the controversy, 'for the Constitution contemplates that in the end our own judgment will be brought to bear on the question of the acceptability of the death penalty under the Eighth Amendment.'"[22] Although other cases had adopted the same position (the subquotation comes from Coker v. Georgia),[23] the gist of those opinions was that the Court's judgment can only confirm popular consensus, not trump it.[24] In these earlier cases, the opinion of the Court on the matter was largely makeweight.[25] In Atkins, in contrast, one gets the sense that the Court's "independent evaluation,"[26] to use Stevens's language, was more important in justifying the decision than the legislative nose-counting. Indeed, in light of the relatively slim legislative consensus against execution of people with retardation, Scalia called this evaluation "[t]he genuinely operative portion of the opinion."[27]

While this latter remark may be an overstatement, there is no doubt that the majority's "independent evaluation" is an essential part of the majority's reasoning. For present purposes, its importance lies in the clues it provides as to how the Supreme Court evaluates the proper scope of the death penalty as it applies to people with mental disability. The core of this evaluation built on the premise, well established by earlier cases,[28] that "retribution and deterrence of capital crimes by prospective offenders [are] the social purposes served by the death penalty."[29] The Court then concluded that, because people with mental retardation have "diminished capacities to understand and process information, to communicate, to abstract from mistakes and learn from experience, to engage in logical reasoning, to control impulses, and to understand the reactions of others," their execution does not "measurably contribute" to either of those goals.[30] Noting that precedent had established that the death penalty was reserved for the most culpable murderers, Stevens stated, "the lesser culpability of the mentally retarded offender surely does not merit that form of retribution."[31] Similarly, compared to the typical person who contemplates murder, people with mental retardation are "less likely [to] process the information of the possibility of execution as a penalty" and thus are less likely to be deterred by that information.[32] *Simmons*, the case prohibiting execution of juveniles, is if anything more insistent than *Atkins* that the death penalty should be reserved for the most culpable and deterrable.[33]

The same types of assertions that *Atkins* and *Simmons* make about people with mental retardation and juveniles can be made about people with significant mental illness. That does not mean, of course, that the *Eighth Amendment* bars the latter's execution. For despite the Court's willingness to look at more "subjective" factors, a determination that evolving standards of decency have been abridged still requires some evidence of statutory evolution,[34] and that evidence simply does not exist with respect to the execution of people with mental illness. Even before Ford v. Wainwright constitutionalized the requirement, every state banned the execution of people whose mental illness rendered them unable to understand the nature of the death penalty.[35] But that rule focuses entirely on the individual's mental state at the time of execution, not at the time of the offense, and it is the latter mental state that is the focus of the retributive and deterrence queries addressed in *Atkins*. In that setting, in contrast to the legislative sentiment ranged against execution of offenders with mental retardation, only one jurisdiction—Connecticut—has banned imposition of the death penalty on those capital offenders who were mentally ill at the time of the offense.[36] At present, no other state is contemplating following Connecticut's lead.

At the same time, the assertion that people with mental illness are similar to people with mental retardation in terms of relative culpability and deterrability is very relevant to equal protection analysis. How strong that similarity must be to force an equivalent ban on execution for people with mental illness depends on how one reads the three Supreme Court decisions that apply that analysis to classifications based on disability. Unfortunately, those cases are not at all clear on that score.

B. Equal Protection and Mental Disability

At first glance, the Supreme Court's application of equal protection analysis to cases involving disability all seem to say the same thing: Mental disability is neither a suspect or a quasi-suspect classification, and the state needs only a rational basis, not a compelling or significant one, for discriminating on that ground. But that would be a misleading characterization of the three most pertinent decisions in this area. In the first of these cases, the Court appeared to apply a more rigorous test than rational basis analysis requires. In the second, it never addressed the proper standard of review for cases involving disability, and in any event gave reasons for upholding the state scheme that might satisfy more heightened scrutiny. In the third, the Court's statement that the rational basis test was the correct one for disability cases appears to have been endorsed firmly by only three of its members, hardly a resounding affirmance. These cases are worth looking at in more detail not only because of their relevance to death penalty jurisprudence, but also because they provide a sense of the law's general views regarding people with mental disability, a topic that permeates this book.

The Supreme Court's first case directly addressing application of the Equal Protection Clause to people with disability was City of Cleburne, Texas v. Cleburne Living Center.[37] There the Cleburne Living Center sued the city of Cleburne for denying it a permit to build and operate a group home for people with mental retardation. The denial occurred under authority of an ordinance that required such permits for "hospitals for the insane or feeble-minded or alcoholics or drug addicts" and for "penal institutions," but did not require permits for other multiperson units, such as medical hospitals, nursing homes, apartment houses, fraternities and sororities, and private clubs. The Living Center's principal contention was that these distinctions violated the Equal Protection Clause because mental retardation was either a suspect classification like race, or a quasi-suspect classification like gender. Either finding would have required the government to advance a strong justification for its discriminatory action which, the Center maintained, it could not do. But the Court refused to find that mental retardation was like either race or gender for equal protection purposes, and thus concluded that the government need only demonstrate a rational basis for the discrimination.[38]

Usually, that would have been the end of it. Under the rational basis test, the Court has stated that a law "must be upheld against Equal Protection challenge if there is any reasonably conceivable state of facts that could provide a rational basis for the classification" made by the law.[39] Further, "a legislative choice is not subject to courtroom fact-finding and may be based on rational speculation unsupported by evidence or empirical data."[40] Indeed, the "burden is on the one attacking the legislative arrangement to negative every conceivable basis which might support it."[41] Laws that do not rely on suspect classifications like race or gender are accorded this strong presumption of validity because the judiciary should not "sit as a superlegislature to judge the wisdom or desirability of legislative policy determinations made in areas that neither affect fundamental rights nor proceed along suspect lines."[42]

In short, losing the suspect classification battle usually means losing the equal protection war. But in *Cleburne,* surprisingly, the Court went on to hold that the Center should prevail. The majority stated that the permit requirement violated the Equal Protection Clause because it rested on "an irrational prejudice against the mentally retarded"[43] and on "mere negative attitudes, or fear, unsubstantiated by factors which are properly considered in a zoning proceeding."[44] In context, these statements belie a rational basis analysis. The trial court had found that the ordinance, as written and applied, was rationally related to the city's legitimate interests in "the legal responsibility of CLC and its residents, the safety and fears of residents in the adjoining neighborhood," and the number of people to be housed in the home.[45] These justifications—particularly the first two—could be said to rely on the same sort of behavioral assumptions that the *Atkins* Court relied on in banning execution of people with mental retardation. If, as *Atkins* stated, people with mental retardation have diminished abilities "to control impulses, and to understand the reactions of others," one could reasonably infer that people with mental retardation living in the community are more likely to behave antisocially, or at least offensively, and thus pose an increased risk of civil and criminal liability. Rational basis review does not require empirical research to back up this kind of inference, but in fact people with mental retardation are at least slightly more likely to engage in violent behavior than members of the general population (albeit not as likely to do so as people who abuse substances and those who are housed in penal institutions, the other two groups subjected to the permit process in *Cleburne*).[46]

These observations suggest that, even if the permit denial was based on prejudice, it was not irrational prejudice, as "irrational" is usually defined in equal protection analysis. The denial may have been based on fear of people with mental retardation. But there was a "rational" basis for that fear, and danger is a factor that "may properly be considered in a zoning proceeding."[47] As others have asserted, the Court in *Cleburne* appeared to be judging the city's action more rigorously than it normally does in rational basis cases; it was applying, at the least, a test that some have called "rational basis with bite."[48]

The second case in which the Court confronted an equal protection challenge to treatment of people with disabilities was Heller v. Doe.[49] There the comparison was not between people with mental disability and others but rather involved the same sort of comparison at issue in this chapter, between people with mental retardation and people with mental illness. Under Kentucky law, the standard of proof for commitment of the first group is clear and convincing evidence, while for the second group the standard is proof beyond a reasonable doubt. A second difference between the two Kentucky commitment schemes is that, in proceedings for people with retardation, close relatives and guardians may participate as parties—with the ability to hire lawyers, cross-examine witnesses, and appeal—whereas in commitment proceedings for people with mental illness the respondent is confronted only by the state. The claim in *Heller* was that both of these differences disadvantaged people with retardation by making it easier to commit them to an institution.

As in *Cleburne,* the Court purported to apply rational basis review in *Heller.* But the way it did so was curious. Given the disability of their clients, advocates for Doe argued for a heightened standard of review. In dismissing that argument, one would think the Court would simply have cited the eight-year-old decision in *Cleburne,* which supposedly established that rational basis review was the proper standard in such cases. Instead, the Court noted that the argument for a heightened review standard had not been presented in the lower courts and that applying such a standard for the first time at the Supreme Court level would disadvantage the state, which had not presented extensive evidence justifying its statutory scheme on the assumption that rational basis review was all that was required in such cases. Reference to *Cleburne* was nowhere to be found in this discussion, suggesting at least some ambivalence about whether the Court meant what it said in that case about disability not being a suspect classification.

Furthermore, in upholding both challenged aspects of Kentucky's commitment scheme, the Court gave reasons that could conceivably meet even a heightened scrutiny standard, at least at the rational-basis-with-bite level. Assuming that mental retardation is easier to diagnose than mental illness, the Court noted that a state might want to protect against the greater risk of error thereby associated with commitment of the latter group through imposition of the heavier, reasonable doubt burden on the state.[50] In other words, the Kentucky scheme could easily be characterized as an attempt to protect people with mental illness, not the result of bias against people with mental retardation, a position that is bolstered by the fact that the clear and convincing standard Kentucky applied to the latter group is clearly constitutionally adequate.[51]

Good reasons also can be given for granting party status to relatives and guardians of people with mental retardation. As the Court pointed out, given the stable nature of retardation and its very early onset, relatives and guardians of people with that condition are likely to have more probative insights about behavioral and dispositional issues than relatives and guardians of people with mental illness, a condition that often strikes for the first time in early adulthood or later and is more changeable. Of course, as the dissent in *Heller* noted, if the primary goal is to assure that relatives and guardians give testimony, the state could simply subpoena them. Testimony may not be the only goal, however. Relatives who have spent years caring for people with retardation may have very strong preferences for a particular disposition (for instance, a community residence as opposed to a distant institution) that are most likely to be implemented through giving them party status. The question in most cases involving people with retardation is not whether commitment will take place but where it will occur.[52] Justice David Souter's assertion in the dissenting opinion, that family members who are given party status are more likely to act as a "second prosecutor," is generally not true in this context.[53]

So *Heller* did not settle the issue of how much protection people with mental disability can expect under the Equal Protection Clause. But there is one more Supreme Court decision addressing the equal protection implications of laws that classify based on mental disability: Board of Trustees of the University of Alabama v. Garrett.[54] There, several states argued, inter alia, that the provisions in the Americans with Disabilities Act (ADA) that require state employers to make "reasonable accommodations" for employees with mental disability are an unconstitutional exercise of Congress's authority to enforce the equal protection guarantee, because they require the states to provide more than plausible reasons for a failure to accommodate disability.[55] In agreeing with that proposition, the Court once again concluded that the appropriate standard of review in disability cases was the rational basis test, and this time it relied heavily on *Cleburne* in doing so. On authority of that case, a five-member majority flatly stated that "states are not required by the Fourteenth Amendment to make special accommodations for the disabled, so long as their actions toward such individuals are rational."[56] This language sounds as if the Court has finally unequivocally settled that disability classifications are governed by traditional rational basis review.

But it has not. First, the Court had no occasion to explicate what it meant by "rational," since it did not address any particular factual situation in *Garrett*; perhaps, as it did in *Cleburne*, application of rational basis review to people with mental disability will morph into "rational basis with bite." More important, two members of the majority wrote a concurring opinion that did not even mention *Cleburne*. Rather, after noting that "[t]here can be little doubt that persons with mental impairments are confronted with prejudice which can stem from indifference or insecurity as well as from malicious ill will," Justices Anthony Kennedy and Sandra Day O'Connor emphasized the absence of proof that any state had engaged in "a pattern or practice" that was "designed" to discriminate against people with disability.[57] When the views of these two justices are combined with the views of the four-member dissent, which expressed a more expansive view of *Cleburne* than the majority,[58] the equal protection status of mental disability remains in some doubt, at least where the state intentionally discriminates based on that classification.

Under such circumstances, there is precedent for an explicit move to heightened scrutiny. Referring to the Court's gender cases, Mark Weber points out that "[h]istory suggests that an erratic pattern of decisions, combined with protests by the Court that it is applying a rational-basis test, may lead to an eventual use of intermediate scrutiny."[59] At least as significant, the Court's case law indicates that when the state's differential treatment affects life or liberty, as it obviously does in the death penalty context, heightened scrutiny is more likely. As a four-member plurality stated in Foucha v. Louisiana, "[f]reedom from physical restraint being a fundamental right, the State must have a particularly convincing reason" for confinement.[60] In short, a strong case can be made that states that continue to execute people with mental illness, now that *Atkins* has been decided, need to demonstrate not just a plausible reason but a good reason for doing so.

C. Why Execution of People with Mental Illness Is Unconstitutional

Combining the conclusions of the previous two sections, execution of people with mental illness should not be permitted unless there is good reason to believe that offenders with mental illness are more culpable or deterrable than offenders with mental retardation. That demonstration might be possible with respect to many forms of "mental illness." But it cannot be made when mental illness is equated with psychosis at the time of the crime. People with psychosis are equivalent to people with mental retardation in all legally relevant respects. Whether the same can be said for people with other types of mental disorder is a subject that is best taken up after considering the equal protection case for people with psychosis.

The classic psychotic diagnosis is schizophrenia. As defined in the DSM-IV-TR, people who suffer from schizophrenia experience "a range of cognitive and emotional dysfunctions that include perception, inferential thinking, language and communication, behavioral monitoring, affect, fluency and productivity of thought and speech, hedonic capacity, volition and drive, and attention." The specific symptoms include delusions, hallucinations, disorganized speech, and grossly disorganized behavior.[61] Put even more functionally, as discussed in Chapter 2, people with schizophrenia have difficulty focusing on essential information, are easily distracted by irrelevant stimuli, often experience "thought blocking" (involving a complete halt to thinking), attribute elaborate meaning to what they see and hear, engage in combinative thinking (involving the reduction of impressions into unrealistic beliefs), and have difficulty forming abstract concepts correctly.[62]

Recall that *Atkins* considered people with mental retardation ineligible for the death penalty because of their "diminished capacities to understand and process information, to communicate, to abstract from mistakes and learn from experience, to engage in logical reasoning, to control impulses, and to understand the reactions of others." The brief description of schizophrenic symptoms above makes clear that people who suffer from psychosis also have great difficulty in communicating with and understanding others, engaging in logical cost-benefit analysis, and evaluating the consequences of and controlling their behavior. If anything, the delusions, command hallucinations, and disoriented thought process of those who are seriously mentally ill represent greater dysfunction than that experienced by most "mildly" retarded individuals (the only retarded people likely to commit crime).

Of course, psychotic symptoms can have mitigating impact during the criminal process. The various insanity tests, the diminished capacity and diminished responsibility defenses, and capital sentencing law itself recognize that these symptoms may significantly affect the ability to understand the nature of one's actions, to differentiate between right and wrong, to formulate intent, and to control behavior.[63] Thus, one might assume that a ban on execution of people with significant mental illness at the time of the offense is likely to have no practical impact.

That assumption would be wrong. Just as people with retardation have ended up on death row despite mitigating characteristics, many people who experienced psychotic symptoms at the time of their crime are sentenced to death. The insanity defense is rarely successful, even (or especially) in murder cases.[64] In most jurisdictions, other defenses that in theory could give mitigating impact to mental illness are either not recognized or are very narrowly defined.[65] And, as Part 2 of this chapter shows, while extreme mental or emotional distress and other abnormal mental conditions are usually explicitly recognized as mitigating factors in capital sentencing statutes, research suggests that presentation of such evidence often acts as an aggravating factor. Apparently, sentencing juries and judges focus more on the perceived dangerousness of such individuals than on their diminished culpability and deterrability. Whatever the reason, the available evidence, noted at the beginning of this chapter, suggests that a sizeable number of people with psychotic symptomatology are on death row. Reported cases also indicate that, analogous to judicial treatment of offenders with mental retardation prior to Atkins, many courts are unwilling to reverse death sentences even in the face of credible evidence of significant mental illness at the time of the crime.[66]

These facts have diametrically opposed implications for the two constitutional doctrines most relevant to the proper scope of the death penalty. They undercut an Eighth Amendment claim, because if they show any consensus, it is that significant mental illness at the time of the crime should not be a bar to execution. But they bolster the equal protection argument, because they show an "irrational prejudice" against people with mental illness that is not justified by any legitimate state goal.

To state the strongest possible equal protection case against execution of people with mental illness, the following discussion will be framed in terms of traditional rationality review. Under that standard, it will be recalled, a state practice "must be upheld against equal protection challenge if there is any reasonably conceivable state of facts that could provide a rational basis for the classification." There are three conceivable bases for supporting continued execution of people with mental illness after *Atkins,* to wit: compared to mental retardation, mental illness is (1) harder to diagnose, (2) less characteriological and more avoidable, and (3) more likely to lead to violent behavior. Good arguments can be made that all three distinctions are specious (and are therefore unreasonable), and they certainly do not withstand the more heightened scrutiny represented by *Cleburne.*

Definition and Proof
Taking a cue from *Heller,* advocates for continued execution of people with mental illness in the wake of *Atkins* might contend that mental illness is harder to define than mental retardation. Mental retardation is measured primarily through objective tests that produce quantified results.[67] Diagnosing mental illness, in contrast, is a relatively seat-of-the pants assessment known to be difficult to carry out reliably.[68] It could be argued, consequently, that the state would not be able to implement a ban on executing people with mental illness in a sensible manner. Furthermore, the amorphous nature of mental illness makes malingering easier. In combination, these difficulties could be said to undermine the state's ability to achieve the retributive and deterrence goals of the death penalty. Mistakes would be made as to who is culpable or deterrable enough to warrant execution, and would-be offenders might calculate that, if caught, they can successfully feign illness and at least escape the death penalty.

There is no doubt that mental illness is an exceedingly vague term. Even when one confines mental illness to psychosis, as I am doing for the moment, the diagnostic nomenclature is slippery. For instance, with respect to delusions, a principal symptom of schizophrenia, the DSM admits that "[t]he distinction between a delusion and a strongly held idea is sometimes difficult to make and depends on the degree of conviction with which the belief is held despite clear contradictory evidence." Similarly, assessment of the "bizarreness" of delusions, also important to a diagnosis of schizophrenia, "may be difficult to judge, especially across different cultures."[69]

But none of this supplies a good reason for differentiating between people with significant mental illness and those with mental retardation. *Heller,* which assumed that mental illness is more difficult to discern than mental retardation, may appear to hold otherwise, but it does not. The type of mental disorder that can provide the basis for civil commitment, which was the legal context at issue in that case, is much broader than the psychoses at issue here.[70] When focused solely on gross impairment related to psychosis, studies show a much higher rate of reliability (that is, agreement between diagnosticians) despite the softness of the criteria,[71] and other research indicates that successful malingering is very difficult.[72] More important, contrary to common belief, diagnosis of mental retardation does not consist simply of adding up scores on an intelligence test to see if the person has an IQ above or below 70 (the widely accepted presumptive cut-off score).[73] Putting aside questions about the reliability of such tests,[74] the DSM notes that "it is possible to diagnose Mental Retardation in individuals with IQs of seventy and seventy-five who exhibit significant deficits in adaptive behavior. Conversely, Mental Retardation would not be diagnosed in an individual with an IQ lower than seventy if there are no significant deficits or impairments in adaptive functioning."[75] As many have pointed out,[76] "adaptive functioning" is at least as amorphous a term as "delusion," "hallucination," or "disorganized speech."

Let us assume, however, that the nuances just discussed do not dissuade courts from adopting the holding in *Heller* that there is a rational basis for believing psychosis is harder to diagnose than mental retardation. The proper response to that concern, as *Heller* itself acknowledged, is to require more convincing proof that the person suffers from significant mental illness. For instance, Oklahoma's rules for implementing *Atkins* provide that the defendant bears the burden of showing mental retardation by a preponderance of the evidence.[77] If a legislature or court is concerned that mental illness is more difficult to discern accurately, the defendant can be required to show its existence by clear and convincing evidence or proof beyond a reasonable doubt.[78] Just as the diagnostic challenge does not prevent the state from committing people with mental illness if they are dangerous to self or others, it should not permit the state to execute them when they are no more culpable than children or people with retardation.

A related objection to equating the two groups, also suggested by *Heller,* is based on the notion that mental illness is a highly variable condition, whereas mental retardation is a permanent status, with relatively constant symptomatology throughout life. As a consequence, the contention might be that a diagnosis of retardation provides probative evidence on mental state at the time of the offense regardless of when it is made (that is, well before the offense, at the time of trial and sentencing, or at any time in between), whereas a diagnosis of psychosis is only relevant to the sentencing question if it pertains to the time of the offense. This contention attributes an impermanency to psychosis that is all too rare. As the DSM states, "[s]chizophrenia tends to be chronic," and "[c]omplete remission (i.e., a return to full premorbid functioning) is probably not common."[79] In any event, the proper response to any concerns about variability is, once again, to place a heavier burden on defendants alleging mental illness to show that they suffered from psychotic symptoms during the relevant time period, rather than simply assume they are more deserving of the death penalty than people with mental retardation.

Given the alternative of raising the standard of proof, the difficulty-of-diagnosis rationale for continuing to allow execution of people with mental illness after *Atkins* clearly does not satisfy heightened scrutiny, which requires that the government's solution be narrowly tailored to the problem.[80] Indeed, the rationale does not even satisfy rational basis review's requirement that the government's aims and the way it chooses to implement them be reasonably related. The state is not acting reasonably if it justifies executing people with mitigating mental illness simply on the ground that it has difficulty identifying who they are.

Accountability for Status

The second possible objection to equating mental illness and mental retardation for purposes of administering the death penalty more directly compares the impact of those conditions on culpability and deterrability. Building on the relative variability notion just discussed, the contention would be something like this: Even if we have sufficient proof of psychosis at the time of the offense, that condition is not as mitigating as mental retardation, because the person with mental illness is more "responsible" for the situation in two ways. First, adults with mental illness, while impaired, are not developmentally impaired; thus, they have greater capacity and more opportunity than people with retardation to develop an understanding of the rules of society and human interaction. Second, mental illness, in particular psychosis, is more easily treatable than retardation, making the person with mental illness at the time of the offense more at "fault" for the impairment and its consequences.

These maturity and treatability differences do exist. But they do not provide good grounds for making distinctions in punishment. With respect to the first difference, it is true that, on average, adults with mental illness are more advanced developmentally than people with mental retardation, because the onset of psychosis usually does not occur until the late teens or early twenties.[81] But, as noted above, once psychosis takes hold, it seldom disappears. More important, the cognitive and volitional impairment associated with active schizophrenia is likely to be much more severe than that which occurs with mental retardation or immaturity.

Consider again the symptoms of psychosis, using the language of the DSM. Delusions involve "misinterpretations of perceptions and experiences." They are usually "clearly implausible and not understandable and do not derive from ordinary life experiences." Hallucinations are usually auditory and often consist of "pejorative or threatening voices." The speech of people with schizophrenia is "tangential" and full of "loose associations," indicating a high degree of disorganized thought. Their behavior ranges from "childlike silliness to unpredictable agitation," is rarely "goal-directed," and leads "to difficulties in performing activities of daily living."[82] As these descriptions indicate, once psychotic symptoms set in, the influence of any real-world knowledge and learning gained from earlier experiences is significantly reduced; as Chapter 2 argued, enough of a sense of societally defined right and wrong may survive to prevent complete acquittal, but the impairment certainly rivals that of a person with mental retardation.

Nor should differences in treatability affect retributive or utilitarian analysis. Antipsychotic medication has vastly improved the treatment of the psychoses, and in many people it can eliminate or substantially reduce the most conspicuous psychotic symptoms in a short period of time.[83] In contrast, habilitation of people with retardation is more time-consuming and less dramatically successful.[84] But to conclude from these facts that people who are psychotic at the time of an offense could have more easily avoided their impaired condition and thus are more justly held accountable is too great a leap. In the usual case, a failure to obtain treatment for psychosis cannot seriously be characterized either as "blameworthy" or as behavior that fear of the death penalty would somehow change. First, many

people with psychosis are not capable of recognizing the benefits of medication or the risks of not taking it (indeed, a principal symptom of schizophrenia is "lack of insight").[85] Second, those who do have such capability
may nonetheless resist medication, because they know it can have serious
side effects, requires long-term maintenance, and is unevenly successful.[86]
Finally, even those who might want medication can have good reasons for
not being on it. As one study indicated, most people with mental disorders
do not seek treatment because they "do not realize that effective treatments
exist, fear discrimination because of the stigma attached to mental illness,
[or are unable to] afford treatment because they lack insurance that would
cover it."[87]

People with mental illness may sometimes be "responsible" for their condition, as Chapter 2 acknowledged. For reasons just suggested, however, such
situations will be rare. Certainly, they will be less common than occurs
among people who have mental retardation. A common characteristic of
such people is a denial of their symptoms and a refusal to seek help.[88] There
can be no rational distinction between these two groups, or at least no distinction that passes a rational-basis-with-bite test, on the ground that people
with mental illness are somehow more accountable for their condition.

Dangerousness

In both *Atkins* and *Simmons,* the Court's "independent evaluation" of
whether imposition of the death penalty violated the Eighth Amendment
focused on the two purposes of punishment already mentioned, retribution and deterrence. As Scalia pointed out in *Atkins,* there is at least one
other "purpose of punishment" that the imposition of the death penalty
might seek to accomplish: (permanent) incapacitation.[89] And, as indicated
earlier, research suggests that it is the perceived dangerousness of the offender, not his or her blameworthiness and not concern about deterrence
goals, that is the most influential factor for many judges and jurors involved
in death penalty proceedings. Thus, a final argument for continuing to execute people with mental illness in the wake of *Atkins* is that they are more
dangerous than people with retardation.

A first response to this argument is that Scalia's assertion about the relevance of dangerousness in death penalty cases is incorrect, at least when
mental disability is at issue. As the next part of this chapter argues, because
mental retardation and mental illness are universally recognized mitigating
factors, they presumably cannot be aggravating factors. Yet that is precisely

what they become when one tries to justify execution on the ground that these conditions make people more dangerous.

Even if incapacitation is a valid consideration in determining the scope of the death penalty for people with mental disability, the claim that people with mental illness are superdangerous is easily debunked. As noted in Chapter 2,[90] the base rate for violence among offenders with severe mental illness is no higher, and is probably lower, than the violence base rate for nondisordered offenders.[91] Even more relevant to the equal protection analysis, people with mental illness are no more likely to recidivate than offenders who suffer from mental retardation.[92]

D. Disorders Other Than Psychosis

A credible Eighth Amendment argument against the execution of capital offenders who experienced psychotic symptoms at the time of the offense cannot be made, because only one legislature in a death penalty state has barred such executions. But that fact simply strengthens the equal protection argument. Because murderers with psychotic symptoms at the time of the crime are no more culpable, or any more dangerous, than murderers who suffer from mental retardation, and are as easily identifiable as the latter group, the only possible basis for the states' continued willingness to execute members of the first group is the type of "irrational prejudice" against which *Cleburne* inveighed.

The next obvious question is whether other types of disorder, besides mental retardation and psychosis, should lead to exemption from the death penalty. As I argued in Chapter 2, a wide array of mental disorders are comparable to psychosis in terms of their effect on volitionality, appreciation of wrongfulness, and rationality. The urges subjectively experienced by many sex offenders are probably as strong as those experienced by people with psychosis. People with psychopathy can have serious difficulty appreciating the wrongfulness of their actions, to the same extent as people with mental retardation, albeit for different reasons. And while people with psychosis may be paradigmatically irrational, people who are subject to violent outbursts, among many others, may also have trouble accessing the right reasons for acting at the time of an offense.

Nonetheless, the equal protection argument is much harder to make with respect to these nonpsychotic disorders. Most of them are readily distinguishable from both mental retardation and psychosis on a number of grounds. Some, in particular the impulse disorders, are much more susceptible to definition and proof problems. Others, especially psychopathy, are more closely associated with dangerousness. Further, people with nonpsychotic disorders might be better equipped to recognize when they need treatment and to seek it out than people with retardation or psychosis.

The probable weakness of the equal protection claim should not obscure, however, the strong policy arguments in favor of expanding the mitigating scope of mental disorder. Stevens stated in *Atkins,* "[i]f the culpability of the average murderer is insufficient to justify the most extreme sanction available to the State, the lesser culpability of the mentally retarded offender surely does not merit that form of retribution."[93] The same can be said not only for murderers who are psychotic at the time of the offense, but also for offenders whose volitionality, appreciation of wrongfulness, and rationality are significantly impaired by nonpsychotic disorders. Of course, at some point the exempted group might become so large that referring to its members as less culpable than the average murderer would no longer be justifiable, simply as a statistical matter; in particular, mitigation based on lack of volition might swallow up the death penalty, a problem addressed further below. But there is no doubt that, in traditional culpability terms, this group's responsibility is significantly diminished compared to the prototypical offender who acts deliberately, while emotionally and rationally aware of the wrongfulness of the action.

Mentioned earlier was the resolution calling for an end to execution of people with mental illness adopted by the American Psychiatric and American Psychological Associations and under consideration by the ABA at the time of this writing. Specifically, the resolution states:

> Defendants shall not be executed or sentenced to death if, at the time of the offense, they had a severe mental disorder or disability that significantly impaired their capacity (1) to appreciate the nature, consequences, or wrongfulness of their conduct, (2) to exercise rational judgment in relation to the conduct, or (3) to conform their conduct to the requirements of the law. A disorder manifested primarily by repeated criminal conduct or attributable solely to the acute effects of voluntary use of alcohol or other drugs does not, standing alone, constitute a mental disorder or disability for purposes of this provision.[94]

Since it recognizes that lack of appreciation, rationality, and volition can diminish responsibility, this language comes close to capturing the group that I think should be exempted from the death penalty.

Two important modifications to the ABA's formulation are necessary, however. First, as Chapter 2 and the next chapter make clear, delineation of the type of volitional impairment that might undermine responsibility is an extremely difficult project, both conceptually and practically. Several commentators have argued that, in the insanity context, a focus on cognitive impairment (that is, lack of appreciation, irrationality) not only is the most philosophically sound approach, but in any event will also capture that group of offenders whom we normally associate with highly impaired volition, such as those with explosive personalities, serious impulse disorders, and addictions.[95] This reasoning also makes great sense at the sentencing stage. Assuming lack of appreciation of wrongfulness and irrationality are recognized as mitigating factors, affording mitigation to those offenders who have a "substantial inability to conform their conduct to the requirements of the law" is neither justifiable nor necessary.

As somewhat of a counterbalance to this modification of the resolution, the word "severe" should also be removed from in front of the phrase "mental disorder and disability." Even most insanity formulations do not require a severe disorder as a predicate. As a result, the resolution is inappropriately narrow, especially so in jurisdictions that use the ALI insanity test where, given the similarity in the language describing the relevant impairments, it may not even cover those who should have been found insane at the trial stage, and at best is congruent with that group.[96] The second sentence of the resolution, excluding from the exemption those whose disorders are manifested "primarily by repeated criminal conduct or attributable solely to the acute affects of voluntary use of alcohol and other drugs," is also unnecessarily constricting, if it is aimed at people with psychopathy and those who are seriously intoxicated at the time of the offense. As Chapter 2 suggested, some people with psychopathy are "morally insane" and do not deserve the death penalty.[97] And people who are seriously intoxicated at the time of the offense to the point of irrationality should probably also be exempted from that punishment, although their role in creating their condition complicates the matter.[98]

As revised, the exemption from the death penalty would read: "Defendants shall not be executed or sentenced to death if, at the time of the offense, they had a mental disorder or disability that significantly impaired their capacity to appreciate the nature, consequences, or wrongfulness of their conduct or to exercise rational judgment in relation to the conduct." This language would have the effect of excluding from imposition of the death penalty any offender who would be excused under the broadest interpretation of modern cognitive insanity formulations described in Chapter 2. The phrase exempting those who lack "rational judgment in relation to conduct" would also encompass offenders with psychosis at the time of the offense, and thus captures all those who should be excused from the death penalty on equal protection grounds as well.

E. The Subtleties of Stigma

Many advocates for people with disability cheered *Atkins* (and presumably would support the expansion of it just described), because it provides a group of disabled people with protection from the harshest punishment imposed by our society. But other disability advocates were dismayed by the decision, not because they are fans of the death penalty, but because they believe that declaring disabled people, as a group, ineligible for a punishment that is accorded all others denigrates those people as something less than human. If people with disability are to be treated equally, these dissenters suggest, they should be treated equally in all areas of the law, including capital sentencing. This concern is closely related to another one, held by liberal and conservatives alike, who are concerned about *Atkins*'s rejection of a case-by-case approach to the determination of whether a person deserves the death penalty.

The joint resolution and my proposed revision of it largely avoid the categorical approach, but they could be vulnerable to these complaints to the extent they exempt from the death penalty the "category" of offenders who suffered from psychosis at the time of the crime. Even so, neither the proposals or *Atkins* are seriously challenged by the stigmatization and group mischaracterization arguments, because both arguments are based on erroneous assumptions. *Atkins* (and its expansion to people with psychosis) will be good for the disability rights movement and for disabled people, because it *accurately* characterizes their relative culpability and because it undermines, rather than exacerbates, typical misperceptions of people with mental disability.

The most prominent "conservative" critic of *Atkins*'s group-based approach is Scalia. His dissent in that case argued that categorical exemptions based on assessments of relative culpability and deterrability do not work in an individualized sentencing context like the one the Court has tried to create in the death penalty setting.[99] As he put it,

Surely culpability, and deservedness of the most severe retribution, depends not merely (if at all) upon the mental capacity of the criminal (above the level where he is able to distinguish right from wrong) but also upon the depravity of the crime—which is precisely why this sort of question has traditionally been thought answerable not by a categorical rule of the sort the Court today imposes upon all trials, but rather by the sentencer's weighing of the circumstances (both degree of retardation and depravity of crime) in the particular case.[100]

More specifically addressing the majority's assertions about the average murderer, he asked "what scientific analysis can possibly show that a mildly retarded individual who commits an exquisite torture-killing is 'no more culpable' than the 'average' murderer in a holdup-gone-wrong or a domestic dispute?"[101]

The related criticism voiced by disability advocates is probably best made by Donald Bersoff, a well-known champion of disability rights. He puts forward two complaints about the stigmatizing impact of *Atkins*. First, it mischaracterizes the capacities of people with mental retardation. As he put it, "[a]s important as it is to protect those who cannot protect themselves, it is equally important to promote the right of all persons to make their own choices and, as a corollary, to be accountable for those choices." Echoing Scalia, he then states, "It is simply untrue that no person with mental retardation is incapable of carrying out a horrible murder with the requisite [degree of] intent or foresight." Second, Bersoff suggests that *Atkins* may even lead to a retraction of the rights and privileges that people with disability currently possess. He asserts, "[i]f we accept the concept of blanket incapacity [that *Atkins* endorses], we relegate people with retardation to second-class citizenship, potentially permitting the State to abrogate the exercise of such fundamental interests as the right to marry, to have and rear one's children, to vote, or such everyday entitlements as entering into contracts or making a will."[102]

If sustained, Bersoff's objections to the *Atkins* majority's "independent evaluation" are potent. I think that his objections are off base, however. With respect to the mischaracterization issue, it is true, as both Scalia and Bersoff state, that some people with serious mental disability can commit murder with intent and even foresight. I also have doubts about the *Atkins* majority's statement that *no* mentally retarded person who murders is as culpable or deterrable as the average murderer. Nevertheless, I think it is clear that *no murderer whose mental retardation or psychosis contributes to the crime is as culpable as the rare murderer who should be put to death.* If we are to have the death penalty, only the most depraved individuals should be executed, as the Court has said over and over again.[103] No person with serious disability is that depraved.

Earlier discussion has amply supported this conclusion with respect to the offender who acts while experiencing psychotic symptoms. But what about Scalia's mentally retarded torturer? Or someone like John Penry, who had an IQ in the 60s, but who cased the residence of his victim to make sure she was alone, forced his way in when she grew suspicious of his repairman story, and stabbed her after deciding she might tell the police about the rape?[104] Or someone like Renard Atkins, a mildly retarded individual who, along with another individual, abducted his victim, forced him to withdraw money from an ATM, then took him to a deserted area and shot him eight times?[105] These people intended, and even premeditated, their crimes, knowing that they were wrong in doing so.

It can be assumed that all these offenders were legally sane at the time of their crime. Because of their retardation, however, people such as Scalia's torturer, Penry, and Atkins lack the full appreciation of wrongfulness that less disabled people have and that should be required before we can execute someone. As recognized most explicitly by the California Supreme Court in the 1960s, culpability is diminished by an inability to "maturely and meaningfully reflect upon the gravity of [the] contemplated act."[106] People with retardation, by definition, are compromised in that ability. According to the DSM-IV-TR, even people with "mild" mental retardation at most can develop academic skills up to approximately the sixth-grade level, amounting to the maturity of a twelve-year-old.[107] By exempting this whole category of people from its purview, Atkins constitutionalized the idea that the death penalty may be imposed only on people who are particularly culpable.

Of course, many people would not draw the line where the Atkins majority did. For instance, three separate juries found that Penry was depraved enough to warrant the death penalty.[108] Atkins, in essence, held that those juries were wrong in defining depravity so broadly. It also implicitly rejected Scalia's position that the brutality of a murder by itself, regardless of the associated mental state, can make a sane person sufficiently "depraved."

In short, Atkins emphasized that the culpability threshold for the death penalty is very high. More important for present purposes, its holding (as distinguished, perhaps, from some of its language about the average murderer) does not mischaracterize the capacities of people with disability in the way Bersoff suggests. Atkins does not say that people with retardation are incapable of committing crime with intent or foresight. Nor, of course, does it say that murderers with serious disability should not be held accountable for their choices, as they still can be given life sentences. All *Atkins* says is that people with retardation, even those who commit a "horrible" murder, can never be as evil as the most evil murderers in our society, and thus that the ultimate punishment may not be imposed on them.

For related reasons, I also disagree with Bersoff's claim that *Atkins* will encourage use of categorical disability-based exemptions in the civil rights setting. While people with serious disability never deserve the death penalty, it is an empirical fact, demonstrated by research examining both people with significant mental illness and mental retardation, that even very disabled people can be competent to make treatment decisions and engage in other decision-making tasks.[109] Nothing in *Atkins* can be used to contest that fact, not even its (possibly erroneous) statement that people with retardation cannot be as culpable as the average murderer. The inquiry in the civil setting is not whether the disabled person is "average," but whether the person meets a minimum level of competence.[110] In other words, even a person whose capacities are "below average" can, under the law, contract, marry, vote, and so on. Thus, neither the holding nor the unnecessarily broad language of *Atkins* sabotages these types of laws.

If *Atkins* does anything in terms of stigma, it *de*stigmatizes people with mental disability, because it diminishes capital sentencing's ability to perpetuate one of the most insidious myths about people with mental disability. Research about attitudes toward individuals with mental illness strongly suggests that most of us erroneously view mentally ill offenders to be abnormally dangerous.[111] Capital sentencing juries, not surprisingly, are no different. An extensive amount of empirical work proves not only that they share this bias, but also allow it to influence their verdicts, despite their oaths to adhere to the law. Although detailed description of this research is deferred until Part Two of this chapter, one such study needs to be noted here, because it shows the particular hostility that capital jurors bear toward offenders with mental illness (as opposed to any other type of offender), and thus helps support the position taken in this chapter that *Atkins* needs to be expanded beyond people with mental retardation.

The study, conducted by Steven Garvey and his colleagues as part of the mammoth Capital Jury Sentencing Project,[112] involved questioning 187 jurors who served on fifty-three capital cases, tried in South Carolina between 1988 and 1997, about their emotional reactions to capital offenders. Regression analysis of their responses revealed that, of the eight emotions studied (including fear, sympathy, anger, and disgust), only "fear" of the offender correlated significantly with the final vote on sentence. The researchers also found that the most feared type of offender was one perceived to be a "madman" or "vicious like a mad animal."[113] The type of offender most likely to fit the "madman" category, of course, is one who exhibits symptoms of mental illness at the time of the offense. Even an offender with mental retardation is likely to be less feared and thus less likely to be irrationally sentenced to death than the person with significant mental illness. Indeed, the researchers found that while jurors were "likely to have felt sympathy or pity" for people with both types of disability, they were more likely to be simultaneously "disgusted or repulsed" only by the latter type of defendant.[114]

Now that people with mental retardation cannot be executed, execution of people who have significant mental illness at the time of the offense is difficult to defend on rational grounds, whether the forum is judicial, legislative, or executive.[115] The primary reason such executions continue is a disproportionate fear of people with mental illness. *Atkins* can and should be interpreted to mean that this equation of disorder with danger is wrong. Its message should be: We cannot execute people (or do anything else to them) simply because we are irrationally scared of them.

II. The Due Process Argument

The due process argument builds on the idea that actors in the criminal justice, in particular jurors and judges, harbor significant misperceptions about people with mental disability when they carry out their duties. The argument is simply stated. Due process of law is clearly lacking when the state fails to follow its own statutory provisions.[116] If, contrary to the law in every death penalty state, mental illness is treated as an aggravating factor in the death sentence determination, a flagrant due process violation has occurred. Given the research about jury biases just alluded to, acceptance of this proposition could be the basis for invalidation of many, if not all, death sentences imposed on those who are mentally ill. Even if one does not believe that the problem identified here is of constitutional magnitude, it should at least count as still another reason, in addition to those advanced in Part 1 of this chapter, for banning execution of people who experienced serious impairment at the time of their crime.

A. Capital Sentencing Law

Every state death penalty statute, either explicitly or implicitly, stipulates that mental illness at the time of the offense be considered as a possible mitigating circumstance.[117] That position is almost certainly constitutionally mandated after Lockett v. Ohio.[118] There, the U.S. Supreme Court stated that "the Eighth and Fourteenth Amendments require that the sentencer, in all but the rarest kind of capital case, not be precluded from considering, *as a mitigating factor,* any aspect of a defendant's character or record and any of the circumstances of the offense that the defendant proffers as a basis for a sentence less than death."[119]

Roughly two-thirds of state capital sentencing statutes explicitly incorporate one or more of the mitigating factors based on mental dysfunction that are found in the Model Penal Code,[120] to wit: (1) the defendant was under "extreme mental or emotional disturbance" at the time of the offense; (2) "the capacity of the defendant to appreciate the criminality [wrongfulness] of his conduct or to conform his conduct to the requirements of law was impaired as a result of mental disease or defect or intoxication"; and (3) "the murder was committed under circumstances which the defendant believed to provide a moral justification or extenuation of his conduct."[121] The first factor mimics the Code's provocation formulation for reducing murder to manslaughter, minus the reasonableness requirement.[122] The second factor uses the Code's insanity defense language (and comes close to the language in the ABA/APAs resolution discussed earlier), but deletes the requirement that the incapacity be "significant."[123] The third factor invites a completely subjective analysis of the offender's motivations.

In short, although no state except Connecticut accepts the exemption position that I advocated in Part 1 of this chapter, most death penalty statutes explicitly state (and, given *Lockett,* the rest implicitly recognize) that the mitigating impact afforded to mental dysfunction should be recognized and broadly defined. Yet research on the behavior of capital sentencing bodies strongly suggests that judges and juries often treat evidence of mental illness in precisely the opposite manner.

B. Juror Attitudes toward Offenders with Mental Illness

One early study in California, which examined 238 capital cases to determine the factors that influenced decisions about capital punishment, found that unsuccessfully raising an insanity defense (a scenario that describes a significant portion of those defendants who use mental illness as a mitigator at the sentencing phase)[124] correlates *positively* with a death sentence.[125] A similar study of 128 cases in Georgia also found a powerful correlation between unsuccessful assertion of an insanity defense and a death sentence. Indeed, a failed insanity defense was one of the most accurate predictors of who would receive the death penalty, ahead of such variables as prior record and commission of another crime at the time of the homicide, and behind only the number of official aggravating factors proven at sentencing.[126]

Research focused on factors explicitly involved at sentencing also indicates that mental illness plays an aggravating role at sentencing. David Baldus and his colleagues looked at 175 capital cases in Pennsylvania in an effort to determine how various statutory aggravating and mitigating factors influenced the fact finder's decision.[127] Based on their regression analysis, the eleven aggravating and eight mitigating factors they studied all correlated with the sentence imposed in the predictable direction, with one exception: "extreme mental or emotional disturbance" correlated *positively* with a death sentence, albeit at a level on the verge of statistical insignificance.[128] A similar study found even stronger evidence of such a correlation, concluding that "[a] defendant's odds of receiving a death sentence increased significantly when the defendant had a history of childhood abuse, drug abuse and/or addiction, and mental and/or emotional disturbance."[129]

A fifth study, using mock jurors, may provide an explanation for these results. The study's author, Lawrence White, speculating as to why he found that mental illness defenses were "so ineffective" in capital cases, noted that the jurors endorsed a number of spurious reasons for their antipathy toward those with mental illness. Many of these reasons were alluded to in the discussion on equal protection: "mental illness is no excuse; he might have fooled the psychiatrist; he should have sought help for his problems."[130] Similarly, a sixth study found that, as compared to mock jurors who expressed scruples about the death penalty and therefore could be removed from a capital sentencing jury,[131] mock jurors qualified to serve on capital sentencing juries under the Supreme Court's case law are much more hostile to defendants with schizophrenia than to defendants with mental retardation and other types of defendants.[132] Again, the subjects' explanation was that mental state arguments by people with mental illness are "a ruse and an impediment to the conviction of criminals."[133]

Garvey's analysis of the Capital Jury Sentencing Project, described at the end of the previous section, provides another explanation for the antipathy toward mentally ill offenders. That research, it will be recalled, found that jurors were "more likely to have found the defendant frightening to be near" when the killing was the "work of a madman" or the defendant was "vicious like a mad animal." To the extent mental illness is equated with "madness," Garvey's findings provide further support for the proposition that mental illness damages, rather than supports, the defendant's case at sentencing.

Related to this last observation are two other sets of empirical results that have already been noted. Probably the most robust finding in research on why juries impose the death penalty is that perceived dangerousness plays a very significant role in the decision to impose the death penalty, even in those jurisdictions in which dangerousness is not recognized as a statutory aggravating factor.[134] In research about attitudes toward people with mental illness, a similarly robust finding is that laypeople view such people as abnormally dangerous. Combining these two lines of research, it is hard to escape the conclusion that mental illness often plays an aggravating role in jury and judge decisions about whom to sentence to death.[135]

C. Legal Implications of the Research

Contrary to statutory command and empirical reality, mental illness is seen as a stigmatizing sign of violence-proneness, not as a mitigating factor. Consequently, death sentences imposed in cases where mental illness is clearly evident are highly suspect. In fact, they should be considered illegal.

One might respond to this conclusion by noting that no death penalty statute explicitly prohibits use of mental illness as an aggravator. But permitting such use may well be unconstitutional. In Zant v. Stephens,[136] the Supreme Court stated that it would be constitutionally impermissible to give aggravating effect to factors such as "race, religion or political affiliation or . . . conduct that actually should militate in favor of a lesser penalty, *such as perhaps the defendant's mental illness.*"[137] Although this statement was dictum and somewhat tentatively phrased, it reflects the well-accepted principle that mental illness diminishes culpability.[138]

Indeed, other courts have gone one step further, holding that even a legitimate aggravating circumstance may not form the basis for a death sentence if the circumstance was "caused" by mental illness. In Huckaby v.

State,[139] the Florida Supreme Court reversed a death sentence because the most significant aggravating circumstance—the heinousness of the offender's crime—was "the direct consequence of his mental illness."[140] Two years later, in Miller v. State,[141] the same court reversed a death sentence imposed by a judge who justified his decision on the ground that the defendant was dangerous as a result of his mental illness. The court noted that dangerousness was not recognized as an aggravating factor in Florida's death penalty statute and went on to state that "[t]he trial judge's use of the defendant's mental illness, and his resulting propensity to commit violent acts, as an aggravating factor favoring the imposition of the death penalty appears contrary to the legislative intent as set forth in the statute."[142]

Carried to their logical end, these cases would make imposition of the death penalty on a mentally ill person difficult, since many aggravating circumstances can often be traced to the person's mental condition. That outcome would also bring a helpful practical advantage. No longer would defense attorneys be put to the Hobson's choice of whether to present evidence of mental illness and risk proving the prosecution's case in aggravation, or instead to refrain from presenting such evidence when it may be the only "mitigating" information available, thereby risking a later ineffective assistance of counsel claim.[143]

It should also be noted, however, that courts could make a distinction between situations where the mitigating and aggravating circumstances both go to culpability, as in Huckaby, and where the aggravating circumstance goes to something else, as in Miller, where the mental illness was used to bolster a finding of dangerousness. While a (mitigating) finding of extreme mental or emotional stress is hard to square with a finding that the killing was heinous (traditionally defined as "hatefully or shockingly evil"),[144] a conclusion that a person's mental illness makes him less blameworthy but more dangerous is not necessarily incoherent.[145]

This latter distinction is not illogical. But it also means that any mitigating impact of mental illness will often be nullified by inaccurate perceptions about the relative dangerousness of people with mental illness. Moreover, even if accepted, it applies only in those states where dangerousness is a legitimate aggravating factor, which amounts to only a few of those states that permit executions.[146] In all other states, like Florida, the considerations outlined above strongly support a complete ban on death sentences for people whose mental illness is evident to the fact finder. Permitting such sentences would ignore both the letter and the logic of capital sentencing statutes.

Moving from that observation to a blanket ban on death sentences for people with mental disability is admittedly a significant step. Not every capital sentencing jury treats mental disability as an aggravating circumstance.[147] And, even when there is proof that the capital sentencing system is not working the way it should, the Supreme Court has been notoriously reluctant to use the Constitution as a corrective.[148] But the Court has also recognized the significant potential for misuse of mental impairment evidence in a number of capital cases.[149] And, as noted at the beginning of this discussion about due process, if the concern about this misuse is not enough on its own to lead to a ban, it should at least supplement this chapter's first argument that people with serious impairments are never sufficiently culpable to deserve the death penalty.

III. The Eighth Amendment Argument

Ford v. Wainright's holding that the Eighth Amendment bars execution of a person who is incompetent left two significant questions unanswered. First, what is the rationale for the competency requirement? Second, what is the content of the competency standard? The response to the first question determines the answer to the second. If, as I argue here, the most plausible basis for the competency requirement is society's interest in retribution, then the standard defining competency to be executed is not as low a threshold as many have suggested, and a significant number of mentally ill people on death row today do not meet it. Furthermore, state efforts to restore with medication those who are incompetent to be executed should be barred by the Eighth Amendment, for they require mental health professionals to engage in unethical practices.

A. The Definition of Incompetency to Be Executed

The Supreme Court in Ford noted at least six reasons, all of them derived from common law dating back to medieval times, that might explain why a person must be competent prior to execution: (1) An incompetent person might be unable to provide counsel with last minute information leading to vacation of the sentence. (2) Madness is punishment enough in itself. (3) An incompetent person cannot make peace with God. (4) Execution of an incompetent person has no deterrent effect on the population. (5) Such execution "is a miserable spectacle . . . of extream inhumanity and cruelty" (quoting E. Coke).[150] (6) The retribution or vengeance meant to be realized by execution cannot be exacted from an incompetent person.[151] The Court avoided settling on any one of these reasons as the sole or principal basis for its decision, simply stating that "[w]hether its aim be to protect the condemned from fear and pain without comfort of understanding, or to protect the dignity of society itself from the barbarity of exacting mindless vengeance, the restriction finds enforcement in the Eighth Amendment [which bans cruel and unusual punishment]."[152]

The majority opinion was even less forthcoming on the competency standard. Indeed, it did not proffer any test. However, Justice Lewis Powell Jr., in concurrence, stated that he "would hold that the Eighth Amendment forbids the execution only of those who are unaware of the punishment they are about to suffer and why they are to suffer it."[153] That language has since become the most widely accepted test for determining competency to be executed.

Because only the retributive rationale makes sense in modern times, Powell's test is the correct one, provided the key word "unaware" is defined to mean a lack of emotional appreciation. The flaws in the other five rationales have been discussed by others[154] and will be only hinted at here. With respect to the first rationale, as Powell noted in his concurrence, the view that competency is required to assist the attorney "has slight merit today," because defendants are entitled to effective assistance of counsel at trial and appeal, as well as to multiple postconviction reviews of the sentence. With respect to the second, even if a lifetime of madness could be seen as sufficient punishment for first-degree murder, the advent of psychotropic drugs means that most mentally ill people will not suffer indeterminately. The third rationale is flawed because the view that competency is required to allow the offender to make peace with God assumes a religious offender (much less likely today than in medieval times), and that it is one's mental state at the time of execution, rather than the tenor of one's life, that is important in heaven. The fourth rationale is also incoherent, even assuming, against significant evidence, that executions have *any* deterrent effect.[155] Executions of people with mental illness are as likely to deter as any other type of execution; indeed, the deterrent effect of the death penalty might even be *enhanced* if the state were to execute those who are psychotic, because the populace would be assured of the state's resolve to kill and because potential criminals who bank on their ability to malinger illness will be faced with the most powerful dissuasion.

The fifth rationale for the competency-to-be-executed requirement works somewhat better. Execution of a person who is unaware that the event is taking place is undoubtedly cruel. But at least as cruel is the execution of someone who knows he or she is about to be killed. If there is any difference in the discomfort we feel observing the execution of an insensate, as opposed to a competent, person, it is best explained as stemming from an unwillingness to exact punishment on someone who does not understand why it is happening—a retributive rationale. Commentators who have closely analyzed the various possible reasons for the competency requirement agree that society's interest in ensuring the offender suffers in proportion to the crime is the most solid traditional basis for the competency requirement.[156]

As harsh as this rationale sounds, it necessitates a definition of execution incompetency that is relatively broad. Mere understanding of the death penalty and why it is being imposed should be insufficient for a retributivist. Rather, the offender must fathom, if not internalize, the nature of the debt that is owed society. As one court put it, an incompetency finding is mandated if the offender, "[when] taken to the electric chair . . . would not quail or take account of its significance."[157]

Barbara Ward objects that this standard "would automatically exempt sociopaths from execution as well as inhumanely require the obliteration of psychological coping mechanisms."[158] Both of her concerns are exaggerated. While the standard might mandate an incompetency finding for some people with antisocial personality disorder (the modern version of sociopathy), it does not require remorse for the crime (a feeling this type of person often lacks), only an appreciation of the penalty. And, if one agrees with the argument made below that people may not be forcibly restored to competency, then treatment may not be used to obliterate the person's "coping mechanisms."

That this "appreciation" standard has teeth is demonstrated by the case of Horace Kelly, found competent by a California jury in 1998. The jury concluded that Kelly was able to describe both the consequence of the death penalty (death) and why he deserved it (he killed two women and an eleven-year-old boy).[159] Thus, he met the austere version of Powell's test. Under a competency standard properly informed by the retributive premise, however, he should not have been found competent to be executed. The evidence indicated that Kelly, who was both mentally retarded and mentally ill, talked in rambling and incoherent sentences; thought that his mother would eventually take him home after one of her visits; and from time to time believed prison was a college.[160] Although Kelly had a cognitive understanding of his legal situation, he did not comprehend the enormity of his punishment or the societal condemnation associated with it. Numerous other individuals, found competent by the courts, would probably not pass the proposed appreciation standard.[161]

In addition to competency to be executed, two other competency issues might arise in the death penalty context. The first, adjudicative competency, focuses on whether a person on death row is able to provide his or her attorney with facts relevant to postconviction proceedings that might prove that person's innocence or lead to reversal on other grounds. The second, decisional competency, focuses on whether a death row inmate's decision to forego such proceedings is valid. Although an offender should be competent in all three respects before he or she is executed, as a practical matter these latter two types of competency issues will normally be resolved well before execution. Further discussion of their scope is deferred until this book's examination of the protection model of liberty deprivation in Chapter 6.

B. Restoration of Competency to Be Executed

For some people with symptoms like those experienced by Kelly, antipsychotic medication can remove delusions and other mental symptoms that cause the incompetency. At issue in Perry v. Louisiana[162] was whether the state may forcibly medicate such individuals when necessary to ensure that Ford's test is met. The U.S. Supreme Court granted certiorari in the case, but then remanded it in light of its intervening decision in Washington v. Harper,[163] which allows forcible medication when "medically appropriate" for prisoners who are dangerous to self or others or gravely disabled. Surprisingly, given the Harper decision and its own earlier rulings, the Louisiana Supreme Court held on remand that forcible medication to render a person competent to be executed is impermissible,[164] relying primarily on state constitutional bases for its decision. Its principal rationale for this decision was that medicating an objecting individual to facilitate execution constitutes cruel and unusual punishment under Louisiana's constitution, because it "imposes significantly more indignity, pain and suffering than ordinarily is necessary for the mere extinguishment of life . . . imposes a severe penalty without furthering any of the valid social goals of punishment, and . . . subjects to the death penalty a class of offenders that has been exempt therefrom for centuries and adds novel burdens to the punishment of the insane which will not be suffered by sane capital offenders."[165]

The U.S. Supreme Court may ultimately reject this reasoning for several reasons. In light of its more recent decision in Sell v. United States[166] (discussed in detail in Chapter 7), the Court could easily find that the state's interests in meting out a justly imposed sentence and in deterring malingering outweigh the extra indignity that forcible medication visits on the mentally ill offender.[167] Moreover, offenders who refuse medication, on their own or through their attorneys, may well be doing so primarily to avoid execution, rather than, for instance, out of a desire to avoid the side effects of medication. If so, the individual interest to be balanced against the state's is entitled to virtually no weight. Finally, and most importantly, if the basis for the competency requirement is society's interest in retribution, the individual's interest in avoiding appropriately titrated medication should count for little or nothing in any event.

It is the societal underpinning of the incompetency requirement, however, that provides the basis for a much more persuasive reason the Louisiana Supreme Court gave to bolster its decision in Perry. Playing off Harper's mandate that forcible medication be "medically appropriate," the Louisiana court concluded that medication given "to facilitate . . . execution does not constitute medical treatment but is antithetical to the basic principles of the healing arts."[168] As the court recognized, there is a clear ethical stipulation in medicine that doctors should do no harm,[169] and the relevant professional organizations' interpret that stipulation to mean that doctors may not participate or assist in executions.[170] In the words of Richard Bonnie, the clinician who restores a prisoner's competency "would be serving a role that is ethically indistinguishable from the physician who administers the lethal injection of barbiturates."[171] Accordingly, the involvement of mental health professionals in the administration of drugs, forcible or otherwise, in an effort to ensure that execution takes place, is constitutionally impermissible under the Eighth Amendment.

The latter conclusion might be read to mean that mental health professionals may not treat even persons who are *charged* with a capital crime and need medication to make them competent to stand trial. But I would not carry the proposition that far. The point at which mental health professionals who treat capital offenders become direct accomplices to the death penalty is when the death warrant is signed. Up to that point the execution is not imminent. Indeed, even when the treatment is of a death row inmate who is incompetent in the adjudicative or decisional senses described above, the Eighth Amendment is not implicated, because restoration in those situations is designed not to facilitate punishment but to aid the inmate in challenging it, either by improving the ability to communicate with an attorney or by ensuring the capacity to make decisions about whether to pursue appeals.

When the death warrant has been signed and execution scheduled, however, the ethical dilemma is crystal clear, and treatment of a person who is incompetent to be executed should be prohibited because of the role in which it places the professional clinician. The fact that the party who is the focus of this argument is someone other than the offender does not prevent state coercion of treatment from being a cruel and unusual method of exacting vengeance. Again, that standard is not defined solely in terms of the offender's interests, but rather takes into account overarching societal mores and "evolving standards of decency." The doctor-patient relationship is an intimate one. Asking a mental health professional to treat someone for the sole purpose of assuring a death sentence is carried out is akin to asking the offender's attorney or relative to assist in that person's execution. When faced with an incompetent capital offender who requires professional treatment to be restored, the state's only option should be commutation of sentence.[172]

IV. Regular Sentencing and the Guilty-but-Mentally-Ill Verdict

The three broad contentions this chapter has made about the role of mental disability in capital sentencing have analogous implications for noncapital sentencing. First, mental disability that causes significant impairment at the time of the offense, as defined in Part 1, should bring a reduction in noncapital sentences as well. Second, mental disability should never be grounds for enhancing a sentence on culpability grounds, for the reasons elucidated in Part 2. And consistent with the reasoning in Part 3, if, after sentence is imposed, a person decompensates to the point of not appreciating why he or she is being punished, that person should not be subjected to such punishment. The appropriate response in the latter situation is treatment in a nonpunitive environment until the person is restored. In the noncapital setting such treatment can be administered ethically, because it alleviates suffering while in confinement, in contrast to the imminent execution context, where it can assure only that the ultimate harm occurs.

The first two prescriptions would require many more downward sentencing departures in noncapital cases than currently occur, at least in determinate sentencing regimes where the offender's culpability is supposedly the only consideration.[173] But that is an obligatory outcome in a punishment model of liberty deprivation.[174] Otherwise, the law is either unjustly ignoring the diminished responsibility of those with mental disability or even more unjustly enhancing their sentences because of it.

To be contrasted with a sentencing system that gives the mitigating effect of mental disorder its due is the widely popular reform proposal known as the "guilty but mentally ill" (GBMI) verdict. GBMI legislation—currently enacted in about a dozen states and periodically considered in others whenever furor erupts over an insanity acquittal or a crime is committed by a released acquittee[175]—provides the fact finder with an additional option to the three traditional verdicts of guilty, not guilty, and not guilty by reason of insanity. If the defendant is found guilty but mentally ill, the court may impose any sentence appropriate for the offense, but the defendant is eligible for treatment in prison or a mental hospital while incarcerated.[176]

The GBMI verdict, put simply, is a hoax. Proponents of GBMI legislation say it will reduce inappropriate insanity acquittals and provide greater protection to the public by offering judges and juries a compromise verdict that ensures both prolonged incarceration and treatment for the offender who is mentally ill. But research results released by the National Center for State Courts back in the 1980s, when the verdict was in its heyday, definitively show that this "reform" achieves none of these aims.[177] It has not affected the insanity acquittal rate or provided more protection for the public, primarily because virtually all offenders found guilty but mentally ill come from the guilty pool, not from those who deserve an insanity defense.[178] Nor has it guaranteed mental health treatment for those who need it, in large part because, for reasons developed below, it does not accurately identify that group.

Most important for present purposes, the GBMI verdict has nothing to do with assessing culpability, which should be the the central issue in a criminal prosecution involving a person with alleged mental problems. Notwithstanding the "guilty *but*" language, the verdict results neither in a reduction of the grade of offense or of sentence length; as noted above, the judge may impose any sentence authorized by law for the crime involved.[179] In fact, sentences imposed on offenders who are guilty but mentally ill do not appear to differ from the sentences imposed on other offenders.[180] Courts have even upheld death sentences imposed on those found guilty but mentally ill, a conclusion that is entirely consistent with the language of GBMI statutes.[181]

A GBMI finding does not even mitigate culpability in the attenuated sense of improving postconviction treatment status for those who are not sentenced to death. In deliberating on the applicability of the verdict, the fact finder's evaluation is limited to the defendant's mental illness at the time of the offense.[182] Although jurors may allow concern about treatability to influence their decision, GBMI legislation appropriately recognizes that the dispositive treatment determination has to be made by experts after conviction, not by lay fact finders at trial.[183] To provide otherwise would force a decision on judges and juries that they have neither the expertise or the relevant facts to make. Not surprisingly, a significant proportion of those found guilty but mentally ill by judges or juries do not need intensive treatment.[184] Nor should they receive treatment priority over offenders who are found simply guilty. Rather, as all states sensibly recognize, treatment should to go those who need it, regardless of label.[185]

In other words, the GBMI verdict is not a proper "verdict" at all. The "mentally ill" component of the verdict serves no identifiable purpose within the theoretical framework of the criminal law. As Ralph Slovenko has aptly put it, the verdict might as well be named "guilty but flat feet."[186]

Accordingly, the GBMI reform should be shunned. As Chapter 2 indicated, there are other ways to address problems with the insanity defense, and all offenders with mental disorder, irrespective of their official verdict, should receive appropriate treatment. As Chapter 4 explains, protecting the public from offenders with dangerous propensities requires a much more nuanced approach than the GBMI verdict takes. And if an offender's responsibility at the time of the offense is diminished by the types of nonexculpatory impairments discussed in Part 1 of this chapter, then he or she deserves a reduction of sentence, not merely a misleading label that has no effect on disposition.

Conclusion

Many people with mental disorder who are convicted on capital charges should not be executed, for one of three reasons. First, those who suffer from serious cognitive impairment at the time of their crime due to mental disability are as undeserving of the ultimate punishment as offenders who are mentally retarded, a group the Supreme Court has exempted from the death penalty. Second, a substantial proportion of death sentences imposed on people with mental illness violate due process, or at least violate statutory prescriptions, because the sentencer has treated the disorder as an aggravating factor, either directly or to bolster a separate aggravating circumstance. Third, many offenders with mental illness who are sentenced to death will be so impaired at the time of execution that they can not appreciate the significance of their punishment and thus cannot be executed under the Eighth Amendment; the latter conclusion is required even if they are restorable through treatment, given the unethical and medically inappropriate role in which such treatment casts mental health professionals.

Analogous claims can be made in connection with noncapital sentencing. But it is in the death penalty context that society's ambivalence about people with mental disorder, noted in the preface to this book and again at the beginning of this chapter, must be most aggressively confronted. While that ambivalence may be unavoidable in everyday life, allowing it to infect the death penalty process—the most awesome exercise of power any society can exert over its members—is inexcusable. As currently implemented, state and federal laws not only violate the spirit of the Constitution by failing to take proper account of a person's mental illness; they also allow misperceptions and prejudices about that condition to *increase* the possibility that a death sentence will be imposed. If it is true that the worth of a society should be judged by the way in which it treats its most vulnerable citizens, then execution of those with mental illness should deeply trouble us all.

— II —

The Prevention Model

— 4 —

A Jurisprudence of Dangerousness

The prevention model addressed in this and the following chapter justifies liberty deprivation not as punishment for past harmful acts but as a means of preventing future ones. Thus, figuring out the role of mental disorder in a prevention regime requires a "jurisprudence of dangerousness"—a set of principles governing when and to what extent the government may deprive a person of life or liberty based on a prediction of harm. At present, this jurisprudence is badly underdeveloped, especially when contrasted to the robust theoretical literature relating to punishment based on retribution and general deterrence. This relative lack of theorizing is unfortunate, because dangerousness determinations permeate the government's implementation of its police power. Death penalty determinations, noncapital sentencing, detention of enemy combatants, sexual predator commitment, civil commitment, pretrial detention, and investigative stops by the police, to name a few examples, often or always depend on dangerousness assessments.[1] In an effort to devise a more coherent jurisprudence of dangerousness, this chapter examines the legitimacy of all of these interventions, not just those that are based on "mental disorder."

A good place to start this examination is with an analysis of long-term, pure preventive detention. Pure preventive detention is a deprivation of liberty that is based on a prediction of harmful conduct and that is not time-limited by culpability or other considerations, such as a pending trial. In the past decade, the law's approach to this type of preventive intervention has changed noticeably, although the change is not as drastic as some have suggested. To understand this point, consider three actual cases.

Leroy Hendricks is on the verge of release from prison after serving his fifth sentence for child molestation. He candidly tells his court-appointed evaluators that, if released, the only sure way he will stop molesting children is "to die."[2]

Garry David, diagnosed with antisocial personality disorder, is nearing the end of his fourteen-year sentence for shooting a woman and two police officers, conduct that occurred just after being released from prison for a previous violent offense. While in prison, he assaulted more than fifteen inmates and guards, conduct that increased his sentence. A court found that, if released, "[h]is underlying anger and resentment would be almost certain to rise to an explosive level as soon as he felt thwarted or subjected to stress."[3]

Zacarias Moussaoui, a French-Moroccan known to have trained in Osama bin Laden's camps in Afghanistan, tried to pay $8,000 for flying lessons before September 11, 2001, stating that he was interested only in learning how to handle an aircraft (not take off or land). He also made several telephone calls to some of the individuals eventually involved in the hijackings of September 11, although the contents of those calls are not known.[4]

Under traditional theory, the government should not be able to detain individuals like these unless it charges them with some (new) crime.[5] That is because, under traditional theory, only people with serious mental disorder (that is, psychosis or something similar) may be subjected to long-term pure preventive detention. As a plurality of the U.S. Supreme Court observed in 1992, the "present system . . . with only narrow exceptions and *aside from permissible confinements for mental illness,* incarcerates only those who are proved beyond reasonable doubt to have violated a criminal law."[6] Hendricks, David, and even Moussaoui may have some types of diagnosable mental disorders, but not disorders that support preventive commitment as classically conceived. Thus, for instance, the Kansas Supreme Court found that, despite his strong antisocial urges, Hendricks was not committable under the Kansas civil commitment standard, a standard similar to commitment laws around the country.[7] Likewise, David, whose case arose in Australia, was not eligible for civil commitment under the common law of that country.[8]

In 1997, however, the Supreme Court appeared to abandon the traditional view that pure preventive detention is reserved for those who are severely mentally ill. In Kansas v. Hendricks,[9] involving the constitutionality of a so-called sexual predator statute, the Court permitted indeterminate confinement of dangerous individuals who have completed their sentences and have committed no new crime, even when they are *not* seriously mentally disordered—as long as they have a personality disorder that renders them unable to adequately control their antisocial conduct.[10] Five years later in a second sexual predator decision, Kansas v. Crane,[11] the Court affirmed its willingness to uphold the institutionalization of nonpsychotic people who meet this "inability to control" threshold.

These holdings are clearly meant to permit the preventive detention of people such as Hendricks, whose commitment was affirmed by the Court in Kansas v. Hendricks.[12] Whether they would authorize preventive detention of someone like David, who may not exhibit the type of inability to control that is popularly associated with sex offenders, remains an open question, and pure preventive detention of someone like Moussaoui is, outside combat situations, undoubtedly not authorized by the Court's case law to date.[13] *Hendricks* and *Crane* opened the door to broader preventive detention more than a crack, but certainly not all the way.

Despite the relatively limited reach of the statute upheld in *Hendricks,* the Court's opinion occasioned a storm of criticism. The attacks on *Hendricks* focus on two aspects of that decision, which I will call the *psychological criterion* and the *prediction criterion.* The psychological criterion describes the psychological traits that distinguish those dangerous people who may be committed from those who may not be. The prediction criterion describes the level of risk that must be shown before preventive detention may take place. The first criticism of *Hendricks* inveighs against its endorsement of the inability-to-control notion as the appropriate psychological criterion for preventive detention. Those who voice this criticism argue instead for some version of the traditional view that only serious mental dysfunction (that is, psychosis or irrationality) permits confinement based on dangerousness. The second criticism concerns the Court's belief, implicit in *Hendricks* and explicit in other cases, that enough evidence can be procured to meet the prediction criterion.[14] Critics of this stripe contend that predicting which individuals will offend with a level of certainty sufficient to justify long-term confinement is impossible, or only possible in a small percentage of cases, and thus invalid detentions and abuse are likely.

Much of this chapter is devoted to assessing the claims and counterclaims made about the psychological and prediction criteria for preventive detention. It concludes that both *Hendricks* and its critics are wrong about the appropriate psychological criterion, but that *Hendricks* is closer to getting it right than those who believe preventive detention should be reserved for people who suffer from psychosis or similarly severe mental disorders. It also concludes that the controversy over the prediction criterion requires significant rethinking.

More specifically, with respect to the psychological criterion, I argue that the core trait that normatively distinguishes the dangerous person who may be preventively detained from the dangerous person who may not be is imperviousness to criminal punishment, or what I shall call *undeterrability*. This condition clearly describes the severely mentally ill person who is oblivious to societal mores or who is irrationally convinced that his or her criminal actions do not violate them. But it might also describe the extremely impulsive individual who, like Hendricks or David, is willing to commit crime despite a very high likelihood of apprehension. It may even apply to someone like Moussaoui, who suffers from neither a major mental disorder nor a volitional dysfunction, but who wants to commit crime so badly he is willing to die for it. When the dangerous person is undeterrable in this sense, society is presumptively entitled to impose preventive detention rather than or in addition to punishment, because then the commands of the criminal justice system not only do not work (a state of affairs presumably descriptive of almost every criminal act), they cannot work.

This chapter also assesses the prediction criterion: the degree of dangerousness necessary to justify preventive detention.[15] The debate on this issue between those who emphasize individual liberty and those who focus on public security has been vigorous, but the two sides often seem to be talking past each other, given their starting points. I do not try to define the prediction criterion precisely, but I do propose two principles on which both sides should be able to agree. The *proportionality principle* requires that the degree of danger be roughly proportionate to the proposed government intervention. For instance, greater proof of dangerousness is needed to impose the death penalty than to conduct a law enforcement frisk. A further, less obvious consequence of the proportionality idea is that preventive detention would be subject to durational limitations, because the longer the government seeks to detain someone preventively, the more proof of dangerousness it would need to produce. The *consistency principle* requires that the prediction criterion applied in the preventive detention context be consistent with analogous manifestations of the government's police power, in particular the implementation of criminal justice. Thus, for instance, the degree of dangerousness required for incarcerative preventive detention ought to be roughly equivalent to the degree of dangerousness that permits conviction for inchoate crimes such as conspiracy, reckless endangerment, and driving while intoxicated, because both preventive detention and these provisions of criminal law authorize significant deprivations of liberty to protect third parties.

As this last comment suggests, application of the proportionality and consistency principles could have significant implications for both preventive detention and the law of crimes. Under these two principles, one could argue that preventive detention based on dangerousness could, at least initially, be justified on a relatively low risk of harm, such as that associated with the crime of driving while intoxicated. Conversely, with some of the most inchoate crimes, such as vagrancy and possession of certain types of contraband, confinement may not be justifiable under any reasonable interpretation of these principles, because the degree of danger posed by such crimes is so minimal.

This chapter develops the psychological and prediction criteria in more detail, as well as the criteria's implications for the criminal law. Before doing so, however, the chapter explores at length a fundamental predicate issue. Assuming the prediction criterion is met, why should society want to impose any additional limitations on the government's authority to incapacitate dangerous individuals? Certainly a primary function of government is to prevent harm to its citizens, and laws that incapacitate individuals simply on evidence that they are likely to cause such harm would seem to be one effective manner of doing so. Indeed, in the next chapter, I argue that such a regime may be superior to our current punishment-dominated one. On the assumption that we are unlikely to abandon our punishment orientation anytime soon, however, an explication of why that orientation cannot coexist with a full-blown preventive regime is necessary to set the stage for the rest of the chapter.

Accordingly, Part 1 discusses the plausibility of a preventive detention regime that jettisons the psychological criterion requirement and instead focuses solely on the prediction criterion. It first concludes that the standard objections to preventive detention—that we cannot predict the future, that preventive detention is an underhanded way of more easily imposing punishment, or that it violates the legality principle because of definitional conundrums—are all rebuttable. But it also concludes that such a regime would violate the fundamental tenet, derivable from deontological, utilitarian, and ethical reasoning, that autonomous individuals who commit criminal acts have a *right to punishment*. If government chooses to detain preventively an individual rather than punish him, it must show the person is not eligible for the right to punishment. Thus, government must demonstrate not only dangerousness, but also that the person is so lacking in the capacity or willingness to adhere to society's most basic prohibitions—in other words, so undeterrable—that punishment is not warranted. Although I recognize an *effect exception* to this proposition—which would permit preventive actions in the absence of psychological impairment if they are consistent with the right to punishment—our current preference for the punishment model as the predominant means of liberty deprivation strongly supports a prohibition on long-term deprivations of liberty based on dangerousness, unless the psychological criterion is also met.

On that assumption, Part 2 of this chapter explores the possible alternatives to the psychological limitation and makes the case for undeterrability as the appropriate inquiry. Part 3 then examines the prediction criterion, and more fully describes the proportionality and consistency principles and their implications for the criminal law. My goal is to explicate and justify a jurisprudence of dangerousness governing the state's implementation of its police power.

I. Dangerousness as the Sole Criterion for State Intervention

Sex offenders are not the only criminals who might routinely recidivate. Burglars, check forgers, and even killers can be repeat offenders. Certainly the state has a compelling interest in protecting its citizens from these types of crimes. Why shouldn't the state be empowered to take preventive action against any individual who is likely to wreak havoc on society?

There are at least four objections to such a preventive regime. The unreliability objection is that we lack the tools to predict criminal behavior with a sufficient degree of certainty. The punishment-in-disguise objection is that a preventive detention regime will allow government to avoid the rigorous procedural protections of the criminal law and perhaps eventually replace criminal justice altogether. The legality objection is that we cannot define the state's power to detain for preventive reasons precisely enough to let the citizenry know its scope or to avoid its abuse by government officials. The dehumanization objection is that deprivations of liberty based on future behavior offend basic precepts of our civilization.

Each one of these objections suggests limitations on preventive detention. None of them, however, requires prohibition of such detention under all circumstances. The following discussion elaborates on these conclusions.

A. The Unreliability Objection

This objection to preventive detention rests on two assumptions. First, government should not be able to deprive a person of liberty on dangerousness grounds unless it demonstrates a high degree of certainty that the person will offend in the near future. Second, such proof is impossible to obtain.

The first assumption expresses a preference for certainty that is analogous to the criminal law requirement that the government prove the essential elements of crime beyond a reasonable doubt. Such a preference is understandable. But it is misguided for three reasons.

First, imposition of the reasonable doubt standard is overly stringent when the state's goal is to prevent rather than to punish. The preference for establishing guilt beyond a reasonable doubt in criminal trials is often expressed through the adage that our system would prefer to let ten guilty people go free than permit one innocent person to be convicted. But assume that six of these hypothetical ten guilty individuals will commit a crime if not confined. On this assumption, Michael Corrado has pointed out the different calculus that exists when the state seeks to prevent rather than convict. The outcome of a crime cannot be changed; in that context, as Corrado states, "[t]he only dangers are those of convicting an innocent person, on the one side, [and] . . . of letting a guilty person off without his proper punishment."[16] In contrast, if we could identify a group of ten people, among whom six will kill in the near future, "surely the likelihood that four will lose their freedom must be weighed against the likelihood that six [victims] will lose their lives."[17] Despite the fact that we can reasonably doubt whether any particular person in this group will commit homicide, preventive detention of the entire group may well be justified given the cost of not doing so.

In any event, the belief that the reasonable doubt standard as applied in criminal adjudications demands *more* than this level of certainty is badly mistaken. Every criminal law professor knows the difficulty of differentiating premeditation from ordinary intent, or recklessness from negligence. Even if agreement can be reached as to the precise definition of these concepts, independent judges and juries applying them are bound to arrive at different results on the same facts; for instance, empirical research indicates that disagreement is highly likely in deciding between first- and second-degree murder, unprovoked and provoked killing, and voluntary and involuntary manslaughter.[18] These disparities are an inevitable aspect of a system that relies on moral judgments about invisible, internal mental states.[19]

In social science terms, this high degree of interrater inconsistency (or unreliability) cannot help but indicate a high degree of inaccuracy (or invalidity) as well. The assertion that we can know, beyond a reasonable doubt, that a person "deserves" a particular verdict and punishment expresses a hope rather than a reality. As the District of Columbia Court of Appeals candidly recognized in Bethea v. United States, "[t]he concept of mens rea involves what is ultimately the fiction of determining the actual thoughts or mental processes of the accused. It is obvious that a certain resolution of this issue is beyond the ken of scientist and laymen alike."[20] And the costs of inaccuracy are huge—a finding of premeditation can result in the death penalty rather than a twenty-year sentence; a conclusion that a defendant's belief was "unreasonable" can mean the difference between conviction and acquittal. If we are willing to countenance these harsh penalty differentials based on such a high degree of uncertainty, we may be hard-pressed to criticize a preventive detention regime on unreliability grounds.

The final reason a high level of certainty may not be necessary in the preventive context rests on the assertion that, when the criminal law punishes conduct because it is dangerous, the degree of danger required is often minimal, especially with respect to crimes such as reckless endangerment, possession, and vagrancy. In other words, as developed in more detail in Part 3 of this chapter, a requirement that predictions of antisocial conduct meet the reasonable doubt standard in the preventive detention context would be, in effect, a more rigorous proof standard than is often found in the criminal punishment context. This observation does not necessarily justify government intervention based on low degrees of danger. It does suggest, however, that a regime that permitted various sorts of preventive action against low-risk individuals would be consistent with our current law of crimes.

Even if a "real" reasonable doubt standard must be met when making predictions of danger, the U.S. Supreme Court is unwilling to accept the assertion that this high level of proof is impossible to meet, a position that substantially undermines the second (impossibility of proof) assumption underlying the unreliability objection. In Jurek v. Texas[21] the Court held that the death penalty—which to be valid requires proof of an aggravating circumstance, presumably beyond a reasonable doubt[22]—may be based on predictions of future violence.[23] In Barefoot v. Estelle,[24] it reaffirmed this position and indicated that even if such predictions are wrong more often than they are right, the adversarial process can be counted on to expose erroneous views.[25] If executions may be based on evidence acknowledged to be this potentially flimsy, presumably preventive detention may be as well.

Although the Court's views on this issue have justly been attacked,[26] its apparent confidence in our ability to predict is not completely misplaced. Due to a number of methodological difficulties in measuring prediction validity, we may never know precisely how accurate the various modes of prediction are.[27] But we can say that prediction science—in particular, methods that utilize actuarial tables or structured interviews—has improved to the point where clear and convincing evidence of dangerousness, if not proof beyond a reasonable doubt, is available for certain categories of individuals.[28] If, as Part 3 discusses in more detail, the quantum of proof necessary to justify exercise of the state's police power need not reach these levels of certainty for some types of detention, then our capacity to make legally valid predictions increases significantly.[29]

The unreliability objection, in short, does not dictate a prohibition on preventive detention. Juxtaposition of preventive detention with the other liberty-depriving manifestation of the police power—the criminal law— suggests several reasons why the threshold necessary to support such detention need not be set at the reasonable doubt level, and that whatever quantum of proof is required, courts assume it can be met, an assumption that current research tends to support for at least some types of individuals. However, the unreliability objection does counsel caution when making predictions of antisocial behavior. Only the best prediction methods should be used,[30] and perhaps other adjustments should be made to compensate for the inevitably speculative nature of prediction.[31] For the remainder of this chapter, I will assume that, under such conditions, dangerousness can be proven with the requisite degree of certainty. That assumption allows focus on the conceptual objections to preventive detention.

B. The Punishment-in-Disguise Objection

In Allen v. Illinois,[32] the Supreme Court presaged *Hendricks* by holding that proceedings under a statute that permits "commitment" of sex offenders in lieu of criminal prosecution do not implicate the privilege against self-incrimination, because such hearings are not "criminal" in nature and thus do not involve incrimination.[33] Similarly, in *Hendricks* the Court held that because such special track sex offender proceedings are not "punitive" in intent, postsentence commitment of sex offenders does not violate the double jeopardy clause's ban on multiple punishments for the "same offense."[34] Such reasoning might also permit courts to declare that the Sixth Amendment's guarantees of counsel, public jury trial, and confrontation during "criminal prosecutions" do not apply in such proceedings.[35]

In his dissent in *Allen,* Justice Stevens expressed concern that the Court's willingness to label preventive detention laws "civil" rather than "criminal" would encourage a proliferation of such statutes.[36] Eventually, he speculated, a shadow criminal code could develop that would give prosecutors the discretion to detain preventively a wide array of dangerous offenders. In his eyes, this alternative code would lead to "evisceration of the criminal law and its accompanying protections."[37]

To date, Stevens's prediction that government will routinely use preventive detention laws to evade the strictures of the criminal law has not come to pass. After *Hendricks* gave the green light to full scale, postsentence preventive detention for sex offenders, the legislative enthusiasm for such schemes rose momentarily but has since abated,[38] and prosecutors in most states with such laws have not rushed to abandon the criminal process in favor of "easier" petitions for commitment.[39] In any event, were such a movement to develop, preventive detention would not thereby be rendered illegitimate, for the Court is right that preventive detention, properly structured, is not criminal punishment.

Much has been written about the criminal-civil distinction.[40] That literature will not be rehearsed here. The strongest argument in favor of the Court's position can be expressed through a simple syllogism. Criminal punishment is based solely on a conviction for an offense and can occur only if there is such a conviction. Preventive detention is based solely on a prediction concerning future offenses and can occur only if there is such a prediction. Therefore, preventive detention is not criminal punishment. Indeed, the concept of "punishment" for some future act is incoherent.[41] Accordingly, to the extent procedural protections depend on characterization of a proceeding as criminal, they are not required in preventive detention proceedings, although the procedural component of the due process clause presumably still applies.[42]

If a liberty deprivation pursuant to a prediction fails to adhere to the logic of preventive detention, however, then it can become punishment. The Supreme Court recognized as much in Jackson v. Indiana,[43] when it declared that "due process [here meaning its *substantive* component] requires that the nature and duration of commitment bear some reasonable relation to the purpose for which the individual is committed."[44] In *Jackson*, that principle mandated that the duration of the government's authority to commit an individual who has been found incompetent to stand trial be limited to that period reasonably necessary to restore the person to competency or to determine that he or she is unrestorable.[45] In the preventive detention context, the reasonable relation principle requires that the commitment match the state's interest in preventing harm.

That general limitation suggests three specific restrictions on preventive detention. The first essential feature of preventive detention—or what might more aptly be called preventive intervention—is that the nature of the liberty deprivation must bear a reasonable relationship to the harm feared. While confinement may be necessary to prevent some individuals from causing harm, conditional release and other less restrictive mechanisms can also be effective at realizing that goal, especially after a period of treatment.[46] Most commitment systems provide for alternatives to institutionalization.[47] If, however, the paucity of such alternatives results in incarceration of those who do not need to be confined, the detention becomes punitive, a position the Supreme Court has tangentially recognized.[48] As Dan Kahan has demonstrated, incarceration is usually equated with punishment in the public eye;[49] unconditional confinement of "dangerous" individuals, especially where treatment is not provided (a scenario discussed below), potently expresses a goal of condemnation, not of prevention, and so must be avoided when possible.

A second principle of preventive detention is that the duration of the commitment must be reasonably related to the prevention of the harm predicted. This restriction requires release once the individual no longer presents the level of danger necessary for preventive detention. A mental hospital must discharge the once dangerous mentally ill person who is "cured"; a police officer must release a person subject to investigative detention if no further suspicion develops during questioning.

Just as important, the duration limitation requires the state to provide treatment that will reduce dangerousness. The Supreme Court, although reticent about announcing a full-blown right to treatment in this setting, has held that a committed person's "liberty interests require the State to provide minimally adequate or reasonable training to ensure . . . freedom from undue restraint."[50] It has also continued to recognize the viability of a due process claim against preventive detention that does not offer treatment.[51] These decisions should be read to confirm that confinement of a treatable individual without providing treatment is unreasonably prolonging detention, in violation of *Jackson*.[52]

This is not to say that the state must prove an individual is treatable before he or she may be preventively confined. As *Hendricks* stated, "incapacitation may be a legitimate end of the civil law."[53] Otherwise, the state's ability to protect itself would depend on the vagaries of treatment science, and the most dangerous individuals might be immune from preventive detention.[54] By the same token, proof of treatability should not somehow *ease* the state's burden in proving the other requisites for preventive detention (contrary to Justice O'Connor's insinuation, in Foucha v. Louisiana,[55] that detention that is "medically appropriate" is more likely to be constitutionally permissible). In short, treatability is irrelevant in determining whether the state may preventively detain a person, but post-detention treatment must be attempted to avoid violating *Jackson's* due process principle.

To ensure that the nature and duration limitations are taken seriously, the third essential component of a preventive system is periodic review of the detention, perhaps every six months and at least annually.[56] Further, the burden should be on the state to demonstrate both the need for continued liberty deprivation and that treatment efforts are being made. Outside of the insanity acquittee context, where special considerations may be present,[57] the Supreme Court has adhered to the sensible rule that the state must show why preventive detention is necessary.[58]

In sum, a preventive detention regime requires efforts at treatment, alternatives to institutionalization, and periodic review. If any one of these three conditions are unmet, then the deprivation of liberty fails to bear a reasonable relationship to the purpose of preventing harm and either must end or be justified through the criminal process. Otherwise, as Stevens feared, preventive detention statutes would become an extension of or replacement for criminal punishment without criminal adjudication.

These limitations may strike some as too few and too easily circumvented. In effect, if not in theory, those who are committed and seek release may be confronted with a presumption of dangerousness that will be hard for them to overcome.[59] The concept of "treatment" is so vague that the state might plausibly argue that even minimal efforts in that regard are sufficient.[60] The expense and relatively less secure nature of institutional alternatives can act as a practical brake on their creation and use.[61] Periodic review may be pro forma, a mere rubber-stamping of opinions proffered by state doctors.

Despite these potential problems with implementing the duration, nature, and review limitations on preventive detention, some civil commitment systems manage to adhere to them successfully.[62] As the next chapter describes in more detail, the popular new therapeutic courts—drug courts, mental health courts, and the like—also operate on preventive principles, with little obvious abuse. That chapter also points out that, if pragmatic objections are to rule the day, then similar objections can be levied at the main competitor to preventive detention, a system of sentencing based on just deserts and determinate sentencing. For reasons suggested earlier, such sentences may well be no more "accurate" than a system based on prediction. Further, in the eyes of many, determinate sentencing is unduly harsh, perhaps to make up for its inability to individualize.[63] Finally, in practice, if not in theory, it results in a considerable amount of disparity and discrimination.[64] In other words, any attempt to exercise the police power is bound to fall short of the ideal. Real-life deficiencies should not sound the death knell for any particular approach unless it will clearly produce more negative consequences than other approaches.

C. The Legality Objection

Let us assume that some sort of preventive detention is permissible in theory, because it is coherently separable from the criminal justice system and because we can predict dangerousness at least as well as we can assess culpability. Many controversies yet remain. Some of the more important swirl around the definition of "dangerousness." The legality objection to preventive detention is that the meaning of dangerousness cannot be satisfactorily cabined, thus allowing the state too much power. Although this objection is probably overstated, it does force careful thought about the scope of preventive detention, and places at least minimal limitations on both the types of danger the state may prevent and the situations in which the state may intervene to prevent them. In doing so, it helps deal with some conundrums that have vexed those who have wrestled with the preventive detention question.

Defining Danger
The principle of legality, famously dubbed the "first principle" of the criminal law by Herbert Packer,[65] means roughly that the government may nei-

ther convict nor punish an individual for an act unless that act was previously defined as criminal by law. The constitutional version of this principle is vagueness doctrine, which as a matter of due process requires invalidation of statutes that do not sufficiently define the offending conduct.[66] The purposes of vagueness doctrine are to ensure citizens have notice of the government's power to deprive them of liberty, and concomitantly to protect against the official abuses and the chilling of innocent behavior that can occur if government power is not clearly demarcated.[67]

Vagueness doctrine should govern the scope of preventive detention laws even if it is assumed, consistent with discussion in the previous section, that such laws are not "criminal" in nature. Indeed, the classic judicial statement of vagueness doctrine came in a civil case.[68] Furthermore, within the criminal setting the vagueness prohibition has been most potent when applied to laws that are, in effect, preventive detention statutes in disguise. Courts most commonly use the doctrine as a justification for invalidating vagrancy statutes that attempt to remove from the streets "undesirables" who might be up to no good.[69] Courts have also declared void on vagueness grounds criminal laws that prohibit particularly amorphous dangers, such as a statute that penalizes "conspiracy to commit any act . . . injurious to public morals."[70]

The legality argument against more explicit (noncriminal) forms of preventive detention is that a statute that permits liberty deprivation based solely on dangerousness is inevitably vague. Consider a law that permits detention of those who are "dangerous to others" or "likely to cause substantial harm to others," with no further definition of dangerousness or harm. This type of language—sometimes still found in civil commitment statutes, albeit always combined with a mental illness predicate[71]—is at least as empty as the phrase "injurious to public morals." It provides no information as to the type of danger a person must pose in order to be committed.

Next consider a law that permits preventive detention of those who are likely to cause "emotional harm" to others. That phrase is commonly used in civil litigation and in connection with child neglect petitions. In these contexts, courts generally reject vagueness challenges.[72] Yet emotional harm, even if qualified by the word "serious" or something similar, is such an open-ended concept that it should not survive a vagueness challenge in the preventive detention setting.[73] Far too much legitimate behavior—ranging from breaking up a relationship to lectures about the meaninglessness of life—could be chilled by a law that permitted the government to deprive people of liberty simply because their actions might cause someone else "serious emotional harm."[74] The latter phrase could easily be construed to include, for instance, suicidal thoughts, frequent nightmares, and general depression.

The most obvious starting point in solving these types of problems would be to describe the risk to be prevented in terms of harms sanctioned by the criminal law. That move would provide relatively specific guidelines to the public and the government.[75] It has the added advantage of incorporating into the definition of dangerousness those harms society considers serious enough to warrant application of the police power.

Vagueness doctrine is thus helpful in limiting the type of predicted harm that justifies preventive detention. But, by itself, the doctrine is insufficient to get the job done. Consider, for instance, the relatively recent development in the United Kingdom known as antisocial behavior orders, the violation of which can result in up to five years in prison.[76] Under this authority, courts have issued orders forbidding designated individuals from making excessive noise, swearing in public, appearing in certain bars, or arguing with their children.[77] The orders use detention in prison, in effect, to enforce a civility code that varies from judge to judge and complainant to complainant. This potential for official abuse of discretion can, once again, be curbed by permitting intervention only when necessary to prevent harms punishable by the criminal law. But vagueness doctrine is not a plausible rationale for this solution, because the behavior prohibited by these orders can often be defined fairly precisely (and in fact courts are supposed to describe the prohibition using "ordinary language").

Here, then, *Jackson*'s due process principle must come into play. If the perceived danger is non-criminal—minor damage to property, excessive noise, swearing in public—then the nature and duration of the government's intervention should be correspondingly minimal, if it occurs at all. Reflecting that insight, many involuntary hospitalization statutes define danger in terms of serious bodily injury.[78] In short, both the procedural (vagueness) and substantive (*Jackson*) components of due process are needed to cabin government efforts at defining the risks preventive detention is aimed at preventing.

Defining the "Point" of Intervention
A second legality problem arises in defining the trigger point for preventive detention. Many preventive detention rules require an overt act before

detention may take place. Sexual predator laws, for instance, require at least a probable cause belief that the subject has committed a sex offense.[79] The typical civil commitment statute, however, does not address this issue, while those few commitment laws that do usually merely require proof of an otherwise undefined act that evidences the danger to be prevented.[80] Vagueness doctrine may have some impact here as well.

The closest criminal law analogue to this situation is the typical endangerment statute, which prohibits conduct that either recklessly or negligently endangers others. An example comes from the Model Penal Code, which penalizes a person who "recklessly engages in conduct which places or may place another person in danger of death or serious bodily injury."[81] Because the Code defines conduct simply as an act or omission,[82] reckless endangerment under this provision could be based on any act or failure to act that creates the requisite danger. Yet these statutes are routinely upheld against vagueness challenges by the courts.[83]

At the same time, the endangerment laws contain their own notice requirement. Reckless endangerment statutes require that the individual be aware of the risk,[84] and negligent endangerment requires proof that a reasonable person would be aware of the risk.[85] Thus, conduct that would not be evidently risky to a reasonable person cannot form the basis for such crimes.

The same should be true in the preventive detention context. Unless the individual engages in conduct that causes legally defined harm or that is otherwise obviously risky, the government should not be permitted to intervene preventively. Only in such situations is the individual functionally (as opposed to officially) on notice that he or she may be subject to government intervention, and only in such situations is the government's police power adequately cabined.

Consider in this regard a not-so-hypothetical situation in which the prediction of dangerousness is based on relatively innocuous variables, such as marital status, age, gender, education, employment, and place of residence.[86] Assume further that the government publishes this list of variables, so that it could be said the public is officially on notice as to when preventive detention may take place. Even with such legally sufficient warning (and putting aside the objection that some of these variables do not amount to "conduct," an issue to be considered below), the fact that these variables are so innocuous should make such a statute void for vagueness.

The Supreme Court's decision in Lambert v. California[87] is relevant here.

Lambert reversed on due process grounds a conviction under a statute that criminalized any felon's failure to register his presence in Los Angeles within five days of arrival in the city. In reaching this holding, the Court mentioned an array of considerations, including Lambert's ignorance of the registration statute, the lack of affirmative misconduct, the absence of criminal intent, and the possibility the statute would be abused by police or prosecutors.[88] As John Jeffries states, "[t]he meaning of [*Lambert*] is subject to infinite disputation."[89] He goes on to assert, however, that *Lambert* most sensibly "stands for the unacceptability in principle of imposing criminal liability where the prototypically law-abiding individual in the actor's situation would have had no reason to act otherwise."[90] The argument from *Lambert*, then, is that a person who avoids acts that a reasonable person would perceive as risky cannot be subject to liberty deprivation even when a statute authorizes it, because a law-abiding individual would behave the same way and literally "would have no reason to act otherwise." Preventive detention based on innocuous predictors that the reasonable individual is unlikely to perceive as indicative of dangerousness is a violation of this precept (which, because it is rooted in due process, applies here as well as in criminal cases).

The proposition that preventive detention is not permissible unless and until harm or otherwise obviously risky conduct has occurred raises three subsidiary issues. The first, alluded to just above, is whether proof of *conduct* is necessary. This issue conjures up the scenario (so far one that occurs only in Hollywood)[91] in which the basis of the government intervention consists solely of risk-predictive characteristics, such as a "violent gene," an inability to empathize, or a biological addiction (all of which might be measurable physiologically, without any reference to behavior).[92] Perhaps these traits are not "obviously risky." But even if they were, detention in this case would run afoul of the legality principle. As Packer asserted, "[i]t is important, especially in a society that likes to describe itself as 'free' and 'open,' that a government should be empowered to coerce people only for what they do and not for what they are."[93] Accordingly, he argued, the law should require proof of an act, "a point of no return beyond which external constraints may be imposed but before which the individual is free—not free of whatever compulsions determinists tells us he labors under but free of the very specific social compulsions of the law."[94] If the state's preventive detention power is not limited by the requirement that it prove some affirmative act that is predictive of a legislatively defined danger, then the government, not the individual, controls if and when the government intervenes. Putting this idea another way, conditions, dispositions, and thoughts, even if highly predictive of danger and identified as such, cannot be the "point of no return" described by Packer because there is no identifiable "point" at which they can be avoided.

Perhaps the government could avoid this trap by alerting the person to his or her dangerousness and demanding that the person take preventive steps; if the person does not take such steps, *that* conduct is the point of no return. Some commentators—trying to reconcile a preference for criminal punishment with a desire to protect society against dangerous people—have proposed what is, in effect, the same approach: we could, they suggest, alert dangerous people to their dangerousness and then convict them for reckless endangerment if they refuse to take preventive action.[95] From the legality perspective, however, this move is a sleight of hand. It allows the government to achieve its aim regardless of what the individual decides; if he declines to take the preventive action, the government takes it for him. In effect, this type of intervention is predicated not on a choice by the individual, but on a choice by the government, which is precisely what the legality principle is designed to prevent.

Note that this interpretation of the legality principle also identifies a distinction between the person with an infectious disease and the predator known to be dangerous, a distinction that has eluded commentators who want to maintain quarantine, but who are not sure about open-ended preventive detention.[96] As soon as the infected person goes into the community, he has engaged in obviously risky conduct that is an imminent threat to others. The same cannot be said for the predator. The latter individual must engage in some further risky or harmful conduct before the state may intervene.

The second subsidiary legality issue concerns the temporal relationship between the triggering event and the detention. For instance, people subjected to postsentence sexual predator commitment may not have engaged in any antisocial conduct for a long period. Should this fact invalidate postsentence preventive detention on legality grounds? Probably not. Functional notice of the specific nature of possible state intervention may well be lacking.[97] But the individual in this situation surely knew the sex offense could trigger some sort of serious government reaction, which is all that vagueness doctrine demands in terms of notice.[98] Further, so long as the act was criminal or obviously risky, it prevents the kind of arbitrariness the legality principle abhors by providing a clear demarcation between when the government may intervene and when it may not.

A final legality issue, which may well be the most important, concerns whether the harm or obviously risky conduct that can act as a trigger for preventive detention must be criminal. If, as I suggested above, the danger to be prevented is to be defined with reference to the criminal law, one might reasonably assume that the triggering criteria should be as well. Yet some obviously risky conduct is not criminal. Numerous examples of this fact come from emergency civil commitment cases involving persons alleged to be dangerous to others.[99] Moreover, the Supreme Court has approved investigative stops based on suspicious activity that does not amount to a crime. In the well-known case of Terry v. Ohio,[100] for example, the Supreme Court approved an investigative frisk of individuals who appeared to be "casing" a storefront and mumbled responses to a police officer's questions about their conduct, activity that was concededly not criminal.[101]

Note, however, that both of these situations involve conduct that, like the conduct associated with the crime of reckless endangerment, suggests anti-social behavior is imminent. What if the conduct is more attenuated from the potential harm? Consider on this score the case of Moussaoui, described at the beginning of this chapter. Moussaoui apparently paid for flying lessons to learn how to pilot planes, but was uninterested in learning how to land or take-off. That conduct does not qualify as either a crime or obviously risky behavior (he may already have known how to take-off and land, or he may have wanted to take one thing at a time). But we also know Moussaoui trained in Osama bin Laden's camps and that he communicated with the participants in the attack on the World Trade Center on September 11, 2001. That intelligence, combined with the flying lessons information, should provide enough evidence of risky behavior in any reasonable person's eyes. Whether it constitutes the crime of conspiracy, however, may depend on the content of the communications with the World Trade Center attackers.[102]

If conspiracy cannot be proven, may the government still preventively detain Moussaoui (assuming the psychological and prediction criteria are met)? In answering this question, it is important to remember that the principle of legality is meant to implement two important objectives. In addition to assuring functional notice, which is presumably present in Moussaoui's case, the legality principle aims to control government discretion.

Thus, if the triggering act for preventive detention is not an immediate precursor to the predicted harm (as with emergency commitment and investigative stops), it must be linked to a statutorily defined crime. Otherwise, the potential for government abuse becomes enormous.

The version of the Moussaoui case described above may tempt one to depart from that precept. But the government's (over)reaction to the events of September 11, including preventive detention of U.S. citizens who remain uncharged,[103] provides a potent counterreason for applying the same legality constraints on preventive detention that apply to inchoate crimes. Rules such as the agreement and overt act requirements in conspiracy and the conduct-beyond-mere-preparation requirement for attempted crimes ought to apply in the preventive context as well.[104] Consistent with this conclusion are the Supreme Court's decisions requiring the government to prove to a neutral tribunal that individuals it has detained as "enemy combatants" are in fact such.[105]

In conclusion, legality and other due process concerns prohibit the state from depriving a person of liberty on preventive grounds unless the harm predicted is serious (physical?) harm and the person has engaged in conduct that causes such harm or otherwise obviously evidences risk that it will occur. Outside of emergency situations, this latter precept requires the commission of criminal conduct. The case for adopting it is substantially bolstered by the final objection to preventive detention.

D. The Dehumanization Objection

Suppose that the state is able to prove by beyond a reasonable doubt that a person has engaged in obviously risky conduct and will engage in serious criminal conduct if not preventively detained. Assume further that the state is prepared, if commitment occurs, to offer rehabilitation in the least restrictive environment consistent with public safety, with periodic review. Is there any ground for prohibiting such detention, in light of the state's compelling need to protect its citizens?

The dehumanization objection to preventive detention is that, even if all the other objections are met, a regime that deprives people of liberty based on what they will do rather than on what they have done shows insufficient respect for the individual. On this view, preventive detention is, in effect, either an assertion that the person does not possess the capacity to choose the good or an assertion that, having such capacity, the person will not do so.

Both assertions, the dehumanization objection posits, are deeply denigrating to the person's status as a self-governing, autonomous human being. This objection has some bite to it, but not in the way one might initially think, as dissection of its logic will reveal.

Preventive Detention's Ambiguous Insult to Autonomy
The first possible meaning of preventive detention—that the individual so detained does not have the capacity to choose the good—is easiest to see as dehumanizing. The capacity to choose one's course is an essential aspect of our notion of what it means to be human. To say that a person lacks that capacity is to treat him like an automaton. For this reason, whatever science may suggest about how "determined" we are by biological or environmental forces, the law, and our society at large, assumes we have free will (for lack of a better shorthand term). Again, Packer put it well:

> People may in fact have little if any greater capacity to control their conduct . . . than their emotions or their thoughts. [But] the idea of free will in relation to conduct is not, in the legal system, a statement of fact, but rather a value preference having very little to do with the metaphysics of determinism and free will.[106]

One dehumanization argument against preventive detention, then, is that it is the legal manifestation of the humanity-denying belief that those detained cannot control their fate.[107]

Preventive detention can also be characterized, however, as an assertion that the detained individual has free will and is simply predicted to exercise it in the wrong direction. This conceptualization appears to avoid Packer's complaint, because it leaves intact the dogma that we control our fate. Consider, for instance, these comments from Ferdinand Schoeman:

> People who have bad eating, smoking, exercise or work habits . . . can be sincere in protesting that they will not do something which we have excellent inductive grounds for claiming that they will. . . . [W]ithout assuming compulsions or anything at all of a pathological nature, and without denying autonomy or choice to individuals, we can see how it is that we might come to discount people's own sincere assertions and resolutions about what they will do. Hence to make such predictions about people and deal with them on that basis does not necessarily involve us in changing our image of what it is to be a person.[108]

In response, the dehumanization objection might be reframed by emphasizing the assumption that autonomous individuals, even when "dangerous," always have the potential for choosing the good, an assumption that also underlies such criminal law doctrines as the mere preparation and abandonment defenses in attempt jurisprudence.[109] The characterization of preventive detention as a prediction that a person will freely choose harm may avoid the automaton image, but continues to assert that the individual will ignore society's clearly stated norms under all circumstances, and thus is internally contradictory. It denies the possibility of autonomous choice while pretending the detained individual is autonomous.

Whether one is convinced by these arguments depends on one's allegiance to the autonomy value. Even as someone who thinks that value important, I am only half persuaded by the dehumanization objection in the abstract, precisely because of its abstractness. What I do find palpably dehumanizing, however, is preventive detention that occurs when both punishment and preventive detention are options, and the state decides to use the second form of social control rather than the first. In that instance, illustrated by the sexual predator regime, the case against preventive detention is much stronger, for reasons suggested below.

The Right to Be Punished

As established in the discussion about legality, preventive detention may not take place unless the individual has either caused harm to another or has engaged in conduct that evidences obvious risk. In cases involving long-term preventive detention, that conduct should always also amount to a crime, either a completed offense or an inchoate one, such as attempt or conspiracy. When, if ever, may the state respond to this conduct through preventive detention rather than criminal punishment? Putting this question another way, under what circumstances, if any, may the state be forced to rely on criminal punishment rather than preventive detention in achieving its police power goals? The short answer is that the state must choose the punishment route unless, consistent with the two situations just described, it can show that the individual lacks the capacity to adhere to society's basic norms or that the individual, even though having such capacity, will ignore those norms regardless of repercussions to himself.

The view that punishment must be imposed on the typical wrongdoer was succinctly voiced by Georg Hegel, when he contended that punishing the criminal vindicates "the formal rationality of the individual's volition."[110] According to Hegel, respect for the criminal entails a right to be punished, because through punishment "the criminal is honoured as a rational being."[111] Conversely, the criminal "is denied this honour . . . if he is regarded simply as a harmful animal which must be rendered harmless, or punished with a view to deterring or reforming him."[112] Several other thinkers in the deontological tradition similarly argue that offenders have the right to be punished.[113]

Within this concept of the right to be punished lies what I consider the most persuasive version of the dehumanization objection to preventive detention. If a person who commits a criminal act is not punished, we fail to treat him as an autonomous human being. If we not only fail to punish him, but simultaneously deprive him of liberty, then, to use Hegel's words, we are treating him simply as a harmful animal. As *Hendricks* and other Supreme Court decisions have held, preventive detention is not criminal punishment. Thus, when the government confronted by a criminal actor chooses the former means of liberty deprivation over the latter, it declares in a very real way that the individual so detained is not a person in the full sense of that word, but rather much closer to Hegel's "harmful animal." Sexual "predator," the label Kansas legislators chose to affix to those committed under the statute at issue in *Hendricks,* brings home the point quite nicely.

The right to punishment advanced by Hegel and others rests on deontological claims about the maintenance of human dignity. The utilitarian might arrive at a similar result, because preventive detention in a dual-track regime could exacerbate, rather than reduce, the public danger, in two ways. First, when the government chooses to label a miscreant a "predator" or "dangerous person" in lieu of punishing him as a "criminal offender," as sexual predator statutes do, it very powerfully announces that the individual either cannot or will not control his behavior. Research on motivation suggests that this type of labeling might become a self-fulfilling prophecy: Individuals shunted into the "predator" system will come to believe that, unlike those who are punished as volitional actors, they are incapable of acting differently, and that belief in turn could well make them more dangerous.[114] Additionally, people who know they are being confined based on speculation about what they will do, while fellow wrongdoers are instead being confined for what they have done, could easily come to believe the system is corrupt (conjecture that finds some support in research concerning attitudes of sexual predators).[115] That kind of loss of respect for the legal system also correlates positively with noncompliant attitudes toward the law and with recidivism.[116] Although these concerns do not give the individual a "right" to be punished rather than preventively detained, they do provide consequentialist support for such a right.

Virtue ethics, a third perspective on the police power of the state, may also be hostile to a separate system of preventive detention. To a proponent of this point of view, criminal punishment is a means of inculcating virtue.[117] It can do so only by identifying, through communal deliberations carried out by the jury, those who are at fault because they have engaged in flawed practical reasoning, and by insisting, through conviction of these individuals, that they are responsible for the character traits that lead to crime.[118] In a system where one offender can be subjected to preventive detention based on dangerousness while another who causes the same type of harm is subjected to punishment based on fault, the law's expressions about good and bad character are obscured; the first individual is likely to be viewed, and likely to view himself, as someone who is not responsible for his personality traits. Again, therefore, punishment is necessary, both as a "right" of the offender to be treated as someone who can control formation of his character and as an obligation of society to educate its citizens about virtuousness.

What I take from this brief discussion of deontological, utilitarian, and ethical reasoning is that a two-track system that differentiates "offenders" from "predators" or "dangerous beings" infringes the right to be punished for criminal conduct. In a dual-track regime, those diverted to the "dangerous offender" track are clearly treated as lesser humans, are more likely to live out the predator prophecy, and are less likely to be perceived as individuals who are responsible for their character. This version of the dehumanization objection to a separate system of preventive detention is more sustainable than the usual abstract claim found in the literature.

The Effect Exception to the Right to Be Punished

Not all liberty deprivations based on dangerousness have the impact just described. Some types of preventive detention do not trench on a person's right to be punished for criminal acts, because they do not in fact deprive the person of such punishment. These types of preventive detention can be said to fall under an "effect exception" to the right to punishment. Other types of preventive detention after criminal conduct are clearly inconsistent with punishment, but are nonetheless legitimate because the psychological characteristics of the person detained divest him of the right to be punished. This section focuses on the effect exception, while Part 2 of this chapter examines the psychological criterion for preventive detention.

Numerous species of preventive detention do not foreclose criminal punishment or do not create a dual-track system and therefore fit within the effect exception I am proposing. For instance, when police stop an individual on the street on reasonable suspicion he is contemplating commission of a crime, they are engaging in preventive detention. Usually, however, the individual has yet to commit a crime, so criminal punishment is not yet an option. In any event, this investigative procedure is merely the first step toward punishment, not a substitute for it.

Other types of pretrial preventive detention may be permissible for the same reason. In United States v. Salerno,[119] the Supreme Court held that pretrial preventive detention of an arrestee, in lieu of bail, does not violate the due process clause, primarily because the duration of the detention is limited (by speedy trial rules) and the intent behind it is not "punitive."[120] The Court's result in Salerno is correct, although neither of its rationales should be dispositive. Any preventive detention of an accused person, however long and whatever its "intent," is suspect if it denies the person the right to contest his or her guilt and the right, if found guilty, to be accorded the respect and dignity inherent in punishment for that act. Typically, however, pretrial detention does not deprive the person of these rights (although it may become illegitimate if its length renders criminal adjudication a sham because, for instance, it exceeds the usual punishment for the offense).

Whether *post*-criminal adjudication dispositions based on dangerousness come under the effect exception depends on whether one adopts a strong or weak view of the right to punishment. The strict deontological position forecloses all use of dangerousness assessments in this context. For instance, as indicated above, Hegel would have prohibited any punishment that is imposed "with a view to deterring or reforming" the offender.

But one can also defend a "weak" view of the right to punishment.[121] The weak view still prohibits preventive confinement when criminal punishment is an option, but does not automatically bar punishment designed to accomplish consequentialist ends. Recall the definition of punishment given earlier: Criminal punishment is based solely on a conviction for an offense and can occur only if there is such a conviction. A weak version of the right to punishment might posit that so long as the disposition occurs because the individual has been labeled a criminal through the appropriate process and with the requisite degree of culpability, the right to punishment has been preserved. That the length of punishment might vary depending on other factors, such as incapacitative or general deterrence considerations, does not challenge the fact that the individual has been found to have autonomously chosen to cause harm.

Both the utilitarian and virtue ethics perspectives are also easily reconciled with this weak right to punishment. If a person who commits antisocial conduct is adjudicated guilty and sentenced at a criminal trial, he will not be saddled with the debilitating predator label. Likewise, once a person has been identified as a person with flawed practical reason through the criminal adjudication, society's interest in publicly defining virtue through the jury has been achieved.[122]

Under the weak version of the right to punishment, therefore, a criminal sentence that falls within the range dictated by retributive considerations would clearly be permissible even if the length of the sentence is calibrated solely through predictions of behavior, as sometimes occurs in sentencing systems that have maintained parole.[123] The retributive range announces and demarcates the punishment for the offender's crime. It thus accords the criminal sufficient respect as an autonomous being.

More difficult to categorize is a criminal sentence that is based entirely on dangerousness, the so-called indeterminate sentence.[124] Functionally, this regime is very similar to a pure preventive detention regime. But two significant traits save it from infringing the right to punishment in its weak form. First, in contrast to a purely preventive regime, in the indeterminate sentence setting the government officially declares that the individual is guilty of a criminal act and that he or she must be punished for it, a declaration that sounds in retribution, not in dangerousness. Second, in contrast to preventive detention schemes such as the sexual predator laws, which exist in addition to criminal sentencing, it avoids the autonomy-denigrating impact associated with assigning the individual to a "dangerous person" track rather than the "offender" track, because there is only one track.

The same cannot be said, however, of preventive detention that exists in lieu of criminal punishment, as is authorized under most sexual predator statutes.[125] Nor can it be said of preventive detention that follows criminal punishment, like that imposed on Hendricks under the Kansas sexual predator law. The right to punishment may seem to be preserved in the latter situation, for punishment for the criminal act does take place. But here—as with preventive detention that functions as a substitute for punishment, and in contrast to indeterminate sentencing—there are two tracks, the punishment track and the predator track. Individuals who, unlike their colleagues in crime, are committed after their sentence is served are again singled out as people who are less than human, confined not for what they chose to do but for what they are, predators. Whatever respect for the person comes with punishment dissipates the moment the state preventively detains him in a regime that is separate from criminal punishment, a reality that is not likely to be lost on the newly designated "predator" himself.

Under the "weak" version of the right to punishment theory, then, preventive detention after criminal conduct is permissible in a wide range of situations where it does not foreclose criminal punishment, but is generally impermissible if the government uses it as a substitute for or in addition to such punishment, because in the latter situations the individual's status as an autonomous human actor is impugned, a fact that is also likely to increase recidivism. Even in the latter situations, however, preventive detention would not be inconsistent with Hegel's injunction to honor the wrongdoer if the wrongdoer is not a "rational being," or should not be treated as one, because then the dehumanizing message sent by preventive detention is more apposite and is likely to have less behavioral impact. Defining the scope of this psychological exception requires more elaborate treatment.

II. The Psychological Criterion for Preventive Detention

The majority opinion in Kansas v. Hendricks indicated, more than once, that dangerousness alone is an insufficient basis for long-term preventive detention. Although the Kansas statute at issue in the *Hendricks* case required proof only of a "mental abnormality or personality disorder which makes the person likely to engage in predatory acts of violence,"[126] the Court construed this language to require proof of a disorder that "prevents [the sex offender] from exercising adequate control over [his] behavior."[127] At other points, the Court defined the requisite impairment as an abnormality that "makes it difficult, if not impossible . . . to control . . . dangerous behavior"[128] and as a condition that renders the offender "unable to control his dangerousness."[129] The Court also stated that it was Hendricks's "admitted lack of volitional control" that "distinguishe[d him] from other dangerous persons who are perhaps more properly dealt with exclusively through criminal proceedings."[130] In Kansas v. Crane,[131] decided in 2002, the Court reiterated that preventive incarceration must generally be accompanied by "proof of serious difficulty in controlling behavior,"[132] although it left open the question of whether dangerousness due to "emotional" impairment might also legitimately form the basis for detention.[133]

The critics of *Hendricks* have argued that the Court's inability-to-control criterion is either meaningless or overbroad. The most commonly proposed alternative psychological criterion is some form of serious mental disorder, akin to that which is required for an insanity defense.[134] That tack would render the typical sexual predator commitment invalid, as most sex offenders, Hendricks included, do not meet traditional insanity tests.

My position is somewhere between the Court's and the critics'. The Court's inability-to-control standard is vacuous to the extent it suggests the state must show some type of "involuntary" behavior or criminal impulse caused by overwhelming urges. At the same time, traditional insanity formulations, although adequate at defining autonomy for the purpose of assessing criminal responsibility, are too narrow when the goal is delineating the psychological criterion for preventive detention. I suggest the focus should instead be on the individual's undeterrability, a standard that would allow preventive detention of some people who are not seriously mentally ill. At the same time, it would stop short of authorizing such detention for all, or even most, who have impulse disorders. In short, the formulation proposed here would encompass people who are lacking in autonomy due to mental disability and the like, as well as that small category of people who are not insane but who can nonetheless be denied the right to punishment because of their manifest obliviousness to society's most important criminal prohibitions.

A. The Inability-to-Control Formulation

Although the Court never clearly provides it in either *Hendricks* or *Crane*, there is at least one plausible rationale for permitting preventive detention based on proof of volitional impairment and dangerousness. It builds, as previous discussion has already suggested, on right to punishment theory. That right exists because we want to treat people as autonomous beings who will choose to avoid commission of crime. But if an individual's urge to commit crime is so strong that he is unable to control it, one can argue that he has demonstrated he is not an autonomous being; a person who is "dangerous beyond [his] control,"[135] to use the *Hendricks* Court's words, is closer to Hegel's "harmful animal" than to a volitional human actor.

Despite its intuitive appeal, the Court's approach is problematic to the extent it relies on the concept of volitional impairment, for reasons that have already been suggested in Chapter 2. Truly "involuntary" acts are rare. Illustrated by epileptic seizures and perhaps some dissociative states,[136] such acts require a disjunction between mind and body that seldom occurs even in people with severe mental illness, much less in sexual predators and similar offenders.[137]

If instead the concept of volitional impairment is meant to refer to conscious control over bodily movements that nonetheless are "compelled" by "irresistible impulses," then as Stephen Morse, Robert Schopp, and others have demonstrated, the concept becomes meaningless, or so expansive that it could include most criminal behavior.[138] Even conduct that the actor perceives to be the product of strong urges is "willed," in the sense that the actor decides to engage in it. The addict who steals to feed a habit, the sexual predator who molests a child, and the psychotic individual who kills all intend, and often plan, their actions. Further, they all probably could have avoided those actions, in the sense that they knew of and were able to choose other options.[139] Finally, for many of these individuals the criminal act is pleasurable, rather than a method of avoiding psychological pain, or is at least a combination of the two.[140] For all these reasons, identifying precisely how such actions are "compelled" is difficult. While such people may seem to have overwhelming urges, they still choose to act on those urges and they do not seem to be compelled in the same way a person acting with a gun pointing at his head is compelled.

Even if one can make sense of the compulsion notion in the abstract, it seems to sweep too broadly in practice. As Michael Moore has noted,[141] all behavior is caused by something not directly in one's control, whether it is biological, environmental, or characterological. Thus, a case can be made that volition is always "impaired." Attempting to draw the line between those who are "compelled" and those who are merely "caused" creates daunting problems. Despite popular perceptions and the Supreme Court's own assumptions,[142] evidence that the impulses experienced by addicts, sexual offenders, and people with psychosis are stronger than those that lead people to commit more typical crimes is hard to come by; burglars recidivate at least as much as sex offenders,[143] and white collar criminals are probably just as likely to be "driven" by urges, albeit for things like wealth, fame, or power rather than (or perhaps in addition to) drugs or sex.[144]

The breadth of the inability-to-control concept has been recognized by researchers and clinicians alike. Representative is the claim by social scientists Robert Plutchik and Herman van Praag. In their paper "The Nature of Impulsivity," they note that impulsivity has been associated with borderline personality disorder, antisocial personality disorder, hyperactive syndrome, alcoholism, substance abuse, brain damage, anorexia nervosa, violent behavior, neurological "soft signs," rage and aggression, homicide, sexual assault, risk taking, error-prone information processing, bipolar disorders, kleptomania, pyromania, addictions, perversion, and some sexual disorders.[145] Any concept that encompasses such a broad array of behavior and conditions is highly suspect, even as a mitigating factor at sentencing (a point noted in Chapter 3), and certainly is useless as a meaningful legal limitation on preventive detention.

In any event, gauging the strength of criminal desires, or the weakness of the will to resist them,[146] is a scientific impossibility at this point. Despite repeated attempts to develop instruments that measure impulsivity, there is no generally accepted, or even partially accepted, formulation of the construct.[147] In contrast to prediction of risk, where major advancements have occurred, instruments for assessing volitional impairment are in a very primitive state.[148]

In short, predicating preventive detention on a showing that a person's dangerousness is something he or she cannot control appears to be a theoretical and practical dead end. It will involve courts in the quagmire of trying to distinguish the impulse that was irresistible from the impulse that was not resisted.[149] The psychological criterion for preventive detention should rest on a sounder conceptual and pragmatic basis.

B. The Insanity Formulation

A promising candidate in this regard is simply to equate the psychological criterion with insanity.[150] The insanity defense is meant to define those who lack criminal responsibility, which describes a group that would seem to coincide perfectly with those who can be preventively detained because their lack of autonomy forfeits the right to punishment. Further, because most modern versions of it focus simply on cognitive impairment,[151] the insanity inquiry is relatively straightforward compared to the assessment of volitional impairment required under *Hendricks*.[152]

Some insanity tests have included a volitional impairment prong as well. If that prong were a necessary component of the insanity defense, then equating the psychological criterion for preventive detention with insanity might rejuvenate all the conceptual and practical difficulties just discussed. But most jurisdictions have rejected the volitional prong (as would the Integrationist Test developed in Chapter 2).[153] Furthermore, as Morse has demonstrated, many cases of volitional impairment can be recharacterized as deficits in cognition.[154] For instance, the person with kleptomania who steals for no apparent reason (because he merely hides what he steals without attempting to make money from it) could be said to have an irrational thought process, as could the person with mania who carelessly spends money in grandiose schemes because of inaccurate beliefs about himself and the world.

Under a cognitively focused insanity defense, the psychological criterion would be defined by such factors as one's ability to distinguish right from wrong, the intelligibility and consistency of one's desires and beliefs, and the nature of one's thought process (the precise focus would depend, of course, on the insanity formulation adopted). These are not easy assessments. But they are more sensible and more manageable than the volitional inquiry. Further, calling such people "dangerous" is not likely to increase their recidivism, either because the label means little to them or because they can attribute their dangerousness to a "disease," which generally can be treated.

Making insanity the psychological criterion for preventive detention thus appears to satisfy both right to punishment theory and the desire for a meaningful standard. Nonetheless, this simple equation does not work, if it means that people who are sane may never be subject to long-term preventive detention. That is because it fails to encompass the second of the two situations in which the right to punishment does not apply—when the actor, though possessing rational capacity, signals a desire to ignore society's most significant norms regardless of the repercussions. The next section explores this objection more fully.

C. Back into the Quagmire: The Undeterrability Formulation

Despite its incoherence, the Supreme Court's inability-to-control formulation does capture a widely shared view that some individuals—including some sex offenders—are sane under the traditional cognitive impairment tests, yet seem to be lacking a fundamental aspect of autonomy. If Hendricks is to be believed, only his death would prevent him from molesting children, despite his acknowledgement that such activity is criminal and would subject him to punishment.[155] This type of dysfunction, whether it is labeled a mental abnormality or simply described in terms of its effects, smacks more of conditioned, animal behavior than human conduct.

For reasons already discussed, trying to describe this intuition in terms of impulse control is futile. Taking a cue from Morse, another way of getting at the "dangerous beyond control" concept is by focusing on cognition—the desires and beliefs that motivate the behavior and the process by which they are formed. But Morse's specific proposal—that claims of volitional impairment should be reanalyzed in terms of the "rationality" of the motivating desires and beliefs[156]—may not get us very far. As Morse himself admits, while "there is something more than a little wacky about wanting anything 'too much' . . . how much is 'too much' will of course depend on the circumstances, including social conventions."[157] To many people, the person who seems to act impulsively, against his own apparent interests, will always be irrational. Indeed, many commentators have noted that impulsivity and irrationality are all but synonymous.[158] If that is the outcome of Morse's proposal—if child molesters, addicts, and people with bad tempers are all seen as irrational[159]—that concept may be as vacuous as control formulations.

I propose, instead, that we should answer the question of "how much is too much" with reference to the most conspicuous and powerful "social convention"—the criminal law. If a person wants to commit serious crime so badly that he is willing to be deprived of liberty or suffer similarly serious consequences for it, then he should be eligible for preventive detention, whether the desire stems from mental illness, subliminal "drives," or cold calculation. This type of person is truly "undeterrable" by the criminal law, and thus is precisely the person who should be subject to its alternative: preventive detention. In contrast, the person who is not willing to suffer punishment in order to achieve his desires is deterrable, and we should respect his autonomy by assuming he will be deterred.

Justice Scalia may have been hinting at this notion in his dissenting opinion in *Crane*, when he tried to defend sexual predator laws by stating that "[o]rdinary recidivists choose to re-offend and are therefore amenable to deterrence through the criminal law; those subject to civil commitment under the [sexual predator act], because their mental illness is an affliction and not a choice, are unlikely to be deterred."[160] Although this moves toward an undeterrability criterion, Scalia's manner of expressing it, like the inability-to-control formulation in *Hendricks*, is incoherent. The justice is right that mental illness is "not a choice." But the behavior that flows from it usually is. Furthermore, recidivists, even "ordinary" ones, are by definition "unlikely to be deterred."

Preventive detention should be aimed at the truly undeterrable. This notion is most meaningfully expressed not in terms of lack of control, irrationality, or the "likeliness" of being deterred, but rather in terms of two other psychological tendencies: (1) unawareness that one is engaging in criminal conduct, or (2) extreme recklessness with respect to the prospect of serious loss of liberty or death resulting from the criminal conduct. The person who is truly undeterrable by the criminal law is one who characteristically either commits criminal conduct not believing it to be criminal or commits the conduct knowing it is criminal but willing to suffer the consequences in order to accomplish his or her criminal aims. Like the irrationality formulation, the language of ignorance and recklessness avoids problematic talk about compulsion; it does not deny that criminal actors generally choose their actions, while aware of their options. But unlike an irrationality test, this language focuses precisely on the desires and beliefs of the actor that make the person undeterrable.

The Unawareness Category of Undeterrability

The lack of awareness category of the undeterrability concept is similar to, if not synonymous with, the cognitive prong of the insanity defense, which traditionally has focused on knowledge of the nature and quality of the act and knowledge of whether the act was wrong. A person who experiences delusions or hallucinations that lead him to think he is shooting a tree rather than a person, or that someone who wants to shake his hand is attacking him, will not be affected by the relevant prohibitions of the criminal law. Numerous other distorted perceptions of reality could render perpetrators oblivious to the criminal implications of their actions or convinced that there are none. Whether the unawareness formulation encompasses all who would be excused under the Model Penal Code's popular "appreciation of wrongfulness" insanity test would depend on how that test is interpreted. But the unawareness group *would* be broader than the group excused under the Integrationist Test advocated in Chapter 2, because some people whose mental illness leads them characteristically to believe their actions are not criminal (for example, Theodore Kaczynski) would not be entitled to an excuse under that test.

One advantage of the unawareness formulation is that it would permit commitment of those who successfully assert an unconsciousness defense, as in sleepwalking and epilepsy cases.[161] Currently this group of people causes significant problems for the criminal justice system, because, having been acquitted on grounds other than insanity, there is no provision for their post-trial commitment.[162] Yet these people should be subject to preventive detention if their unconsciousness is likely to cause further harm, because in that state they are truly undeterrable.

The Recklessness Category of Undeterrability

The recklessness category of undeterrability describes an entirely different set of people—"sane" people who know they are committing a crime and are aware of a significant risk of apprehension and long-term deprivation of liberty, but who commit it anyway. The old "police officer at the elbow" test puts the matter succinctly.[163] A person who is likely to commit a crime while observed by law enforcement officers or in situations that are similarly likely to lead to apprehension is, by definition, on the far end of the undeterrability spectrum. In contrast, the typical recidivist will avoid committing a crime under such conditions.

In short, the recklessness subcategory of undeterrability identifies people who prefer crime to freedom. I would also require, however, that the anticipated/ignored loss of freedom be substantial. That caveat ensures that the person is truly undeterrable, as opposed to someone who could be deterred with significant enough disincentives.

Note that this formulation does not necessarily exclude offenders or potential offenders who try to avoid apprehension. Even people with very strong desires to commit crime will try to evade detection before they commit their act; otherwise, they will not be able to commit it. And after the act is complete and their desire is sated, they will presumably try to elude detection. This formulation does require, however, that the individual is the type of person who commits crime while aware of a very substantial risk that he or she will be caught and subjected to a serious deprivation of liberty or death. That is what distinguishes these people from the typical burglar, murderer, rapist, or car thief. Given a choice between punishment and foregoing crime, the typical criminal will choose the latter option.

Very few people would fit in the recklessness category so defined, but those who do might be divided into two types. The first group would be composed of those who commit the crime primarily to achieve their own ends. These would include the individual with mania whose grandiosity leads him to commit rape in full view of the public,[164] the individual who rapes while being actively pursued by the police,[165] and the individual (like Hendricks?) who routinely commits sexual acts in situations where it is "almost inevitable" (to use the phrasing of one court wrestling with this issue) that he will be caught.[166] These examples, taken from actual cases, all involve sex offenders. But cases involving other types of offenders can be imagined; in particular, individuals who routinely engage in homicidal assaults in public fora, like David (described at the beginning of this chapter), are apparently unaffected by a very high likelihood of apprehension. All these people can be considered undeterrable, even though they are not insane under traditional definitions, because their desire for the "benefit" they receive from crime is demonstrably greater than their fear of significant punishment.

The second group that might be said to be undeterrable because of recklessness toward the prospect of punishment commits crime to achieve goals that are largely unselfish. Into this category might fall those who want to kill abortion clinic doctors,[167] assassinate prominent political leaders,[168] or commit terrorist acts in full view of others, knowing escape is unlikely.[169] These people are neither mistaken about the prohibitions of the law nor forgetful of them, but rather believe them to be irrelevant. They know they will either be caught or die, but are convinced their ideological agenda justifies their actions and glorifies their punishment or death.

Does this formulation mean that political activists could be subject to preventive detention for their complaints against government? Perhaps so, in totalitarian states where dissent will in any event result in serious punishment. But in democratic societies, where political speech cannot be criminalized, the stipulation that only obliviousness to *serious* punishment can trigger intervention will prevent this use of preventive detention. Believers in environmental justice or abortion rights may commit trespass or harassment in aid of their protests,[170] but seldom engage in murder or other serious harms for the cause. If the latter type of conduct *is* the predicted harm, however, they would be subject to preventive detention under my scheme.

Despite its narrow scope, preventive detention in lieu of or in addition to criminal punishment is most likely to be resisted in connection with this second category of individuals who are reckless about punishment. As noted above, those who choose crime over freedom for their own ends seem remarkably similar to conditioned animals. In contrast, those who choose crime over freedom to achieve political or ideological goals appear to be acting more "volitionally." To use Morse's language, the latter group appears to be more "rational." Thus, the argument might go, the dehumanization objection (which I have assumed is valid at least in a dual-track regime) should apply to preventive detention of this second group.

Recall, however, that preventive detention eludes the dehumanization objection if the government can show the individual so detained lacks autonomy *or* it can show that person will exercise his or her autonomy in the antisocial direction regardless of circumstance. Proof of this second type of undeterrability can never be certain, but neither can we be sure a person lacks autonomy; if a showing of insanity is a good enough proxy for an absence of autonomy, proof of a commitment to harm others even when it brings substantial harm to oneself should be a good proxy for the recklessness component of undeterrability. In short, those who are willing to choose extremely serious crime over freedom forfeit their right to be punished, regardless of how we evaluate their "volitionality" or "rationality."

Consider in this regard those who executed the attack on the World Trade Center. They were probably not insane, but they were undeterrable, in that they preferred crime to life itself. The same might be said of Moussaoui, who was once dubbed the "twentieth hijacker." Moussaoui has declared himself a "slave of Allah," who prays for the destruction of the United States and wants to "fight against the evil force of the federal government."[171] In court papers filed in March 2003, Moussaoui stated "I will be delighted to come back one day to blow myself into your new W.T.C. if ever you rebuild it."[172] That people like Moussaoui are committed to ending innocent lives in disregard of international legal principles and any threat to their own life distinguishes them from the "deterrable" common criminal.

Some Residual Issues

The Moussaoui case is also helpful in explicating two other aspects of the jurisprudence of dangerousness espoused in this chapter. First, the psychological criterion for preventive detention need not be associated with any type of mental disorder. That may seem antithetical not only to the traditional approach to long-term preventive detention but also to *Hendricks* as well. But consider that, under well-established law, if the government can prove that a person like Moussaoui is an enemy combatant—a status that has nothing to do with mental disorder—then preventive detention is clearly permitted.[173] Although that outcome cannot be explained under traditional dangerousness jurisprudence, which requires some sort of mental aberration, it is perfectly consistent with the psychological criterion for preventive detention developed in this chapter: Given their orders, enemy combatants are by definition undeterrable.

The second aspect of the proposed scheme that Moussaoui's case illustrates, whether it occurs in military or civilian courts, is the breadth of the government's options. If the psychological criterion is equated with insanity, then an offender is eligible either for punishment (if sane) or preventive detention (if insane), but not both. Under the scheme proposed here, in contrast, when an offender is impervious to the dictates of the criminal law because of mistake or recklessness but is not excusable (because, for instance, like Moussaoui or Kaczynski, he "knows" the act was wrong), he is eligible for prosecution *and* for preventive detention. In such an instance, is the government free to choose between the two? And may it pursue *both* options, one after the other?

Although *Hendricks*'s holding that the double jeopardy ban does not prohibit preventive detention would appear to require affirmative answers to both of these queries, I would answer the first question no, at least when the triggering act violates a serious criminal prohibition.[174] In serious cases, such as Moussaoui's, the government should have to pursue criminal prosecution rather than preventive detention because of the right to punishment. Although I have argued that people who are undeterrable do not have such a right, I also think it is sensible to presume that, along with innocence, everyone is deterrable. That presumption fits better with our legal system's preference for autonomy, and prevents unnecessarily unleashing the repugnant labeling effects associated with the preventive detention option. It also ensures that government does not pick preventive detention simply because it appears to be the easiest route to getting someone off the streets.

A prosecution-first rule should not mean that preventive detention may never *follow* criminal prosecution, however. Of course, in a case like Moussaoui's, where a life sentence or execution is a very high likelihood, government might not see any reason to avail itself of this type of power. Sentences based primarily on just desert are not always of long duration, however, even when the crime involved is serious (as it would have to be to invoke the proposed regime).[175] In such cases, if the undeterrability and prediction criteria can be met, preventive detention may be a viable postsentence option, an option, it should be noted, that might alleviate some of the pressure to ratchet sentences upward on general incapacitation grounds.

If, rather than conviction and sentence, criminal prosecution results in acquittal, preventive detention should also be an option. But in this instance the principle of legality will often stymie the prosecutor who wants to use preventive detention as a backup. Again, take Moussaoui's case as an example. If the prosecution fails because the government cannot show the agreement necessary for conspiracy, preventive detention should be impermissible as well, because no predicate offense occurred. Any abortion of prosecution on evidentiary insufficiency grounds should usually mean the case is over from both the criminal and commitment perspectives.

D. Summary

Undeterrability, as I have defined it, is the characteristic tendency to be "unaffected by the prospect of punishment."[176] It comes in two forms. Undeterrability through mistake bears a close resemblance to the cognitive insanity tests. It identifies those individuals who are characteristically unaware of the prospect of punishment for contemplated antisocial action because they misperceive its antisocial nature. Undeterrability through recklessness essentially restates the traditional "police officer at the elbow" test, without the mental illness predicate. It identifies those who would choose crime despite the high likelihood of a significant loss of freedom or death if the crime were committed, and includes both those who act for their own ends and for the ends of others. Using the lingo relied on by the Supreme Court in Kansas v. Crane,[177] the mistake category of undeterrability would be coextensive with "emotional abnormality," while "volitional" impairment would be parallel to the recklessness category. But the mistake-and-recklessness language is preferable to Crane's amorphous terminology.

The undeterrability predicate for preventive detention is fully consistent with the view that punishment is necessary to show respect for those who commit crime. While most wrongdoers can be said to possess the "right" to punishment, that right can justifiably be denied to the subset of wrongdoers who lack autonomy or who will choose the bad regardless of the consequences. The mistake and recklessness components of undeterrability capture precisely these two concerns. Although subjecting these people to preventive detention in addition to or in lieu of criminal punishment may treat them as less than human, that treatment is justified by their demonstrated inability or unwillingness to make the right choice.

The undeterrability formulation is also superior to the "gap-filler" justification that is sometimes advanced in support of preventive detention. As expressed by Stephen Schulhofer,[178] this justification exists "when the state has a compelling interest that cannot be met through the criminal process."[179] His preeminent example of gap-filling through preventive detention is the commitment of people with serious mental illness, who cannot be punished and thus who could harm society in the absence of such commitment.[180] But this type of thumb-in-the-dike justification proves too much, for it would also permit commitment of any dangerous convict who has served his or her sentence and can no longer be confined through the criminal process, something Schulhofer clearly does not endorse.[181] The undeterrability criterion better describes the "gap" population that cannot be addressed by the criminal law—those people who are impervious to its dictates.

This undeterrability formulation of the psychological criterion for preventive detention is narrower than the Court's inability-to-control criterion and broader than the cognitive insanity formulation. It would significantly limit the types of offenders who could be committed under sexual predator statutes because most are neither mistaken about the criminality of their actions nor willing to flaunt them brazenly. For the same reason, it might reduce the number of people subject to police power commitment under traditional civil commitment laws, which normally define mental disorder relatively expansively, as a "substantial disorder of the person's emotional processes, thought or cognition which grossly impairs judgment, behavior or capacity to recognize reality."[182] At the same time, this latter definition, in contrast to the undeterrability formulation, does not permit commitment of nonmentally ill people who are undeterrable in the recklessness sense, a small group likely to be comprised of particularly aggressive sex offenders, psychopaths, and terrorists; in fact, some statutes expressly preclude commitment of individuals who exhibit only personality disorders.[183] The concern behind these limitations may be that these latter individuals do not belong in a mental hospital. That concern is understandable. But the state should not be precluded from preventively detaining truly undeterrable individuals in some type of facility, if they meet the prediction criterion.

III. The Prediction Criterion

Debate over the degree of dangerousness the state must prove before it may preventively detain an individual has been heated. Representative is an exchange between Alexander Brooks and John LaFond. Brooks stated that even if the risk of violent recidivism by a particular individual is only

50 percent, preventive detention is permissible, because "[a] mistaken decision to confine, however painful to the offender involved, is . . . simply not morally equivalent to a mistaken decision to release . . . One is much less harmful than the other."[184] LaFond responded:

> Suddenly, the fundamental assumption of American criminal justice that it "is far worse to convict an innocent man than to let a guilty man go free" has been transformed into a first principle worthy of George Orwell's 1984. Now, according to Professor Brooks, it is far better that at least half, and maybe more, of the people confined to a psychiatric prison indefinitely be harmless in order to "incapacitate" those who may commit a future crime. Even better, why not convert our criminal sentencing system into a game of chance? Release from prison could be decided by a flip of a coin. At least this lottery will be more accurate than the one Professor Brooks embraces.[185]

If the psychological criterion for preventive detention is undeterrability, defined as a characteristic ignorance that one's criminal activity is criminal or a characteristic willingness to commit crime despite near certain and significant punishment or a high risk of death, then the individual's dangerousness will often seem evident. Whether the person with such characteristic beliefs or desires will translate them into action, however, still requires prediction. Various psychological and situational variables—including the strength of the beliefs or desires, the availability of targets, and the effect of constraints other than liberty deprivation—must be considered.[186] If the psychological criterion is defined more broadly, as with the Court's inability-to-control formulation, then dangerousness is even less apparent, and false positives are more likely. Finally, in many situations (for example, stop and frisk, pretrial detention, sentencing), no psychological criterion is or should be required. In these latter situations, the prediction may be even more vulnerable to attack.

In the following discussion I do not reach definitive conclusions as to how likely the risk of antisocial conduct must be before preventive detention in all its variations is permitted. I do propose two principles for guiding debate on this issue, however. The first is the proportionality principle, which states that the degree of dangerousness required for preventive detention should be roughly proportionate to the degree of liberty deprivation the state seeks. The second is the consistency principle, which states that the degree of dangerousness required for preventive detention should be similar to the degree of dangerousness sufficient to authorize like liberty deprivations associated with other manifestations of the state's police power, in particular criminal dispositions.

A. The Proportionality Principle

Government interventions based explicitly on dangerousness vary enormously both in nature and duration. Commitment as a sexual predator involves confinement in a prisonlike setting[187] that is renewable periodically and that will often be long-term; indeed, it may amount to a lifetime disposition, given the relative untreatability of some of these offenders.[188] Pretrial preventive detention of suspects occurs in jail and is limited by speedy trial laws, but can still easily last for one hundred days even when the defendant pushes for trial.[189] Typical civil commitment of those with serious mental illness occurs in a less confining institution and is both much shorter, on average, than either sexual predator commitment or pretrial detention, primarily because treatment is more efficacious at reducing the danger.[190] Police stops occur in a public setting and should last no longer than fifteen or twenty minutes.[191]

Generally, the law requires a lesser showing of dangerousness as one moves down this hierarchy of interventions. Sexual predator statutes usually require proof beyond a reasonable doubt;[192] pretrial detentions require proof by clear and convincing evidence or some similar standard;[193] civil commitment also requires clear and convincing evidence;[194] short-term (forty-eight-hour) commitment pending the commitment proceeding may be based on probable cause;[195] and police investigative stops require reasonable suspicion.[196] In general, this proportionality approach is sensible.[197] It hides two important problems, however.

The first has to do with the interaction of the standard of proof and the definition of dangerousness. One might think that proof of dangerousness beyond a reasonable doubt requires a showing that the individual is extremely likely to engage in crime if not detained. Some statutes define dangerousness in less absolute terms, however, speaking instead of whether the person is "likely to" engage in antisocial conduct.[198] This definition has the effect of lowering the state's burden, because it only requires that the government demonstrate by the requisite standard (beyond a reasonable doubt, clear and convincing evidence, and so on) that the person is likely to offend.[199] An analogous approach, made popular with the advent of actuarial approaches to prediction, is to label a person "dangerous" if the state can show by the relevant standard of proof that the person belongs to a particular group for whom a specific likelihood of risk can be identified, even if that likelihood is relatively low.[200] Both of these moves are sleights of hand to the extent they purport to require a high level of proof that the person will offend.

The second problem with the hierarchical approach to proof of dangerousness is that the hierarchy itself is not as clear as it seems at first glance. I have assumed, for instance, that commitment of sexual predators is longer than typical civil commitment. Yet some individuals subjected to civil commitment are as resistant to treatment as the "incorrigible" sex offender is.[201] Some sex offenders, in contrast, may be rendered less dangerous through chemical treatments or cognitive therapy programs.[202] To a very large extent, in other words, the length of confinement depends, or at least should depend, on the individual rather than the state or a statutory provision. Thus, the standard of proof the state must meet should not be based solely or even predominantly on the type of commitment, but should instead depend primarily on its length.

This conclusion has important implications for the scope of preventive detention. Although each new commitment at the periodic review need not be preceded by a new antisocial act (because, if effective, the intervention should prevent such acts, and because the justification for preventive detention is dangerousness, not behavior), it should be permitted only upon increasingly more stringent proof of dangerousness, whether the setting is criminal or civil commitment. Evidence of resistance to treatment, recent overt acts, and other new indicia of dangerousness can meet this burden under some circumstances. At some point, however, release should be required simply because the requisite certainty level demanded by the proportionality principle has become so high it cannot be met by any type of evidence. That proposition might require, for instance, automatic release after a certain period unless new evidence of dangerousness is forthcoming.[203]

Another important implication of this reasoning concerns sentencing. Dangerousness is no longer a major consideration under most sentencing schemes and is considered irrelevant in many, at least in theory.[204] However, when dangerousness is a legitimate sentencing criterion, as in indeterminate sentencing regimes, the proportionality principle should apply in this setting as well. In light of the liberty deprivation to which prisoners are subjected, that means that a relatively high degree of dangerousness must be proven before a sentence may be imposed, and that, as with commitment, release should be required after a certain period of time, unless the state can demonstrate a new basis for a dangerousness finding or the sentence is based on additional considerations such as deterrence or desert. On the same ground, the death penalty should never be based on a finding of dangerousness,[205] unless the prediction can be made with virtual certainty.

B. The Consistency Principle

The consistency principle works in tandem with the proportionality principle. The proportionality principle provides a method of graduating the prediction criterion, through assessment of the nature and length of the preventive detention. The consistency principle provides a baseline for the prediction criterion, through assessment of the proof required to sanction other government interventions based on dangerousness.

The most obvious place such intervention occurs is in the criminal justice system where, either explicitly or implicitly, assumptions about dangerousness are pervasive. Thus, application of the consistency principle would require that the prediction criterion for preventive detention conform to the prediction criterion in criminal law provisions that contemplate liberty deprivations. In making this inquiry, consistency analysis would look solely at comparisons with crimes that do not require proof of any particular harm, for once harm occurs other considerations besides dangerousness come into play.[206] The somewhat surprising outcome of this way of thinking about the prediction criterion is that preventive detention might be justifiable, at least as an initial matter, upon a minimal showing of risk.

Among the most conspicuous illustrations of crimes that do not require harm but that do incorporate a risk assessment are the classic "inchoate crimes," attempt and conspiracy. These offenses do not occur unless there is sufficient conduct to show the ultimate harm is likely to be committed. For attempt, as noted earlier, mere preparation is insufficient and something akin to "dangerous proximity" to the completed act is often required.[207] For conspiracy, an agreement and, in many jurisdictions, an overt act in furtherance of the agreement must be proven.[208] More important, the government must show the alleged attempter or conspirator intended to carry out the criminal act; mere awareness that the act will occur is usually insufficient.[209] In combined effect, these *actus reus* and mens rea requirements

mean that, to obtain conviction, the state must show the act would have occurred had it not been for the incompetence of the perpetrator or the competence of law enforcement. In short, proof of a high degree of danger is
incorporated into the definition of inchoate crimes.[210]

If attempt and conspiracy were the only crimes based on a dangerousness
assessment, endorsement of the consistency principle might require a very
high likelihood of harm before preventive confinement could occur. But
these inchoate offenses are not alone. Other nonresult crimes, which might
be called "anticipatory" offenses, allow conviction on proof of a much lower
risk of harm.

Consider first vagrancy statutes. Older versions of these statutes permitted conviction based on acts such as a refusal to identify oneself or standing
on a street corner with no apparent purpose, acts that have only a tenuous
relationship to public harm of any sort.[211] For related reasons, these laws
have usually been found invalid on vagueness grounds.[212] However, newer
versions of these statutes, which prohibit conduct such as loitering within
thirty feet of a cash machine or congregating in areas known for drug traf-
ficking, have withstood such challenges even when a mens rea requirement
is absent, perhaps because they are more obviously associated with a real
public menace.[213] Even so, that association is usually trivial; certainly, the
chance that any person standing near a cash machine or in a high-crime
area will cause serious harm to others is negligible. The "danger" these
statutes are trying to prevent appears to be deterioration in the quality of
life.[214] Until "damage to the quality of life" is made a crime, however (and
the legality principle should prevent that), the danger sought to be prevented by these laws is so diffuse as to be nonexistent, unless the law also requires, as some do, proof of intent to harm a person or property.[215]

Even more explicit in their reliance on suspect dangerousness assessments are endangerment laws. Here, too, the degree of dangerousness required does not approach that required for attempt or conspiracy. Under
the Model Penal Code, as noted earlier, a person commits a misdemeanor if
he or she "recklessly engages in conduct which places or may place another
person in danger of death or serious bodily injury."[216] The words "may
place . . . in danger" obviously contemplate a less-than-rigorous standard
of proof with respect to risk.[217] Along the same lines is the popular crime of
driving while intoxicated.[218] The chance that a drunken driver will actually
kill or hurt someone is fairly low. Once again, the dangerousness requirement inherent in this type of crime is minimal.

A final type of anticipatory offense is possession, a crime that comes in many varieties. In most states, for instance, it is a crime to possess burglary tools and, in some jurisdictions, this offense occurs even if the only items possessed are more likely to be used innocently than criminally, such as crowbars and screwdrivers.[219] In contrast to inchoate offenses such as attempt and conspiracy, conviction for this type of crime does not require proof of intent to commit any particular harm, but rather only knowing possession under "suspicious" circumstances.[220] Similarly, in simple drug possession cases, the prosecution often only needs to show knowing possession (and sometimes not even that); it never needs to prove that the perpetrator's possession of the drug will cause some identifiable harm.[221] In gun possession cases, conviction is usually automatic if the possessor is a felon or an alien, or does not have a license; in none of these three situations is "good moral character" or something analogous a defense.[222] All these crimes are based on explicit or implicit dangerousness assessments, and none require demonstration of a high degree of danger. Indeed, with respect to possession of a small amount of drugs and possession of a gun without a license, one is hard put to identify what third-party interests the state is attempting to protect.[223]

In short, a large number of crimes not only do not require proof of any harm, but are also based on very weak predictions of harm. That suggests that if the state's police power were to be consistently instituted, initial preventive detention could justifiably be based on very weak predictions as well. A closer look at these anticipatory crimes suggests a more nuanced conclusion, but ultimately also suggests that this general statement is correct.

Anticipatory crimes seem to fall into one of three categories, illustrated by the three types of offenses just described. The first category—exemplified by vagrancy laws—carries trivial penalties, generally involving little or no actual liberty deprivation.[224] If this were the only baseline, application of the consistency principle might lead to the conclusion that the government should not have the option of preventively depriving people of liberty when the risk of it occurring is low.

But that conclusion fails to take into account the second and third categories of anticipatory crimes. The second group of such offenses—exemplified by drunken driving and reckless endangerment—is more likely to bring significant incarceration,[225] even though it too may be associated with minimal risk. Thus, application of the consistency principle might permit preventive detention in similar low-risk situations. At the same time, a fact that distinguishes this second category of anticipatory offenses is that it is aimed at avoiding significant, imminent harm. That suggests, under consistency reasoning, that low-risk individuals may be preventively confined only when the harm feared is very serious and near at hand, two elements that, together, place substantial limitations on the threshold for intervention.[226]

Still left to consider, however, is the third category of anticipatory crimes. Illustrated by possession crimes, it can lead to significant sentences,[227] even though the feared harm is unlikely to occur and is neither imminent nor serious. Under the consistency principle, this suggests that preventive detention can be based, at least initially, on a showing of moderate or even minimal risk regardless of the nature of the harm threatened. Only as the confinement becomes prolonged would the proportionality principle require proof of a high level of danger.

A retributivist might argue that using the level of dangerousness inherent in criminal statutes as a baseline for preventive detention in the manner just described is nonsensical, because crimes are by definition backward-looking assessments. When defining crime, the retributivist might contend, the focal point of the inquiry is culpability, not the degree of dangerousness inherent in particular acts. As a result, the fact that certain anticipatory crimes might not require a high level of dangerousness is not a pertinent indicator of the state's police power interest. The only important factor a retributivist regards as important is whether the perpetrator recognizes, or should recognize, the danger that does exist or, under the most subjective approaches, whether the perpetrator thinks the danger exists, regardless of whether it actually does.

The problem with the retributivist argument is that, under any of the anticipatory crimes just discussed, subjective awareness of the degree of risk is virtually or entirely irrelevant. A person will be convicted of gun or drug possession, drunk driving, or vagrancy if he meets the act requirement, regardless of whether he was aware of the risk he created (or lack thereof). Even in a reckless endangerment prosecution, where awareness of risk is relevant, the degree of risk actually created is likely to play a much more significant role than the risk perceived by the actor.[228] The gravamen of these crimes is not what the person thought, but the objective risk posed. In many cases, that risk is not very high, and in some it is nonexistent, but the state exerts its police power anyway.

A second argument against adopting the consistency principle is based on the practicality that crimes must be defined legislatively. Given this fact, one might contend, we must allow prosecution and conviction of people who do not cause any identifiable harm and are not obviously dangerous—for example, the harmless vagrant or gun owner—to ensure that we also nab the really dangerous loiterer or weapons possessor; criminalizing the behavior of the first group is the inevitable consequence of a preference for generalized, before-the-fact rule making. In the preventive detention context, in contrast, we are able to individualize the dangerousness assessment, and thus we should do so, despite the likelihood that we will end up requiring greater proof of danger than we do in analogous criminal adjudications.

To my mind, this latter contention is not an argument against the consistency principle, but rather an indictment of how we think about defining crime. The logic of the consistency principle does not dictate that the degree of risk required for preventive detention correlate with the currently low levels associated with many anticipatory crimes. It could just as easily be used to reform crime definition. Because preventive detention forthrightly and conspicuously bases liberty deprivation on predictions of dangerousness, courts have traditionally required the government to demonstrate a high degree of risk in that setting. In contrast, as just discussed, the criminal law blithely permits conviction and punishment of individuals who have caused no harm and are not very dangerous. Perhaps that should change.

In Addington v. Texas,[229] the Supreme Court held that the loss of liberty associated with civil commitment requires clear and convincing evidence of dangerousness. While Addington rejected the reasonable doubt standard as unnecessarily stringent where nonpunitive confinement is concerned, it also repudiated the lower preponderance of the evidence standard of proof in that setting.[230] The primary reason the Court gave in support of this holding is revealing: "[t]he individual should not be asked to share equally with society the risk of error when the possible injury to the individual is significantly greater than any possible harm to the state."[231]

That conclusion could have significant implications for the criminal law. If civil commitment, which Addington confirms is a less onerous burden on liberty than criminal conviction, requires proof that a person is more likely than "more likely than not" to cause harm to another, criminal laws that base liability and incarceration on danger rather than harm should, at the least, require the same.[232] Judges should demand proof of a high degree of dangerousness from prosecutors pursuing inchoate and anticipatory crimes, or dismiss charges and reduce sentences. Legislatures should avoid vagrancy, possession, and endangerment formulations that do not demand similar proof.[233] Whether implemented judicially or legislatively, actus reus elements should require conduct that is clearly risky, and mens rea elements should likewise require intent to cause harm (as the attempt and conspiracy offenses do), or at least willful blindness to the risk. That would be the legacy of proactively applying the consistency principle.

Conclusion

Preventive detention is a pervasive, routine occurrence in our society. Its most conspicuous guise may be the relatively new sexual predator laws. But it is also the key feature of civil commitment and police stops on the street, as well as a significant component in many criminal sentences and an intrinsic element of crimes such as possession and endangerment. Given their ubiquity, courts and lawyers need to pay much more attention to how and why we justify these deprivations of liberty based on dangerousness.

This chapter has explored some of the commonalities and distinctions between these various exercises of the state's police power in the hopes of furthering their rational implementation. The jurisprudence of dangerousness it has advanced is based on three significant assertions. The first is that, while preventive detention is generally inconsistent with a preference for autonomy when criminal punishment is an option, it is acceptable both for those who are unaware of the criminality of their actions and for those who are committed to crime and are aware that this commitment will very likely mean a significant loss of freedom or death. The second assertion is that potential abuses associated with a preventive detention system can be minimized—or at least reduced to a level no higher than exists in any alternative police power regime—through periodic review, rules requiring treatment and detention in the least restrictive manner feasible, a threshold requirement of obviously risky conduct, and increasingly heavier burdens of proof as the detention lengthens.

The final assertion underlying the jurisprudence of dangerousness described here is that we can predict danger adequately for legal purposes. That assertion is based in part on improvements in prediction science, but stems mostly from the belief that we cannot justifiably demand more accuracy in the preventive detention setting than we do in the criminal law. This same idea, however, could also lead to the position that we should demand more certainty than we currently do in making those predictions sought by the law of crimes.

These conclusions would require significant change in both the law of preventive detention and the law of crimes. The scope of *Hendricks* and *Crane* would be cabined, the threshold and conditions of commitment would need to be revamped, and possession and other anticipatory crimes would need to be redrafted or at least subjected to more intense judicial scrutiny. Perhaps most important, the law would recognize that a jurisprudence of dangerousness is an essential aspect of regulating government power.

— 5 —

The Civilization of the Criminal Law

The previous chapter argued that a two-track regime that simultaneously permits punishment and preventive detention of "deterrable" individuals is repugnant to our society's most fundamental premises, precisely because it consists of two tracks. Such a system strongly fosters the perception—a perception that can become a self-fulfilling prophecy—that those who are shunted off the punishment track to the commitment track are less than human. Under this type of system, those relegated to commitment are treated, not as autonomous actors who deserve to be punished for their choices, but as harmful, uncontrollable beings who must be caged under a special detention law.

By this logic, however, the dehumanization objection would not obtain if intervention based on dangerousness were the government's *only* liberty-depriving response to antisocial behavior. Then invidious comparisons with a second, "autonomous" group worthy of blame cannot occur. A system of liberty deprivation that takes the dangerousness criterion as the sole predicate for intervention would not shadow the criminal code but instead constitute it.

In this chapter, I explore the jurisprudential and practical feasibility of such a system, what I will call a "preventive" regime of justice. More specifically, this chapter examines an updated version of the type of government intervention espoused four decades ago by thinkers such as Barbara Wootton,[1] Sheldon Glueck,[2] and Karl Menninger.[3] These individuals—the first a criminologist, the latter two mental health professionals—envisioned a system that is triggered by an antisocial act but that pays no attention to desert, or even to general deterrence. Rather, like sexual predator regimes, the sole goal of the system they proposed is individual prevention through assessments of dangerousness and the provision of treatment designed to reduce it. However, unlike the sexual predator scheme at issue in *Hendricks*, a preventive regime would not countenance a two-track system involving "punishment" and "commitment"; the intervention would take place immediately after the antisocial act, rather than after completion of a criminal sentence. A preventive regime is also different from a system that follows conviction with an indeterminate sentence, because it considers gradations of culpability irrelevant at the threshold of intervention as well as at the dispositional stage. As Wootton imagined it, once the "obsession with the punitive [is] dispelled, the courts could be free to deal with every lawbreaker in whatever way, consonant with the moral standards of the community, seemed best calculated to discourage future lawbreaking. Their eyes would be on the future, not on the past."[4]

Some modern modifications of Wootton's proposal, mostly semantic, need to be made. Today, social scientists talk about risk assessment, not predicting dangerousness, to connote the idea that the potential for violence is not something that resides solely in the individual, but rather stems from the interaction of biological, psychological, and social variables.[5] A clinician evaluating someone in a prevention regime would look for "risk factors" that correlate with antisocial behavior, some of which are static—such as age, gender, and prior antisocial history—and some of which are dynamic or changeable—such as rage reactions, substance abuse, family and peer dynamics, and the proximity of certain people.[6] As detailed later in this chapter, risk assessment techniques, long lambasted for their inaccuracy, have improved substantially in recent years.

Social scientists also talk about "risk management," not incapacitation or control, which gets across the notion that the best disposition is the one that manages the dynamic, or changeable, risk factors.[7] The ultimate goals of risk management, in terms that a student of the criminal law would understand, are specific deterrence, rehabilitation, and incapacitation. Interventions under a risk management approach need not occur in a confined space, but rather can take place in the community—albeit sometimes under strict monitoring—and in any event are ongoing and flexible rather than set at the front-end. The permissible dispositions are legion. In addition to formal rehabilitation programs and prison, they can include restitution, fines and forfeitures, community service, contempt-backed peace orders, and other probationary conditions, as long as the focus remains individual prevention. Thus, the system examined in this chapter is one that rejects culpability assessments, and instead looks at whether an offender's risk factors indicate a potential for harm to others, in which case appropriate management in the community or, if necessary, through incapacitation in an institution occurs. The contours of this prevention system will be fleshed out in subsequent pages.

The ultimate objective of this chapter is to present a defense of a prevention system as a replacement for, rather than in addition to, our current criminal justice system. The Supreme Court upheld the sexual predator scheme in Kansas v. Hendricks, despite its forward-looking nature, because it deemed the scheme "civil" rather than "criminal."[8] Assuming some significant modifications of the model the Court sanctioned, a preventive system may indeed be a more civil method of dealing with antisocial conduct than the current desert-based approach, a notion captured by Menninger's famous title, The Crime of Punishment.

Such a defense of a purely preventive regime has been rare in the legal literature since the 1960s, when just-deserts philosophy became popular and preventive approaches fell into disrepute.[9] Since then, a number of conceptual and empirical advances have made the issue even more complex. The case for a preventive regime nonetheless deserves serious consideration in the twenty-first century, as an increasing number of jurisdictions adopt harsh determinate sentencing based on desert principles,[10] and in the wake of the American Law Institute's recent announcement that its planned revision of the Model Penal Code will forsake the original Code's focus on reform of prisoners and instead endorse a just-deserts approach to sentencing.[11]

Part 1 of this chapter looks at jurisprudential objections to a prevention regime, which all center on the regime's perceived failure to do "justice." It contends that such a regime would neither slight human dignity nor undermine the general deterrence and character-shaping goals of the criminal law. Part 2 examines concerns about the feasibility of a preventive system, including questions about the accuracy of predictions, the efficacy of treatment, and the costs of a reform-oriented justice system. It concludes that these concerns are overstated, and in any event are less serious than the practical problems that afflict the punishment model. Part 3 summarizes the reasons for favoring prevention over traditional punishment. Its principal point is that a preventive regime is much better at assimilating the proliferation of scientific findings that call into question humans' ability to control their actions, which is the central premise of a punishment system based on desert.

The view taken in this chapter is exploratory, however. For a number of reasons, legal and sociological, one might be ambivalent about instituting a full-blown preventive regime, at least in the immediate future. Accordingly, the conclusion to the chapter, Part 4, suggests a transitional compromise, which maintains culpability as the threshold for government intervention, and reserves application of the preventive model for disposition, in what amounts to a modern version of indeterminate sentencing.

I. Jurisprudential Objections to Preventive Intervention

The most fundamental argument against a prevention regime is simply that it goes against everything we stand for. This argument has several versions, deontological, quasi-consequentialist, and straightforwardly consequentialist. Here it is subdivided into contentions made by retributivists (those who view punishment of offenders as morally obligatory), rule utilitarians (those who subscribe to general deterrence theories), and virtue ethicists (those who believe punishment is justified because it inculcates virtue).

A. Retributivist Objections

Michael Moore puts the deontological case most forcefully with his arguments in favor of noninstrumental retributivism. He arrives at his position in favor of backward-looking desert-driven intervention primarily through thought experiments, one of which explicitly contrasts a preventive regime with a retributive one. Imagine, he hypothesizes, that a psychiatrist discovers that a particular patient has extremely dangerous propensities. The patient also happens to be the accused in a criminal trial but, it turns out, is completely innocent and has never committed any crime. Under utilitarian theory, Moore notes, as long as the judge is the only one who knows about both the psychiatrist's opinion and the patient's innocence, and as long as the prediction is reliable and the harm predicted is sufficiently serious, the person should be punished. Yet Moore conjectures that most of us would consider that conclusion inappropriate, because it would involve punishing an innocent person.[12]

Moore is probably right that even many adamant utilitarians would not want to punish an innocent person who is merely predicted to be harmful, except perhaps when the utility of doing so is tremendous. But he skews the issue by using the word "punish." By definition, we *cannot* punish people unless they committed a crime, or at least we say they have committed one.[13] That does not mean that we are unwilling to authorize coercive government intervention against an innocent person. Consider a more realistic thought experiment, involving an individual who has molested children on several occasions and has been convicted for those crimes. The term of his last sentence, based on desert, is just about to expire. Psychiatrists believe that if released he will molest again, and indeed the person himself says that the only way he will stop abusing children is "to die." These are the facts of *Hendricks*,[14] and many of us would vote enthusiastically for a stringent risk management program in his case, even if he were innocent of any unpunished crime.

Of course, under the prevention regime examined in this chapter, Hendricks's child molestation would have subjected him to risk management *immediately*. Although Hendricks would not be "innocent" under this scenario (for he has not yet served a sentence for his crime), Moore and many retributivists would still object to any intervention based on a prediction of danger. To them, as discussed in the previous chapter, this type of "nonpunitive" disposition would violate Hendricks's right to be punished or at least breach society's obligation to punish. Moore's case for this requirement of punishment is based on an assessment of our emotional reaction to crime,[15] a topic discussed below. The more widely cited explanation for this stance comes from other commentators, using a somewhat more instrumental set of arguments than Moore. For instance, Herbert Morris would insist on desert-based punishment because it is necessary to affirm the dignity of the offender through recognition of him as a responsible human actor,[16] while Jean Hampton argues that punishment is required as a societal affirmation of the victim's worth in the face of the criminal's demeaning attack.[17]

Neither the dignity of offenders nor of victims is dependent on desert-based punishment, however. Risk management, properly conducted, explores the causes of antisocial behavior and continuously stresses the offender's ability to change that behavior through cognitive restructuring, avoidance of risky behavior (such as drinking or fraternizing with gang members), and adjusting relationships.[18] As modern rehabilitative efforts routinely demonstrate, a regime based on prediction does not have to insult the notion that past choices have consequences and that the offender is responsible and held accountable for them.[19] There *is* a difference in message, however. The punishment model says to the offender: "You have done something bad, for which you must pay." The prevention model says: "You have done something harmful, which you must not let happen again." In terms of how they treat their children, many parents would probably prefer the latter message to the former; arguably government officials in charge of responding to antisocial behavior should as well.

The message that the offender has caused harm should also affirm the worth of the person who was harmed. Indeed, restorative justice programs designed to facilitate prevention through reintegration of the offender into the community transmit this message much more concretely than the traditional punishment model ever could, by organizing group conferences at which both offender and victim are present. A primary goal of such conferences is "to give offenders a sense of the consequences of their actions and an understanding of how victims feel" in an effort to humanize and dignify both offender and victim[20] (which in turn has been found to reduce recidivism by increasing remorse, reconciliation, and self-esteem).[21]

For a subset of victims, the message a prevention regime sends is even more complex, in a way that is, again, probably preferable to the message a punishment regime communicates. The punishment model often sets up a false dichotomy between the victim and the offender by suggesting that the offender deserves blame, while the victim is, well, innocent. In fact, much crime is intrafamilial or results from other types of prolonged interaction between offender and victim.[22] In some of these situations, a risk management approach might involve the "victim" as well as the offender, and both would have to accept proportionate responsibility for their actions; this is, of course, a common premise in marital and other types of dyadic therapy. In other words, the prevention model treats crime in context, not as an isolated event or the result solely of one individual's actions. To social scientists that is a much more accurate perspective on our "crime problem" and one that therefore ought to be communicated.[23]

This discussion of offenders and victims does gloss over some important tensions triggered by the prevention model, however. First, most of the time the victim truly is innocent and the offender clearly is the only harming actor, yet on some of these occasions the offender will not be considered a risk. If the government avoided intervention in such cases, as the prevention model counsels, then no government affirmation either of the offender's responsibility or of the victim's worth occurs. Conversely, some offenders, because they are dangerous, would be subject to intervention under a prevention regime even though they lack the relevant mental state or were justified in their actions. As in Moore's unlikely but nonetheless possible hypothetical, a person might also be considered dangerous even though he has *never* committed an antisocial act.

In these situations, the moral message communicated by a prevention system would admittedly be ambiguous. Using these kinds of examples, Paul Robinson has posited that a system that ignores the human urge to gauge blame—to condemn or withhold condemnation based on assessments of culpability—would lack "moral credibility" with the public.[24] Dissatisfaction with the law and with authorities who intervene (or fail to intervene) in ways the public perceives as unjust might, in turn, lead to less willingness to comply with rules set by those authorities.[25] These are plausible speculations. But there is simply not enough information about how people think about crime to say much more than that.

Take first the claim that preventive detention is repugnant to the typical layperson. Evidence for that assertion is slim. Even the current two-track system that accentuates the difference between a desert-based regime and a preventive one does not seem to have caused much public concern. The electorate has fervidly endorsed sexual predator laws that explicitly eschew assessments of blameworthiness and recidivist statutes that implicitly do so.[26] Nor is it likely that a public obsessed with its safety, as ours is,[27] would be very upset by elimination of defenses based on excuse and elimination of subtle gradations of mens rea. As it is, many people had a hard time understanding why John Hinckley was "acquitted,"[28] and do not seem to be bothered by significant sentences based on negligent actions, as Robinson's own empirical work demonstrates.[29]

That being said, modification of the prevention regime to take into account some of the stronger intuitions of the public might be wise. For instance, one could supplement the act threshold required by Wootton[30] by limiting intervention to those who have committed or attempted a harmful act that is both nonaccidental and unjustified. As an empirical matter, a person who has not done (or tried to do) anything harmful or whose harmful act is inadvertent or justifiable is unlikely to be considered a risk in any event, and a person who does meet these conditions is likely to pose some risk. Regardless of empirical considerations, however, limiting intervention to those who commit or attempt harm and lack objective justification for doing so might be warranted as a method of minimizing the public dissatisfaction Robinson hypothesizes. It is also more congruent with the principle of legality described in the previous chapter.

This type of "shallow" prohibition is probably as far as one needs to go to address Robinson's concerns about preventive detention, however. Indeed, this approach is not inconsistent with Robinson's own suggestion that the best method of informing the public about criminal law norms is through what he calls "rules of conduct," which state in simple language the criminal law's prohibitions.[31] Under Robinson's scheme, more complex "adjudication rules," which would incorporate the gradations required by desert, would govern prosecutions of offenders, but only conduct rules would constitute the criminal law as far as the rest of the public is concerned. And, as Robinson notes, "most mental elements are culpability mental elements, which function as principles of adjudication,"[32] not rules of conduct. Thus, Robinson's conduct rules would simply stipulate that people should not kill, rape, or steal, or try to kill, rape, or steal, without the fine-tuned mens rea terms currently found in criminal codes.[33] That is precisely what a code in a preventive regime would look like.

With these adjustments, public discontent with a government that refuses to play the blame game is most likely to arise, not from confinement of the "nonculpable," but from failure to treat harshly enough relatively nondangerous persons perceived to be "culpable." Here again, however, we must speculate, and what little evidence we have suggests that outrage over "lenient" treatment of serious offenders would not be extensive. The current criminal justice system routinely dismisses charges or reduces sentences on lack-of-danger grounds without significant social disgruntlement.[34] As Chapter 3 indicated, death penalty research consistently finds that even the decision to forego imposition of the ultimate punishment rests on assessments of relative dangerousness more than any other factor.[35]

None of this is meant to deny that desert analysis often plays a prominent role in lay evaluation of the appropriate disposition of individual cases.[36] But surveys suggest that, when asked to view dispositional issues in the abstract, the American public believes that specific deterrence and crime reduction is at least as important as giving offenders what they deserve.[37] At best, it is unresolved whether a system explicitly devoted to the former goal would undermine public confidence in the criminal justice system, much less its willingness to comply with the law, especially given the close relationship of dangerousness and moral culpability.[38]

Furthermore, we should ask whether the government ought to be complicit in endorsing retributive notions, however universal they may be, given their proximity to the coarse emotions of vengeance and hatred.[39] Instead, perhaps, the government's treatment of antisocial behavior ought to educate the citizenry about the extent to which human behavior is a function of social as well as personal factors, many of which may be beyond the immediate control or awareness of the individual at the time of an offense.[40] Less willingness to look to internal phenomena in apportioning blame may in turn result in reduced perceptions of injustice, anger arousal, and the desire to punish or inflict harm, not just on "criminals" but on any person who is viewed as in the "wrong."[41] As Neil Vidmar has suggested, punitive reactions may beget punitive reactions, initiating a cycle of recrimination and violence.[42] The fact that everyone has these emotions does not mean we should privilege them.[43]

B. Deterrence-Based Objections

Retributivists are not the only group uncomfortable with the preventive model of criminal justice. Henry Hart lodged a number of objections to it, all centered around the goal of general deterrence. His first concern was that the preventive approach would tend to undermine deterrence because, given its forward-looking focus on the dangerousness and treatability of individuals, it underemphasizes general formulations of prohibited conduct.[44] But a government invested in prevention could easily generate a code which straightforwardly sets out the harms that, if committed nonaccidentally and unjustifiably, would be the subject of intervention. That list of harms could be based on the same sort of societal assessment of human and property values that goes into drafting today's codes and, as noted above, probably would look little different from today's criminal statutory framework, except that most mens rea terms and the excuses would be absent.

Hart's second deterrence-related objection to a prevention regime is more powerful. He wondered if the "public interest" would be adequately protected "if the legislature is allowed only to say to people, 'If you do not comply with any of these commands, you will merely be considered to be sick and subjected to officially-imposed rehabilitative treatment in an effort to cure you' [or, as a variation,] 'your own personal need for cure and rehabilitation will be the predominant factor in determining what happens to you.'" An effective deterrent, he suggested, is likely to exist only if the legislature is enabled to say, "'If you violate any of these laws and the violation is culpable, your conduct will receive the formal and solemn condemnation of the community as morally blameworthy, and you will be subjected to whatever punishment, or treatment, is appropriate to vindicate the law and to further its various purposes.'"[45]

Hart failed to consider a fourth option that comes closer to the legislative pronouncement that would occur in a preventive regime: "If you do not comply with these commands, you will be subject to intervention designed to prevent you from violating them again, which may consist of restrictions on liberty as well as treatment designed to ensure protection of the public." Because disposition is individualized in a preventive regime, the would-be first-time offender cannot know how the government will react if he is caught, which may maximize deterrence.[46] Multiple offenders, in contrast, will probably guess (often correctly) that the government's response will be relatively tough if they are caught recidivating. If three-strikes laws have had any crime-reducing effect at all, it is because two-time offenders are well aware of the consequences of a third strike.[47]

Deterrence is an overrated rationale for punishment in any event. With the exception of a short period in the 1990s, crime rates in the United States have been in an upward surge since the mid-1960s, apparently unaffected by either indeterminate or determinate sentencing approaches.[48] Numerous authors have questioned the fundamental premises of deterrence theory, especially with respect to its assumptions that incremental changes in punishment affect behavior and that we can figure out how much deterrence we want.[49] Empirical research is equally unsupportive of nuanced deterrence theory. Tom Tyler's studies indicate that most law-abiding people avoid crime not because of a fear of punishment, but because of their respect for the law and the authorities who promulgate it,[50] a finding that perhaps argues for the sorts of community-sensitive modifications in the prevention model that have already been discussed, but also suggests that deterrence should not be the centerpiece of a crime-prevention system. And a considerable amount of research indicates that those people who tend *not* to be law abiding pay virtually no attention to the criminal law.[51] A recent contribution to this literature by David Anderson is particularly potent because it relies on interviews of prisoners themselves. Anderson found that the vast majority of the 278 criminals he sampled "either perceive no risk of apprehension or have no thought about the likely punishments for their crimes" and that virtually all "are undeterred by harsher punishments because drugs, psychosis, ego, revenge, or fight-or-flight impulses inhibit the desired responses to traditional prevention methods." Only 11 percent of the violent criminals and only 24 percent of the entire sample seemed responsive to the prohibitions of the criminal law.[52]

In other words, most criminals are not the rational actors favored by economic models.[53] Thus, even if a preventive regime is, in theory, a less effective deterrent than the current system, in practice it may well be no worse. Furthermore, as discussed below, its behavior-shaping effects on third parties (rational or not) may be augmented by its relatively greater impact in social influence terms. In the meantime, risk management aimed at dealing with individual substance abuse, mental disorder, and antisocial behavior patterns are much more likely than a punishment model to prevent further crime by the types of individuals Anderson describes.

Note that, by eschewing general deterrence as a rationale for government intervention, the preventive regime also avoids one of the main complaints about typical utilitarian approaches to punishment. Government intervention meant to be an incentive for *others* to avoid crime can result in "using" offenders, sometimes in a manner disproportionate to either their culpability or dangerousness.[54] A preventive regime, in contrast, is not justified by its effects on third parties. Preventive intervention may have a general deterrent effect, but its focus is on reducing a specific offender's propensity to commit crime.

C. Objections Derived from Virtue Ethics

Hart was aware of the "imperfect" nature of the punishment model as a deterrent; to him, a concern "more serious by far" than the objection that a preventive regime might defeat deterrence was that it "would undermine the foundation of a free society's effort to build up each individual's sense of responsibility as a guide and a stimulus to the constructive development of his capacity for effectual and fruitful decision."[55] This line of reasoning is consistent with virtue ethics theory, which views punishment as a demand that each person develop and exhibit good character traits, and thus is critical not only of the prevention model, but also of classical retributivists.[56]

To use an example proffered by Kyron Huigens,[57] a proponent of virtue ethics would punish a person for rape even if the person honestly thought, because of his drunkenness and the fact that the victim's husband had told him she would be aroused by forcible intercourse, that the protestations of the victim were feigned. A retributivist interested in culpability might have trouble with this position because of the lack of culpable intent.[58] But Huigens also considers relevant to the analysis the defendant's "severe voluntary intoxication, his poor choice of friends, his ability to make himself believe whatever he finds it convenient to believe and a general moral obtuseness, as evidenced by his failure to perceive not only a woman's genuine resistance to forced sexual intercourse, but also the fact that even a simulated rape is an act degrading to human dignity."[59] Such a person should be punished both because he is at fault for having "inadequate and flawed practical judgement" and because "the justifying purpose of the criminal law is the inculcation of sound practical judgment—a quality which is also known as virtue."[60]

This latter point, which echoes Hart, greatly exaggerates the importance of and need for the criminal law in shaping the character of the general populace. Family, peers, schools, churches, and various other institutions are likely to be much more effective at achieving that aim.[61] Nor is punishment likely to be the best way to inculcate sound practical judgment in individuals who cause harm. Even assuming a generic jury verdict can get the message across, telling the "rapist" his punishment is due to his various character traits as well as his acts seems like a relatively blunt instrument for doing so. An individualized prevention regime, focused on the types of risk factors that Huigens identifies, would be much better at developing good judgment.

As to whether punishment is nonetheless mandated when one fails to develop a capacity for such judgment on one's own, that question threatens to plunge us into the middle of the determinism–free-will debate, which is taken up in Part Three. It will suffice to say at this point that behavioral scientists who promote the prevention model find difficult enough the retributivist claim that intentions are the principal causes of behavior (a recent symposium issue of *American Psychologist* was titled "Behavior—It's Involuntary").[62] They would find even more problematic assertions that people who commit crime are responsible, *ex ante*, for their moral obtuseness or personal acquaintances. Rather than condemn the individual for these traits, it makes more sense to behavioral scientists, both from the crime prevention and human dignity perspectives, to confront the morally bankrupt, relationship-poor individual and help him structure his life in a more satisfactory manner. If antisocial behavior persists, then prolonged incapacitation might be necessary, not as a matter of desert (which is ambiguous at best) or in an effort to teach others (who either are not listening or already know better), but as a preventive measure.

II. Implementation Objections to the Preventive Model

This discussion leads to the major practical objection to the prevention model: it simply is not feasible. We do not have the tools of prediction, nor have we developed the methods of rehabilitation, to implement an effective risk management system and, even if we did, it would be far too expensive. These objections are plausible, but are not particularly persuasive when ranged against analogous problems associated with the punishment model.

A. Inaccuracy and Its Consequences

Twenty-three years ago the Supreme Court—quoting the "leading" researcher on violence prediction, John Monahan—voiced the standard statement about our ability to predict dangerousness: at least two out of three individuals the experts label "dangerous" will *not* commit a violent act.[63] But within a year of the Court's statement, Monahan himself had suggested that, in light of new research using more sophisticated methodology, predictions of dangerousness made by mental health professionals are closer to fifty percent accurate.[64] He has also noted that any estimates of predictive accuracy are likely to be skewed downward by the fact that the research on which they are based almost always uses samples of people who are immediately institutionalized after a positive prediction, thus making impossible observation of their actions had they been left alone, which is the true test of the prediction.[65]

In any event, prediction science has improved immensely since 1983. The MacArthur Research Network, of which Monahan is a member, has done outstanding recent work on risk assessment. Using "iterative classification trees" (akin to an actuarial flow chart), experts can now identify groups of individuals with recidivism rates of 76 percent, 52 percent, and so on, down to a group that has a 1 percent chance of recidivism. The classifications depend on factors that are relatively easily to calibrate, such as age, psychopathy (measured on a highly reliable instrument), prior arrests, serious child abuse, alcohol or drug use, violent fantasies, and legal status.[66] Developers of an instrument called the Psychopathy Checklist-Revised can identify a group that has a 77 percent chance of recidivism over a three-year period.[67] Various other researchers claim their predictive methods are similarly accurate with a wide array of criminal populations.[68]

Opponents of a preventive regime will note, however, that these developments in prediction technology, as impressive as they are, still do not amount to proof beyond a reasonable doubt. Thus, the argument goes, any regime that relies on prediction, at least when that prediction results in incarceration, is illegitimate. There are several responses to this oft repeated observation.

First, as the previous chapter indicated, many of the current system's threshold determinations are at least as flawed as the predictions that would need to be made in a preventive regime. To begin with, as any criminal law expert knows, huge disagreement exists over the types of *mentes reae* that merit punishment, even for serious crimes such as homicide (with particular heat generated over whether punishment is warranted for felony murder, which imposes murder liability even for accidental killings).[69] Putting those irresolvable conundrums aside, experience and research demonstrate that judicial and jury conclusions about core culpability concepts—such as premeditation, recklessness, and insanity—differ significantly across individuals and across juries. Given this unreliability, many of these conclusions about blameworthiness cannot possibly achieve the 90 to 95 percent degree of accuracy normally associated with the reasonable doubt standard. That should not be surprising, given the ill-defined scope of legal mental states,[70] and the difficulty of investigating subjective beliefs and desires.[71] But it is disturbing: as Chapter 4 noted, these unreliable assessments can spell the difference between a conviction for manslaughter and eligibility for the death penalty, or between a prison term and indeterminate institutionalization in a mental hospital.

For many crimes—say taking someone's purse, where the doing of the act often permits confident assessments of mental state—inaccuracy of this sort is generally not a problem. But even for these types of crimes, arriving at a consensus on the appropriate sentence—whether the metric is just deserts, deterrence, or practical reasoning skills—is similarly impossible.[72] On what basis, for instance, can retributive, deterrent, or ethical theory distinguish between a two-year sentence, as opposed to a two-month sentence or any sentence in between, for petty theft? The vagaries in scientific investigation that bedevil the risk management approach are trivial compared to the calibration chores that afflict a retributivist regime bent on ascertaining degree of culpability, a deterrence-based system that purports to modulate the penalty based on cost-benefit analysis, or a virtue ethics scheme that tries to measure fault for character.[73]

Another type of inaccuracy associated with the punishment model has to do with the form, rather than the length, of disposition. Imprisonment, which is the most common type of punishment, is in a deep sense not commensurate with blame; depriving individuals of virtually all their freedom because they raped, robbed, or assaulted someone is a gigantic moral non-sequitur. If we are really interested in retributive punishment, the biblical eye-for-an-eye shibboleth comes much closer to getting it right, and if we are really interested in repaying society or the victim then, as restorative justice advocates argue,[74] reparation is more appropriate. Yet the first response is rightly viewed with repugnance, and the second response, most desert theorists would say, is insufficiently punitive.[75] The result is that most dispositions under a desert-based punishment model bear only a tenuous relationship to their rationale.[76]

Risk management, in contrast, is structured to achieve the precise aims of the prevention model. Each intervention is individualized, based on the need to deal with specific risk factors. Institutionalization makes perfect sense on this view (although, as noted below, only if no other less restrictive intervention will prevent the perceived harm). Restitution to and communicating with the victim also is consistent with the prevention premise, at least to the extent that it helps the offender restructure his or her behavior by gaining an understanding of the true harm caused by the offending act.

A third response to the inaccuracy point is that the *cost* of a mistake in a risk management regime is likely to be much lower than the cost of a mistake under the punishment model. Under the latter model, once culpability is assessed, the fix is in; the degree of blame determines the type and the length, or at least the range, of liberty deprivation. Under a prevention regime, in contrast, risk is constantly monitored and, if considered low enough, release occurs; such periodic review is probably constitutionally required.[77] Furthermore, as just noted, the dispositional emphasis is on community-based programs, which are a viable alternative even for some violent offenders.[78] Indeed, community dispositions are both legally and pragmatically necessary to a preventive regime. As a constitutional matter, Chapter 4 pointed out, the degree of liberty deprivation should be limited to that necessary to achieve the government's prevention aims. As a practical matter, it is almost impossible to predict or change behavior in the community when a person is sitting in a prison.

Those familiar with the sexual predator programs—which routinely incarcerate and rarely release—may be skeptical of these latter claims. But, as their postsentence focus indicates, the sexual predator programs of today are really appendages of a punishment regime, not a bona fide implementation of the prevention model. Under the sex psychopath programs of the mid-twentieth century, which operated in *lieu* of a sentence, release and conditional release were quite common.[79] The better illustration of the risk management approach is the drug court, which uses incarceration as a last resort. As Michael Dorf and Charles Sabel note, these courts are truly "experimentalist," in the sense that they constantly modify dispositions to maximize behavior change in the offender.[80] In contrast to a punishment model, where the concept of experimentation is incoherent (since the crime definitively establishes the sanction received), the flexible nature of a risk management regime makes confinement just one of many options, relied on only when necessary to achieve specific deterrence or prevent harm. Further protection against indeterminate confinement can be guaranteed if, as I argued in Chapter 4, government's authority to prolong incapacitation is conditioned on increasingly more convincing showings of serious danger. This requirement would place practical limitations on the duration of liberty deprivation for all offenders, and especially for petty and relatively low-risk criminals.[81]

More will be said about model risk management programs below. For now, the important points are that, compared to a punishment regime, mistakes under such a program are probably no more likely, and in any event visit less deprivation of liberty and are more easily corrected.

B. Efficacy Issues

A second major source of discomfort about a preventive regime stems from the belief that, no matter how much verbal allegiance we give to the least drastic penalty notion, the default disposition will be long-term confinement, given our ignorance about how to manage risk in any other way. Although written more than twenty years ago as a review of rehabilitative efforts up to that time, Francis Allen's book *The Decline of the Rehabilitative Ideal* is still one of the best statements of this view. First, Allen noted, efforts at establishing reformation-oriented systems "have tended to inflict larger deprivations of liberty and volition on its subjects than is sometimes exacted from prisoners in more overtly punitive programs," and have ended up looking little different than the prison regimes they sought to replace. Second, these systems have usually given release decision-making authority to nonlegally trained parole boards and mental health professionals with no clear criteria for release or accountability, leading to unequal treatment, demoralization, and cynicism among offenders. Third, in Allen's straightforward words, "we do not know how to prevent criminal recidivism through rehabilitative effort."[82] That these are not simply historical observations is borne out by the current experience with sexual predator statutes that, as just noted, routinely result in long-term institutionalization, often with little or no treatment and subject only to periodic review based on vague standards.

The experience with sexual predator laws, however, should not obscure the fact that risk management techniques, like risk assessment methods, have improved immensely during the past decades.[83] In general, researchers have found that programs based on fear, punishment, or psychotherapy—the bread and butter of older rehabilitation programs—are much less likely to reduce recidivism than programs "that are highly structured and behavioral or cognitive-behavioral, that are run in the community rather than an institution, that are run with integrity and enthusiasm, that target higher-risk rather than lower-risk offenders, and that are intensive in terms of number of hours and overall length of program."[84] For instance, "multisystemic therapy," which involves intense family, school, and peer-based interventions over a four-month period, can reduce recidivism among violent juveniles by as much as 75 percent compared to matched control groups that receive no treatment or traditional treatment in prisons.[85] The same type of intensive, ecological treatment works well with many adult offenders.[86] Thus, drug treatment courts that closely monitor the offender's performance in the program, as well as of the program itself, typically cut drug use-related recidivism in half.[87] Even treatment of child molesters modeled on these principles can work, although not as dramatically. Research conducted in the past ten years indicates that cognitive therapy may reduce recidivism rates of child molesters by up to 25 percent.[88] Among all offenders involved in rehabilitation programs that meet the above criteria, the average reduction in recidivism is between 20 and 40 percent.[89]

In short, the sentencing reform mantra of the 1970s and 1980s that "nothing works" is not true.[90] Indeed, the author of the meta-review from which that famous phrase derives disavowed it within five years of its publication.[91] These findings significantly undermine one of the primary motivations behind policy makers' rejection of a reform-oriented system.

The preventive model of justice may also be relatively effective at encouraging law-abiding behavior in those who are *not* the subject of government intervention. This is not an argument from classical deterrence, which earlier discussion suggested is a weak justification for such intervention. Rather it is based on social influence theory, which claims that people tend to behave consistently with their surroundings.[92] One might think that removing criminals from the community, the usual result of punishment, would be the best method of stemming negative social influence. But there is good reason to believe that the modern criminal justice system's reaction to crime may actually increase influences toward antisocial behavior, by causing resentment toward authority, unwillingness to cooperate with law enforcement, and the dismantlement of families and other institutions that act as a brake on crime.

This is the argument of Darryl Brown, who contrasts the current punitive approach to street crime with our predominantly preventive approach toward white collar, and in particular corporate, crime.[93] Brown notes that, rather than routinely resorting to imprisonment, prosecutors working white collar cases often rely on "civil" remedies such as restitution, enforcement of compliance programs, and other attempts to restructure the corporate culture. In doing so, they implicitly recognize the force of social influence on would-be wrongdoers, as well as the unnecessary damage a punitive approach would wreak on employees and shareholders. Brown contends that the government's response to street crime could follow the same "preventive, compliance-oriented" path it takes with respect to corporate crime: "It could take advantage of, rather than ignore and contradict, knowledge about social influence: it could more fully assess and minimize the social costs of punishment." His examples of how this social influence approach would work are the same types of risk management programs described above—drug treatment courts, victim-offender mediation, and "survivor-centered" domestic violence policies—which together target "a broad slice of the criminal justice system" (drug offenders, property offenses among neighbors, and violence among intimates).[94] Brown's work suggests that an individual-centered preventive system has a better cost-benefit ratio than a punitive one even when crime-related costs and benefits are defined broadly, to include interests beyond those associated with reducing the recidivism of the individual criminal.[95]

Risk management programs probably cannot eliminate the abuses of discretion, the disparity in dispositions, and the demoralization effects that Allen rightly associates with the rehabilitative agenda. But, again, comparison with the punishment model suggests that a modern preventive regime might well be an improvement on all three counts.

Abuse of discretion occurs in any system. In a preventive regime it is most likely to occur during disposition, while under the punishment model it occurs during the charging stage. Given the discretion granted prosecutors, the latter process can produce wildly irrational results; for instance, whether a person receives a life sentence or a few years in prison may depend entirely on whether he or she is willing to "deal."[96] Even worse, the charging and bargaining process is notoriously difficult to monitor.[97] In contrast, risk management decisions are much more transparent, not only because a public hearing is held periodically, but because risk assessment will usually be based on statistically derived factors that result from peer-reviewed research, and therefore can more easily police for use of illegitimate factors such as race.

As to disparity, that is in the eye of the beholder. To some, treating all armed robbers alike makes sense.[98] But, in fact, the desert visited by a particular term of imprisonment varies from robber to robber, depending on the conditions of imprisonment and the nature of the offender.[99] Thus, a system that stresses consistency of treatment for those who represent similar risks may be more equitable. The intense judicial resistance to the desert-based federal sentencing guidelines seems to indicate that many judges favor the latter form of equality.[100]

The demoralization claim about risk management approaches is most plausible when they require indeterminate, potentially lifelong confinement to be effective at prevention (and there certainly would be such cases).[101] But here, too, the claim can be exaggerated. Offenders subjected to this type of confinement, although not always told a time certain when they will cease being a managee, *are* given specific goals they must achieve, such as completion of vocational programs, or satisfactory behavioral control during a conditional release.[102] Compared to waiting out a period that bears no necessary relationship to their ability to function in a law-abiding manner, that approach may be psychologically less demanding. It is also more likely to enhance individual responsibility; time of release in a preventive regime is to a significant extent controlled by the offender, which should not only enhance rehabilitative success, but also energize those with the potential to be law-abiding.[103]

C. Costs

A third pragmatic objection to preventive regimes is their fiscal impact. As Allen put it, advocates of penal reform have often displayed "a splendid disregard for the fact of scarce resources."[104] Again, the sexual predator experience suggests Allen's observation is still true today. The state of Illinois estimated that initiation of a sex offender program in that state would cost $1 billion over ten years.[105]

Again, however, the modern sexual predator program is the wrong paradigm for many types of offenders. Multisystemic therapy, described above, costs $29,000 less per juvenile than boot camp, and less still than traditional detention.[106] Drug court dispositions are significantly less expensive than prison terms for small-time drug dealers and addicts.[107] For many other types of offenders, halfway houses, day programs, furloughs, and other types of community arrangements are cheaper than more secure dispositions, as well as more effective at reducing recidivism.[108]

None of this should suggest that a preventive regime would be inexpensive. Secure confinement would need to be maintained as an option at the same time more intermediate and community programs would need to be developed. But it should also be recognized that, under a regime that is focused on prevention rather than punishment or deterrence, the demand for secure confinement would be reduced. *Selective* incapacitation, which is the focus of individualized risk management, will always be less costly than the *general* incapacitation that results from the punishment model's focus on culpability. The most conspicuous example of general incapacitation—the "three strikes and you're out" statute—is a serious burden on the fiscal integrity of many state correctional systems.[109] Yet if proof of past crime is the gravamen of intervention, three-strikes laws are an unsurprising, if not inevitable, reaction to rising crimes rates. A preventive regime, in contrast, can limit costly confinement to those with three strikes (or two or four) who are the most dangerous.[110]

When one expands the notion of cost to include the harm to others incurred as a result of preventable crime and the need to prosecute it, the prevention regime should do even better by comparison to the current system, for reasons already suggested. The sole goal of a preventive regime is to reduce crime. By definition, that is not the only goal of a regime based on just deserts.

III. The Impending Lessons of Science

To this point, this chapter has proceeded largely by defending the preventive model against criticisms that have been leveled at it. Along the way, however, it has noted several positive aspects of the model, including its treatment of the offender as an individual worthy of respect, its potential for self-correction, and its efficacy at crime reduction. At least one other benefit of a preventive regime deserves special attention: the ease with which it can assimilate new scientific discoveries about human behavior. This capacity may be its single most important advantage in achieving criminal "justice."

A. The Implications of Hard Determinism

The increasing accuracy of prediction based on demographic and situational factors, described earlier, is one of many pieces of evidence that behavioral scientists rely on in arguing that all human behavior is determined by biology, upbringing, and the current environment. As Chapter 2 noted, a significant amount of evidence more directly supports this proposition. Very briefly described here, it suggests that our actions are wholly caused by factors over which we have no control (hard determinism), or at least that we are strongly predisposed to act in certain ways (soft determinism).

A number of studies indicate that genes, organic processes, and early childhood experiences play a very influential role in criminal behavior. Research on animals has found that the presence or absence of particular genes and hormones has a significant impact on levels of aggression.[111] Twin and adoption studies point to heredity as a major determinant in the development of criminal behavior, which environmental factors can exacerbate.[112] Frontal lobe impairments, low serotonin levels and variations in dopamine receptors have been associated with increased aggressive and impulsive behavior.[113] When these anomalies are combined with abuse as a child, antisocial behavior is even more likely.[114] Although no one gene or biological trait is going to explain violent or other antisocial behavior, some scientists believe that a mixture of such factors, triggered by environmental stimuli, may well do so.[115]

Social and cognitive psychology research has also produced insights into the link (or lack thereof) between thought process and behavior. Unconscious, automatic processes dominate human cognition, from the initial perception of events to responses to them[116] (which is not surprising, given the degree of reflexive behavior in animals). More specifically, phenomena such as personality type, heuristic ways of thinking, and neural pathways that develop in response to external stimuli determine the information or events we notice and the way we interpret them.[117] Moreover, we frequently are not aware of these bases for judgment,[118] and often are wrong in our explanation for our choices and behaviors.[119] Research also suggests that the "reasons" for a particular action may well follow, rather than precede, the unconscious processes that produce the behavior, and sometimes may even follow the action itself, acting as an unconscious rationalization of it.[120] In other words, our intentions and motivations are not only often caused by processes of which we are not aware but may not even be the direct impetus for our actions.

As many have pointed out,[121] if the full implications of this research turn out to be true of human behavior, the premises of a desert or general-deterrence model of government intervention become much more tenuous, if not unsupportable. If our acts result from phenomena over which we have no control, the claim that we "deserve" to be punished for our antisocial conduct or can be deterred from it by general proscriptions of conduct is difficult to sustain, even if the conduct is "intentional." Compatibilists (those who think that the free will paradigm and determinism can be reconciled) argue that, even if determinism is true, people may still justifiably be held responsible for actions that are caused by intact practical reasoning.[122] But, without regurgitating the full debate or trying to resolve the ultimate issue, it is easy to see why many have concluded their logic is faulty: Even assuming that reasons do cause behavior, determinism (which compatibilists accept arguendo) dictates that reasons are determined as well. Nor can we easily say, as virtue ethics theorists posit, that we are responsible for our character, if the way we perceive and respond to the world depends on our character. In addition to this serious chicken-and-egg conundrum, these theorists have to deal with the extensive research literature indicating that most character formation occurs in the developmental years leading up to age fourteen, when the person can hardly be held responsible for how he or she turns out.[123]

B. The Implications of Soft Determinism

The determinist hypothesis has not yet been proven, and may never be; certainly, many of us intuitively reject it, based on our daily experience, and the academic debate has, to date, resulted in a stalemate.[124] But one does not have to subscribe to hard determinism to recognize that discoveries about the causes of antisocial conduct can (and should) create substantial stress within the criminal justice system. As Chapter 2 indicated, serious arguments have been made in favor of defenses based on chromosonal abnormalities, psychopathy, rotten social background, cultural differences, black rage, TV "intoxication," battered women syndrome, and a host of other genetic and situational phenomena, a list ultimately limited only by the imagination.[125] Some of these defenses are based on very weak empirical evidence, but all have some logic and science to them.[126] At the least, these various assertions suggest that many people who commit crime find avoiding it very difficult.

A system based on desert ought to take this fact into account, but our current criminal justice system, perhaps due to fear of psychiatric minefields or perhaps simply out of moral blindness,[127] is very reluctant to do so. The insanity defense is limited to an extremely narrow set of offenders, typically recognizing an exculpatory claim only in cases involving a psychotic-like cognitive impairment.[128] And, in a large number of jurisdictions, the rest of the criminal code continues to adhere to objective "reasonable person" tests for mistake and affirmative defenses that contemplate little or no mitigation for behavioral deficiencies.[129] The Model Penal Code's attempt to define mens rea is even more revealing because, as noted in Chapter 2, the Code represents one of the most rigorous efforts to subjectify the blameworthiness inquiry.[130] In its definitions of the provocation defense, duress, and recklessness (the latter of which is also relevant, in some circumstances, to the scope of defenses such as self-defense), the Code speaks in terms of what a person in the actor's "situation" would have perceived or experienced.[131] That term is intentionally left undefined in the black letter of the Code, so that it could, on its face, include virtually any aspect of the individual's personality or environment, including impairments due to genetics, psychopathy, trauma, and all of the other factors that behaviorists think contribute to behavior. Yet, with the possible exception of the provocation defense (which in any event only applies to homicide),[132] the Code's commentary on these provisions states that the interpretation of "situation" in these contexts should allow consideration only of "[s]tark, tangible factors" such as "size, strength, age or health," not "[m]atters of temperament."[133] Elsewhere, the commentary indicates that "heredity" and "intelligence" are also not to be encompassed within the actor's "situation" in appraising these mental states.[134]

The Code's unwillingness to contemplate "internal" factors, particularly in assessing recklessness, which is the Code's default mens rea for both offenses and defenses,[135] contradicts its commitment to blameworthiness based on subjective desert. It may be easier to discern size and age as compared to intelligence or temperament, but there is no culpability-based reason for the kinds of distinctions the Code makes. As a theoretical matter the line-drawing exemplified in the Code is arbitrary; it evades, rather than faces, the logical consequences of a desert-based system.

The contention is sometimes made that any culpability-mitigating circumstances not considered at trial can be given due weight at sentencing, which is the tack this book takes in Chapter 3.[136] But this gambit admits that culpability is only of secondary importance in defining crime, prevents juries from playing the role they are best suited to fill in a desert-based system, and, given the low visibility of sentencing, hides the core decisions about punishment from the public.[137] If sentencing statutes could make clear the extent to which various mitigating factors affected disposition, at least the implications of desert-based punishment would be clarified. But, as already noted in this chapter and throughout this book, there are no clear criteria for making these types of distinctions, whether they take place at trial or at sentencing.

In a recent article, Stephen Morse, a leading retributivist, concedes as much. Morse agrees both that current criminal law takes insufficient account of diminished responsibility due to mental and behavioral impairments, and that the jury, rather than the sentencing judge, ought to decide whether responsibility is diminished.[138] But because "we have only the limited ability to make the fine-grained responsibility judgments that are possible in theory," he eschews any attempt to grade culpability in a nuanced fashion. Instead he proposes a generic "guilty but partially responsible" defense that would reduce sentence by the same amount for every defendant whose "substantially diminished rationality . . . substantially affected [the] criminal conduct." As he states, "[t]his proposal would lump together for the same degree of reduction defendants convicted of the same crime but who have disparately impaired rationality and consequently different responsibility." Although he admits that "[t]his may seem a denial of equal justice," the "failure to provide perfect justice in this imperfect world is not a decisive, or even weighty, objection in this instance."[139] Evaluations of weightiness aside, Morse's admissions that the present desert-based system largely ignores the mitigating impact of biology and situation, and that even his reform requires significant compromise, suggests that the punishment model literally cannot do justice to the variety of human motivations for crime.[140]

A preventive regime, in contrast, neither ignores the biological and situational causes of crime nor arbitrarily limits their relevance. Rather, its individualized dispositions explicitly experiment with means of reducing their impact. As scientific knowledge about crime advances, a desert regime will either have to abandon its own premises or resort to clumsy adjustments, while a preventive regime is well situated, both in theory and in practice, to integrate new information into the intervention calculus.

Conclusion

The punishment model of the criminal law is currently threatened by the newly popular prevention model of intervention, a model of intervention based on predictions of risk uncabined by culpability assessments. This chapter has argued that this trend is not necessarily a bad thing; it may be time to swing the pendulum back toward a preventive model, albeit with some modifications. A preventive regime that is limited to interventions after nonaccidental, unjustified harmful acts, and that engages in competent risk assessment and risk management, might well be superior to the current system of criminal justice, or to any system of criminal justice based primarily on desert, deterrence, or ethical philosophy. Such a preventive regime would be more effective at preventing crime and assimilating new scientific information about human behavior, and probably would be no more inaccurate or costly than the punishment model.

Of course, there may be serious constitutional problems with a preventive model of criminal justice. Although *Hendricks* upheld the sexual predator regime, it did so on condition that the state prove that a "mental abnormality" causes the dangerousness underlying the commitment.[141] As Chapter 4 noted, that phrase is virtually meaningless as a limitation on commitment. But by no stretch is it ambiguous enough to cover every person who commits an antisocial act. Another possible constitutional obstacle to a preventive regime is its nonchalance toward mens rea. In Morrissette v. United States, for instance, the Court stated that "[t]he contention that an injury can amount to a crime only when inflicted by intention . . . is as universal and persistent in mature systems of law as belief in freedom of the human will and a consequent ability and duty of the normal individual to choose between good and evil."[142] Procedure-related obstacles to a preventive regime might also arise under the Constitution. In particular, a system that depends on expert assessment of risk and treatability could diminish the role of jury decision making, which the Sixth Amendment requires for all "criminal prosecutions."[143]

The latter two objections probably do not pose insurmountable obstacles to a preventive regime. *Morrissette* notwithstanding, the Supreme Court has been quite ambivalent about requiring particular mental states as a matter of due process;[144] in any event the regime proposed here would not permit intervention for nonnegligent or justified acts. And although a preventive system would rely heavily on experts, it would not have to derogate the roles of juries and judges, contrary to the claims of some of its opponents.[145] Juries should be instrumental in determining whether a person committed a nonaccidental, unjustified harm, and judges should be involved in monitoring risk assessment and risk management, as occurs in drug courts. Ultimately, the degree of risk necessary to authorize intervention, and the restraint on liberty and intrusiveness of treatment legitimated by a given degree of risk, are moral/legal questions that laypeople and legal experts, not clinical ones, should decide.[146]

The decision in *Hendricks* that confinement based on dangerousness may take place only when linked to abnormality—affirmed by the Court in Kansas v. Crane[147]—is not so easily finessed, however. If that decision stands, immediate implementation of a preventive regime may not be possible, at least for adults.[148] Added to this constitutional impasse are the related psycho-social concerns that were discounted but not dismissed in the foregoing pages. First, it is possible, as Robinson suggests, that an abrupt end to blaming practices would undermine the criminal law's legitimacy.[149] Second, even if determinism is true, a criminal law that appears to endorse the notion that people cannot control their fate might have a significant debilitating impact.[150] Although this chapter contends that a preventive regime should not have these effects (and that, in any event, the criminal law is only one among many behavior-shaping institutions in society), as of yet we do not know enough to evaluate these claims.

Thus, even if one agrees with the general thrust of the arguments made here, legal and sociological considerations may counsel that some aspects of the punishment model be maintained, at least for a transitional period. Specifically, culpability determinations might remain a fixture at the trial stage; their retention as a liability predicate probably satisfies *Hendricks*,[151] and their visibility would assure the public that the criminal justice system still takes blame seriously. However, once conviction occurs, disposition should be based on risk management principles; no minimum or maximum terms would be imposed. Routine risk assessment, periodic review, community placements, and rehabilitation efforts would be the focus of the postconviction process. That version of indeterminate sentencing, although not a pure preventive model, might be a significant first step toward civilizing the criminal law.

—III—

The Protection Model

— 6 —

Competency in the Criminal Process

Recall that the third model of liberty deprivation—the protection model—authorizes government interventions to ensure autonomous decision making. For reasons developed in Chapter 1, government should generally allow people to make their own decisions when the consequences of the decision do not pose substantial harm to others. That preference for autonomy derives from the Millsian notions that people are ordinarily better than government officials at judging their own interests and that, in any event, maintaining individual decision-making rights is the best means of assuring that decision-making capacities are developed (a valued objective in democratic societies). The preference for autonomy also flows from the Kantian principle that taking away the opportunity to decide would show insufficient respect for the person.

Conversely, when a person *lacks* autonomy, society is not required, and may even be obligated, to override his or her choices, even if they affect no one else. Because the latter, "incompetent" people are deemed unable to understand their own interests, we are more willing to ignore their decisions, even if doing so will make them feel minimized. To take an extreme example, suppose a man is unable to control his bodily movements and is unable to speak. When asked a question, his head nods "yes" or "no" completely randomly. Most would agree that taking some important action—say, giving or withholding experimental but potentially life-saving treatment—based on such a nod would be improper. There is no necessary correlation between the nod and the person's "true" desires. Indeed, the nod is not really a "choice" in any sense of the word; acting on it could be viewed as an insult to him. Therefore, consistent with the autonomy preference, the state is justified in attempting to enable him to respond in a meaningful fashion and, if that fails, in making the decision for him if a decision is necessary.

A second justification for refusing to honor the man's "decision" and allowing government intervention under these circumstances is more general in nature. Acting on a random nod would not only be insulting to the individual, it would also make a mockery of the concept of autonomy itself. It would suggest that society sanctions random decision making. Thus, ensuring competency protects not only individual interests, but those of society at large.

As the next chapter explains, the protection model's authorization of government intervention over incompetent decision makers is related, but not necessarily congruent with, the traditional parens patriae power,[1] which is said to justify a number of government "civil" interventions, including involuntary hospitalization of those who are dangerous to themselves, guardianship proceedings, and forcible psychiatric treatment. In the criminal adjudication setting, the topic of this chapter, the model is operationalized through several different competency requirements. For instance, a criminal defendant must be competent to stand trial, competent to plead guilty, competent to waive rights, and competent to undergo the sentencing process. If a person is incompetent in one or more of these respects, both current legal doctrine and the protection model advanced in this chapter presumptively authorize the state to take any one of a number of steps, including rejection of the defendant's decision, continuance of the proceedings and, at least when the crime is serious, forced hospitalization and treatment to restore competency.[2]

Many of the nuances that arise when the protection model is applied to criminal cases came to the fore in one of the more well-known federal prosecutions of the 1990s. In January 1998, Theodore Kaczynski, the self-named Unabomber, was indicted on capital murder charges as a result of deaths caused by "letter bombs" he sent through the mail.[3] Even before he was taken into custody, his "Manifesto" fueled speculation about his mental state.[4] After his arrest, suspicions were confirmed that he was a highly intelligent but mentally disturbed individual. Evaluators for both the defense and the court unanimously concluded that he suffered from paranoid schizophrenia.[5] Not surprisingly, his lawyers decided that Kaczynski's best defense at trial would be some form of mental state defense, and that, if he were convicted, the case in mitigation at sentencing should be based on mental abnormality.[6]

Kaczynski, however, had other ideas. He repeatedly refused to allow psychiatric defenses to be posed on his behalf, and threatened to fire his attorneys if they persisted in that strategy.[7] Although his preferred defense strategy was never clear, Kaczynski may have wanted to assert some type of "necessity" defense,[8] to the effect that his letter bombs were a justifiable effort to put a stop to the depredations of technology (all his victims were in some way connected to technological innovation).[9] Furthermore, it appears that Kaczynski was willing to pursue his aims without legal representation if necessary.[10]

To the relief of many, Kaczynski's case never went to trial. An airing of a necessity-type defense, with Kaczynski representing himself, might have resulted in a fiasco not unlike the trial of Colin Ferguson, a psychotic man accused of gunning down six people on a Long Island Railroad train who fired his attorneys and argued, despite several eyewitnesses' testimony to the contrary, that he was not the perpetrator.[11] On the other hand, allowing Kaczynski's attorneys to proceed with a defense based on mental abnormality over their client's objection would probably have resulted in periodic confrontations between Kaczynski and his lawyers, if not complete pandemonium in the courtroom (Kaczynski's one courtroom outburst occurred when he came to believe that the judge and his attorneys were going to force him to raise a mental state defense).[12] Perhaps concerned about the spectacle a full-blown trial of such an individual might create,[13] the government eventually offered a life sentence without parole, an offer Kaczynski accepted.[14]

The Kaczynski case casts in stark relief the tension created by a criminal justice system that insists on client autonomy at the same time it claims to convict only those who deserve punishment. Out of respect for Kaczynski's autonomy, society may feel obligated to honor his decision to abandon legal claims bottomed on assertions of mental abnormality. Yet out of concern that only the culpable be convicted, we may also feel uneasy about convicting and sentencing to death someone like Kaczynski without at least airing the impact his mental illness had on his criminal liability.

For similar reasons, the Unabomber case also raises serious issues about the role of the defense lawyer in criminal prosecutions. The traditional view is that the client determines overall goals or ends, while the lawyer is in charge of determining the tactics or means necessary to achieve the goal.[15] Are the insanity defense and similar defenses "ends," or "means" for achieving ends, such as an acquittal or a reduced charge or sentence? If a defense based on mental abnormality is an end, and therefore controlled by the client, can the court or defense attorney nonetheless dictate the use of a mental abnormality defense over the defendant's objection when the client is suffering from mental disability (which will often be the case when a mental state defense is being considered)? If so, how does the attorney decide when a client is sufficiently impaired due to mental illness to justify overriding the client's decision? Assuming the lawyer concludes the client is incompetent to make decisions, what steps should the lawyer take? If, instead, the client is competent, does an ethical commitment to client autonomy mandate that lawyers always defer to the client's preferences, regardless of concerns for decorum or the likelihood that, as was probably true in the Kaczynski case, the client's decision would make a death sentence inevitable?

This chapter provides a framework for answering such questions. The foundation for that framework is a conceptually sound definition of competency. Because a client who is competent is presumptively entitled to make fundamental decisions regarding his or her case, while an incompetent one is not, the competency construct is an essential component of the criminal justice system's approach to resolving the conflict between autonomy and culpability. I argue in this chapter that, when the issue is whether a client is competent to waive a mental state defense, plead guilty, or waive the right to an attorney, the competency test should focus on "basic rationality and self-regard." This test requires the client to have an understanding of the rudiments of the criminal process, the ability to give nondelusional reasons for the decision in question, and enough self-regard to consider alternative reasons. The basic rationality and self-regard formulation is probably more demanding than the test the U.S. Supreme Court requires (depending on how one construes the Court's decision in Godinez v. Moran,[16] discussed in detail below), but is significantly less stringent than what some lower courts have mandated.

Once a client's competence is assessed with some degree of certainty, the defense attorney is confronted with three possible scenarios, each of which produces its own set of controversies. First, the attorney may believe the client is incompetent. In this situation the attorney has an ethical obligation to ensure the client receives treatment to restore competency, even if that obligation requires raising the incompetency issue in court. Although that prescription may seem obvious, a number of commentators have suggested otherwise, given the negative consequences of an incompetency determination (for example, psychotropic medication or prolonged hospitalization). A preference for autonomy and a number of practical considerations dictate the more traditional response to the incompetent client.

Second, the client may be considered competent, either as an initial matter or after receiving treatment to restore competency. In this situation, the client's decisions should usually govern, at least in the three areas on which this chapter focuses: pleading guilty, waiving mental state defenses, and waiving the right to an attorney. I also suggest, however, that the competent client's decision on these matters may be overridden when compelling state interests in assuring the reliability or dignity of the proceedings are at stake. Thus, for instance, in the case of Kaczynski (whom the court found competent), the defense attorneys' strategy should have prevailed despite Kaczynski's preference, if the defense attorneys had believed that the insanity defense was the only viable defense, that it had a good chance of success, and that it was clearly in Kaczynski's best interests to assert it. It must also be noted, however, that the likelihood that all three of these criteria will be met in a given case (including Kaczynski's) is extremely low.

The third competency-related scenario confronted by the defense attorney occurs when a good faith effort at restoring the client to competency is unsuccessful. In this situation, I argue that, despite constitutional precedent to the contrary, dismissal of the charges is not always necessary. Rather, when only the client's decision-making competency is at issue, the lawyer should be authorized to assume control of the case, because in this situation the client's autonomy is nonexistent.

The first part of the chapter describes and critiques the current state of the law regarding criminal competencies, focusing on the Supreme Court's decision in *Godinez*. The second part then sets out the basic rationality and self-regard competency formulation in more detail and explains its benefits. The final part examines the defense attorney's ethical obligations to the incompetent client who may be restorable, the competent client who disagrees with the attorney, and the client whose competence is unrestorable.

I. The Legal Landscape

As noted above, there are numerous "criminal competencies," including competency to stand trial, competency to plead guilty, and competency to waive an insanity defense. An issue that has bedeviled the courts is whether these different competencies require different levels of cognitive ability. The Supreme Court's decision in *Godinez* apparently answered that question in the negative, but in the course of doing so has raised even more questions.

A. Godinez v. Moran

Prior to *Godinez,* which was decided in 1993, most courts held that a person who is competent to stand trial is also competent to plead guilty. A few courts, however, required a greater capacity in the latter setting, as well as when the defendant waives counsel. One court in this minority was the Ninth Circuit Court of Appeals, which issued a major decision on the issue ten years before *Godinez* in Sieling v. Eyman.[17] In line with the Supreme Court's opinion in Dusky v. United States,[18] *Sieling* acknowledged that defendants are competent to stand trial if they have "a rational, as well as a factual, understanding" of the proceedings and are capable of assisting their counsel.[19] But the Ninth Circuit also declared that defendants are competent to plead guilty or waive counsel only if they also have the "ability to make a reasoned choice among the alternatives presented to him."[20] Under this standard, *Sieling* explained, a person who is competent to stand trial is not necessarily also competent to plead guilty or waive counsel.[21] As the Ninth Circuit subsequently put it in its opinion in Godinez v. Moran: "[c]ompetency to waive constitutional rights requires a higher level of mental functioning than that required to stand trial."[22]

The rationale for this differentiation between competencies, according to *Sieling,* is that competency should be assessed "with specific reference to the gravity of the decisions with which the defendant is faced." Trial competency, the court further asserted, is not a sufficient basis for finding that the defendant is able to make decisions of "very serious import."[23] In the latter category the court included both the decision about whether to represent oneself and the choice about whether to plead guilty and thus surrender the rights to trial counsel, jury, confrontation of accusers, and remain silent.[24]

In contrast, as noted above, the majority of courts equated the competency to stand trial and competency to plead guilty standards.[25] These courts seem to be motivated primarily by practical concerns. As one court stated, a dual competency standard would "create a class of semi-competent defendants who are not protected from prosecution because they have been found competent to stand trial, but who are denied the leniency of the plea bargaining process because they are not competent to plead guilty."[26]

In *Godinez* the Supreme Court resolved this controversy, at least as a federal constitutional matter. Disagreeing with the Ninth Circuit's approach, it held that, under the Due Process Clause, a person who is competent to stand trial is competent both to plead guilty and to waive counsel in federal court. (States are still free to require a "greater" level of competency in their courts.)

The Court's analysis with respect to the competency required to plead guilty was straightforward. According to the Court, "the decision to plead guilty . . . is no more complicated than the sum total of decisions that a defendant may be called upon to make during the course of a trial."[27] Similar to those who plead guilty, defendants undergoing trial may have to decide whether to waive the right to a jury, to confront certain accusers, and to take the stand (thereby surrendering the right to remain silent).

The Court's analysis with respect to competency to waive counsel was somewhat different. The Court recognized that self-representation might involve more complicated decisions than those involved in standing trial or pleading guilty. Yet this fact was irrelevant to the Court, because "the competence that is required of a defendant seeking to waive his right to counsel is the competence to waive the right, not the competence to represent himself."[28] The majority pointed out that Faretta v. California,[29] the Supreme Court case that recognized the right to represent oneself, had emphasized that "technical legal knowledge . . . [is] not relevant"[30] to determining whether a defendant is competent to proceed *pro se* and that a court must honor a competent defendant's decision to do so even though he "may conduct his own defense ultimately to his own detriment."[31] Thus, "a criminal defendant's ability to represent himself has no bearing upon his competence to *choose* self-representation."[32]

Although the *Godinez* Court held that one size competency fits all, it also required, consistent with long-established precedent, that any waiver of constitutional rights, such as occurs with a guilty plea or waiver of counsel, be "knowing and voluntary."[33] The Court explained the difference between the competency standard and the waiver standard as follows:

> [t]he focus of a competency inquiry is the defendant's mental capacity; the question is whether he has the ability to understand the proceedings. The purpose of the "knowing and voluntary" inquiry, by contrast, is to determine whether the defendant actually does understand the significance and consequences of a particular decision and whether the decision is uncoerced.[34]

Under *Godinez*, then, the following rules apply in federal court (and those state courts that follow *Godinez*). A defendant is competent to stand trial, plead guilty, waive counsel, and, presumably, waive any other rights or defenses (such as the insanity defense) if he or she meets the *Dusky* competency-to-stand-trial standard. That standard, again, requires a rational and factual understanding of the proceedings and an ability to assist counsel in the defense. Prior to *Godinez,* most courts and state statutes interpreted this language to mean that, at a minimum, a defendant must have some capacity to: (1) understand the essence of the charges; (2) understand the potential outcomes of the criminal process; (3) understand the nature of the adversary process (for example, the roles of the judge, jury, prosecutor, and defense attorney); and (4) communicate to the attorney (and, if necessary, the court) facts pertinent to the offense.[35] After *Godinez,* the courts must also ensure, if they did not already do so in connection with the third factor, that defendants have the capacity to understand the rights to silence, jury trial, confrontation, and trial counsel. Additionally, if the defendant waives any constitutional rights, he or she must not only have the capacity to understand, but also must actually understand the consequences of the waiver decision and arrive at the decision voluntarily.

B. An Analysis of *Godinez*

Godinez's equation of competency to stand trial and competency to plead guilty makes sense. The Court correctly noted that a defendant who decides to go to trial rather than plead guilty may subsequently want to waive the right to a jury trial, forego confrontation of accusers, or relinquish the right to remain silent by taking the stand, and is otherwise implicitly or explicitly deciding to retain those rights. Accordingly, defendants who proceed to trial as well as defendants who plead guilty must understand these basic guarantees. As suggested above, if this analysis changes the law in any way, it raises the threshold for competency to stand trial.

The Court's equation of competency to waive counsel with competency to stand trial may be more problematic, depending on how the Court's opinion is interpreted. As noted above, in explaining when a waiver is "knowing" the Court stressed that the defendant must "actually . . . understand the significance and consequences of [the] particular decision." This language signals that the defendant wishing to waive counsel may need to understand more facts, or different facts, than the defendant who is deciding whether to go to trial or plead guilty. Yet the Court also stated that "there is no reason to believe that the decision to waive counsel requires an appreciably higher level of mental functioning than the decision to waive other constitutional rights."[36] If, as has apparently occurred in some lower courts,[37] this latter language is interpreted to mean that any defendant capable of comprehending the facts necessary to be competent to stand trial or plead guilty can also make a valid waiver of counsel, then *Godinez* significantly undermines the autonomy preference.

Justice Harry Blackmun suggested why in his dissenting opinion in *Godinez*, stating that "[c]ompetency for one purpose does not necessarily translate to competency for another purpose."[38] The mental acuity of a person who merely meets the minimum threshold of competency to stand trial or competency to plead guilty does not approach the competency we should require of someone who wants to waive counsel. The latter individual must not only understand that, after such a decision, counsel will no longer be available to point out options, provide information about the law, and help make decisions,[39] but should also demonstrate some understanding of the details of those options, the relevant types of information, and the variety of decisions that must be made. If, for instance, the defendant cannot explain the nature of the state's evidence and the nature of his own evidence (relevant to plea negotiations as well as to going to trial), he cannot be said to "actually . . . understand the significance and consequences" of a decision to proceed without counsel. The same would be true of the defendant who cannot fathom the role an attorney plays in making opening and closing arguments, conducting direct and cross-examination, raising timely objections, and proposing precise instructions to the jury.

This is not to say, as does Blackmun in his *Godinez* dissent,[40] that defendants are competent to waive counsel only if they are competent to represent themselves. *Faretta*'s clear mandate, which flows from the autonomy preference, is that defendants should be able to waive their right to counsel to their "own detriment."[41] Thus, as the *Godinez* majority suggests, the issue in determining competency to waive counsel is not how well the person would represent himself, but rather whether the person understands "the significance and consequences" of conducting his own defense.

My concern with the majority opinion is not the test it propounds, but with the Court's apparent willingness to conclude that a low level of competency is sufficient to meet it. First, that position is inconsistent with *Faretta*. Although that case stated that a defendant need not understand technical legal rules, it also made clear that judges must ensure that defendants who wish to waive the right to counsel are "aware of the dangers and disadvantages of self-representation, so that the record will establish that 'he knows what he is doing and his choice is made with eyes open.' "[42] To the extent *Godinez* is interpreted to equate the mental capacity to stand trial with the mental capacity to waive counsel, defendants might be allowed to waive counsel even when, in effect, their eyes are "closed" to the effects of their decision, in which case it may as well be random. Such an interpretation is similar to saying that a person who can understand the significance and consequences of undergoing surgery also understands the significance and consequences of conducting that surgery oneself.[43] Yet it is far easier to comprehend the risks and benefits of properly conducted medical procedures (for example, "I know there is a 1 in 10,000 chance I could die from the surgery, but the only option is to go blind") than to comprehend how difficult it would be to choose, without the benefit of medical training, the precise procedures to use and how to carry them out.[44]

A second ambiguity in *Godinez* about competency to waive rights—one that exists whether the interest waived is the right to counsel or the rights waived when pleading guilty—concerns not what the defendant must understand but what the defendant does with the information that is understood. More specifically, the majority opinion left unclear whether a defendant's *reasons* for choosing a particular course of action are important in determining competency. The opinion starts off well enough in this regard by endorsing the *Dusky* competence standard, which requires, inter alia, "a rational as well as factual understanding of the proceedings."[45] Use of the word "rational" in addition to the word "factual" in this formulation suggests that a mere ability to describe the nature of the criminal process and the legal posture of the case is insufficient. The *Godinez* Court, however, never refers to this standard again in the opinion. Rather, as indicated above, it speaks of the person's "understanding" of the proceedings and "understanding" of the significance and consequence of any decisions made. Read literally, this latter language focuses simply on the defendant's comprehension of certain facts, not on his or her belief structure.

To understand this point, imagine a person who understands the charges against him, accurately describes how the criminal justice system works, and knows the rights he will waive if he pleads guilty, but who also believes that he should plead not guilty because he is growing smaller every day and will be invisible by the time a trial date is set. Is such a person competent to plead under the *Godinez* standard? One could say that his plea is invalid because his belief about his diminishing size means he does not understand the true consequences of his decision to plead not guilty. But one could also plausibly conclude that he *does* comprehend the "significance and conse-quences" of his decision, given his accurate perception of the legal system, the rights at stake, and the implications of giving them up.

Unfortunately, the latter interpretation of the *Godinez* standard seems to be the one actually applied by the Court in resolving the *Godinez* case itself. The defendant in *Godinez*, Richard Moran, was charged with three counts of capital murder. Nonetheless, he fired his attorneys, pleaded guilty against the advice of counsel, and presented no evidence at the capital sentencing proceeding.[46] Evidence adduced at his habeas proceeding made clear that, although he was competent to stand trial (he understood his situation and the consequences of particular decisions), he was extremely depressed at the time he made these decisions, to the point where he had no desire to de-fend himself.[47] The Supreme Court did not even mention this latter fact in its opinion, and it reversed the Court of Appeals finding that Moran was in-competent to plead guilty and waive counsel.[48] These aspects of the major-ity opinion suggest that trial courts need not consider the nature of the defendant's objectives when they determine competency.

A failure to inquire into the reasons for pleading guilty or waiving an at-torney is antithetical to a preference for autonomy. A person who under-stands his or her legal situation can still act for senseless reasons (for example, "I'm going to plead guilty because I'm getting smaller") and for reasons that demonstrate a complete lack of self-regard (which, as I argue below, was the case with Moran), as well as for no reason at all (as might be the case with the man who could only nod "yes" or "no," described at the be-ginning of this chapter). Honoring such "decisions" undermines both goals animating the preference for autonomy alluded to earlier: the goal of re-specting people's true desires and beliefs and the goal of acknowledging that doing so is an important value in our society.

Godinez should thus be interpreted to require, as *Dusky* seems to man-date, a full exploration of a defendant's reasons for waiving or asserting rights, and trial courts should base their competency decisions on the ra-tionality of those reasons. That is not what all lower courts have done, how-ever. For instance, as described below, the trial courts in the Kaczynski and Ferguson cases, both of which purported to apply *Godinez*, appeared to adopt the narrow view of *Godinez*'s understanding test.

In summary, significant questions about the appropriate approach to competency in criminal cases persist after the Supreme Court's decision in *Godinez*. In particular, the decision left unclear both the degree of competency required to waive counsel and the role reasons should play in determining competency. The next part aims to resolve these ambiguities, particularly the latter one.

II. Toward a Better Competency Standard

Richard Bonnie has developed a conceptual framework for thinking about competency in criminal cases that helps explain how *Godinez* should be interpreted.[49] Although I disagree with some of his ultimate conclusions, an understanding of his work is important to set the stage for a comprehensive analysis of competency in the criminal setting.

The most fundamental component of Bonnie's analysis is the differentiation between "competency to assist" counsel (what I will call "adjudicative competency") and competency to make specific decisions (what Bonnie calls "decisional competency," a term I will also use). Adjudicative competence requires that the person understand the criminal process and be able to communicate relevant facts to the players in the system (in other words, it is identical to competency to stand trial as typically defined by the courts). Decisional competency, in contrast, is only required when the defendant is entitled to make a decision about his or her case, such as whether to plead guilty.[50] The flaw in *Godinez* is that it conflates, or at best does not adequately distinguish between, adjudicative and decisional competency. The two types of competency requirements exist for different reasons and have different criteria.

Adjudicative competency is required, Bonnie explains, to promote dignity and reliability. To proceed against "[a] person who lacks a rudimentary understanding of the nature and purpose of the proceedings against her . . . offends the moral dignity of the process because it treats the defendant not as an accountable person, but as an object of the state's effort to carry out its promises."[51] Furthermore, "[t]o proceed against a defendant who lacks the capacity to recognize and communicate relevant information to his attorney and to the court would be unfair to the defendant and would undermine society's independent interest in the reliability of its criminal process."[52] Thus, to adjudicate a person on criminal charges, the person must understand the process and his or her role in it, and be able to communicate relevant information.

Decisional competency, in contrast, is required to implement the goal of promoting autonomy. As Bonnie argues, "[a] construct of 'decisional competence' is an inherent, though derivative, feature of any legal doctrine that prescribes a norm of client autonomy."[53] Such legal doctrines permeate the legal system and include the three areas of interest in this chapter— pleading guilty, waiving an insanity defense, and waiving the right to counsel.

Bonnie also provides a useful framework for determining the content of the decisional competency standard. Borrowing from the treatment decision-making literature,[54] he proposes five levels of competency, each of which subsumes the preceding level(s): (1) the ability to express a preference (the preference test); (2) the ability to understand relevant information (the understanding test); (3) the ability to give a reason for the decision that has a plausible grounding in reality (the basic rationality test); (4) the ability to give reasons that are both plausible and avoid being "powerfully influenced by delusional beliefs or pathological emotions" (the appreciation test); and (5) the ability to demonstrate a rational manipulation of the information (the reasoned-choice test).[55]

These tests are discussed further below, but are briefly distinguished here. The preference test requires nothing more than an assent or negative response to the proposed course of action. The understanding test is similar to the narrow view of the *Godinez* standard discussed above: the defendant must be able to understand the supposed costs and benefits of the proposed course of action (as well as possess the ability to express a preference based on that understanding), but the defendant's reasons for acting need not be considered. In contrast, the remaining tests require an understanding of the nature and consequences of the proposed action and some ability to deal with those facts in a rational manner. A defendant meets the basic rationality test so long as he or she subscribes to nondelusional reasons for acting, while the appreciation test further requires the absence of any other significant cognitive or emotional problems. Finally, the reasoned-choice test (reflecting the language used by the Ninth Circuit in *Sieling* in constructing its test for waiver of constitutional rights) requires the absence of significant pathology as well as evidence of an ability to manipulate rationally the relevant information.

Following several other commentators,[56] Bonnie argues that different standards should apply in different settings. For Bonnie, the primary variable in this regard should be whether the client's decision is in accord with, or contrary to, counsel's advice. On the assumption that counsel's recommendations can be trusted, he would require only the understanding threshold for client decisions that are in accord with counsel's advice, except for the decision to plead guilty, where he would require basic rationality in order to ensure the moral dignity of the process.[57] For decisions that run counter to defense counsel's advice, Bonnie concludes that, at a minimum, competency at the appreciation level is required and that, in some situations, a reasoned choice is mandated, on the theory that where the client and attorney disagree reliability of outcome is more likely to be threatened if the defendant's wishes are allowed to prevail.[58]

Bonnie's competency framework is extremely helpful. First, it resolves the confusion created by *Godinez* and the cases leading up to it, which failed to distinguish between adjudicative and decisional competency. Second, its competency hierarchy allows sophisticated discussion of decisional competency issues. Most important, perhaps, is its recognition that the standard for adjudicative competency is meant to protect reliability and dignity interests, while the decisional competency threshold implements the autonomy preference.

Because Bonnie fails to adhere consistently to this latter insight, however, I part company with him in some respects. Bonnie is correct that reliability and dignity interests (as distinguished from autonomy rights) must play a pivotal role in establishing the standard for adjudicative competency. On that assumption, a criminal defendant cannot be competent in the adjudicative sense unless he meets the understanding test (i.e., understands the process and can communicate relevant facts to his attorney). Even if the lesser expression-of-a-preference were considered to be sufficiently competent as a matter of autonomy, society would be entitled to prohibit prosecution of such a person to prevent convictions based on unchallenged evidence that the accused does not understand, during proceedings that he cannot fathom and in which he cannot participate.

Decisional competency, in contrast, should be concerned solely with autonomy. The societal interest in assuring a reliable and dignified process should play no role in determining when a person has the capacity to make a decision about his or her rights or prerogatives. Although Bonnie initially indicates that this is his view, his discussion of decisional competency standards, briefly described above and discussed in more detail below, makes clear that he ultimately believes otherwise, and that is the nub of our disagreement. His manipulation of the decisional competency threshold depending on whether attorney and client agree improperly injects reliability concerns into the analysis.

A preference for autonomy does not allow for variation on such grounds.

Rather, the basic rationality standard, supplemented by what I call a "basic self-regard" requirement, should be the competency test in *all* the criminal settings discussed here. Basic rationality, as noted above, requires nondelusional reasons for the decision (in addition to the ability to express a preference and an understanding of the relevant information). Basic self-regard requires a willingness to exercise autonomy, which can usually be demonstrated by a willingness to consider alternative scenarios. To explain this conclusion further and explore in more detail how these various tests work, the following discussion considers the two contexts emphasized by Bonnie—when the client and attorney agree, and when they disagree—as well as *Sieling*'s "decisional importance" rationale for adopting varying competency standards.

A. Attorney-Client Agreement

Bonnie argues that when the client and the attorney agree on a decision, the client's reasons are likely to be rational and thus the inquiry into reasons required by the basic rationality and self-regard test is unnecessary. To refrain from such an inquiry, however, ignores the client's motives, however irrational they may be. Perhaps, for instance, the client wants to assert an insanity defense, not for the reasons the attorney considers prudent, but because the defendant thinks that otherwise the attorney will shoot him. Perhaps he wants to plead guilty, in accord with the attorney's recommendation, because he doesn't care what happens to him and thus decision making falls by default to the attorney. In such situations, concluding that the defendant has "competently" waived the defense is disrespectful both to him and to the concept of autonomy. In the first case, the defendant's patently false belief cannot be considered grounds for an autonomous decision. In the second case, his unwillingness to consider alternatives or even affirmatively delegate to the attorney the choice between them demonstrates a surrender of autonomy.

A second argument for a lower standard when client and attorney agree is purely pragmatic. In essence, the contention is that a determination of incompetence results in negative consequences that manipulation of the competency standard can avoid.[59] For instance, a finding of incompetence to assert an insanity defense might delay adjudication and subject a defendant to prolonged hospitalization and forcible medication to "restore" competency. Furthermore, once rendered competent the defendant is likely to accede to the attorney's decisions about the defense in any event. Thus, the argument goes, insistence on the basic rationality and self-regard test does more harm than good when the client agrees with the attorney.

If these types of pragmatic concerns are to predominate, however, then a mere expression of preference for, or even a failure to object to, the attorney's position should be sufficient. The better way to deal with these concerns is not to lower the competency standard arbitrarily, but to ensure that the consequences of an incompetency finding are not onerous. The most obvious reform in this regard is to ensure that both evaluation and treatment takes place on an outpatient basis whenever feasible. Although at one time most states relied on long-term hospitalization for both purposes, in the past two decades there has been a significant movement toward the outpatient approach.[60]

More important, the "pragmatic" rationale for concluding that the defendant's competency should be a minor concern when he agrees with the attorney miscalibrates the costs and benefits of an incompetency finding. Assume, for instance, a defendant agrees with counsel that an insanity defense should be asserted, but for wildly irrational reasons. Contrary to the pragmatic claims made above, the hospitalization and delay that are likely to accompany an incompetency finding in such cases will rarely be any worse than the consequences of pretending the defendant is competent. In the latter instance, one of two results will usually occur: either acquittal on insanity grounds, which is likely to result in the same "negative consequence"—hospitalization and forced medication—sought to be avoided through imposition of a low competency standard, or conviction, which is presumably no better than hospitalization. Any delay in these dispositions that might be occasioned by a finding of incompetency will often be factored into the disposition itself: if convicted, the person may (and should) receive credit for time spent involuntarily hospitalized as incompetent,[61] and if the person is instead acquitted on insanity grounds, any treatment already received to restore competency will help reduce, if it does not eliminate, the need for hospitalization.[62] Furthermore, of course, the "delay" due to treatment brings the benefit of ensuring that we know whether the client rationally agrees with the attorney once the delusions are eliminated.

The same type of analysis applies in the guilty plea context. A defendant who agrees with the attorney's recommendation that a plea is appropriate for irrational reasons should be treated, not convicted. First, there is no reason to believe that a defendant who pleads guilty after restoration of competency will receive a worse disposition than if the guilty plea had occurred initially, while he or she was incompetent. Further, as discussed above, time spent in the hospital being restored to competency should count against time to be served in prison after the plea is made (assuming the person is even sent to prison; transfer back to a hospital after conviction may occur as well).[63] Also worth noting is the fact that even competent defense counsel, when pressured by prosecutors, judges, and docket concerns, have been known to arrange plea deals that are not in the client's best interests;[64] clients of questionable competency are most likely to be oblivious to, and therefore harmed by, such actions. In sum, it is not clear that there are any practical advantages to a low competency standard when counsel and client agree on decisions about waiving rights.

B. Attorney-Client Disagreement

The basic rationality and self-regard test should not only be the standard when the client and counsel agree, but should also apply when they disagree, whether the issue is pleading guilty, pleading insanity, or self-representation (which presumably will always be against counsel's wishes). As noted above, Bonnie argues for a heightened competency standard in these instances because of reliability concerns, and ultimately endorses the reasoned-choice test "when the defendant waives representation by counsel or insists [on] acting without counsel or against the advice of counsel."[65] Bonnie is right that a client who is incompetent under the appreciation or reasoned-choice tests is more likely than one who is competent under those tests to make decisions that will lead to erroneous determinations. Changing the competency threshold for this reason, however, trivializes the autonomy preference because it again makes the competency test dependent on factors that have nothing to do with mental capacity. If reliability is the concern, the strategy that will achieve the most reliable result should be selected and the client's wishes ignored. As argued in later parts of this chapter, concerns about reliability may on rare occasions affect the determination of when a competent client's wishes may be overridden, but they should not affect the predicate determination of decisional competence.

While these points explain why reliability concerns should be irrelevant to the competency standard, they do not establish why basic rationality and self-regard, as opposed to appreciation, reasoned choice, or some other more rigorous standard, is sufficient for autonomous decision making when clients and attorneys disagree. For that purpose, I rely on the work of Elyn Saks, who has written extensively about competency in the psychiatric treatment context.[66] Saks argues that requiring any degree of rationality beyond that demanded by the basic rationality standard is inappropriate, in light of the "pervasive influence of the irrational and the unconscious" in everyone's decision-making process. As she notes, "[p]sychiatrists and psychologists have demonstrated convincingly the ever-present influence of primitive hopes, wishes, and fears on the mental lives of us all."[67] Under a heightened rationality test (as opposed to a "basic rationality" test), too many decisions would be considered incompetent. As Saks, along with her coauthor Stephen Behnke, states in another work:

> It is unclear that pure or pristine reasoning plays an essential role in all effective decision making. Intuitive and idiosyncratic processes may actually improve decision making in certain instances (consider cases in which people dream of solutions to difficult mathematical problems, or police officers who solve a case on a "hunch"). Perhaps more important, even generally effective decision makers who indisputably have the ability to form accurate beliefs misuse statistics, misunderstand probabilities, and accord undue weight to vivid examples. They may also be profoundly affected by irrational and unconscious factors. Unless we are willing to declare most people incompetent, declaring only the mentally ill who lack reasoning skills incompetent risks unjustifiably discriminating against individuals on the basis of mental illness.[68]

That reasoning, if accepted, means that the reasoned-choice standard is too demanding. Only if a defendant provides very good reasons for a decision is this test likely to be met when the decision conflicts with the attorney's, especially if the person applying the test is the attorney. Of particular concern is the likelihood that, under this test, any such reasons given by a person perceived to be "mentally ill" will be considered incompetent without any inquiry into whether the illness is substantially affecting the decision. Bonnie emphasizes that the reasoned-choice test focuses on a person's ability to process information rationally, rather than the actual decision reached. He also concedes, however, that "if others consider an outcome to be misguided or irrational, this may signal a problem with the defendant's reasoning process."[69] Duncan Kennedy put the matter more forthrightly and more accurately: once one moves beyond the "extreme" cases, "the question of capacity is hopelessly intertwined with the question of what [the lawyer] wants to do in this particular case."[70]

The appreciation test—which, as Bonnie would define it, renders incompetent a person who is "powerfully influenced by delusional beliefs or pathological emotions"—is not as clearly submissive to the lawyer's opinion or as dismissive of the mentally ill person's. But that is precisely why the cognitive part of that test (referring to delusional beliefs) is problematic. Any standard that tries to split the difference between basic rationality and "reasoned" rationality is too vague to provide meaningful guidance, and thus it too is likely to lead to findings of incompetency that are unmerited. Additionally, it is a well-known feature of mental disorders that a person who has delusions about some things can be perfectly rational about others.[71] By definition, a person who fails the appreciation test but meets the basic rationality test has no delusional beliefs about the decision being made; calling that decision incompetent would again be tantamount to saying that no person with significant mental illness can make competent decisions about anything.

The "affective" component of the appreciation test, having to do with whether the individual is influenced by "pathological emotions," is also very vague. But it does encompass an important aspect of autonomy—impairment of volition (as opposed to impairment of cognition). Rather than speaking of decisions "powerfully influenced" by such impairment, I prefer the tighter basic self-regard formulation. As will be demonstrated below, that test avoids most of the problems associated with evaluating volition that were discussed in Chapters 2 and 4, because it focuses attention solely on a client's willingness to consider alternatives. It does not require proof that the reasoning process be a product of "free will," but only proof that such a process took place. Nor does it require the type of value judgment contemplated by the appreciation standard's inquiry into whether decision making was "powerfully influenced" by "pathological" factors.

C. The "Importance" of the Decision to Be Made

A second rationale for varying competency levels rests not on whether attorney and client agree but on the "import" of the decision to be made. This was the basis, it will be recalled, of the Ninth Circuit's opinion in *Sieling* (later nullified by *Godinez*) establishing the "reasoned choice" standard for pleading guilty and waiving counsel. Because of the constitutional gravity of these decisions, the Ninth Circuit concluded, a particularly rigorous level of competency must be met before they may be honored.

This rationale does not fare any better than Bonnie's, if the decisional competency standard is viewed as a method of implementing autonomy. As earlier discussion illustrated, some decisions, such as waiver of counsel, require an ability to understand more complex information than other decisions. In this sense, the required competency level *should* be heightened with respect to certain decisions. But a rule, like *Sieling's*, that requires more competence, simply because the decision is viewed as more "important" in some objective sense, suffers from the same problem as Bonnie's approach—it improperly minimizes the defendant's desires.[72] For some individuals, for instance, the choice about whether to plead guilty or proceed without counsel may be, contrary to *Sieling's* assertion, of virtually no consequence, perhaps because the defendant believes he is guilty or the charge is trivial. Other individuals may value the ability to voice their concerns in their own way much more than the supposed benefits of pleading guilty or having an attorney. Preventing otherwise competent defendants from achieving these types of goals because their choice does not appear to be "reasoned" is rank paternalism.

A preference for autonomy dictates that the defendant—not the judge, the attorney, or an appellate court—determine the significance of a particular decision. Because that determination will not be the same for every defendant, varying competency thresholds based on the decision's importance is impossible. Again, the basic rationality and self-regard test should be applied in *all* criminal competency settings, since it enables defendants to control their case except when they are so irrational that they cannot recognize or act on their interests.

These various points are admittedly abstract. They are best explicated through an analysis of recent instances in which competency was an issue.

D. Competency in the Unabomber Case and Other Cases

The Kaczynski case illustrates the differences between the competency standards just outlined, as well as the difficulties inherent in any attempt to evaluate competency. Kaczynski's lawyers decided very early on that the only viable defense for their client was some type of mental abnormality claim. Kaczynski, however, opposed such a defense.[73] At one point he and his attorneys did reach an agreement that discarded the insanity defense but allowed the attorneys to argue that his mental illness negated his intent to murder. As part of this agreement, the attorneys stipulated that they would call only lay witnesses, not psychiatric experts, during the trial stage.[74] Even this limited arrangement gave Kaczynski significant pause, however. As he stated to the trial judge, "Your Honor, as you know, I do not agree with counsel concerning major strategic decisions, but I've become aware that legally I have to accept those decisions whether I like them or not."[75]

What lay behind Kaczynski's resistance to mental state defenses? Unfortunately, information about Kaczynski's thought process concerning the psychiatric claims, his plea of guilty, and his desire to represent himself is incomplete, perhaps because the trial judge's allegiance to the five-year-old decision in *Godinez* led him to deemphasize the need for information about motivation. From what is available to the public, it appears that the primary reason for Kaczynski's resistance to his lawyer's strategy was what his attorneys called "a deep and abiding fear" that he would be perceived as mentally ill, a fear he had possessed "for his entire life."[76] Bolstering this theory are statements in his famous Manifesto, suggesting that he would rather die than be subjected to the indignity of being called mentally ill.[77]

Was Kaczynski's apparent willingness to trade death for diagnosis proof of incompetence? If this were the only evidence, the answer should be no. Kaczynski's desire to forego his only viable defense, although perhaps not a choice most people would make, is not grossly irrational. Indeed, one could argue that this reasoning suffices to meet even the reasoned-choice test, given the stigma attached to mental illness and mental state defenses.[78]

Psychiatrists, however, would not stop the inquiry at this surface level. The evidence suggests that Kaczynski not only did not want to be labeled mentally ill, but also that he truly believed he was not mentally ill (a phenomenon clinicians often call "lack of insight").[79] That belief, psychiatrists might say, was false in light of the large number of mental health professionals, from both the defense *and* the prosecution, who concluded that Kaczynski was suffering from paranoid schizophrenia. Such a conclusion would make Kaczynski incompetent to make a decision about the insanity defense under Bonnie's standard, which requires a high degree of competency when the defendant disagrees with the attorney, as occurred here. Any decision to waive the insanity defense that is based on a denial of a diagnosis agreed on by both sets of experts could not be considered the product of reasoned choice, and is clearly influenced by "pathological" processes (thus failing the appreciation test as well).

The outcome under the basic rationality standard is not as clear, however. That is because the conclusory label "mental illness," and even the diagnosis "paranoid schizophrenia," are not objective facts that can be proved or disproved. The unreliability of psychiatric diagnoses is well docu-mented;[80] the amorphous and politically charged nature of the term "men-tal illness" is also well recognized.[81] More important, diagnoses and the concept of mental illness are constructs that are not empirically verifiable, but rather exist solely as convenient methods of describing certain constel-lations of behavior.[82] Given these facts, a belief that one is not "mentally ill," even one that is contradicted by all the experts, cannot by itself be said to be patently false.

Assume instead that the evidence that Kaczynski is suffering from men-tal problems is at the symptom level. That is, assume that Kaczynski is shown to believe that the people to whom he mailed bombs were out to ex-terminate him personally, despite the absence of any objective evidence to that effect. This belief is demonstrably false. If part of the reason he rejects the insanity defense is because he insists on his victims' ill will toward him, then he fails even the basic rationality test. We have no indication, however, at least from public records, that Kaczynski was delusional in this sense. In the absence of such evidence or any other evidence of clearly false beliefs,[83] and assuming he understands the relevant information, he was competent to make decisions about mental state defenses and to fire attorneys who in-sisted on such a defense.

As this analysis demonstrates, the basic rationality and self-regard stan-dard is easier to meet than the appreciation or reasoned-choice standards. It will still result in numerous incompetency findings, however, because it still requires that the client be able to express a preference, that the client understand and consider the relevant information, and that the client have no patently false beliefs about that information or the reasons for the deci-sion. The following discussion demonstrates this point by looking at the facts of Godinez v. Moran,[84] which illustrates the basic self-regard concept, and People v. Ferguson, which permits elaboration of the basic rationality idea.[85]

As previously noted, Moran fired his attorneys, pled guilty, and refused to present evidence in mitigation at sentencing.[86] Both evaluating psychia-trists, as well as all the courts that considered the matter, agreed that Moran understood his legal situation.[87] He also undoubtedly knew that a failure to present evidence at sentencing would not improve his chance of avoiding a death sentence. In other words, he was competent in the adjudicative sense and met the understanding test with respect to pleading guilty; he probably also met the understanding standard with respect to waiving counsel, al-though that conclusion is more doubtful.[88]

More ambiguous are the "reasons" for his actions. To the extent they can be gleaned from the record, they appeared to be based on a conclusion that he deserved the death penalty and a sense that nothing, not even his life, was worth fighting for.[89] While these reasons might be considered irrational (thus failing the reasoned-choice test), and while his decisions appeared to be "powerfully influenced" by his depressive emotions (thus failing the appreciation test), they were not based on clearly false assumptions. Moran may indeed have deserved the death penalty, and the value of his life is not something that can be calculated with any certainty. Under the basic rationality test, then, the outcome of the competency analysis is the same as that reached by the *Godinez* Court (although under the basic rationality test, in possible contrast to the Court's test, substantial inquiry is made into the reasons for Moran's decision).

The analysis of Moran's competency should not end there, however. There is a strong argument that even if Moran met the basic rationality standard he did not meet the basic self-regard standard, because he was unwilling to consider the alternatives of going to trial and presenting evidence at sentencing. As he subsequently stated, "I guess I really didn't care about anything . . . I wasn't very concerned about anything that was going on . . . as far as the proceedings and everything were going."[90] Had his thought process involved an evaluation of the evidence against him, he would have been competent under this standard. Instead, his reasoning appeared to represent a complete abdication of autonomy. (Moran's suicide attempt a few months before the plea hearing is also noteworthy in this regard.)[91] Moran is representative of numerous individuals who, suffering from anhedonia or major depression, waive their right to post-conviction hearings, due to apathy rather than consideration of their options.[92]

Colin Ferguson, like Moran, was charged with several counts of murder and, like Moran, fired his attorneys.[93] The prosecution's case was based on the reports of a staggering number of eyewitnesses, all of whom claimed that Ferguson boarded a commuter train in Long Island and shot at a large number of people (six were killed and nineteen wounded).[94] His attorneys had wanted to assert a "black rage" insanity defense, to the effect that Ferguson had been driven into psychosis by an oppressive white society. Ferguson rejected both the attorneys and their theory, however, and instead insisted that a white man had stolen his gun and carried out the crimes.[95] Given these actions, Ferguson's competence became a major issue. But both psychologists who evaluated his competency found Ferguson to be an articulate, well-educated person who, while suffering from paranoid personality disorder, was competent to stand trial.[96] The trial judge conducted his own inquiry of Ferguson and, apparently influenced by *Godinez*, found him competent to stand trial and competent to waive his right to counsel.[97]

Ferguson proceeded to represent himself in a fashion that observers unanimously considered bizarre. For instance, he told the jury there were ninety-three counts against him because the year was 1993. He also announced that he would call as "a witness a parapsychologist and exorcist who would testify that government agents had planted a microchip" in his head, and asked the state's ballistics expert whether the bullet fragments had been tested for "alcohol or substance abuse."[98]

Ferguson's case exposes even more clearly than Moran's why the Supreme Court's decision in *Godinez* should not be interpreted in the narrow sense outlined earlier.[99] The focus of both the experts and the court in Ferguson was whether Ferguson understood the criminal process and the consequences of representing himself. Little attention was paid to Ferguson's reasons for wanting to forego the insanity defense and proceed pro se.

Had there been such an inquiry, as structured by the basic rationality and self-regard test, it is likely Ferguson would have been found incompetent. Although information about Ferguson's reasons for avoiding an insanity plea and wanting to represent himself is scarce, one of the psychologists who evaluated Ferguson opined to the press that these decisions were "an obvious choice on his part," because going to jail with sane inmates for a determinate period of time was preferable to spending the rest of his life in a mental hospital, and because "he doesn't wish to be viewed as a crazy person."[100] If those were Ferguson's sole reasons for waiving the insanity defense and counsel, he would be competent in both the adjudicative and decisional senses to the same extent Kaczynski was. Ferguson also appeared to believe, however, that he did not commit the crimes, despite overwhelming evidence to the contrary. If one of the reasons for rejecting the insanity defense was a belief that he did not shoot the victims, and his reason for firing his attorneys was that they would not pursue that line of defense, his decisional competency is in much greater doubt. Under such circumstances, *Godinez* notwithstanding, he should have been found incompetent to waive counsel.

These applications of the basic rationality and self-regard test illustrate not only the substance of that standard, but also the complex nature of mental disorder and its relationship to competency. Unfortunately, reaching an understanding as to how competency is to be defined in the criminal context is only the beginning of the task. Still necessary is a framework for deciding who makes the competency determination and what should happen when a person's competency is suspect. The remainder of this chapter argues that the defense attorney should play a crucial role both in investigating competency and in assuring that appropriate steps are taken when competency is at issue.

III. The Role of the Lawyer Representing a Mentally Disabled Defendant

As noted in the introduction to this chapter, a defense attorney who has a client with mental disability should be prepared to make three types of decisions. The first involves deciding whether the client's competency is suspect and, if so, whether the court should be alerted to that fact to obtain treatment for restoration of competency. The second requires choosing whether to override the competent client's wishes with respect to a particular aspect of representation, a scenario that could occur with nonmentally disabled clients, but is more likely to occur with those clients who suffer from mental disability. The third involves deciding how to represent a client whose competence is not restorable.

A. The Obligation to Raise the Incompetency Issue

Assume a defense attorney believes or suspects that the client is incompetent, in either the adjudicative or decisional sense. What should the lawyer do? The American Bar Association's *Model Code of Professional Responsibility,* one of the three primal sources of rules governing attorney ethics, provides no answer. It merely states that when an impaired client has no guardian the lawyer may be compelled to make decisions on the client's behalf, but then warns that "a lawyer cannot perform any act or make any decision which the law requires his client to . . . make."[101] The more recent ABA *Model Rules of Professional Conduct* are somewhat more helpful, stating that when the client is incapable of making a decision, the lawyer "may seek the appointment of a guardian or take other protective action."[102] The Model Rules might therefore be read to permit the defense attorney to seek treatment for the incompetent defendant, either through a guardian or more directly. Ultimately, however, the Model Rules, like the Model Code, provide no definitive guidance for the attorney.

The ABA's *Criminal Justice Mental Health Standards* are more forthright. Standard 7–4.2(c) states that "[d]efense counsel should move for evaluation of the defendant's competence to stand trial whenever the defense counsel has a good faith doubt as to the defendant's competence," and permits such a motion even over the defendant's objection.[103] The commentary to the standard states that this position is mandated by the lawyer's obligation to maintain the integrity of the judicial process and the attorney's duty to the court, as well as by the need to ensure defendants are not deprived of their right to make fundamental case decisions while competent. Most courts take the same view.[104]

Many commentators, however, have a different view. They argue that the attorney whose client is incompetent may have an ethical duty to refrain from alerting the court to that fact under some circumstances. Given the possibly adverse consequences of such a motion, they contend, the attorney must make a nuanced decision as to which course of action—notification to the court or surrogate decision making for the client—is in the client's best interest.[105]

I share the overall goal of achieving the incompetent client's best interest. I am not sanguine, however, about attorneys' ability to ascertain what that interest is in the case of the incompetent client. Accordingly, with two important caveats, I argue below that an attorney is ethically obligated to seek appropriate treatment for the incompetent client, even if that goal requires alerting the court to the client's mental problems and possibly triggering involuntary hospitalization. Although similar to the ABA's stance, this position is not identical to it. While the ABA requires a formal motion to the court when the attorney suspects a client is incompetent, the primary focus of my approach is on seeking treatment in that situation. Such treatment might be obtainable through extrajudicial means (especially if the defendant has insurance), although as a practical matter a court order may be necessary in many cases involving indigent defendants.

I have already suggested the practical reasons for imposing a duty to seek treatment for the incompetent defendant. The avoidance of coerced psychiatric treatment achieved by failing to raise the issue will usually be a pyrrhic victory, given the likelihood the client will be subject to such treatment in any event (in prison, after transfer from prison, due to an insanity verdict, as part of a plea bargain, or after dismissal through civil commitment). Those who believe that incompetency should sometimes be hidden from the court are particularly concerned about defendants charged with petty misdemeanors who are found incompetent. They assert that these individuals may spend more time in the hospital being restored than they would spend in jail once convicted, because misdemeanor convictions often result in much less confinement. What this analysis omits, however, is the likely disposition of a minor case if there is no incompetency finding: either jail time in a facility that is unlikely to have good treatment resources[106] or civil commitment or probation in exchange for a dismissal or reduction of charges. While the probation disposition may seem preferable to hospitalization on incompetency grounds, probation violations, which are quite frequent when the defendant is mentally ill,[107] will often result in jail time.[108] An incompetency plea in minor cases, in contrast, often is a precursor to dismissal of charges or withholding of adjudication if the defendant complies with the treatment program.[109]

Furthermore, treatment to restore a person to competency does not have to entail a significant deprivation of liberty. As noted above, today, in contrast to the practice several years ago when most of the commentators who are cautious about competency motions were writing, many jurisdictions require outpatient intervention when feasible. In minor cases, such evaluation and treatment is standard practice in most jurisdictions.[110] Hospitalization, if it is ordered, is constitutionally limited to the time necessary to restore the individual to competency,[111] which should be less than six months in virtually all cases,[112] and should count as time served if a sentence is imposed. While both the outpatient option and the rules regarding the duration of hospitalization are frequently ignored,[113] that is due as much to the negligence of defense attorneys as to the inertia of the system.[114] Finally, of course, failing to obtain treatment can in some cases seriously harm a person's mental health.[115] In short, if the lawyer is careful in the initial decision about client competency and vigorously monitors the legal system's treatment of the client, concerns about liberty interests alone should not deter the attorney from raising the competency issue.

Nonetheless, a number of commentators believe lawyers should avoid competency motions when their client objects, regardless of the client's competency. Rodney Uphoff is one. He cites the case of a mentally ill, clearly incompetent defendant who is charged with intentionally breaking a store window; because the defendant engaged in similar conduct in the past, the prosecutor refuses to drop charges but does offer a sentence of "time served" if the defendant pleads guilty.[116] To Uphoff, the offer is preferable to an incompetency determination, and thus the attorney should avoid raising the latter issue. But, as indicated above, an incompetency motion does not have to result in hospitalization. More important, the plea that Uphoff believes is preferable is no guarantee that civil commitment will be avoided; indeed, the facts suggest that the defendant will commit further crime if not treated in some fashion. Finally, one wonders whether the suggested disposition is really in the client's "best interests," given his clear mental difficulties.

Uphoff is also concerned about the possibility that attorney-client confidences will be disclosed when the attorney makes a competency motion (since the reasons for it will generally have to be explained).[117] He adds that a competency evaluation and ensuing treatment might reveal incriminating information that the prosecution could use against the defendant.[118] His fears are not unfounded, but they are insignificant. In virtually every state, information revealed pursuant to a competency motion and evaluation may legally be used only for the purpose of resolving competency issues.[119] The likelihood that the prosecution will somehow still be able to obtain incriminating information is too minimal to outweigh the benefits of treatment and assuring autonomy.

Bruce Winick, another commentator who believes that the lawyer should generally not raise the competency issue when the client does not want it raised, argues that the incompetency label has debilitating psychological "side effects" beyond what might be associated with forced treatment. In particular, he asserts that the incompetency label can become a self-fulfilling prophecy, acting to diminish self-esteem, inhibit initiative and motivation, and cause depression.[120] Winick's assertions, although somewhat speculative, are persuasive enough to provide reasons for defining incompetency as narrowly as possible. But they do not justify defining that term so narrowly that autonomy is rendered irrelevant. To the extent Winick would allow the attorney to ignore a client's restoration needs based merely on the client's ability to express a preference for the attorney's desire to proceed,[121] he does just that.

Residual concerns relating to the adverse consequences of defense attorney efforts to assure competency may be alleviated by several observations. First, the number of defendants affected by such consequences would be kept to a minimum if attorneys raised the issue only when there was strong reason to believe the client was incompetent;[122] in this regard, it is worth emphasizing that it would be unethical for a lawyer to raise an unfounded claim of incompetency.[123] Second, the number of defendants subjected to intervention would be reduced even further if courts adopted and attorneys accepted the low competency threshold advocated here (rather than the appreciation or reasoned-choice test). Third, there should be no objection, ethical or otherwise, to methods of avoiding involuntary evaluation and treatment that are consistent with the obligation to ensure a client's competence. For instance, as noted earlier, an attorney could privately arrange for treatment to restore competency on an outpatient basis without triggering a state evaluation or treatment. And once an attorney does alert the court to a client's suspect competency, Winick's proposal calling for a series of trial continuances contingent upon proof that the defendant is seeking treatment and is progressing toward restoration of competency may be a good substitute for involuntary hospitalization of a person who is found incompetent.[124]

Finally, while this chapter argues that a lawyer is always obligated to ensure *adjudicative* competence, there are two narrowly defined situations in which the attorney need not raise the *decisional* competency issue. The first is when the lawyer, rather than the client, has clear authority to make a particular decision. The second is when the client has authority to make the decision but there are compelling reasons for pursuing a particular path regardless of how rational the client's wishes are.[125] These two exceptions are the subject of the next section.

B. When Client Decisions May Be Ignored

Up to this point, this chapter has assumed that the competent client's decision must always be honored. That, of course, is not the law. Many courts have suggested that decisions about matters that are tactical or strategic rather than "fundamental" are for the lawyer to make, regardless of the client's wishes. Ethical rules also appear to state that clients control only the "end" of litigation, not the "means" by which it is achieved. The topic of lawyer-client autonomy is a large and complex one that this chapter does not try to resolve. It does, however, explain why the client should normally control decisions about mental state defenses.

At the same time, even a competent client's decision about a matter that the client should control, such as whether to assert the insanity defense, is not necessarily sacrosanct. The attorney's duty to society may demand that, in narrow sets of circumstances, the wishes of a competent client be ignored. The scope of this exception to the autonomy preference is fleshed out through further examination of the Kaczynski, Moran, and Ferguson cases.

Which Decisions Are Presumptively the Client's?

A survey of the relevant law, ethical rules, and commentary suggests three possible approaches to the issue of when lawyers should defer to a competent client's wishes. The first has been called lawyer-centered, because it gives the lawyer control in most situations. The second, dubbed client-centered or client-controlled, confers the predominant authority on clients.[126] The third, which is a spin-off of the second approach but more conciliatory toward the first, might be called delegation-centered. It requires the lawyer to seek the client's consent to make decisions in specified areas, such as presentation of evidence or legal arguments.

At the constitutional level, the Supreme Court has sent mixed signals as to which approach it endorses in the criminal context. In Jones v. Barnes,[127] the Court conceded that a criminal defendant has the authority to decide whether to plead guilty, waive a jury trial, testify on his or her own behalf, and take an appeal.[128] But it strongly implied that virtually all other decisions could be left to the attorney without violating the Constitution.[129] Strickland v. Washington,[130] the Supreme Court's leading case on effective assistance of counsel, is similar in tone. Although the Court stated that "[c]ounsel's actions are usually based, quite properly, on informed strategic choices made by the defendant,"[131] the spirit of the opinion is more accurately reflected in its earlier statement that counsel's "strategic choices made after thorough investigation of law and facts relevant to plausible options are virtually unchallengeable."[132]

In contrast, remember that the case that established the right to self-representation, Faretta v. California,[133] stated that a defendant should be allowed to "conduct his own defense ultimately to his own detriment."[134] Referring to the Sixth Amendment's "assistance of counsel" language, it also stated that "an assistant, however expert, is still an assistant."[135] Other language in *Faretta* appeared to adopt the delegation approach, by referring to the "tradition" of allocating to counsel "power to make binding decisions of trial strategy in many areas," provided the defendant consents, "at the outset," to accept the counsel as his or her representative.[136]

The organized bar is also not entirely clear about which approach it endorses, but it appears to lean toward the lawyer-centered approach. The Model Code seems to grant the client considerable power in the lawyer-client relationship, but also states that a lawyer may "[w]here permissible, exercise his professional judgment to waive or fail to assert a right or position of his client."[137] The Model Rules similarly provide that the client controls the "objectives and means of representation" (including decisions about pleas, the jury right, and whether to testify) but state in commentary that "a lawyer is not required to pursue objectives or employ means simply because a client may wish that the lawyer do so" and then states that "[a] clear distinction between objectives and means sometimes cannot be drawn."[138] The ABA's *Standards for Criminal Justice* (hereafter called the Standards) provide that a defendant has control over what pleas to enter, whether to accept a plea agreement, whether to waive jury trial, whether to testify, and whether to appeal, but then states that "[s]trategic and tactical decisions should be made by defense counsel after consultation with the client where feasible and appropriate."[139]

The behavior of practicing attorneys appears to reflect the principles set out in the ABA Standards. One study of almost seven hundred attorneys in two major jurisdictions indicated that virtually all attorneys believe the client should decide whether to accept or reject a plea bargain, waive a jury trial, and testify.[140] Much smaller proportions, however, believe the client should "make the call" on whether to: waive a preliminary hearing (78.2 percent); initiate a plea bargain (68.6 percent); request a lesser included instruction (37 percent); raise an affirmative defense (27.3 percent); file a suppression motion (17.8 percent); use peremptory challenges (16.7 percent); decide which defense witnesses to call (11.4 percent); request appointment of an expert witness (8.1 percent); or interview prosecution witnesses (4.9 percent).[141]

In short, outside of a few well-defined areas, significant confusion exists about which decisions are for the client to make and which should be left to the attorney. Fortunately, with respect to two of the three decisions on which this chapter has focused, the confusion is muted, at least in the formal rules. As indicated above, there is consensus that the decision to plead guilty is the client's, and *Faretta* appears to raise to constitutional status the client's right to make the decision to waive counsel.

The decision whether to raise the insanity defense and related defenses is not as clearly demarcated as one the client should make, however. A majority of courts hold that the trial court may not impose an insanity defense over the defendant's objection, but a sizeable minority hold that this decision is within the trial judge's (and therefore the attorney's) discretion.[142] Courts are also split on the issue of who has decision-making control over the introduction of psychiatric evidence relevant to criminal intent (as opposed to insanity). At least two state appellate courts,[143] as well as Judge

Garland Burrell in Kaczynski's case,[144] have concluded that the attorney controls this decision, but at least one other court has found to the contrary.[145] Similarly, courts disagree about whether the decision to present mitigating psychological evidence at capital sentencing proceedings is up to the attorney, although the trend appears to be toward client direction of that decision.[146]

Of particular interest is whether a competent defendant has the authority to refuse assertion of a mental state defense even if, as may have been the case with Kaczynski, it is the only viable defense. This scenario is especially complex, given the likelihood that even competent defendants in such cases are denying the very mental illness that both bolsters the insanity defense and makes it difficult for them to see its advantages. It appears that, in practice, attorneys often ignore their client's wishes on this matter. For instance, in the survey reported above, only 27.3 percent of the attorneys believed that the client should control decisions about affirmative defenses, and only 8.1 percent believed clients should determine whether an expert witness will be appointed.[147] It is possible that those surveyed were not thinking about the insanity defense and psychiatrists when they answered these two questions. But other research suggests that attorneys are quite capable of failing to consult their clients about the insanity issue. A study of 114 cases in which the insanity defense was raised found that "[i]n more than one-third (36%) of the cases . . . the attorneys appear to have pre-empted their clients' participation in the decision-making process."[148]

This practice is impermissible, if the client is competent. Indeed, consistent with the preference for autonomy and the theory behind client-centered counseling, one might argue that, where feasible, *all* nontrivial decisions about the course of representation should be left to the client, if he or she is competent to make them. This position would mean that, contrary to the apparent practice, clients should be consulted and permitted to make decisions about suppression motions, witnesses, instructions, and a host of other issues. One need not go that far, however, to conclude that decisions about mental state defenses—the insanity defense, mitigating evidence at sentencing, and lack of mens rea arguments—ought to be the client's.

We can begin with the insanity defense. The most significant argument against leaving the decision about this defense to the client is the deleterious effect its waiver might have on the integrity of the criminal process. As Judge David Bazelon stated in his dissent in Whalem v. United States:[149]

One of the major foundations for the structure of the criminal law is the concept of responsibility, and the law is clear that one whose acts would otherwise be criminal has committed no crime at all if because of incapacity due to age or mental condition he is not responsible for those acts . . . In the courtroom confrontations between the individual and society the trial judge must uphold this structural foundation by refusing to allow the conviction of an obviously mentally irresponsible defendant, and when there is sufficient question as to a defendant's mental responsibility at the time of the crime, that issue must become part of the case. Just as the judge must insist that the corpus delicti be proved before a defendant who has confessed may be convicted, so too must the judge forestall the conviction of one who in the eyes of the law is not mentally responsible for his otherwise criminal acts.[150]

Many courts have rejected this argument on two grounds. The first ground, reflected in *Faretta*, is the client's autonomy interest. The second ground, more specific to the insanity defense, is that a conviction can be preferable to an insanity verdict for a number of reasons: (1) the confinement after an insanity acquittal is often longer than imprisonment after conviction for the same offense;[151] (2) prison conditions may be preferable to the conditions in mental hospitals, which include forced treatment and association with people who are severely mentally disordered; (3) the stigma associated with an insanity verdict (which incorporates a finding that a crime was committed) may be worse than the stigma of conviction; and (4) an insanity plea might trivialize any political or religious message the defendant is seeking to impart to the jury and the public.[152] These considerations suggest that the insanity defense is rarely a good idea when conviction would result in only a few years imprisonment, and they could even support rejection of the defense when the charge is serious.

Neither the *Faretta* principle nor observations about the reality of an insanity verdict directly responds to Bazelon's argument, however. Even if a person autonomously rejects an insanity plea, Bazelon reasoned, the criminal justice system cannot convict a person who is clearly not responsible for the crime due to mental disability, just as it should not allow a factually innocent person to plead guilty.[153] This moral imperative, he concluded, overrides the dispositional and other potentially negative consequences of an insanity verdict.[154]

One might challenge Bazelon's central assumption by asserting that, in contrast to factual guilt, sanity is not a condition of criminal responsibility.[155] That assertion is rejected in most jurisdictions, however.[156] A stronger response to Bazelon, one based on assertions made in Chapter 2, is that insanity is rarely so obvious that conviction of a person who is mentally ill would amount to a travesty of justice in the same way conviction of an innocent person would. The determination of insanity is dependent upon self-reported invisible mental states that are interpreted by laypeople and experts, rather than based on "objective" criteria.[157] Because of the moral ambiguity of the concept, juries have convicted even those who have presented overwhelming evidence of mental disability at the time of the offense.[158] One could be sure of an insanity verdict only if the judge guaranteed it, and even then there would be no objective way of determining whether that result is "correct."

This moral ambiguity is even greater when the issue is whether to present evidence of mental state at sentencing. The Supreme Court has held that the state may not bar capital defendants like Kaczynski from presenting such evidence at the sentencing proceeding to support the case in mitigation.[159] No matter how powerful such evidence is, however, a jury can always lawfully decide that it is outweighed by the evidence in aggravation. Furthermore, as Chapter 3 noted, research suggests that many types of mental state evidence presented at sentencing have an aggravating effect on juries, which apparently often equate mental illness with dangerousness. Thus, again, a court could not justify forcing a defendant to present mitigating evidence on the ground that manifest injustice would otherwise result.

The mental abnormality defense that gives rise to the strongest argument in favor of leaving the waiver decision in the attorney's hands is the diminished capacity, or lack of criminal intent, defense. Although a number of states do not even recognize such a defense,[160] a persuasive argument can be made that prohibiting evidence of mental illness that negates mens rea is unconstitutional.[161] In those cases where such evidence strongly suggests that the defendant did not intend to carry out the criminal act, a court might be justified in overriding a client's objection to its presentation; this situation most closely parallels that in which there is no factual basis for a guilty plea. These cases are extremely rare, however,[162] and when they do occur the mental illness is usually so severe the prosecution rarely attempts to convict. In the more typical diminished capacity case, represented by Kaczynski's situation, the evidence that the defendant lacked criminal intent is much weaker, and a failure to raise the defense can hardly be called a travesty of justice. Moreover, like the insanity defense and evidence of mental disorder presented at sentencing, the diminished capacity defense is stigmatizing, undercuts any political message the defendant might want to impart, and can even result in prolonged hospitalization, depending on the charges involved.[163]

For these reasons, the decision whether to present evidence of mental state should generally be left up to the client.[164] Even if one subscribes to the lawyer-centered approach to decision making, the uniquely personal considerations associated with decisions about mental state defenses strongly support the conclusion that they should be an exception to that approach.

When Deferral to the Competent Client's Wishes Is Unethical

The analysis is only halfway complete at this point, however; still to be considered are societal interests that may dictate lawyer or judicial control of such decisions. As Bazelon suggests and as this chapter noted earlier, society has interests both in reliable outcomes and a dignified process, interests that are not waivable by a defendant. More specifically, society has an interest, independent of the defendant's, in ensuring that the criminal justice system accurately assesses the culpability of those it prosecutes and that its procedures are not ignored or abused.[165] While these interests should normally not trump the autonomy preference, serious threats to these interests may justify a refusal to defer to the client.

The guilty plea example noted earlier makes the point most clearly. Presumably all would agree that the criminal justice system should not accept a guilty plea (at least outside of the plea bargain context) from a person who is provably innocent,[166] regardless of the person's desires or competency level. Such an outcome would seriously undermine the integrity of the system, because it is neither reliable nor respectful of the criminal justice system's adjudicatory processes.

Now consider three other examples, drawn from cases discussed earlier in the chapter. The first is Kaczynski's, in which a mentally ill person faced with capital murder charges, the validity of which is not in dispute, refuses to permit expert testimony about his mental state either at trial or at sentencing, despite his attorneys' belief that it is the only viable defense. The second is Moran's, in which a severely depressed person, also charged with capital murder, insists on pleading guilty and conceding the prosecution's case at sentencing. The third is Ferguson's, in which a clearly psychotic individual fires his attorneys and makes the claim, against overwhelming evidence to the contrary, that he did not commit the murders with which he is charged.

I have argued that, although all three of these individuals were competent in the adjudicative sense, neither Moran nor Ferguson were competent in the decisional sense and Kaczynski's decisional competence is not free from doubt. Assume now, however, that all three are competent for all relevant purposes (an assumption that is consistent with the view of the courts involved in those cases). On this assumption, do society's interests in reliability and dignity trump the defendants' decisions to waive mental state defenses, plead guilty, and waive the right to counsel that occurred in these cases?

Because of the strong preference for autonomy that informs the analysis of this chapter, society's interest in promoting reliability in these three contexts should prevail over the defendant's autonomy interests only if the defendant is clearly "innocent" and is taking a position that will lead to a clearly less desirable disposition. Therefore, a defendant's rejection of a mental state defense should be overridden on enhancement-of-reliability grounds only in the unlikely event that three factors co-occur: (1) the mental state defense is the only viable one; (2) it is very likely to prevail; and (3) a successful defense would do the client more good than harm (for example, by assuring a shorter time in confinement). In cases that do not involve serious felony charges, the third criterion may never be met. In the three homicide cases at issue here, the first and third criteria may have been met, but the second criterion was not. Indeed, for reasons discussed above in dismissing Bazelon's arguments, that criterion will virtually never be satisfied.

The nullifying effect of society's interest in a dignified process must also be carefully cabined. The Supreme Court has recognized that certain fundamental rights, among them the right of the defendant to be present at his own trial[167] and the right of the press to observe the trial,[168] can be trumped by concerns about decorum. That interest should be particularly compelling in this context, however, because otherwise we are ignoring the decision of a competent defendant merely to ensure a tidier proceeding.

Ferguson's self-representation presents the hardest question on this score. Given his delusions, the bizarre nature of his trial was predictable. Perhaps to protect both his dignity and the integrity of the trial process, he should not have been allowed to proceed pro se, or to make the argument that he did not commit the crime.

One might also argue that allowing Moran to plead guilty, fire his attorneys, and leave the prosecution's sentencing case uncontested made a mockery of the system, by signaling that our purportedly adversarial process, devoted to determining the precise culpability of those whom society sentences to death,[169] is a meaningless myth. Here the concern is not, as in Ferguson's case, abuse of the system, but neglect of it. If, however, Moran's guilty plea and waiver of counsel and sentencing evidence were (contrary to my earlier assumption) exercises of will rather than an abdication of it, then he chose to streamline the process in a manner similar to a guilty plea.[170] Assuming this was a stable decision by a decisionally competent individual, it deserves dispositive weight.

Kaczynski, like Ferguson and unlike Moran, clearly planned to defend himself using the adversary process. Yet his trial probably would not have resulted in the same surreal atmosphere that characterized the Ferguson trial; Kaczynski certainly was not as overtly psychotic as Ferguson and in fact may have been willing to allow an attorney to make a necessity case (or some other argument) for him. In light of these facts, and assuming Kaczynski was decisionally competent, he probably should have been allowed to pursue the defense as he saw fit.

In short, concerns about reliability or dignity should rarely trump a competent individual's decision about pleading, self-representation, or mental state defenses. Only when these societal interests are extremely compelling does the attorney have an ethical obligation to ignore the competent client's wishes and try to convince the court that it should override those wishes as well.

C. The Permanently Incompetent Defendant

The final scenario that might confront the defense attorney with a client who has a mental disability involves balancing reliability, dignity, and autonomy concerns when the defendant cannot be restored to competency. Again, the ethical rules do not provide clear guidance in this situation, leaving it up to the attorney to decide what protective action should be taken. The law, in contrast, appears to require that charges be dismissed whenever competency is unrestorable, a result that comports with the autonomy preference but has been criticized as insufficiently protective of society's interests in preventing recidivism.[171] The solution to this puzzle depends on whether the person who is unrestorably incompetent is incompetent in the adjudicative or the decisional sense. If the former, the present legal practice of dismissing charges is appropriate. If only decisional competence is impaired, however, adjudication should proceed.

In Jackson v. Indiana,[172] the Supreme Court held, on equal protection and due process grounds, that if a person is not restorable to competence only two options remain: release or civil commitment. The Court reasoned that a person who is unrestorable to trial competency cannot be convicted and thus must be treated similarly to any other unconvicted person, meaning that the state may confine such a person only if it can show that he or she meets the criteria for civil commitment (typically, mental illness and dangerousness).[173] The Court also held that, once unrestorability is demonstrated, continued confinement on the grounds of incompetence would violate the Constitution because the "nature and duration of [the] commitment [would] bear [no] reasonable relationship to [its] purpose."[174]

Jackson has been ignored in a number of jurisdictions, probably because the government does not want to be limited to the options of releasing or maintaining in relatively insecure civil confinement incompetent persons charged with serious crime.[175] To deal with this situation, various proposals for trying unrestorable individuals, usually calling for heightened procedural safeguards, have been proposed.[176] Applying this chapter's analysis, however, *Jackson* makes sense, at least when the person's *adjudicative* competence cannot be restored. Prosecution of a person who does not understand the charges or the system, or who is unable to communicate with counsel about the offense, can seriously undermine the integrity of the process, in terms of both reliability and dignity. Moreover, in the wake of the Supreme Court's decision in Kansas v. Hendricks,[177] a civil commitment regime is certainly capable of adequately protecting society from those who are undeterrably dangerous, as Chapter 4 explains.

Assume, however, a defendant (like Moran, Ferguson, and perhaps Kaczynski) who is competent in the adjudicative sense but not in the decisional sense. Assume further that the person's decisional incompetency cannot be remediated despite diligent treatment efforts. Should charges against such a person be dismissed? *Jackson* did not directly address that question. *Godinez* may have. If, as conjectured earlier, that opinion requires only adjudicative competence (that is, an understanding of the process, with no need to inquire into reasons) before a person can undergo adjudication, then it may permit trial of such an individual.

That result is correct, although for different reasons than the Court gives. Suppose a person is unrestorably incompetent to make a decision about waiving the insanity defense, but is competent in the adjudicative sense. Because such an individual understands the trial process and can communicate relevant facts to the attorney, neither dignity interests nor reliability would be undermined by pursuing adjudication. Less obvious, even the autonomy preference would not be slighted by proceeding to trial. Unlike a policy that permits decisions to be made for the incompetent client who has not yet been treated, surrogate decision making in this situation occurs only after society has made a good faith effort to restore the individual's decision-making capacity. In other words, autonomy has been given its due.

Thomas Litwack has objected to this position on the ground that it fundamentally contravenes the client's autonomy and may well be adverse to the client's long-term interests as well.[178] Of course, if the client's competency is not restorable, there is no autonomy to "contravene." Allowing the lawyer to make decisions for the decisionally incompetent defendant is no different from allowing a guardian to make treatment decisions in the civil commitment context, where liberty can also be at stake. The other options are to dismiss the charges despite the defendant's ability to understand and respond to them or, as Litwack seems to prefer, to allow the defendant to proceed on his own theory, however delusional (as occurred in the Ferguson case). Under the latter option, conviction is highly likely (although the jury might, after observing the defendant's antics in the courtroom, find him insane over the defendant's objection). It is not clear how that option better serves the client's "long-term interests" than a criminal trial in which a lawyer seeks to secure an insanity acquittal or perhaps an outright acquittal for the defendant.

When it is the client's *decisional* competence that is not restorable, defense attorneys should act as the ultimate fiduciary, and be authorized to act as guardian.[179] If the lawyer representing such a client believes a guilty plea is preferable to trial, the plea should be made and the court should accept it, regardless of the client's wishes. If instead the lawyer believes an insanity defense is the best defense after a sensitive appraisal of the countervailing factors described earlier, it should be raised, again regardless of the client's wishes. And presumably no waiver of counsel should ever be granted to such a client.

Conclusion

The defense attorney has a multifaceted duty toward the client with mental disability. That duty requires, first and foremost, respect for the autonomy of the client. The lawyer shows that respect not only by heeding the wishes of the competent client but also by refusing to heed the wishes of the incompetent client. A coherent approach to the competency construct is therefore important. Following Bonnie's lead, this chapter has broken competency into two components: adjudicative competency and decisional competency. It has defined the former concept in traditional terms, as an understanding of the criminal process and an ability to communicate relevant information, while arguing that the latter concept should be defined in terms of basic rationality and self-regard.

If the defense lawyer's duty to respect client autonomy is assumed, it follows that the lawyer with a client who has mental illness must assess the client's competency in both the adjudicative and decisional senses. Furthermore, if the client appears to be incompetent in either sense, the lawyer must assure that attempts are made to restore competence; if doing so requires alerting the court to the defendant's mental problems, that step must be taken. If, however, the client is competent, the attorney should generally accede to his or her wishes, at least with respect to pleading guilty, assertion of mental state defenses, and waiving the right to counsel. Occasionally, however, the lawyer's fiduciary duty to the client merges with society's interest in assuring a reliable and dignified process; in the extremely rare instances when these interests are compelling (for example, it is clear that the client who wants to plead guilty is factually innocent, or the trial of the client will make a complete mockery of the system and of the defendant), the attorney is ethically obligated to override the competent client's wishes. Furthermore, the lawyer should act as a surrogate decision maker when a defendant is competent in the adjudicative sense but unrestorably incompetent in the decisional sense.

A subtext of this chapter has been that the lawyer also owes a duty to the client to assure the system works as it should. The lawyer should resist using a competency motion for purposes other than evaluation and treatment, and, if a competency motion is made, the lawyer should ensure that any resulting intervention occurs in the least intrusive manner possible. Outpatient treatment should be the usual method of restoring competency, and hospitalization, if necessary, should never be prolonged and should be credited toward sentence. A failure to pursue these latter strategies increases the temptation of the defense attorney to ignore the client's autonomy interests out of concern about the possible consequences of a competency motion or of a plea the defendant favors, even though the attorney's calculations about possible outcomes may be off base, short-sighted, or ultimately less solicitous of the client's treatment needs.

The ethical quandaries created by cases like Theodore Kaczynski's, Colin Ferguson's, and Richard Moran's are extremely complex. The thousands of less-conspicuous cases involving defendants with mental illness can be just as daunting to defense attorneys who want to do right. The competency standard outlined here provides lawyers who are not trained in such matters with relatively clear yardsticks. The client-centered preference for autonomy establishes a strong presumption in favor of the competent client's decisions on pleas and waiver of counsel. In combination, these prescriptions define and appropriately limit the scope of the protection model in the criminal context.

— 7 —

Treatment Decision Making

This chapter is an exploration of the state's authority to force psychiatric treatment, in particular psychotropic medication, on people with mental disability. The nature of this authority depends on the legal category in which the person with disability falls. The "right to refuse treatment" (the most common way of describing the issue) varies according to whether the proposed intervention is designed to restore competency to proceed, to treat those considered unable to care for themselves, or to reduce dangerousness to others. Determining the scope of the right for the first two categories of people requires further elaboration of the protection model of liberty deprivation, while figuring out the nature of the right for those considered dangerous to others necessitates revisiting the prevention model.

The reader might wonder why discussion of the treatment refusal issue belongs in a book about deprivations of liberty. It is true that nonconsensual treatment of these groups does not *always* involve a physical deprivation of liberty. But when the treatment is psychotropic medication or something equally invasive, some type of confinement is usually involved, especially at the outset as a means to ensure a stable environment in which the proper treatment modality and dosage can be ascertained.[1] Putting this point another way, more often than not involuntary government detention of people who have a mental disability is for the express purpose of treating them. In any event, forcible psychiatric treatment, particularly in the form of medication, behavioral therapy, or psychosurgery, also clearly affects mental liberty. Thus, an analysis of laws that deprive people with mental disability of their liberty would be seriously incomplete without a discussion of the extent to which government may involuntarily treat its populace.

Much has been written about the right to refuse treatment, and especially the right to refuse psychotropic medication,[2] but the issue is particularly germane now, for two reasons. First, most of the literature on the right to refuse was written against the backdrop of a treatment regime that depended heavily on "neuroleptic" medications, which are associated with significant relapse rates and extremely negative side effects for some individuals. The recent development of "atypical" antipsychotic medications, which are purportedly more effective and have significantly fewer side effects, could be changing the terms of the debate (although I argue below it should not do so).[3]

The second reason the right-to-refuse issue is particularly topical is that recent judicial developments have thrown the governing legal regime into a state of flux, especially in connection with those found incompetent to stand trial. Until 2003, most courts held that the state's interest in trying defendants charged with crime trumped the defendant's autonomy interest in making decisions about treatment; accordingly, they permitted forcible medication of any defendant found incompetent, in either the adjudicative or decisional sense.[4] In that year, however, the Supreme Court decided Sell v. United States,[5] which has changed the constitutional calculus significantly, at least in theory. In Sell, the Court held that medication may not be used to restore competency to stand trial over objection unless there is a compelling state interest for doing so, and also concluded that the interest in ensuring that a defendant can stand trial, by itself, will not always be compelling. This holding has raised a number of questions about the state's authority to treat this category of people.

Even murkier is the doctrine surrounding the right to refuse treatment in connection with civil commitment (whether on danger to self or danger to others grounds). Some lower courts have announced that every competent individual who is not imminently dangerous to self or others has a right to refuse psychotropic medication.[6] Others seem to have adopted the position that even competent people may be forcibly medicated, not only when they are dangerous to others, but also when they are dangerous to self, and have further permitted "danger" to be defined broadly.[7] The Supreme Court appears to side with the latter group of courts, but Sell may end up having an impact here as well.

The first part of this chapter looks at the right to refuse treatment for those who are considered dangerous to others. It consists primarily of an application of the prevention model principles developed in Chapter 4 to the treatment refusal context. The second part describes the law pertaining to treatment refusals by those who are incompetent to stand trial, and then reaches conclusions about the appropriate scope of the right to refuse in that setting. In particular, it points to serious practical and logical problems with the *Sell* decision. Part 3 follows the same methodology in appraising the right to refuse treatment for those who are considered dangerous to self or unable to care for themselves. Although the focus in Part 3 is on the right to refuse, its analysis is also meant to develop more general limitations on the state's parens patriae power to deprive people of liberty in an effort to protect them.

A constant theme throughout the latter two parts is that the Supreme Court, and courts generally, have paid insufficient attention to incompetency as the threshold for treatment intervention, and thus have slighted the autonomy principle. Part 4 concludes the chapter by discussing how incompetency should be defined in connection with treatment refusals (as well as in connection with *consent* to proposed treatments). To some extent, this discussion repeats the arguments in Chapter 6, because it concludes that the basic rationality and self-regard test developed there should also apply in this setting. But the chapter fine-tunes those arguments through a critique of the most sophisticated effort to date at defining competency in the treatment decision-making context—the MacArthur Treatment Competence Study. Assessment of this work helps surface for the courts, lawyers, and mental health professionals the most important components of the competency concept.

I. Persons Considered Dangerous to Others

The U.S. Supreme Court's first opinion concerning the right to refuse psychiatric treatment was Washington v. Harper.[8] There the Court considered a prison policy that permitted forcible medication of inmates who pose a "substantial risk" of "physical harm" to themselves, others, or property, or who are "gravely disabled," if they also suffered from "mental disorder" (defined as "any organic, mental, or emotional impairment which has substantial adverse effects on an individual's cognitive or volitional functions"). Harper had been forcibly medicated because he was experiencing psychotic symptoms that, the state alleged, made him a threat to other people in the prison. But Harper argued that prison authorities should not be able to treat him over his objection unless they could also show he was incompetent to make treatment decisions, a showing that could not be made simply through proof of "mental disorder" as that term was defined in the policy. Assuming that Harper was in fact competent, the Court nonetheless held that his "suggested rule takes no account of the legitimate governmental interest in treating him where medically appropriate for the purpose of reducing the danger he poses."[9]

The Court is right, at least in its assertion that incompetence should not be a threshold requirement for state intervention on prevention of violence grounds. As Chapter 4 explained, government is generally entitled to prevent harm to others through coercive intervention if doing so does not violate the right to punishment. If the preventive intervention occurs after conviction, as it did in Harper's case, that right is not violated. Nor is it violated when it occurs before or in the absence of conviction, if the target of the intervention is undeterrable, as will often be the case with people who are seriously mentally ill and are either civilly committed as dangerous to others or committed after an acquittal by reason of insanity. If the government's aim is to prevent harm to others, the protection model, as implemented through the competency construct, is irrelevant in these contexts.

That conclusion does not necessarily mean that Harper himself could be forcibly medicated, however. Chapter 4 also developed limiting principles on the state's ability to engage in otherwise permissible preventive intervention, two of which call into question the Court's resolution of Harper's case. First, under Jackson v. Indiana,[10] the nature of the intervention must be reasonably related to its purpose, meaning it must achieve its goal without causing unnecessary liberty deprivation. As noted above, the *Harper* Court did insist, in apparent agreement with this principle, that medication to reduce dangerousness be "medically appropriate." But, as Justice Stevens pointed out in his dissent in *Harper,* there was significant evidence in Harper's case that medication did not reduce his dangerousness, such as it was. The one incident report in his record (an assault on two nurses) occurred while he was on medication; further, according to one of his doctors, Harper was "irritable" and "uncooperative" when receiving medication, while off it he was psychotic but nonassaultive.[11]

Even if the medication did reduce his antisocial behavior, it was probably not a reasonable means of doing so. As Stevens noted, the medication Harper received, one of the older neuroleptics called Prolixin, had several deleterious effects. The well-known adverse reactions to these drugs can include drowsiness, restlessness, hypertension, nausea, vomiting, loss of appetite, dry mouth, headaches, constipation, eczema, muscle spasms, and, in their worst guise, catatonic-like states, tardive dyskinesia (an irreversible syndrome of uncontrollable movements), and neuroleptic malignant syndrome, which is fatal to 30 percent of those who suffer from it.[12] Harper experienced enough of these effects to state at one point that he would rather die than take the medication.[13] That, combined with the fact that administrative segregation and disciplinary sanctions had been successfully used on Harper in the past,[14] suggests that the medication was hardly the least restrictive means of achieving the state's goal of reducing danger. Stevens summed up the point well when he stated, "A rule that allows prison administrators to address potential security risks by forcing psychotropic drugs on mentally ill inmates for prolonged periods is unquestionably an 'exaggerated response' to that concern."[15]

Even if Harper's treatment was medically appropriate and the least intrusive means of reducing his antisocial behavior, it may not have been justified. The second principle that *Harper*'s holding may have violated is the consistency principle, which requires that preventive intervention be based on proof of dangerousness equivalent to that required by analogous interventions under the criminal law. As Chapter 4 explained, with few exceptions (exceptions that Chapter 4 argues should not exist), inchoate and anticipatory crimes require proof of a high probability of imminent harm to others, unless the predicted harm is significant, in which case the likelihood of its occurrence need not be as high. Neither type of danger appears to have been shown with respect to Harper. As noted above, when not on medication Harper had no history of serious antisocial behavior in the institution; thus he did not appear to be immediately physically threatening to other inmates or to jail personnel when unmedicated. On the record before the Court, Harper left untreated was at most a nuisance, not a serious, imminent risk.

Forcible administration of treatment to prevent danger to others, then, is permissible under two conditions: (1) the person poses a moderate risk of imminent, serious harm or a high risk of less serious imminent harm; and (2) the proffered treatment is an effective way of reducing the risk without unreasonably harming the individual. Conversely, if the second condition is not met—the proposed treatment is not "medically appropriate" because it is not efficacious at reducing the danger or it is an exaggerated response to the danger—then the individual's refusal should be honored even if the individual represents a significant danger to others. However, as developed in the next two sections, the absence of the first condition—the requisite level of danger—does *not* necessarily prevent forcible treatment, if it is an effective way of restoring an individual found incompetent to stand proceed or of preventing an individual who is incapable of making the necessary treatment decisions from harming himself.

II. Defendants Found Incompetent to Proceed

Two years after *Harper*, the Supreme Court decided Riggins v. Nevada,[16] which involved a defendant who had been convicted of capital murder and sentenced to death while he was on very high dosages of Mellaril, a potent antipsychotic medication. Although Riggins argued he should have had a right to refuse the medication, the Court avoided that issue. Instead, it granted relief to Riggins on narrower grounds. First, the Court noted that, unlike in *Harper*, there had been no showing that "treatment with antipsychotic medication was medically appropriate and, considering less intrusive alternatives, essential for the sake of Riggin's own safety or the safety of others" (language that nicely sums up the principles described in the previous section, although I believe, for reasons indicated there, that no such showing was made in *Harper* either).[17] More important for present purposes, the Court also emphasized that the medication may have compromised Riggins's legal rights. The Court was particularly concerned about the possibility that the medication's tranquilizing impact on Riggins could have adversely affected "the substance of his own testimony, his interaction with counsel, or his comprehension of the trial."[18]

Riggins rightly stressed that if a criminal defendant is medicated, the treatment must not compromise his or her Sixth Amendment rights to a fair trial, confront accusers, and effective assistance of counsel. Clinicians, lawyers, and judges are obligated to ensure that medication does not impair the defendant's demeanor, memory, ability to testify, or ability to communicate with the attorney.[19] Using the terminology of Chapter 6, medication, forced or not, should not be allowed to undermine the reliability or dignity of the trial, or the autonomy of the individual, interests that the individual and the government share.

Assuming that goal can be accomplished, is it then permissible to medicate over objection a criminal defendant when, as will often be the case with defendants who are mentally ill, the medication is the only way to restore competency? As noted at the beginning of this chapter, until recently most lower courts answered this question affirmatively, perhaps aware that a negative answer might cause major disruption to the prosecution process. According to one estimate, for instance, roughly 75 percent of forensic clients refuse medication at one time or another.[20]

Nonetheless, the Supreme Court declared in Sell v. United States that forcible medication of defendants found incompetent to stand trial should be "rare," at least when the state admits that the purpose of the medication is to restore competency.[21] In that situation, Justice Stephen Breyer stated for six members of the Court, the treatment can occur only if it facilitates achievement of an "important" state interest. And, he continued, the interest in prosecuting a criminal accused, by itself, will often not be important enough.[22] For instance, Sell had been charged with fifty-six counts of mail fraud, six counts of Medicaid fraud, and one count of money laundering, but the Court did not consider seeking conviction on those charges a sufficiently compelling interest to warrant medicating him over his objection. Even prosecution of more serious crimes might not outweigh the individual's autonomy interest, Breyer suggested, if the government can commit the individual and thus protect the public without having to go to trial.[23]

But there is far more to Sell than that. While purporting to establish a strong right to refuse for defendants found incompetent to stand trial, the Court also reiterated Harper's holding that the state may forcibly medicate criminal defendants who are dangerous to self or others.[24] The Court did not directly address whether this exception applied to Sell, because it felt bound by the lower courts' holding that Sell was not presently dangerous. But it strongly suggested that, had it been deciding the case de novo, it would have permitted medication of Sell over his objection, given reports of his assaultiveness and undisputed expert testimony that he was dangerous.[25]

As a result, however radical Sell might appear as a matter of law, its practical impact on prosecutions of people with mental disability could well be minimal. Trial judges who want to ensure that an incompetent defendant is medicated and tried can often find evidence of dangerousness to self or others somewhere in the record. Even if they cannot, judges may be able to conclude that prosecution of the charges is an "important" state interest, at least if the charges are more serious than those in Sell. While that option will not be available when the defendant is charged with a misdemeanor or a minor felony, in these cases Sell at most will only accelerate the already popular practice of diverting defendants with mental disability who are not dangerous and who are charged with low-level crimes out of the criminal justice system.[26]

That Sell might not lead to numerous unwanted charge dismissals does not mean it will have no detrimental effects, however. For one thing, the decision creates an incentive for virtually all the players in the criminal process to act pretextually. Worried about dismissals, judges will be tempted to find incompetent defendants competent, or to find incompetent defendants dangerous to self or others when they are not. Similarly, prosecutors may be prone to overcharge to make the government's interest more "important." Clinicians working at forensic facilities will be asked to treat "dangerousness" but will know the real purpose of the referral is to restore competency (and in those cases where the treatment modalities might differ depending on whether reduction in danger or restoration of competency is the goal, clinicians will be pressured to pursue both). Defense attorneys might be more likely to raise the competency issue even when competency is not in doubt, because a finding of incompetency and treatment refusal can lead to dismissal of charges. For the same reason, defendants will be tempted to refuse medication, even when they are not concerned about side effects, simply as a means of evading prosecution. In other words, everyone involved in criminal prosecution of a person who has been found incompetent will pretend restoration of competency is not the issue, when in fact it is the only issue.

Second, in those (few?) serious cases where a refusal is honored and charges are dismissed, one of two dispositions will follow, neither of them good. The theoretically correct disposition is complete release from government custody, even for individuals who are mentally ill and have been charged with a felony, since by definition they are not dangerous to self or others (otherwise they could be forcibly medicated under *Harper* and tried). The disposition that may be more likely, however, is commitment. Although that should not be an option under appropriately narrow commitment standards of the type espoused in this book, Breyer implied that it would be, when he noted in *Sell* that "[t]he defendant's failure to take drugs voluntarily . . . may mean lengthy confinement in an institution for the mentally ill."[27] If so, in retaliation for refusing treatment the state may detain these people well beyond the time they would have received if sentenced, something that, as Chapter 6 indicated, is already going on even for those who are *truly* unrestorable (in clear violation of Jackson v. Indiana).[28]

At least as serious as these practical problems with *Sell* is the decision's failure on a conceptual level, for the opinion both unduly minimizes the state's interest and exaggerates the individual's. Except when the charge is a means of dealing with nuisance cases (in which case diversion out of the criminal justice system is the proper response, for reasons given in Chapter 4),[29] the state's interest in prosecuting people charged with crime is obviously a significant one. Breyer's attempt to discount this interest by pointing to the civil commitment option is incoherent. First, as noted above, it is not clear that civil commitment *is* an option in those cases where refusal is permitted, since these people are not dangerous. More important, it is wrong to imply, as the *Sell* Court does, that the state's primary goal in prosecuting individuals is protection of the public. While that would be true if the proposals in Chapter 5 were adopted, today's criminal justice system is largely focused on punishing the blameworthy. As one court put it, the argument that civil commitment can achieve the state's goals as adequately as forcible medication and trial "ignores the retributive, deterrent, communicative, and investigative functions of the criminal justice system, which serve to ensure that offenders receive their just deserts, to make clear that offenses entail consequences, and to discover what happened through the public mechanism of trial."[30] That is true whether the crime is murder or a low-level felony.

Sell also gives undue weight to the individual's interest in refusing medication. First, any harm to the individual is substantially reduced if *Harper* and *Riggins* are adhered to—that is, if the medication is truly medically appropriate and is the least restrictive way of restoring competency without impairing Sixth Amendment rights. More important, virtually all defendants who are incompetent to stand trial are also incompetent to make treatment decisions, a status that, as the next part of this chapter reiterates, eliminates the right to refuse. A person who does not meet the basic rationality and self-regard standard proposed in Chapter 6, or the even lower criminal competency threshold apparently announced in *Godinez*, is unlikely to be able both to understand the risks and benefits of particular treatments and to give nondelusional reasons for refusing them. There are insinuations in *Sell* that the Court understood this point,[31] but it veered away from explicitly recognizing it, perhaps because it did not want the right it was creating to be stillborn.

If all of this is correct, defendants charged with a nontrivial crime who are incompetent to stand trial or to proceed with some other aspect of the criminal process should not have the right to refuse medication when the treatment meets the necessity and appropriateness requirements of *Harper* and *Riggins*. These latter requirements are not insubstantial. But if they are satisfied, so are the dictates of the reliability, dignity, and autonomy principles outlined in the previous chapter.

III. Persons Considered Dangerous to Self

The treatment refusal policy at issue in *Harper*, it will be recalled, permitted forcible medication not only of those disordered prisoners who were dangerous to others, but also of those who were dangerous to self or gravely disabled. The policy defined danger to self as "[a] substantial risk that physical harm will be inflicted by an individual upon his own person, as evidenced by threats or attempts to commit suicide or inflict physical harm on one's self." Gravely disabled was defined as "[a] condition in which a person . . . (a) [i]s in danger of serious physical harm resulting from a failure to provide for his essential human needs of health or safety, or (b) manifest severe deterioration in routine functioning evidenced by repeated and escalating loss of cognitive or volitional control over his or her actions and is not receiving such care as is essential for his or her health or safety." If one or more of these conditions was associated with "mental disorder," the policy permitted forcible medication.[32]

This book will not attempt an elaborate analysis of the type of danger to self that may trigger state intervention, a project that has been ably carried out by others.[33] As with the danger to others construct discussed in Chapter 4, a risk of harm to self should generally not be grounds for state intervention unless the harm is imminent and significant. With those understandings, the definition of danger to self provided by the policy at issue in *Harper* is adequate.

More attention must be paid, however, to the role of "mental disorder" in determining the right to refuse for those who are a risk to themselves. According to *Harper*, that term need not be equated with incompetency to make treatment decisions; *Harper* held that a person who is mentally disordered and dangerous to self may be medicated over objection even if competent to make treatment decisions. Of course, the focus of *Harper* was on forcible medication of persons who are dangerous to others; thus, any innuendo in the opinion about medication of other categories of individuals might be considered dictum. Furthermore, *Harper* involved treatment in prison rather than via the civil commitment process, which is the typical setting in which the parens patriae power is invoked. One might argue that the state has more leeway inside prison, where security concerns are heightened and the "patient" is a convict, than in other settings.

These attempts to minimize *Harper*'s implications for forcible treatment in the parens patriae context may not work, however. The government's interest in preventing self-harm is not any greater inside a prison than it is inside a mental hospital, nor does an individual lose whatever interest he has in avoiding the effects of medication simply because he has been convicted (unless, perhaps, the medication is imposed as part of the punishment, which was not the case in *Harper*). Moreover, earlier Supreme Court cases that more explicitly deal with the state's parens patriae authority in the civil commitment context are at best ambiguous on the scope of that authority; none of them explicitly require an incompetency finding. In O'Connor v. Donaldson, the first Supreme Court decision in this vein, the Court stated, without elaboration, that "the State may arguably confine a person to save him from harm."[34] Chief Justice Warren Burger's concurrence in that case suggested that state intervention is permissible if it is in "the best interests of the affected class and . . . its members are unable to act for themselves."[35] And in Addington v. Texas, the Court declared simply that "[t]he state has a legitimate interest under its parens patriae power in providing care to its citizens who are unable because of emotional disorders to care for themselves."[36] Unless one stretches the concept of "inability to care for self" beyond recognition, these pronouncements fail to mandate proof of incompetency before the state may intervene under the parens patriae power.

Sell, which does not purport to deal with civil commitment, nonetheless muddies the waters further. At one point in that opinion, Breyer asks, "Why is it medically appropriate forcibly to administer antipsychotic drugs to an individual who (1) is not dangerous and (2) is competent to make up his own mind about treatment?"[37] But he never addresses the question, thus leaving unsettled whether incompetency is a predicate for parens patriae treatment. In any event, most civil commitment statutes do not require a finding of incompetency. Instead, like the policy in *Harper,* they merely mandate that the inability to care for self be the result of mental disorder.[38]

These statutes, and Supreme Court case law to the extent it is consistent with them, are deficient. Proof of danger to self is only a necessary condition, not a sufficient one, for authorizing forcible treatment under the parens patriae power. The state should also have to show that the individual is incompetent to make decisions about the treatment. The rationale for this position should be clear by now. The autonomy principle requires the state to honor all competent decisions that do not harm others, even if they will result in significant harm to self.

However, it bears repetition—especially for those Millsian diehards who believe the state should be able to detain only those who threaten others—

that honoring an *in*competent decision to harm oneself also shows insufficient respect for the person and for the concept of autonomy. Thus the state can ignore such a decision if the predicted harm is significant enough and the intervention is medically appropriate and the least intrusive means of reducing the harm. In short, much rides on the definition of competency, which is the subject of the next section.

IV. Competency in the Treatment Setting

The test for competency in the treatment decision-making context should be the same basic rationality and self-regard standard that defines the decisional competency standard in the criminal context. In both settings the person should have to understand the relevant facts, be free of any fixed, false beliefs about those facts, and be willing to exercise decision-making authority. Of course, because the settings are different, application of the basic rationality and self-regard test will differ in the criminal and treatment contexts. While basic rationality in the criminal setting requires understanding of the charges, the criminal process, and a nondelusional grasp of the individual's criminal case, that standard in the treatment context requires an understanding of the risks and benefits of treatment and a nondelusional appreciation of how the treatment will affect the individual. But with these necessary variations recognized, in neither setting should the standard be set any lower or higher than basic rationality and self-regard.

The standard should not be any lower because if the individual cannot understand the relevant facts, is too apathetic to consider them, or has fixed, false beliefs about them, then any decision made will have little or no basis in reality. As Chapter 6 explained, honoring such a decision would sanction random choices and make a mockery of the autonomy concept. Kenneth Kress has interestingly suggested that the basic rationality and self-regard standard is too high if it would invalidate a decision to delegate one's decision-making authority to another (say, a doctor or a lawyer) by one who does not feel equipped to make the decision himself.[39] Such a decision would be invalid under the proposed test, however, only if the individual did not understand the consequences of the delegation or delegated for irrational reasons. If, instead, the individual realizes he does not have the capacity to grasp the relevant facts about treatment options, but does understand that the options can result in varying consequences and is able to give nondelusional reasons for trusting another person to make the choice, the basic rationality and self-regard test will likely be met. (In any event, the ultimate outcome in this situation is no different than if the person were found incompetent, since the delegatee will function as a guardian.)

Treatment competency should also not be set any higher than the basic rationality and self-regard standard. For reasons similar to those canvassed in Chapter 6, requiring the absence of all significant pathology or a "reasoned choice" before a treatment decision will be honored gives insufficient sway to the person's choices. These more demanding standards come too close to making some other person the repository of wisdom about what is best for the individual. For instance, these are the standards at work when psychiatrists find people incompetent simply because they deny they are mentally ill or reject the psychiatrist's treatment recommendations.[40] As Elyn Saks notes, people may persist in a denial of mental illness despite a confirmed diagnosis for a number of reasons besides "incompetency": they may not believe in the concept of mental illness, they may be unwilling to admit that such a stigmatizing label attaches to them, or, most important, they may just not feel ill.[41] In the latter instance, those who disagree with the treating doctor may simply be expressing "a legitimate preference for the symptoms over the cure" or "may be saying merely that they are not suffering—and on this, surely, it is they who are the final authorities."[42] Similarly, failure to agree with a doctor's treatment recommendation should not be dispositive of the competency issue. As Saks states, "while the doctor's belief, perhaps as well as the treatment's typical effects, may be indisputable, what effects it will have on a particular individual are not so clear, and failure to agree with the doctor does not amount to a gross distortion of reality."[43] On the latter score, she is not alone; the few existing treatment competency cases seem to adopt the same position.[44]

Analogous to Richard Bonnie's suggestion that the criminal competency standards vary depending on whether attorney and client agree, some commentators have suggested that treatment competency should also vary, depending on where the decision falls along two axes: the intrusiveness and efficacy of the treatment, and whether the individual wants or rejects the treatment.[45] For instance, voluntary hospitalization, because it is perceived to pose few risks and significant benefits, might be permitted if the individual is simply able to evidence a choice in favor of the hospital, even if he or she does not understand the risks and benefits, or wants to be hospitalized for "crazy" reasons. In contrast, a "reasoned choice" might be required before a person can consent to psychosurgery, given that treatment's experimental, highly intrusive, and irreversible nature. At the same time, on this view treatment *refusals* ought to be treated in the opposite fashion: a refusal of hospitalization would require a high degree of competency before it will be honored, whereas a refusal of psychosurgery will be adhered to almost automatically.

This variable-competency scheme for treatment competency does not work for the same types of practical and theoretical reasons it does not work in the criminal competency setting. A fair lexical ordering of treatments, which is what the variable competency approach requires, is not possible. For some people, hospitalization can be a horrible experience[46] and psychosurgery can be extremely effective.[47] A definition of competency based on any variable other than the individual's basic rationality and self-regard means that doctors, legislators, or some other third party, not the individual seeking or rejecting the treatment, is in effect making the decision. It may be that, with certain types of treatment such as psychosurgery or medication, we want to be particularly certain about the individual's competency, and thus will want to require more rigorous procedural protections to ascertain that fact.[48] But the substantive standard should not change merely because a particular treatment is viewed as more or less beneficial by a third party.

That is why recent advances in antipsychotic medication should not modify the right to refuse analysis. First, of course, the relative benefits and side effects of the atypical medications is still a matter of some dispute.[49] But even assuming the new medications are much more effective and much less risky than the older drugs, they should not be forced on an individual who is not dangerous to others unless he or she is incompetent under the basic rationality and self-regard test. If the drugs truly are superior to the older drugs, most individuals with psychosis who meet this test will probably accept them.

As in the criminal competency context, it is not enough to discuss these issues in the abstract. Analysis of some concrete examples can help flesh out the normative inquiry and the consequences of these various standards. Thus, this chapter ends with an analysis of the treatment competency research instruments developed by the MacArthur Research Network, which provide a rich setting in which to explore treatment competency issues.

A. The MacArthur Treatment Competence Study

Building on work started by Loren Roth and his associates,[50] the Mac-Arthur Treatment Competence Study, led by Paul Appelbaum and Thomas Grisso, began by carefully parsing the competency construct. Through years of laborious research and trial and error, the group developed three psychometrically sound instruments that measure as many as thirteen aspects of functioning relevant to that concept.[51] The Understanding Treatment Disclosures (UTD) instrument tests the individual's ability to grasp information about five elements (disorder, treatment, benefits of the treatment, risks of the treatment, and alternative treatment and its risk and benefits). The Thinking Rationally about Treatment (TRAT) instrument assesses the quality of the individual's processing of the information. Finally, the Perceptions of Disorder (POD) instrument consists of two subtests that assess individuals' "appreciation" of two aspects of their situation: their disorder and the benefit of the proposed treatment.

The following discussion focuses on the POD, because it raises the most interesting issues about treatment competency and is an excellent vehicle for surfacing differences in the decisional competency tests. The first subtest of the POD, the Nonacknowledgment of Disorder (NOD), inquires into: (1) patients' acknowledgment of symptoms as provided to them from their hospital chart; (2) patients' beliefs about the severity of their symptoms (which are then compared to the person's rating on the Brief Psychiatric Rating Scale [BPRS]); and (3) patients' acknowledgment of the formal diagnosis in their chart. Scores of zero are given if the person does not acknowledge the symptoms or the disorder, or if the person states that the symptoms are not severe when, according to the BPRS, they are.

The second subtest of the POD, the Nonacknowledgment of Treatment Potential (NOT), assesses acknowledgment of the importance of obtaining treatment for one's condition; the potential benefit of a specific proposed treatment; and the lesser likelihood of improvement without the treatment. On this second subtest, a person who does not acknowledge treatment potential in the initial questioning is asked why, and then given a hypothetical that "nullifies or challenges the respondent's original belief."[52] Only patients who "rigidly disavow" their treatment potential in the face of this nullifying hypothetical receive a low score (zero) on this subtest.

The POD is a wonderfully sophisticated instrument. But its two subtests are based on a conceptualization of competency that is significantly flawed, if one accepts the basic rationality and self-regard standard as the correct treatment competency standard. That standard requires an assessment of reasons for treatment decisions. In contrast, the first subtest of the POD does not assess a person's reasons for refusal at all, and the second subtest focuses on the rigidity with which those beliefs are held, rather than whether they have any basis in fact.

After explaining these conclusions in more detail, I suggest ways of revising the POD to conform to the normatively appropriate competency standard. It should be acknowledged at the outset, however, that the POD was intended merely as a research instrument. Indeed, the MacArthur group itself has substantially revised its approach to competency issues.[53] Thus, the following comments about the POD are best seen as a method of delving into the competency concept, rather than a direct criticism of the MacArthur project.

B. An Analysis of the POD's Conceptual Underpinnings

The premise of the NOD subtest is that a person is "impaired" if he or she does not acknowledge the symptoms or disorder assigned in the chart or believes that the symptoms are not "severe" when, as measured on the BPRS, they are. Yet, for reasons suggested above, the fact of denial, by itself, should be only the starting point. Much more important in evaluating competency are the reasons for denying one is disordered and whether any of those reasons are clearly wrong. While an individual's reasons for denial are supposed to be elicited during administration of the NOD, they do not affect the ultimate score on this subtest.[54] Thus, persons who, contrary to chart information and the BPRS, deny their illness or its severity simply because they want to avoid the mentally ill label or do not "feel" sick are nonetheless found to be impaired on this subtest.

One way to understand the problems this approach poses is to compare how the NOD would be applied to a patient who is physically ill. Assume a patient, John, who has been diagnosed as having angina. The first component of the NOD would assess whether John is willing to acknowledge that he has "angina." If he is not, he receives a score of zero on this part of the NOD. But suppose that, even though he recognizes he is experiencing sharp chest pains (and indeed has reported them to the doctor), John disagrees with the doctor's diagnosis because similar pains in the past have turned out to be indigestion or because he is simply a "positive thinker" who prefers to block out unpleasant thoughts (a defense mechanism that research has shown can be related to recovery).[55] Even if his "diagnosis" is much less likely to be correct than the doctor's, neither of these reasons for such a conclusion suggest a lack of reality-testing so serious that John should be considered nonautonomous and incompetent.

Now consider Sam, a person diagnosed with schizophrenia who rejects that label. For reasons suggested in the previous chapter's discussion of Theodore Kaczynski's case, Sam may have an even stronger "rational" reason than John for eschewing his diagnosis. First, a diagnosis of schizophrenia is likely to be wrong more often than a diagnosis of heart disease.[56] Second, as the "consumer/ex-patient" movement has persuasively asserted, psychiatric diagnoses—much more so than diagnoses of most physical illnesses—can be dehumanizing, erosive of self-esteem, and so stigmatizing that they ruin relationships, disrupt employment, and prevent a normal life.[57] Yet the NOD considers these types of reasons irrelevant.

The component of the NOD that attempts to determine whether the patient acknowledges the severity of the symptoms is suspect for the same reason. Here again, a simple disagreement should not suffice for a finding of incompetency with respect to either of our hypothetical patients. Even if his doctors believe his heart disease is "advanced," John may prefer to think otherwise. Perhaps, as conjectured above, he believes positive thinking is the best approach in such situations. Or he may just disagree with the doctors' definition of severe, a term that is, after all, susceptible to many interpretations. Sam, our psychiatric patient, may have even less reason to agree with his doctors' assessment. Even more so than with a diagnostic pronouncement, a declaration that symptoms are "severe" is significantly more subjective where mental, as opposed to physical, phenomena are concerned. Although the MacArthur group attempted to "objectify" the severity measurement by resorting to the BPRS, even a cursory look at that instrument reveals the amorphous, ultimately subjective nature of its inquiry. For instance, the interviewer using the BPRS is supposed to rate on a numerical scale ranging from one to seven the presence of symptoms such as anxiety (defined as "worry, fear, or overconcern for present or future"); conceptual disorganization (defined as the "degree to which the thought processes are confused, disconnected, or disorganized"); and excitement (defined as "heightened emotional tone, agitation, increased reactivity"), constructs that are not susceptible to meaningful quantification.[58]

Finally, the third aspect of the NOD examines whether the person acknowledges his or her symptoms. This inquiry is on much firmer ground, because discovery of symptoms usually relies on concrete observation or testing of the patient. In the physical illness context, such third-party observation can provide highly reliable evidence. Assume, for instance, a valid laboratory shows that John has clogged arteries. Even Saks would agree that a refusal by John to accept these results is indicative of incompetency, because the patient is so clearly wrong. Analogous reasoning applies in the mental health setting. If Sam denied, despite contradictory chart evidence, that he talks to people who are not there, significant impairment is clearly present. If instead he insists that the nonexistent people *are* present, or declares that he is Napoleon, an unwillingness to acknowledge that these perceptions are hallucinations or delusions (that is, obviously inconsistent with reality) would also indicate a significant lack of appreciation of his condition. In both the physical and mental treatment settings, focusing on acknowledgment of symptoms shifts the inquiry from the subjective issue of whether the patient is "sick" to a more objective inquiry into whether the patient is wrong about demonstrable facts.[59]

Even here, however, the physical and mental arenas differ. Mental "symptoms" can range from descriptions of behavior (rapid pacing, hearing of nonexistent voices, statements that "I am Napoleon") to categorical traits, such as "anxiety" or "depression." The latter terms are obviously much more value laden than typical symptoms of physical illness, and patients who deny they apply to them are more likely to be "right." Categorical terms like delusion and hallucination are less subject to misapplication, but even they can be wrong, especially when based on third-party observation rather than self-report (for example, a conclusion that a patient is hallucinating based on the fact that the patient is talking to himself or herself). It is not clear whether the NOD takes these concerns into account. The "symptoms" about which a patient is quizzed are supposed to be taken from the chart, but that term is not otherwise defined in the manual.[60] If the chart is typical, symptoms are often described categorically rather than behaviorally. To ensure that competency is measured reliably, the interviewer should describe the symptoms in functional terms ("the chart says you believe you are Jesus Christ"), and then ask whether the individual adheres to that belief.

This focus on denial of specific functions rather than on denial of diagnosis or symptom severity is also superior to the common practice among many mental health professionals of labeling "incompetent" individuals who are thought to "lack insight" about their "illness." This practice is a true catch-22: agreement with the doctor means the person is mentally ill, but so does disagreement. Recent research does suggest that anosognosia, a neurological condition that results in unawareness that one is ill and a compulsion to prove that one is sane, is highly prevalent among people with schizophrenia.[61] But if this condition truly is present, it should lead not only to a denial of blanket claims of mental illness, but also to a denial of functional symptoms; only in the latter case is a finding of incompetency warranted.

In contrast to the NOD, the NOT requires assessment of one's reasons for refusing treatment in making the impairment determination. Recall that the only people who are subjected to inquiry under the NOT are those who state that treatment will not, or will probably not, help them. Furthermore, once a reason for this stance is elicited, only those people who insist on it in the face of a hypothetical that nullifies or challenges their reason for nonacknowledgment are considered incompetent. The hypotheticals all take the form of asking the person to assume that treatment has been developed that helps 90 percent of the people in the patient's situation. For instance, if the reason a person gives for not wanting treatment is that he or she is "just too sick," the challenging hypothetical goes like this: "Imagine that a doctor tells you that there is a treatment that has been shown in research to help 90 percent of people with problems just as serious as yours. Do you think this treatment might be of more benefit to you than getting no treatment all?"[62] Only respondents who answer "definitely not" or "probably not" to this question receive a score indicative of incompetency.

Although the NOT comes much closer than the NOD to the type of inquiry the basic rationality and self-regard test envisions, it too is deficient. First, for it to work, one must assume that abstract hypotheticals are taken seriously and that words like "benefit" have a universal meaning. The latter is a particularly risky assumption; for instance, those who believe the side effects of medication outweigh its reduction in symptomatology might have real trouble saying the medication will benefit them.

A more important objection is that a belief that one is among the 10 percent of those who are "too sick" to benefit from a particular treatment—a belief that the NOT suggests is evidence of incompetency—should *not* be considered irrational. Indeed, even people with no disorder are often willing to assume they are in a small minority, for all sorts of reasons. For instance, people tend to give less weight than warranted to base rate statistics (like the 90 percent hypothetical in the NOT) and, correspondingly, more weight than warranted to diagnostic information (in this setting, the patient's self-diagnosis).[63] Particularly relevant to situations where the reason for denying treatment has to do with side effects is research indicating that people greatly overestimate dramatic and sensational causes of death, such as accidents, homicide, and cancer (which in our setting would be replaced by concerns about malignant neuroleptic syndrome or tardive dyskinesia).[64] And research on "information framing" indicates that choices often depend on how information is presented. For instance, patients are more likely to opt for a risky treatment if it is described as a means of preventing the patient's current state from deteriorating rather than, as is true under the NOT, as a way of improving an otherwise dismal prognosis.[65] For these sorts of reasons, only if the person expresses a view about the treatment that is manifestly wrong—for instance, that the hypothesized medication would never help anyone or that it causes pregnancy—should a finding of incompetency be contemplated.

Yet the NOT instrument consistently permits a finding of incompetency on a much lesser showing. Consider these other representative examples of statements that, if persistently held in the face of the relevant hypothetical, are indicative of incompetency under the NOT: "I've had treatment for so many years and nothing has changed"; "I don't really need [the treatment]. Many people get better without it"; "How could [the treatment] help if nothing else in my life changes?"; "It's in the hands of God. Who knows?"; "The only thing that will work is if you just convince yourself that you are going to get better"; "I don't need any treatment as long as I'm busy, make a lot of friends, keep my mind off things"; "Those medications just make you feel worse"; "I just think it won't help."[66] Even if given by our angina patient, John, many of these reasons would be an insufficient basis for an incompetency finding (at least if my law students, whom I queried on the issue, are any guide).[67] With Sam the case for incompetency is even weaker, because psychotropic medication is not as successful as, and is more likely to have significant side effects than, heart medicine. Yet the NOT would suggest both individuals are incapable of making treatment decisions if these sorts of reasons are given. Indeed, with the exception of those who give religious or cultural explanations for refusing to acknowledge treatment potential, everyone who continues to deny they can be helped by medication during the second-stage inquiry of the NOT is found impaired.[68] This group includes those who believe the well-known side effects of the medication outweigh its benefits.[69]

In short, the two subtests of the POD define impairment too broadly for treatment competency purposes. The POD focuses too much of its attention on one's willingness to go along with medical opinion about diagnosis and treatment and not enough attention on the quality of the reasons for refusing to acknowledge this opinion. If these conclusions are correct, the remaining question is whether an instrument can be developed that takes them into account.

C. Refining the POD

One response to the above arguments might be to eliminate the POD entirely. The competency assessment could be based solely on a person's ability to understand and reason as measured by the UDT and the TRAT. This remedy is too drastic, however. For one thing, while the UDT or a similar manner of ascertaining understanding of treatment options is fundamental to the competency determination, the TRAT's focus on reasoning process requires capacities well beyond those the basic rationality and self-regard test demands (a point developed further in the next chapter). More important, abandonment of the "appreciation" inquiry contemplated by the POD would eliminate a crucial element of the competency inquiry: as the basic rationality and self-regard test recognizes, people who have patently false beliefs about their own situation should not be considered competent even if they fully understand such a situation in the abstract and even if their reasoning process is reasonably intact. Finally, assuming these conclusions are correct, an empirically based and normatively sound method of assessing the appreciation component of competency is obviously preferable to one that relies on intuitive judgments that may be based on stereotypes (for example, anyone who is mentally ill is incompetent) or paternalism (for example, anyone who rejects treatment is incompetent). Thus, the MacArthur group's attempt to develop a psychometrically sound instrument that measures appreciation is a useful one.

Nonetheless, in light of the foregoing arguments, the POD instrument should be modified. The NOD subtest, focusing on one's acknowledgment of disorder, should be reduced to the one component that focuses on denial of symptomatology. As discussed above, this part of the NOD is not as questionable as those components that assess acknowledgement of diagnosis and illness severity, because the presence or absence of many symptoms, when defined behaviorally, can be objectively affirmed, and because denial of obvious symptoms is relevant to treatment competency. Only obvious symptoms, such as those associated with loose associations, hallucinations, and delusions, should be used for this purpose, however. Moreover, a simple denial of such symptoms cannot end the matter: A patient could refuse to acknowledge even obvious symptoms for a "rational" reason, namely, fear that such acknowledgement will lead to unwanted treatment.[70] Conversely, some people who acknowledge their symptoms may nonetheless prefer them to treatment and, again, one must determine whether the reasons for this preference are patently false in the sense demanded by the basic rationality test.

Thus, the NOT subtest, which addresses views about treatment, should be retained as well. One possible refinement of this instrument would be to rely on the same types of hypotheticals it does but substitute a 100 percent figure for the 90 percent figure. A person who denies the helpfulness of a treatment with a 100 percent success rate for similarly situated patients could be said to hold a belief for which there is no evidence, at least hypothetically. The problem, of course, is that the 100 percent figure is just a hypothetical. A person might continue to deny treatment efficacy on the plausible ground that such a success rate (or even a 90 percent rate) is simply not feasible. The difficulty of assuring that answers to such esoteric questions are meaningful counsels for a less elegant approach. Thus, if the person continues to deny any treatment potential after the hypothetical, the reasons for doing so should be more fully explored.

Contrary to what the reader may be thinking at this point, the types of reasons for rejecting treatment that would fail the basic rationality and self-regard test are legion. Several examples can be found, for instance, in Grant Morris's description of his experience as a hearing officer charged with determining the treatment competency of mental health patients in California.[71] Many of the fifty patients Morris found incompetent appeared unable to understand the risks and benefits of treatment, and thus the appreciation issue was secondary. Others found incompetent understood risks and benefits but gave one of the following reasons for refusing medication: a belief the medicine was poison; a belief that the medication would harm the patient's fetus, even though the patient was not pregnant; an inability to articulate a reason why the patient could take medication in pill but not in liquid form; a belief that the patient was not assaultive, when in fact he was; an unwillingness to consider small dosages of medication even though refusal was based on fear that large dosages would hurt one's stomach; a belief that the medication would have no effect; a denial of clear physical illness; a statement that the reason for refusing medication was "because it creates an illusion and that's Walt Disney;" a belief that the doctors were delusional; a belief that the doctors were practicing witchcraft. All these reasons, if adhered to in the face of clarifying questions, are clearly based on false perceptions of reality. It should also be remembered that the person who does not evidence a choice or who, due to apathy, is "non-protesting," would be incompetent under the self-regard component of the basic rationality and self-regard standard.

However, when reasons *are* given for refusing (or consenting) to treatment, and the factual predicate of the reasons *cannot* be easily disconfirmed (as with statements that the same treatment has not helped in the past or that the treatment hurts more than it helps), they are an insufficient basis for denying the authority to make treatment decisions, even if "rigidly" held. Contrary to the implicit assumption of the NOT, a fixed belief is not necessarily a wrong or irrelevant belief. Again, the ultimate inquiry should focus on the extent to which the person believes "facts" for which there is no evidence, not "facts" that change depending on whether one is the patient or the doctor. In short, the appropriate standard in the psychiatric medication context is the basic rationality and self-regard test.

Conclusion

Treatment refusal is a difficult, highly emotional subject. Civil libertarians inveigh against "chemical straitjackets" while treating professionals complain about patients "rotting with their rights on."[72] The "patient" is sometimes lost in the heat of battle. The individual's autonomy cannot be slighted, but neither should the incompetent individual's treatment needs be ignored. Accordingly, treatment should always be medically appropriate and essential to achieving the legitimate purposes of the state. Those purposes are limited to preventing imminent, significant danger to others, restoring the competency of defendants charged with nontrivial crimes, and treating individuals who evidence significant danger to self and fail the basic rationality and self-regard test.

A pragmatist might observe that the basic rationality and self-regard standard dooms some people to repeated cycles of refusal and decompensation until gross delusion sets in, at which point treatment will occur only until those delusions are removed and the person once again refuses it. The pragmatist might also point out that this standard could have the practical effect of burdening society with untreated people who are unable to survive without significant, expensive assistance. A pragmatist should also note, however, that psychiatric treatments are not always effective and carry significant risks;[73] that people treated against their will do not fare as well as those who accept treatment;[74] that experiencing decompensation may trigger the necessary motivation to try treatment;[75] that lifelong medication is also a very expensive proposition;[76] and that some untreatable people who are presently in hospitals should not be there.[77] Further, a robust right to refuse encourages dialogue between doctor and patient that is all too rare when the patient is mentally disabled.[78] My own feeling is that practical concerns are a wash and that the normative inquiry about government's authority to force treatment is the dispositive one.

It must also be acknowledged, however, that this book's efforts at this normative inquiry have ignored two other threats to the protection model of liberty deprivation, both of which will be briefly examined here. The first has to do with the concept of "mandated treatment." In today's legal regime, people with mental disability are often forced to agree to psychiatric treatment as a condition of receiving "benefits," such as public housing, welfare, or reduced sentences.[79] In discussing government's authority to engage in this practice, concepts of autonomy and the like have often been neglected, with the debate instead centering on whether the benefit sought is a "privilege" or an "entitlement."[80] On this view, privileges can be conditioned on an agreement to undergo treatment, whereas entitlements may not be.

But this manner of approaching the issue is misguided. First, distinguishing between privileges and entitlements can be extremely difficult. (Into which category does welfare fall?) In any event, that inquiry has the wrong focal point—the nature of the benefit sought. The focus instead should be the nature of the interest that government wants the individual to sacrifice. Government should be able to make receipt of a benefit conditional upon treatment only when the person does not have a right, as defined in this chapter, to refuse that treatment; thus, a person who is dangerous without treatment can be told he will not get public housing unless he agrees to treatment, and a person who is incompetent to make treatment decisions can be required to undergo treatment as a condition of receiving Social Security payments. Conversely, however, government should never be able to force nondangerous, competent individuals to undergo psychiatric treatment to obtain a benefit, regardless of whether the benefit is denominated a privilege or an entitlement.

The mandated treatment debate is connected to an even larger debate about whether the concept of autonomy should continue to be conceptualized as something centered in the individual. Liberal "progressives" argue that if, as Mill suggested, the ultimate goal of society is the promotion of freedom in decision-making, then individual choices may be limited when they are destructive of the individual's own freedom, even if they harm no one else. Thus, for instance, even Mill held that government should be able to prevent a person from enslaving himself, regardless of his "competence."[81] Social constructivists even more forcefully reject an individual-centered concept of autonomy, on the separate ground that individual choices are better viewed as the product of social forces.[82] As author J. L. Hill notes, "[i]n the extreme versions of this view, no choices are truly authentic, and government intervention is justified not only to prevent the individual from making bad choices, but . . . to 'construct' individuals to make better choices and thereby to be better citizens."[83]

A comprehensive response to the progressive-constructivist position will not be attempted here, but a few observations can be made. As applied to people with mental disability, the progressivist-constructionist way of thinking about autonomy would substitute for the right to refuse treatment, exercised by the individual, a right to "good" treatment, as defined by experts. It would disregard the individual's own desires about treatment any time those desires are considered "dangerous" to the individual—not just dangerous in the physical sense, but dangerous mentally, in the sense of potentially undermining mental freedom. In effect, the progressivist-constructivist position would replace the protection model of liberty deprivation with a prevention model.

The tension between this outcome and the autonomy principle is obvious, despite progressive attempts to reconcile the two. This is apparent even when considering consensual enslavement, Mill's paradigmatic example of when a person's will may be ignored: One person's "enslavement" can be another's act of penance or sole means of survival (furthermore, any brutality associated with such an arrangement should trigger government intervention against the "enslavor").[84] The constructivist's relativism about autonomy also wrings hollow, at least when incompetency is defined, as I have defined it, in terms of beliefs that are clearly false; under this definition, there is little or nothing to be relative about.

None of this is meant to imply that paternalism is an unmitigated evil; the progressive-constructivist position may be justifiable in many contexts, ranging from motorcycle helmet laws to food and drug legislation.[85] But that position cannot be sustained when the issue is state authority to deprive people of liberty. As Chapter 5 contemplated, the prevention model of liberty deprivation might be a worthwhile substitute for the *punishment* model. But expanding its reach to eliminate the incompetency limitation on detention of citizens whenever it is considered necessary to "protect" them from themselves—in other words, creation of a true therapeutic state—grants government far too much power.

—8—

Conclusion: Rethinking Legally Relevant Mental Disorder

As this book has made clear, the law insists on maintaining mental disorder as a predicate for a wide array of legal provisions, in both the criminal justice system and the civil law. Among adults, only a person with a "mental disease or defect" can escape conviction for an intentional, unjustified crime on grounds of cognitive or volitional impairment.[1] Only people with "mental illness" or "mental abnormality" may be subjected to indeterminate preventive commitment based on dangerousness.[2] Under the laws of many states, only people with a mental disorder are prevented from making decisions about treatment, criminal charges, the right to counsel, and a host of other important aspects of life.[3]

What is it about "mental disorder" that merits such special legal treatment? Why are people with mental disorder singled out by the law in so many different contexts? These questions can only be answered by first figuring out what the law is trying to accomplish in those areas in which it makes mental disability relevant. That has been the task of this book, in those settings in which mental disorder is a predicate for either avoiding or imposing a deprivation of life or liberty. It is in these situations, where the stakes are the highest, that it is most important to determine precisely what the law means and should mean when it uses the term mental illness and like terminology.

Chapter 1 described how the behavioral sciences have defined mental disorder. Generally, that chapter pointed out, clinicians have described mental disorders in terms of their *effects* (for example, shortened life span, reduced fertility), *processes* (for example, irrationality), or *causes* (for example, organic etiology). These categories are vague and expansive, leaving the law plenty of working room. This chapter begins by summarizing how the *law* treats the concept of mental disability. In general, the law's definitions of this phenomenon have been equally vague, and are often nonresponsive to the law's own normative objectives.

That conclusion leads to a discussion, in Part 2 of the chapter, of what the goals of liberty deprivation law *should* be, which allows summarization of the major themes of this book. Specifically, the argument is that mental disorder is relevant to laws that deprive people of liberty only to the extent it diminishes culpability (when punishment is the issue), deterrability (when prevention is the goal), or competency (when protection is the objective). Part 2 is not solely a regurgitation of previous chapters however. It also parses from them a common theme—that in determining whether a person lacks culpability, is undeterrable, or is incompetent, the law should focus on the *content* of the person's thoughts. Aberrant thought content can be distinguished from a number of other characteristics of mental illness, most prominently an aberrant thought *process.* Analysis of one's thought process might include an examination of thought content but would also require examining the consistency and coherence of the person's beliefs and desires and perhaps a number of other variables. This book argues that, in deciding whom to deprive of liberty for the purposes of punishment, prevention, or protection, the content of the person's thought process is the relevant consideration, not how he or she arrives at that content or other mental phenomena.

Finally, Part 3 explores the advantages and disadvantages of a content-based approach to legally relevant mental disorder. The advantages include: a strong reaffirmation of most people's responsibility, deterrability, and competence; a concomitant destigmatization of mental disorder; and more precise legal standards. At the same time, a content-based definition of legally relevant mental disorder might represent an uncomfortable departure from lay understandings about mental disorder, make some legal determinations more subject to manipulation by litigants, and lead to an emphasis on autonomy values that some might argue should be downplayed given our increasing knowledge about the causes of human behavior.

There are two overarching theses to this concluding chapter, and thus to this book as a whole. The first is that the choice as to how mental disorder should be defined for legal purposes should be based on pragmatic as well as normative concerns, since normative analysis leaves so many questions unanswered. A related thesis is that mental disorder is such a vacuous phrase that the law should consider dispensing with it as an independent criterion for intervention and instead simply identify as precisely as possible the types of mental dysfunction it wants to treat specially.

I. Legal Approaches to Mental Illness

As Chapter 1 noted, no less an authority than the U.S. Supreme Court has counseled that judges and legislators, not psychiatrists or other mental health professionals, should define the scope of legally relevant mental disorder.[4] DSM also cautions that its nosology does not necessarily map onto legal constructs.[5] Those sentiments are wise. Unfortunately, however, in detailing the scope of mental disorder for legal purposes, legislatures and courts have often fallen down on the job or inappropriately delegated it to others, at least in those settings involving potential deprivations of liberty.

A. The Insanity Defense

One would think that the law would be most interested in accomplishing the task of demarcating legally relevant and irrelevant mental illness in connection with the insanity defense, the most conspicuous, if not the most commonly used, legal arena for determinations of mental illness. But despite centuries of law, the usual test for insanity still speaks simply in terms of "mental disease or defect," without further elaboration.[6] The result is enormous vagueness about the predicate for the insanity defense, despite its importance to the punishment model of liberty deprivation.

Of course, in order for an insanity claim to succeed, the mental disease or defect must cause significant cognitive or volitional impairment at the time of the offense. In the words of the popular American Law Institute (ALI)/Model Penal Code test, it must result in a lack of "substantial capacity either to appreciate the wrongfulness of [the] conduct or to conform [the] conduct to the requirements of the law."[7] A well-known criminal law treatise asserts that this language is the gravamen of insanity, and that the mental disease or defect predicate is not meant to serve any significant limiting role.[8] But the consequences of that view would be dramatic, at least in theory. As Chapter 2 pointed out, many conditions not normally associated with "insanity" correlate with substantial cognitive or volitional impairment. Psychopaths, dependent personalities, and people with mild mental retardation might not appreciate the wrongfulness of their actions. Pedophiles, people with explosive personalities, and people who commit crime to feed addictions may have trouble conforming their behavior to the requirements of the law. Since, using the DSM as our guide, any one of these people could be said to have a mental disease or defect, the term needs more content than simply equating it with a substantial lack of appreciation or control if these types of people should be held responsible for their criminal acts.

In recognition of this problem, some legislative and judicial formulations have narrowed the universe of mental disorders that can form the basis for an insanity defense. The ALI insanity formulation, for instance, includes a paragraph meant to exclude psychopathy as a ground for excuse,[9] a clause that many states have adopted.[10] Several states have gone further, prohibiting insanity claims based on any type of personality disorder.[11] Apparently along the same lines, the federal insanity statute requires a "severe" mental disease or defect.[12] Case law in some jurisdictions has expressly prohibited insanity based on conditions that are solely the result of "passion" or of substance abuse.[13] Finally, a few states have adopted definitions tied to their civil commitment statutes. For instance, Michigan defines mental illness or defect for insanity purposes as "[a] substantial disorder of thought or mood that significantly impairs judgment, behavior, capacity to recognize reality, or ability to cope with the ordinary demands of life."[14]

While these latter formulations do limit the scope of the insanity defense, they are either under- or overinclusive. Excluding psychopathy, substance abuse disorders, or some other narrow category of disability still leaves large numbers of individuals eligible for an insanity defense who probably should not be. In contrast, the blunderbuss approach—exemplified by the exclusion of all personality disorders (a category that includes paranoid, schizotypal, and borderline disorders)—prevents people with very bizarre thought content and process from arguing for an excuse.[15] The federal test's use of the word "severe" may raise the same problem, but since the word is not defined further, it is hard to know.

Michigan's formulation is the most interesting. It does not depend simply on undifferentiated diagnosis but on specific dysfunctions. Using the clinical categorizations described in Chapter 1, it looks at effects (impairment in coping ability) and process (impairment in judgment). But it is still far too imprecise, because it could encompass virtually any mental condition, a fact that Michigan courts have recognized.[16] Indeed, the Michigan definition of mental illness for insanity purposes is identical to that used in that state's guilty-but-mentally-ill statute,[17] a law that, as Chapter 3 pointed out, is routinely applied to garden-variety criminals and results in a verdict that has no mitigating impact in terms of ultimate disposition.[18]

B. Civil Commitment

The same types of observations can be made about the definition of mental disorder in the civil commitment context. As recently as the 1980s, many state civil commitment statutes did not bother to define the term at all or defined it tautologically, as a condition in which "mental health is substantially impaired."[19] Today most states use language similar to Michigan's[20] (which, it will be recalled, contemplates "a substantial disorder of thought or mood that significantly impairs judgment, behavior, capacity to recognize reality, or ability to cope with the ordinary demands of life"). That language—which I shall continue to call, for brevity's sake, the "Michigan" formulation—is clearly an improvement over the older tautological language, but it still is fatally lacking in precision in this context as well.

The reasoning necessary to reach that conclusion requires breaking commitment into its two components, police power commitment and parens patriae commitment, which substantially overlap with what this book has referred to as the prevention and protection models of liberty deprivation. In neither setting has the law's definition of mental disorder corresponded to its stated rationale for depriving people of liberty.

Police power commitment permits involuntary detention of those who are mentally disordered and dangerous to others.[21] As Chapter 4 noted, many commentators have suggested that, in this setting, mental disorder ought to be reserved for those who would be found insane were they prosecuted for a crime. Even those who do not subscribe to this notion, which includes the Supreme Court justices who were in the majority in Kansas v. Hendricks,[22] require that people subject to police power commitment suffer from a "mental abnormality" that makes them "dangerous beyond their control."[23]

Commitment laws that simply list various diagnoses as the predicate for intervention obviously do not capture either notion. The Michigan language improves on the diagnostic approach somewhat, but not much. Consider first whether the language captures those who would be excused on insanity grounds if they committed crime. In Michigan, as already pointed out, this language also describes those who are guilty "but mentally ill," which suggests that it is applied to many who would not be excused were they to commit a crime. Putting aside that fact, which could be due to legislative oversight, the language making eligible for commitment those who have substantial impairments of judgment and behavior also easily applies to people with antisocial personality,[24] individuals rarely found insane when they commit crime and therefore, presumably, people who generally should not be committable under the excuse rationale.

Indeed, such individuals are not even "dangerous beyond their control" in the sense that phrase is used in *Hendricks*. The Supreme Court has indicated that this language should distinguish between noninsane individuals who are detainable preventively and noninsane individuals who are simply ordinary felons.[25] Yet the ordinary felon is often diagnosed with antisocial personality disorder,[26] which, as just pointed out, is subsumed under the Michigan definition. A solution to this problem might be to retain the Michigan language but exempt antisocial personality or perhaps all personality disorders from its coverage, as some civil commitment statutes do. But, as already noted, some people with personality disorders do suffer from conditions that might excuse or make them dangerous beyond their control.

Perhaps all this sounds too finicky, but these definitional issues have real consequences. A huge percentage of the population could be considered "dangerous to others," including most of those who are released from prison.[27] The definition of mental disorder may determine whom among them is subject to further commitment. Since the resurgence of sexual predator statutes in the 1990s, literally hundreds of judicial decisions have grappled with the definition of mental abnormality in connection with commitment of sex offenders who have completed their prison terms.[28] Some courts have required a specific finding that the person subject to commitment be severely volitionally impaired,[29] while others have been satisfied with a finding that "mental abnormality" and "dangerousness" are linked, or do not require any special showing at all.[30] Riding on the outcome of this debate is the liberty of thousands of sexual offenders. In the future, we are sure to see "predator" commitment statutes outside the sex offender area (indeed there already are such laws),[31] making the issue addressed here even more important.

Let us turn now to the parens patriae component of civil commitment, which focuses on danger to self and on inability to provide for basic needs (or "grave disability").[32] Here, too, the precise scope of legally relevant mental disorder is an important limiting criterion, for all sorts of behavior—ranging from smoking, drinking, and overeating to attempts at suicide—can be classified as self-harming and often imminently so (in the sense that intervention is necessary to prevent further harm); without some limiting factor, a huge segment of our population would, in principle, be subject to state intervention. As they have with respect to police power commitment, commentators and the Supreme Court have diverged on the meaning of mental disorder in this setting. Commentators have tended to view the primary focus of the inquiry to be the competency of the individual to make the relevant decisions,[33] whereas, as Chapter 7 pointed out, the Court has spoken of the parens patriae power in terms of the state's interest "in providing care to its citizens who are unable . . . to care for themselves."[34]

Once again, simple diagnostic definitions of mental disorder are useless here. Nor does the ubiquitous Michigan formulation adequately capture the legal agenda. With one exception, its multipart definition of mental disorder (focusing, remember, on impairments in (1) judgment, (2) behavior, (3) ability to recognize reality, and (4) ability to cope) fails to operationalize either incompetency or inability to care. Anyone who has a DSM-IV diagnosis and who engages in seriously self-harming behavior could be said to have one of the first two dysfunctions (a "substantial disorder that significantly impairs judgment [or] behavior") since no one in their "right mind" would intentionally harm themselves. Yet despite their self-harming behavior, many of these people might well be "competent" to make the decisions they are making (think of heavy smokers diagnosed with "nicotine use disorder,"[35] or the recluse with "social phobia").[36] Likewise, many of these people are probably capable of caring for themselves, as is true of many "mentally ill" people who choose to be homeless.[37] The same can even be said of people with significant impairments in their "capacity to recognize reality" (the third part of the Michigan formulation). As a number of studies have shown, many people with psychosis are able to give competent reasons for refusing treatment,[38] and, as just noted, they can often survive on their own. It is more difficult to say that people who are significantly impaired in their mental "ability to cope with the ordinary demands of life" are competent or able to care for themselves, but if that is the definition of mental disorder, it collapses into the grave disability commitment criterion found in virtually every commitment statute,[39] and thus has no independent significance.

C. Competency in Criminal Proceedings

The final type of liberty deprivation in which mental disorder plays a significant role is in connection with determinations of incompetency to stand trial and related issues. As Chapter 6 indicated, to be competent to deal with the criminal system, a criminal defendant must be able, in the words of the Supreme Court's decision in Dusky v. United States, "to consult with his lawyer with a reasonable degree of rational understanding" and have "a rational as well as factual understanding of the proceedings against him."[40] Dusky itself does not mention mental disorder in connection with this test, but most state statutes assume that mental illness and mental retardation are the usual causes of incompetency.[41] Given Dusky's language, the apparent purpose of requiring proof of mental disorder in this context is to ensure that any inability to understand the criminal process or make decisions about it is the result of irrationality rather than ignorance or intransigence.

If mental disorder is defined at all in competency statutes, it is described in language similar to that found in the jurisdiction's commitment statute. In this setting, the Michigan language is somewhat better at implementing the law's objectives, at least with respect to "adjudicative competency," which, it will be remembered from Chapter 6, looks at the individual's ability to understand and communicate about the process. A person who cannot understand the charges or talk to his or her attorney because of substantial impairments in "judgment" or the "ability to recognize reality" is in all likelihood "irrational" in the sense used by Dusky.

The language is not very helpful, however, in determining who is lacking in "decisional competency," that is, competency in the context of making an important decision in the criminal process. Assume the defendant wants to plead guilty or waive an insanity defense and that the decision is against the attorney's advice. How do we figure out when such decisions are "irrational"? The Michigan language is useless in this situation. It does not tell us who among those who are significantly impaired in judgment, behavior, or ability to recognize reality should have their control over these decisions taken away, unless we say that all these people, because of their resistance to their attorney's advice, are irrational. The tautological nature of that solution suggests the problem with the definition, which once again proves too imprecise.

*   *   *

Current laws dealing with mental disability and deprivations of liberty do not do a good job defining legally relevant mental disorder. They do a bad job because they are insufficiently attentive to the specific role mental disorder plays in specific contexts. Any attempt to revise the definition of legally relevant mental disorder needs to begin with a better conceptualized view of these roles.

II. A Summary of Several Proposals

The legal objectives sought to be achieved by the insanity defense, police power commitment, and civil and criminal incompetency determinations are obviously and importantly different, as this book's tripartite division into sections on the punishment, prevention, and protection models of liberty deprivation is meant to emphasize. The insanity inquiry takes place at a criminal proceeding where the law's primary goal is to determine whether punishment is merited. Police power commitment is a "civil" process aimed not at punishment but at specific deterrence, incapacitation, and, perhaps, rehabilitation. Competency determinations, whether they take place in connection with civil commitment or the criminal process, are meant to ensure autonomous decision making. The first inquiry is retrospective, the second prospective, and the third focuses primarily on present mental status.

Beyond these basic propositions, much is hotly disputed, as this book has made clear. Reactions to the insanity defense have ranged from proposals to replace it with a narrow mens rea alternative[42] to judicial formulations that excuse any crime that is the "product" of mental disease or defect.[43] Some have advocated abolition of civil commitment on the ground that people with mental illness are not especially lacking in control,[44] while others think it should be expanded to permit detention of any dangerous person with a mental abnormality,[45] and still others believe it should extend to any mentally ill person who needs mental health treatment, dangerous or not.[46] Some believe incompetency should be defined in terms of whether the person can register a choice,[47] while others come close to adopting the position that any person who disagrees with a doctor or lawyer is incompetent.[48]

Despite the highly contested nature of these disputes, one should not forgive the law for failing to define mental disorder precisely. The law's continued vague assertions that people with mental disorder can be treated differently, without identifying more clearly in what sense they are different for legal purposes, has resulted in normatively unsatisfying judgments, unnecessary deprivations of liberty, and unfair stigmatization. The task of figuring out legally relevant differences between those we call "disordered" and those we do not is a hard one, but worth the effort.

This book has offered my take on these issues. Here, the arguments will only be outlined to remind the reader of their gist. The primary purpose of this exercise is to compare and contrast with other approaches the types of dysfunction that I think are relevant in the insanity, commitment, and criminal competency contexts.

A. Insanity: Integrationism

In general terms, the purpose behind the mental disorder predicate in insanity cases is clear. Mental disorder is thought to diminish culpability, determination of which is the primary focus of criminal punishment. As Chapter 3 argued, that is why the guilty but mentally ill verdict, which assigns no relevance to the "mental illness" part of the verdict, is incoherent, and why mental disorder should have significant mitigating impact at sentencing. But the role of mental disorder in determining whether an offender should be excused *entirely* from criminal liability requires much more careful delineation than the law currently provides; at present, as shown in the previous section, a fundamental gap exists in the theoretical edifice of criminal justice.

In Chapter 2, I argued that the insanity defense should be abolished and that mental illness should be relevant to culpability determinations only to the extent it leads to a lack of mens rea or to beliefs that sound in justification or duress. More specifically, I contend that, assuming the individual is not knowingly responsible for them, there should be four, and only four, excusing conditions: (1) the absence of intent with respect to an element of the crime (that is, the lack of mens rea defined subjectively, in terms of what the defendant actually knew or was aware of); (2) a mistaken belief about circumstances that, had they occurred as the person believed, would amount to legal justification; (3) a mistaken belief that conditions exist that amount to legally recognized duress; and (4) ignorance of the concept of crime (as in the case of infants). Any of these conditions might result from "mental illness," but they might also exist in the absence of any type of mental disorder.

I call this approach "integrationist" because it accords people who suffer from mental illness the same defenses available to people who are not mentally ill under modern subjectively oriented criminal law statutes, no more and no less. Because these modern statutes provide an excuse for offenders who do not intend or understand the consequences of their actions and for those who honestly believe justificatory or coercive situations exist, they provide a wide array of grounds for exculpation of offenders who are mentally ill (for instance, people like Daniel M'Naghten or Andrea Yates). In contrast, individuals who might be insane under current insanity tests because of a "lack of appreciation" or "lack of control," but who intended to commit their crime and lacked motivations that sounded in justification or duress (offenders like John Hinckley or Charles Manson) would not be excused under this approach.

The central justification for integrationism is that the special defense of insanity is no longer normatively required now that modern criminal codes have subjectified mens rea and the traditional affirmative defenses. Those defenses are necessary and sufficient grounds for recognizing the exculpatory effect of mental illness. In contrast, people with mental illness who commit crime with the requisite mens rea and in the absence of justificatory or coercive rationales are not provably different in terms of their perceptions or control over their behavior than many "normal" individuals who commit crime, such as those who offend because they do not like the victim, "lose it" momentarily, or act under the influence of other, more dominant offenders. The intuition that people with mental illness are qualitatively different in terms of their ability to avoid crime is undermined by the fact that they offend at no greater rate than many other segments of the offender population; even most of those with serious symptoms do not recidivate.

Chapter 2 defended the integrationist approach at length. There are two aspects of it that I want to emphasize here. First, this version of excuse does not require proof of a particular "mental disease or defect" or, for that matter, any mental disease or defect; the important variable is the motivation for the crime, not the diagnosis. Second, following from the first point, the focus of culpability analysis under the integrationist approach is the precise content of the offender's thought, not whether, to use the Michigan language, there is a "substantial impairment" in judgment, emotions, ability to recognize reality, or control of behavior. The latter considerations are relevant only to the extent they cast light on the extent to which the offender possessed the mens rea or was motivated by beliefs that sound in justification or duress.

B. Police Power Commitment: Undeterrability

In the previous part of this chapter it was noted that there is significant dispute over the proper role of mental disorder in justifying police power commitment. Many commentators have argued that if preventive detention is permissible at all it is justifiable only for those who are so lacking in autonomy that they would be considered insane if they committed an offense. In contrast, the Supreme Court in *Hendricks* held that even noninsane individuals may be subject to long-term police power commitment if they have a mental abnormality that renders them "dangerous beyond their control." Since the Court clearly contemplated that convicted sex offenders would be committable under this standard, it rejected the proposition that mental dysfunction akin to that required for insanity is a prerequisite to commitment.

As Chapter 4 makes clear, my position falls somewhere between these two stances. I believe that police power commitment is permissible only for those who are undeterred by the prospect of serious punishment. Most criminal actors would not commit crime if they knew they would be caught and subject to such punishment. But two categories of individuals commit crime even when apprehension is likely, and thus are undeterrable in the sense used here: those who engage in criminal conduct unaware that it is criminal or convinced that it is not, and those who engage in criminal conduct despite awareness of a very high likelihood they will suffer a serious loss of liberty or death as a result. The people in these two categories either cannot or will not abide by the law, and thus are undeserving of the respect that criminal punishment—which is premised on the assumption that people have the capacity to be law-abiding and will act accordingly—grants most individuals.

The first group would be comprised primarily of individuals who suffer from serious mental disability, one that leads them characteristically either to be unaware they are engaged in antisocial conduct or to believe their crimes or contemplated crimes are justified or excused. Included in this group might be anyone who is excusable under the integrationist approach, but it might also include those who believe they are justified in acting even though those beliefs would *not* sound in justification or duress (which may have been the case with John Hinckley, for instance). The people in this category are not deterrable by the prohibitions of the criminal law because they (erroneously) think their contemplated actions are not wrongful. Thus, they can be committed as dangerous, even though some of them (like Hinckley?) could also be punished if they were to commit crime.

The second group of undeterrable individuals would be comprised of individuals who know their conduct is criminally prohibited but are characteristically willing to commit it despite being virtually certain of serious punishment or similar consequence. Captured by the "policeman-at-the-elbow" rubric, it would apply only to a small group of especially blatant sex offenders and other individuals who are willing to choose crime over freedom. Within the latter group might be included terrorists and "enemy combatants" who are willing to commit crime despite a very high risk of death. All these individuals are unaffected by the prospect of punishment, and thus are undeterrable in the sense used here.

The undeterrability predicate for police power commitment, like the insanity predicate preferred by commentators and the Court's inability-to-control concept, is deeply controversial. Chapter 4 defends it, and critiques other approaches. The important point for present purposes is the nature of the inquiry posed by the undeterrability notion. The goal is not to discover a particular diagnosis or a more global "significant impairment" in cognition or volition, but rather to discern whether the individual is likely to believe that his criminal actions are not criminal or is likely to choose to commit them even knowing of a high risk that his life or liberty will be sacrificed. As with the integrationist approach to culpability assessments, the content of the person's motivations is the focus of the undeterrability evaluation.

C. Competency Determinations:
Basic Rationality and Basic Self-Regard

Virtually everyone agrees that to be competent to make decisions about treatment or about matters that arise in a criminal trial, the individual must understand the basic risks and benefits of the decision and its alternatives. The more difficult determination concerns when a particular decision is "rational," to use *Dusky*'s language. In Godinez v. Moran,[49] the Supreme Court came close to holding that an understanding of the risks and benefits is *all* that is necessary for a rational decision. At the other end of the spectrum is the position that only a "reasonable" decision, defined as one the reasonable doctor or lawyer would make, is rational. In between are at least two other standards. The "basic rationality" standard requires a finding of competency unless the reasons for a decision are based on a clearly false assessment of the risk and benefits. The "appreciation" standard takes a more global approach, examining whether the decision is significantly affected by pathological processes.

Not surprisingly, given its focus on the reasons for acting, I favor the basic rationality approach, but with a twist. More specifically, as argued in Chapters 6 and 7, competency to make decisions ought to be defined in terms of "basic rationality and basic self-regard." Basic rationality requires nondelusional reasons for the decision (in addition to an understanding of the relevant information). Basic self-regard requires a willingness to exercise autonomy, which can usually be demonstrated by a willingness to consider alternative scenarios.

To remind the reader of how this standard would work, under the basic rationality and self-regard standard, Colin Ferguson's decision to fire his attorneys on the ground that they would not insist on his innocence demonstrated his incompetence, because he fervently believed he did not commit the crime, despite overwhelming evidence that he gunned down six individuals on the Long Island Railway. Richard Moran, the petitioner in Godinez v. Moran, would also be incompetent because he "wasn't very concerned about anything" when he pleaded guilty to four capital murder charges and sat through his capital sentencing hearing without presenting evidence. Ferguson lacked basic rationality, while Moran lacked basic self-regard. Because of their incompetency, they can be prevented from acting on their decisions. In contrast, Ted Kaczynski's refusal to allow mental illness defenses to be raised in his capital murder case did not demonstrate incompetence under this standard, if the reasons for his refusal were, as he suggested in his Manifesto and elsewhere, that he would rather die than be labeled "mentally ill." On the latter assumption, Kaczynski did not hold any clearly false beliefs, just unusual ones.

Kaczynski probably *was* incompetent under the appreciation test. But a standard based on the existence of pathological process (which is the gravamen of the appreciation test) pays too little warrant to the person's desires and suggests that a person with serious illness can never make a competent decision about anything. Similarly, a standard based on "lack of insight" (the test often used by clinicians) can easily become a proxy for a straightforward reasonableness inquiry. The person's specific reasons for a given decision must be demonstrably false to render him incompetent under the basic rationality and self-regard standard.

The same standard would apply to parens patriae civil commitment. On the one hand, a person who refuses treatment because he believes he is Jesus Christ and immune from disease, both patently false beliefs, would be incompetent under the basic rationality standard. As a result of this incompetence, the faux Jesus could be involuntarily hospitalized and treated under the parens patriae commitment authority. On the other hand, a person who rejects treatment because of its acknowledged side effects is not incompetent under the basic rationality standard even if, contrary to the opinions of all the "experts," he also asserts he is not mentally ill. The latter assertion, standing alone, is not provably false; only if the person denies obvious specific symptoms might basic rationality be lacking.

Further defense of the basic rationality and basic self-regard approach is undertaken in Chapters 6 and 7. Once again, the important point for now is that the test rests on an assessment of thought content. Incompetency exists only if a person acts for delusional reasons or is unwilling to give any reasons or to consider alternatives. Pathology is relevant only to the extent it is associated with these types of aberrant thought content.

III. Four Models of Legally Relevant Mental Disorder

The previous section made clear that the inquiries that I think ought to take place in implementing the punishment, prevention, and protection models of government-sponsored liberty deprivation—the integrationist, undeterrability, and basic rationality and self-regard inquiries—all depend on an assessment of thought content. It should also be clear by now that the account these proposals give of when a person should be held responsible for crime, subject to preventive detention, or considered incompetent is a relatively thin one. Using the language of the Michigan formulation, the focus is primarily on the individual's capacity to recognize reality. Given little weight in these proposals are a number of other factors that might be considered relevant to these determinations, including the quality of the person's thought process and the person's character and emotional makeup.

For instance, a number of commentators have argued that criminal responsibility—and therefore preventive detention under schemes that require that intervention be reserved for the insane—should focus on the consistency and coherence of one's thoughts, rather than simply the reasons one might give for the conduct.[50] Similarly, those who have tried to conceptualize competency have thought it important to measure a range of cognitive skills, including the person's ability to seek information and to imagine the consequences of his or her decisions.[51] Using the Michigan formulation for mental disorder, these approaches are concerned about whether there is a "significant impairment in judgment," although they operationalize that concept somewhat more precisely.

Others' accounts of criminal responsibility and competency, as well as the Supreme Court's account of undeterrability, additionally contemplate some attempt to measure the strength of one's urges, either toward criminality or toward harming oneself.[52] A person is mentally disordered if his or her actions, whether they involve commission of crime, resisting treatment, or waiving an attorney, are "compelled" or strongly influenced by psychological or characteriological forces, which in turn may be the product of biology or the environment.[53] In the Michigan formulation's terms, these approaches attempt to determine whether there is a "significant impairment in behavior."

Still other legal authorities have appeared to look solely at the externally discernible dysfunction that results from the disorder. Thus, some commentators and courts have advocated giving exculpatory effect to any identifiable disorder that causes crime.[54] In the parens patriae setting, a few courts have defined mental disorder simply in terms of whether it causes inability to provide for one's basic needs.[55] The analogue to the latter approach in the Michigan formulation is its reference to significant impairment in the ability "to cope with the ordinary demands of life."

For simplicity sake, I am going to refer to these competing approaches as the *process, predisposition,* and *external* models of disorder, and to my approach as the *content* model of disorder. This section looks at these models more closely. It does so first from a philosophical perspective. It then discusses practical concerns, specifically issues relating to ease of application and the impact of these various approaches on the lives of people with mental disorder.

A. The Legal Relevance of the Four Models

At the risk of some confusion, note first that the process, predisposition, and external models of legally relevant disorder match the three approaches to clinically defined disorder described in Chapter 1 and briefly noted at the beginning of this chapter (which I called the process, etiological, and effects categorizations). The content model, in contrast, has no direct clinical analogue. More important for present purposes is the extent to which each of the four models captures the *legally* relevant considerations connected with mental disorder. That issue is best addressed by looking at the predisposition model first, followed by the external, process, and content models.

The primary philosophical problem with the predisposition model of disorder, as several chapters in this book have explained, is that it does not fit well with a legal system premised on free will and autonomous decision making. All behavior is caused, if not by biology or character, then by environment. While some behavior may seem "over-caused," in fact predispositions and compulsions cannot be sensibly distinguished from mere "causes" (outside of those situations where a person is literally not in control of his or her body).[56] Consider the following questions: Is a person with severe schizophrenia who commits rape more "compelled" than a person with pedophilia or a person who rapes out of stress and anger? Is a person who reports strong urges to act or to make a particular decision more volitionally impaired than a person who is unaware of his or her urges?[57] Is a person who commits a criminal act that is "out of character" (ego-dystonic) acting less autonomously because the conduct is so out of the ordinary, or is that person acting volitionally, again because the conduct is so out of the ordinary? Is the ego-*syn*tonic act relatively uncontrollable because it is "programmed," or does it merely reflect an individual's characteristic "willed" choices?[58] These questions are probably unanswerable. Yet given its tendency to ascribe behavior to one's biology, character, or environment, the predisposition model of mental disorder pushes in the direction of characterizing every act and every decision as "compelled," thus rendering the concepts of culpability, deterrability, and competency meaningless.

The external model of mental disorder undermines the premises of the legal system in a similar way. It attempts to avoid the difficulties of plumbing one's internal psychological processes by looking solely at its manifestations in the outside world—whether a crime is committed or whether a person has become unable to care for himself. Yet because of this focus on conduct, distinctions about culpability, deterrability, and competency assessments are glossed over. Unless we want to say that all crime (even premeditated burglary) and all grave disability (even that associated with homeless people who like to be homeless) is the result of disorder, we need some method of distinguishing between causes that are "disordered" and those that are not. That analysis presumably requires resorting to some assessment of the mental states that accompany crime and grave disability.

Of course, the legal system could jettison the free will premise and the preference for autonomy, a notion that Chapter 5 explored at length. It could accept the assertion that intentionality is a myth, an ex post explanation of actions that are caused by forces beyond our control. It could adopt the position that because all behavior is caused by biology, character, and/or environment, no one is culpable and no decisions are truly one's own. But these are not the law's assumptions today, and they will not be the law's assumptions any time in the foreseeable future, regardless of what science tells us about the causes of behavior. In the meantime, the law should assume that one's choices are the proximate causes of behavior and define mental disorder accordingly.

Both the process and content models of mental disorder seek to accomplish that task. As already noted, the process model looks at a person's mental states in relatively global terms. As described by Michael Moore, one of its progenitors, the process model examines the intelligibility of the desires and beliefs motivating the action, as well as the consistency and coherence of those desires and beliefs.[59] The content model, in contrast, focuses on the intelligibility of desires and beliefs, while relegating the consistency and coherence inquiries to secondary status. Another way to understand the contrast is through consideration of the MacArthur Research Network's conceptualization of competency to make treatment decisions. As Chapter 7 noted, in its experimental work on competency the Network developed three assessment instruments: one that measures understanding of the situation; one that measures the accuracy of the premises underlying the reasons for making a decision; and one that gauges the ability to make rational inferences (that is, the ability to seek information; generate, consider, and compare the consequences of particular decisions; and engage in transitive and probabilistic thinking). The process model of disorder would consider all these measures relevant, whereas the content model would rely solely on the first two.

If the type of mental disorder that the process model suggests the law should privilege had to be described in a single sentence, it would perhaps best be captured not by the Michigan language, the amorphous nature of which has been discussed, but the American Psychiatric Association's definition of mental disease or defect in the insanity context: "[T]hose severely abnormal mental conditions that grossly and demonstrably impair a person's perception or understanding of reality."[60] The content model, instead, looks at the precise way in which the person's perception or understanding of reality was or is impaired. More specific examples of the contrast have already been suggested. Hinckley would probably be excused under the process model but not under the content model. Kaczynski would probably be incompetent under the process model but not the content model. Those few people who are undeterrable because they would choose crime over freedom are committable under the content model but not the process model, while a large number of people who are "substantially impaired in judgment or behavior" could be committed under the latter model but not the former.

My hunch is that the process model more closely conforms with the lay notion of mental illness. Yet it also assumes that a person with severe pathology cannot act culpably, is undeterrable under all circumstances, and is significantly compromised in terms of autonomy. For reasons provided throughout this book, I am not convinced. Again, a severely impaired person who intentionally kills, motivated by desires and beliefs that do not sound in justification or duress, is often as culpable as many other nonmentally ill people and may be just as deterrable. A severely impaired person who nonetheless is able to refuse treatment or insist on waiving an insanity defense for nondelusional reasons is just as competent as many nonmentally ill people. The intuition that irrational thought process captures the essence of legally relevant mental illness is just that—an intuition, based on unproven beliefs about people with mental illness on the one hand, and on misinformed assumptions about normality on the other.

Because behavioral science cannot provide us with the necessary information, choosing between the two models is a normative/pragmatic decision, not a scientific one. I choose the content model because exculpation or detention under the process standard fails to give credence to the fact that even severely impaired people can engage in isolated actions—whether they are crimes, decisions about treatment, or waivers of criminal rights—based on nondelusional reasons. It is a well-known feature of mental disorders that a person who has delusions about some things can be perfectly rational about others.[61] Similarly, severely impaired people can still give good reasons for making certain decisions.[62] Such choices should count for more than they do under the process model. Under the content model, the person's precise motivation for acting is the important variable, not the extent to which he or she suffers from significant pathology.

It should also be noted that, compared to the process model, the content model will result in fewer findings of legally relevant mental disorder. Bruce Winick has argued that if we are serious about our preference for autonomy, we ought to prefer narrow legal definitions of mental disorder, not just on deontological grounds but because the mental disorder label undermines self-esteem and the willingness to change.[63] While some civil libertarians may be bothered that fewer people would be found insane under the content model than under the process model, they may be comforted by the fact that fewer will be committed and found incompetent. It is also worth remembering that the consequences of an acquittal on insanity grounds are often more serious than the punishment that follows conviction.[64]

B. Reliability under the Process and Control Models

For reasons discussed above, the predisposition and external models of mental disorder do not map onto the foundational premises of the legal system. The rest of the discussion will thus focus on the process and content models. Addressed here is a second consideration in choosing between the two: What is the relative feasibility of determining when a particular person is irrational (under the process model) and when a person acts for reasons that suggest a lack of culpability, deterrability, or competency (under the content model)?

On the face of it, determining a person's reasons for acting should be easier than assessing the various, additional types of cognitive functioning that are relevant to the process model. The mental phenomena to be evaluated under the process model are much more complex than those that need to be assessed under the content model. Consistent with this logic, the MacArthur Research Network found that, in administering the three measures described earlier, interrater reliability was lower for the instrument meant to gauge reasoning process than for the other two instruments.[65]

That is not to say that making accurate determinations under the content model will be simple, however. First, the reasons people give for acting may be inaccurate in both a shallow and a deep sense. They are inaccurate in the shallow sense when the person lies about his or her motivations, which is not uncommon in the forensic context.[66] They are inaccurate in the deep sense when even honest accounts do not appear to explain one's actions or decisions. A Freudian can have a field day determining one's true motivations.[67]

Even if we can be reasonably sure we can trust a person's account of his or her motivations, we may often find there is more than one reason given. That is not a serious problem when the reasons all suggest nonculpability or incompetency or, conversely, when they all suggest culpability or competency. But more than occasionally that is not what happens. At one point, Andrea Yates said she killed her children because otherwise they would go to hell. At another point, she said she killed them because she did not want them to grow up to be bad teenagers.[68] Mary Northern refused an operation on her gangrenous foot, despite the high possibility she might die in the absence of surgery, both because she was aware that the surgery itself was life-threatening (although less so than foregoing the surgery) and because she thought the black color of her foot was due to soot.[69] These types of cases could bolster an argument for the process model, which places more emphasis on inconsistent, incoherent reasoning. But the impairments demonstrated by Yates and Northern would be dispositive under the content model as well. If one of the reasons that seem to explain a particular action or decision suggests legally relevant disorder, it makes sense to conclude that legally relevant dysfunction exists.

All things considered, the content model is probably only marginally easier to apply than the process model. But that is still an argument in its favor.

C. Stigma and Discrimination under the Process and Content Models

A final consideration is the impact of the two models on those who are labeled mentally disabled. The three groups of people discussed in this book are the most stigmatized, maligned groups in society.[70] Called "criminally insane," "dangerous madmen" or "predators," and "incompetent," they are perceived as and treated like outcasts.

One argument for the content model, already alluded to, is that it subjects fewer people to these stigmatizing labels than does the process model. But the positive impact of the content model may go deeper. In particular, under the integrationist approach to culpability assessments, there would no longer be a special defense for people with mental illness; they would be exculpated or convicted on the same basis as those who are not mentally ill. People excused in this regime would not be "criminally insane" but acquitted because they honestly believed they were justified or did not intend their acts, grounds that should be easier for the public to swallow than a verdict of "not guilty because of mental illness," and thus grounds that are less likely to inspire disdain or repulsion.

To a lesser extent, the content model's application in the prevention and protection settings should also alleviate the current system's tendency—which the process model would not alleviate—to single out people with mental illness as a special, reviled class. Undeterrability analysis of the type advanced here would base commitment of dangerous people not on mental disorder but on obliviousness toward punishment, which would encompass not only those whose mental confusion leads them to believe antisocial acts are justified, but also those "rational" individuals, such as terrorists or enemy combatants who characteristically choose harming others over freedom. A regime that permits preventive confinement of individuals who are obviously not mentally ill, at the same time it minimizes preventive confinement of those who are, is less likely than today's commitment law (which insists on mental disorder and defines that term broadly) to feed the public's preconception that mental illness and abnormal dangerousness are synonymous. Similarly, the basic rationality and self-regard test would find incompetent only those whose decisions are based on patently false beliefs, suggesting, contrary to current law, that mental illness and incapacity are not inevitably linked.

None of this, by itself, will eliminate the stigma associated with mental disorder or the discrimination that results from that stigma. But at least the content model of mental disorder minimizes the law's contribution to that stigma. Indeed, it moves far in the direction of erasing "mental disorder" as a discrete predicate for laws that authorize government deprivations of liberty.

Conclusion

Elimination of "mental disorder" and like terms from the legal lexicon may be too radical a step at this point in time. But, as a substantial move in that direction, it is worth considering the abolition of the special defense of insanity and the orientation of commitment and competency determinations toward an evaluation of thought content and away from amorphous assessments of predispositions, dysfunction, or irrational thought process. Those modifications would be far preferable to the law's current haphazard and underconceptualized definitions of mental disorder. They also would be more consistent with the norms that currently drive the punishment, prevention, and protection regimes than models of disorder based either on predisposition or dysfunctional conduct, and at least as consistent with those norms as a process model of mental disorder. Finally, compared to the process model of disorder, the content model would be easier to implement and less stigmatizing and thus, in the long run, more beneficial to all who are unfortunate enough to be labeled "mentally ill."

Notes

1. The Clinical and Legal Landscape

1. American Psychiatric Association, *Diagnostic and Statistical Manual of Mental Disorders*, Fourth Edition-Text Revised [hereafter noted as DSM-IV-TR] (2000), xxi.
2. Ibid.
3. See Kenneth Mark Colby and James E. Spar, *The Fundamental Crisis in Psychiatry: Unreliability of Diagnosis* (1983), 214 (calling DSM "a politically motivated compromise between differing interpretations of the data, outright dogma, and propaganda"). See generally Stuart A. Kirk and Herb Kutchins, *The Selling of DSM: The Rhetoric of Science in Psychiatry* (1992).
4. DSM-IV-TR, xxi.
5. For detailed descriptions of these and other disorders, see DSM-IV-TR.
6. See Herb Kutchins and Stuart Kirk, *Making Us Crazy* (1997), 243 (summarizing a National Institute of Mental Health study applying DSM diagnostic criteria that found that 32 percent of American adults have one or more psychiatric disorders in their lifetime and that 20 percent have a disorder at any given time); R. C. Kessler et al., "Lifetime and 12-Month Prevalence of DSM-III-R Psychiatric Disorders in the United States," 51 *Archives of General Psychiatry* 8 (1994) (finding that, within a year period, 50 percent of the population reported at least one disorder during their life and 30 percent reported at least one current disorder).
7. R. E. Kendell, "The Concept of Disease and Its Implications for Psychiatry," 127 *British Journal of Psychiatry* 305 (1975).
8. Ibid., 307.
9. Michael Moore, *Law and Psychiatry: Rethinking the Relationship* (1984), 244–245. See also Christopher Boorse, "What a Theory of Mental Health Should Be," 6 *Journal of Theory of Social Behavior* 61, 63, 72 (1976).

10. Moore, *Law and Psychiatry,* 244–245.

11. See testimony of Park Elliot Dietz in the John Hinckley trial, reported in Ralph Reisner, Christopher Slobogin, and Arti Rai, *Law and the Mental Health System: Civil and Criminal Aspects,* 4th ed. (2003), 423. See also *Mental Health: A Report of the Surgeon General* (1999), 44.

12. Many people with manic-depression, for instance, lead long and productive— albeit very intense, disrupted, and disrupting—lives, even when left untreated. See generally D. Jablow Hershman and Julian Lieb, *Manic Depression and Creativity* (1998) (describing Newton, Dickens, and Picasso as people with manic-depression).

13. DSM-IV-TR, xxi.

14. Eric R. Kandel, "A New Intellectual Framework for Psychiatry," 155 *American Journal of Psychiatry* 457, 460 (1998).

15. Ibid.

16. For a description of the medical, psychoanalytic, behavioral, and social models of mental disorder, see Paul Lazare, "Hidden Conceptual Models in Clinical Psychiatry," 288 *New England Journal of Medicine* 345 (1973).

17. Thomas Szasz, *Ideology and Insanity* (1970), 12.

18. Ibid., 21.

19. Ibid., 16 (emphasis in original).

20. See Michael Moore, "Some Myths about Mental Illness," 18 *Inquiry* 233 (1975).

21. Barry R. Furrow et al., *Health Law: Cases, Materials and Problems,* 4th ed. (2001), 2 (contrasting physical "disease," which is "a deviation from the biological norm of natural function," from physical "illness," which is "a socially constructed deviance").

22. Ralph Slovenko, *Psychiatry and Criminal Responsibility* (1995), 54.

23. DSM-IV-TR, xxii.

24. Kansas v. Hendricks, 521 U.S. 346, 359 (1997).

25. Stephen J. Morse, "A Preference for Liberty: The Case against Involuntary Commitment of the Mentally Disordered," 70 *California Law Review* 54, 58 n. 14 (1982); Susan Stefan, *Unequal Rights: Discrimination against People with Mental Disabilities and the Americans with Disabilities Act* (2001), xv.

26. DSM-IV-TR, xxiii.

27. See generally Jacobson v. Mass., 197 U.S. 11, 26–27 (1905) (describing police power); Hawaii v. Standard Oil, 405 U.S. 251, 257 (1972) (describing parens patriae authority).

28. United States v. Morrison, 529 U.S. 598, 618 (2000) ("we can think of no bet-

ter example of the police power . . . than the suppression of violent crime and vindication of victims"); Addington v. Texas, 441 U.S. 418, 426 (1979) ("the state has a legitimate interest . . . under its police power to protect the community from the dangerous tendencies of some who are mentally ill").

29. *Addington,* 426 ("the state has a legitimate interest under its parens patriae powers in providing care to its citizens who are unable because of emotional disorders to care for themselves"); Schall v. Martin, 467 U.S. 253, 263 (1984) ("the state has a parens patriae interest in preserving and promoting the welfare of the child, which makes a juvenile proceeding fundamentally different from an adult criminal trial").

30. Gary Melton et al., *Psychological Evaluations for the Courts: A Handbook for Mental Health Professionals and Lawyers,* 2d ed. (1997), 308.

31. Immanuel Kant, *The Metaphysical Elements of Justice* (1797), trans. John Ladd (1965), 120.

32. Georg W. Hegel, *The Philosophy of Right* (1820), trans. T. M. Knox (1962), 69.

33. Michel Foucault, *Discipline and Punishment: The Birth of the Prison* (1977), 3–16.

34. Paul Robinson, "The Criminal-Civil Distinction and the Utility of Desert," 76 *Boston University Law Review* 201, 211 (1996).

35. Ibid., 211–212.

36. Dan Kahan, "The Secret Ambition of Deterrence," 113 *Harvard Law Review* 413, 419–426 (1999).

37. The exception is with respect to strict liability crimes, which are generally reserved for regulatory violations and usually do not involve significant penalties.

38. For a discussion of the objective and subjective approaches to culpability, see Herbert Wechsler, "The Challenge of a Model Penal Code," 65 *Harvard Law Review* 1097, 1108–1110 (1952).

39. Jeremy Bentham, *An Introduction to the Principles of Morals and Legislation,* eds. J. H. Burns & H. L. A. Hart (1988), 170–171.

40. See generally Moore, *Law and Psychiatry,* 233–239 (contrasting these purposes of punishment, designed to reduce crime, with retributivism). Moore and others call these goals "purposes of punishment" but, as Chapter 4 explains, use of that word is misleading: punishment is a reaction to a past act, not an attempt to prevent a future one.

41. This type of preventive regime would encompass denunciation (sanctions to ensure social cohesion around certain justice principles) and maintenance of stability (sanctions to ensure citizens do not engage in vigilante justice). Both purposes are forward-looking deterrence mechanisms, although the basis for

intervention may be triggered by desert-based considerations such as revenge. See Moore, *Law and Psychiatry*, 233–234.

42. See Richard A. Posner, "An Economic Theory of the Criminal Law," 85 *Columbia Law Review* 1193, 1221–1223 (1985). Posner also notes that the types of actions most likely to lead to accidental or negligent crime (for example, driving a car) are often legitimate actions that harsh punishment may overdeter. Ibid., 1206.

43. See, for example, Model Penal Code §1.02(1) (1962) (describing eclectic mix of purposes for criminal punishment).

44. Immanuel Kant, *Foundations on the Metaphysics of Morals* (1785), trans. Lewis White Beck (1959), 59–67.

45. John Stuart Mill, *On Liberty,* ed. C. Shields (1956), 9.

46. Ibid., 104.

47. See Bruce Winick, "On Autonomy: Legal and Psychological Perspectives," 37 *Villanova Law Review* 1705, 1715–1725 (1992).

48. Mary Ellen Waithe, "Why Mill Was for Paternalism," 6 *International Journal of Law and Psychiatry* 101 (1983).

49. Jackson v. Indiana, 406 U.S. 715, 738 (1972).

50. Addington v. Texas, 441 U.S. 418, 426 (1979).

51. For a description of the debate, see Janet E. Ainsworth, "Re-Imagining Childhood and Reconstructing the Legal Order: The Case for Abolishing the Juvenile Court," 69 *North Carolina Law Review* 1083 (1991). At one time, I planned to include a chapter on juvenile justice in this book, but the subject is tangential to this book's focus on people with mental disability and would have made an already overlong book even longer. For my views on this topic, written with two behavioral scientists, see Christopher Slobogin, Mark R. Fondacaro, and Jennifer Woolard, "A Prevention Model of Juvenile Justice: The Promise of Kansas v. Hendricks for Children," 1999 *Wisconsin Law Review* 185.

52. Henry J. Steadman and Jeraldine Braff estimated that only 1,625 people were hospitalized after an acquittal by reason of insanity in 1978, before a number of states significantly narrowed the scope of their insanity test in response to the acquittal of John Hinckley in 1981. Henry J. Steadman and Jeraldine Braff, "Defendants Not Guilty by Reason of Insanity," in *Mentally Disordered Offenders: Perspectives from Law and Social Science,* ed. John Monahan and Henry J. Steadman (1983), 110.

53. One relatively recent estimate is that there are 87,000 people with severe mental disorders in prison. T. Howard Stone, "Therapeutic Implications for Incarceration for Persons with Severe Mental Disorders: Searching for Rational Health Policy," 24 *American Journal Criminal Law* 283, 285 (1997). A second es-

timate puts the number at 285,000. The Impact of the Mentally Ill on the Criminal Justice System: Hearing Before the House Judiciary Subcomm. on Crime, 106th Cong. (2000) (testimony of Congressman Ted Strickland). For data on the number of people with mental disability on death row, see Chapter 2.

54. See generally W. Lawrence Fitch and Debra A. Hammen, "The New Generation of Sex Offender Commitment Laws: Which States Have Them and How Do They Work?" in *Protecting Society from Sexually Dangerous Offenders*, ed. Bruce J. Winick and John Q. LaFond (2003).

55. The daily census in state hospitals has been reduced considerably in the past fifty years. James R. Walker, "Getting the Mentally Ill Misdemeanant Out of Jail, 6 *Scholar: St. Mary's Law Review on Minority Issues* 371, 378 (2004) ("By 1998, the number of state hospital patients was down from 559,000 institutionalized patients out of a population of over 165 million [in the mid-twentieth century] to 57,151 patients out of a population of over 275 million"). Because length of hospitalization is so much shorter, however, the number of people hospitalized annually (some more than once) is in the hundreds of thousands. See Bruce J. Winick, *Civil Commitment: A Therapeutic Justice Model* (2004), 7 ("If we assume an average patient stay of 30 days and that the census of public mental hospitals is 55,000, then as many as 660,000 patients per year may be subject to involuntary commitment").

56. See Richard J. Bonnie and Thomas Grisso, "Adjudicative Competence and Youthful Offenders," *Youth on Trial: A Developmental Perspective on Juvenile Justice*, ed. Thomas Grisso and Robert G. Schwartz (2000), 78 ("A conservative national estimate . . . would be sixty thousand pretrial competence assessments per year."). An earlier study found that approximately 25 percent of those assessed for competency end up hospitalized. Henry J. Steadman and Eliot Hartstone, "Defendants Incompetent to Stand Trial," in *Mentally Disordered Offenders*, 40–41.

2. The Insanity Defense

1. Sheldon Glueck, *Mental Disorder and the Criminal Law* (1927), 187–188.
2. Michael Perlin, *The Jurisprudence of the Insanity Defense* (1994), 1.
3. See, for example, Abraham L. Halpern, "The Politics of the Insanity Defense," 14 *American Journal of Forensic Psychiatry* 3, 4 (1993); Joseph Weintraub, "Insanity as a Defense: A Panel Discussion," 37 *Federal Rules of Decision* 365, 372–373 (1964).
4. Abraham Goldstein, *The Insanity Defense* (1967), 214–219; Richard Bonnie, "The Moral Basis of the Insanity Defense," 69 *American Bar Association Jour-*

nal 194, 197 (1983) (arguing for abolition of the volitional prong of the defense); American Bar Association, *Criminal Justice Mental Health Standards*, Standard 7–6.1 and accompanying commentary (1988) (same).

5. See Joel Feinberg, *Doing and Deserving* (1970), 272–273. Some courts have come close to adopting this approach, but with virtually no explanation. Cruse v. State, 580 So.2d 983 (Fla. App. 1991).

6. 8 Eng. Rep. 718 (H.L. 1843). A good description of the *M'Naghten* trial is found in Thomas Maeder, *Crime and Madness* (1985), chap. 3.

7. Deborah W. Denno, "Who Is Andrea Yates? A Short Story about Insanity," 10 *Duke Journal of Gender Law and Policy* 1, 37 (2003). See also, Associated Press, "Yates Claimed She Killed Kids to Keep Them from Going to Hell," March 1, 2002, www.courttv.com/trials/yates (accessed 4/11/04).

8. Ralph Reisner, Christopher Slobogin and Arti Rai, *Law and the Mental Health System: Civil and Criminal Aspects* (4th ed. 2004), 548.

9. For descriptions of the Jeffrey Dahmer case and the verdict, see "Found Sane," *Time Magazine,* February 24, 1992, 68.

10. See, for example, McElroy v. State, 242 S.W. 883 (Tenn. 1922) (defendant who believed his act was commanded by God found sane); State v. Cameron, 100 Wash.2d 520, 674 P.2d 650 (en banc 1983) (finding of insanity based on similar facts).

11. People v. Schmidt, 216 N.Y. 324, 110 N.E. 945, 950 (1915) (Cardozo, J.).

12. See Model Penal Code §2.01.

13. The term "automatism" is often used to describe application of the involuntary act doctrine to those who have mental disorder. Wayne LaFave, *Criminal Law,* 3d ed. (2000), 405. LaFave also notes that although the defense "is sometimes explained on the ground that such a person could not have the requisite mental state for commission of the crime, the better rationale is that the individual has not engaged in a voluntary act." Ibid. Be that as it may, for reasons of parsimony this chapter will continue to include involuntary acts in the lack-of-mens rea category. For a discussion of the effect of frontal lobe dysfunction on intent and inhibitions, see Jonathan H. Pincus, "Aggression, Criminality, and the Frontal Lobes," in the Human Frontal Lobes: Functions and Disorders 547, eds., Bruce L. Miller and Jeffrey L. Cummings (1999).

14. See, for example, Richard Bonnie et al., *Criminal Law* (1997), 456–465 ("The Case of Joy Baker").

15. This example is based on People v. Wetmore, 22 Cal.3d 318, 149 Cal.Rptr. 265, 583 P.2d 1308 (1978).

16. This example is based on the case of John Barclay, who killed a friend for £3 and a watch, vaguely knowing it was wrong to do so, but also believing that

there was no difference between killing a human and killing an ox. Isaac Ray, *A Treatise on the Medical Jurisprudence of Insanity,* ed. Winfred Overholser (1962), 93.

17. LaFave, *Criminal Law,* 440–441.

18. In medieval times, the insanity finding was implemented not through a formal verdict after judicial instructions, but via pardon from the king. There are several accounts of pardons before the sixteenth century, but the precise grounds for these actions are not clear. See, for example, Maeder, *Crime and Madness,* 4–5.

19. See Donald H. J. Hermann, *The Insanity Defense: Philosophical, Historical and Legal Perspectives* (1983), 23–26.

20. Anthony Platt and Bernard L. Diamond, "The Origins of the 'Right and Wrong' Test of Criminal Responsibility and Its Subsequent Development in the United States: An Historical Survey," 54 *California Law Review* 1227, 1235–1237 (England); 1250–1257 (United States).

21. See Maeder, *Crime and Madness,* 9–22. See also Ray, *Treatise on Insanity,* 188.

22. Platt and Diamond, *The Origins of the Right-Wrong Tests,* 1251–1256 and 1260 (table II).

23. 27 How. St. Tr. 1281 (1800).

24. M'Naghten's Case, 8 English Reports 718, 722 (1843).

25. Ibid., 723.

26. For a summary of nineteenth-century views on this matter, see Parsons v. State, 81 Ala. 577, 2 So. 854, 856–857 (1886). These types of views continued to be espoused in the twentieth century. See Benjamin Cardozo, "What Medicine Can Do for Law," in *Law and Literature and Other Essays and Addresses* (1931), 70, 106, 108 (1931); United States v. Freeman, 357 F.2d 606, 617 (2d Cir. 1966).

27. Writing in 1943, Gregory Zilboorg, a psychiatrist, argued that if *M'Naghten's* language were taken seriously, "it would excuse only those totally deteriorated, drooling hopeless psychotics of longstanding, and congenital idiots." Gregory Zilboorg, *Mind, Medicine and Man* (1943), 273. See also Sheldon Glueck, *Law and Psychiatry: Cold War or Entente Cordiale?* (1966), 43–46.

28. At its peak in the 1920s, the "irresistible impulse test" formed part of the insanity defense in eighteen jurisdictions. Goldstein, *The Insanity Defense,* 241–242 n. 1 (collecting cases). Traditional insanity defense history has it that volitional tests developed after cognitive ones. Note, however, that a number of states developed insanity formulations focusing on lack of volition at virtually the same time they adopted lack-of-knowledge tests. See Henry Weihofen, *Mental Disorder as a Criminal Defense* (1954), 100–103.

29. Goldstein, *The Insanity Defense,* 49.

30. Model Penal Code §4.01(1).

31. The drafters stated that "[t]he adoption of the standard of substantial capacity may well be the Code's most significant alteration of the prevailing tests." American Law Institute, *Model Penal Code and Commentaries* to §4.01 (1985), cmt. 3, 172.

32. Ibid., 169. ("The use of 'appreciate' rather than 'know' conveys a broader sense of understanding than simple cognition.")

33. More specifically, "criminality" in the Code formulation was meant to refer to the illegality of the act, whereas "wrongfulness" was meant to refer to a community or personal belief that the act was wrong. Ibid.

34. 214 F.2d 862 (D.C. Cir. 1954).

35. See Henry Weihofen, *The Urge to Punish: New Approaches to the Problem of Mental Irresponsibility for Crime* (1956), 5.

36. United States v. Brawner, 471 F.2d 969, 1032 (D.C. Cir. 1972) (Bazelon, C. J., concurring and dissenting).

37. Herbert Fingarette and Ann Hasse, *Mental Disabilities and Criminal Responsibility* (1979), 218.

38. Michael Moore, *Law and Psychiatry: Rethinking the Relationship* (1984), 245.

39. Stephen Morse, "Immaturity and Irresponsibility," 88 *Journal of Criminal Law and Criminology* 15, 24 (1997).

40. Benjamin Sendor, "Crime as Communication: An Interpretive Theory of the Insanity Defense and the Mental Elements of Crime," 74 *Georgetown Law Journal* 1371, 1415 (1986).

41. Robert Schopp, *Automatism, Insanity, and the Psychology of Criminal Responsibility* (1991), 215.

42. See, for example, Morse, "Immaturity and Irresponsibility," 29; Schopp, *Psychology of Criminal Responsibility,* 203.

43. New Hampshire retains the product test. See State v. Abbot, 503 A.2d 791 (N.H. 1985).

44. See Michael Perlin, *Mental Disability Law: Civil and Criminal,* vol. 3 (1989), §15.07, 302.

45. Reisner, Slobogin, and Rai, *Law and the Mental Health System,* 535–536.

46. Idaho Code §18–207; Kansas Statutes Ann. §22–3220; Montana Code Ann. §46–14–201; North Dakota Statutes §12.1–04.1–01; Utah Code Ann. §76–2–305. See also Pouncey v. State, 297 Md. 264, 465 A.2d 475 (1983) (arguably abolishing the insanity defense in Maryland). Nevada's legislature tried to abolish the defense, but the Nevada Supreme Court found the statute unconstitutional. Finger v. State, 117 Nev. 548, 27 P.3d 66 (2001).

47. Francis Bowes Sayre, "Mens Rea," 45 *Harvard Law Review* 974, 981 (1932).
48. Ibid., 981–982.
49. Hermann, *The Insanity Defense*, 22.
50. As Sayre put it, mens rea in this period "smacked strongly of general moral blameworthiness." Sayre, "Mens Rea," 988. With respect to homicide "[t]he line between murder and manslaughter was unknown; there was no legal distinction between voluntary and involuntary homicide." Ibid., 994.
51. Ibid., 996.
52. Ibid., 999–1003; LaFave, *Criminal Law,* 238–239 (describing the "traditional view" with respect to specific and general intent).
53. Even as late as 1946, at most nine states permitted such evidence, and at least two of these did so only in dictum. Henry Weihofen and Winfred Overholser, "Mental Disorder Affecting the Degree of a Crime," 56 *Yale Law Journal* 959, 965–966 (1947).
54. See Peter Low, "The Model Penal Code, the Common Law, and Mistakes of Fact: Recklessness, Negligence, or Strict Liability?" 19 *Rutgers Law Journal* 539, 556 (1988) (describing the Model Penal Code's subjective approach to mistake of fact as a "reject[ion of] a judgment expressed in a common-law rule that was centuries in the evolution").
55. The "prevailing rule" in the first half of this century was that there be "a reasonable ground" for the belief that defensive action was necessary. *MPC Commentaries* to §3.04, cmt. 2 and cases cited in n. 3, page 35.
56. Peter Ashworth, "The Doctrine of Provocation," 35 *Cambridge Law Journal* 292, 293 (1976).
57. LaFave, *Criminal Law,* 474.
58. For instance, as to provocation, LaFave states that under the traditional test "[i]t is quite uniformly held that the defendant's special mental qualities . . . are not to be considered." Ibid., 711–712.
59. "It was believed to be unjust to measure liability for serious criminal offenses on the basis of what the defendant should have believed or what most people would have intended." *MPC Commentaries* to §2.02, cmt. 2, 235.
60. Model Penal Code §4.02(1).
61. Under the Code, murder occurs when a person is killed purposely, knowingly, or extremely recklessly, and manslaughter occurs when a person is killed recklessly, Model Penal Code §§210.2; 210.3, with recklessness requiring an awareness of the risk of death. Model Penal Code §2.02(2)(c).
62. See American Bar Association, *Criminal Justice Mental Health Standards,* 352–353.

63. Model Penal Code §3.04(2)(b) (emphasis added).

64. Model Penal Code §210.3(1)(b) (emphasis added).

65. Model Penal Code §2.09(1).

66. *MPC Commentaries* to §2.09, cmt. 3, 380.

67. The major caveat to this view of the Model Penal Code is that, when negligence is grounds for criminal liability, as it is for negligent homicide under the Code, see §210.4, then a negligent mistake as to the elements of the self-defense or duress also leads to liability. See §3.09(2). More is said about negligence as a basis for liability later in the chapter.

68. Only a "few" states have adopted the Code's approach to self-defense; however, a "substantial minority" have adopted its provocation formulation, and a "very distinct majority" abide by its duress test. LaFave, *Criminal Law*, 494–495; 713; 472.

69. Oliver Wendell Holmes, *The Common Law* (1881), 43.

70. See, for example, Jerome Hall, "Negligent Behavior Should Be Excluded from Penal Liability," 63 *Columbia Law Review* 632 (1963); Glanville Williams, *Criminal Law: The General Part*, 2d. ed. (1961), 32–34, 123.

71. DSM-IV-TR, 13–14 (listing disorders).

72. See, for example, American Psychiatric Association, *American Psychiatric Glossary*, 7th ed. (1994), 153. (Defining "personality disorder" as "[e]nduring patterns of perceiving, relating to, and thinking about the environment and oneself that begin by early childhood and are exhibited in a wide range of important social and personal contexts. These patterns are inflexible and maladaptive, causing either significant functional impairment or subjective distress.")

73. See Lee N. Robins et al., "Antisocial Personality," in *Psychiatric Disorders in America: The Epidemiological Catchment Area Study*, ed. L. N. Robins and D. Reiger (1991), 273; Myrna M. Weissman, "The Epidemiology of Personality Disorders: A 1990 Update," 7 *Journal of Personality Disorders* 44, 50, table 3 (1993).

74. In 1985, for instance, it was estimated that roughly 35 percent of the prison population suffered from character disorders alone, and an additional 9.5 percent to 29 percent were suffering from retardation. Samuel Brakel et al., *The Mentally Disabled and the Law* (1985), 736–737. A number of studies indicate that the prevalence of antisocial personality disorder, stringently defined, is almost 40 percent among prison populations. See, for example, Robert D. Hare, "Diagnosis of Antisocial Personality Disorder in Two Prison Populations," 140 *American Journal of Psychiary and Law* 887, 888 (1983); Robins et al., "Antisocial Personality," 274.

75. See Stephen D. Hart and Robert D. Hare, "Psychopathy: Assessment and Association with Criminal Conduct," in *Handbook of Antisocial Behavior*, ed. E. M. Stoff et al. (1997), 24 (finding that between 15 percent and 30 percent of offenders and forensic patients meet strict criteria for psychopathy).

76. Deborah W. Denno, "Human Biology and Criminal Responsibility: Free Will or Free Ride?" 137 *University of Pennsylvania Law Review* 615, 619–645 (1988) (summarizing studies).

77. Ibid.

78. See David M. Stoff and Robert B. Cairnes, eds., *Aggression and Violence: Genetic, Neurobiological, and Biosocial Perspectives* (1996); Adrian Raine, *The Psychopathology of Crime: Criminal Behavior as a Clinical Disorder* (1993), 79.

79. Raine, *The Psychopathology of Crime*, 91 (reviewing studies showing a correlation between aggressive offenders and low serotonin levels, with the percentage of such offenders ranging from 20 to 50 percent, depending on the study).

80. DSM-IV, 427–428 (discussing post-traumatic stress disorder); 424 (noting that "military combat" and "violent personal assault" can produce the trauma leading to post-traumatic stress disorder).

81. See Christopher Slobogin, "Psychiatric Evidence in Criminal Trials: To Junk or Not to Junk?" 40 *William and Mary Law Review* 1, 5–12 (1998) (describing various new psychiatric defenses).

82. For example, DSM-IV reports studies indicating that the prevalence of post-traumatic stress syndrome in the general population is 1 to 14 percent DSM-IV, 426.

83. Gary Melton et al., *Psychological Evaluations for the Courts*, 2d ed. (1997), 217 (table summarizing six studies showing that proportion of those found insane who were diagnosed with a "major psychosis" ranged from 67 to 97 percent).

84. See, for example, DSM-IV, 522–523 (the "essential" feature of a paraphilia [for example, pedophilia, exhibitionism, sexual sadism] is "recurrent, intense sexually arousing fantasies, sexual urges, or behaviors generally involving (1) non-human objects, (2) the suffering or humiliation of oneself or one's partners, or (3) children or other nonconsenting persons"); 616 (pathological gamblers "may resort to antisocial behavior [for example, forgery, fraud, theft, or embezzlement] when their "borrowing resources are strained").

85. See DSM-IV, 654 (listing one criterion for borderline personality disorder as "inappropriate, intense anger or difficulty controlling anger"); 84 (listing one criterion of attention-deficit/hyperactivity disorder as "often 'on the go' or acting as if 'driven by a motor'").

86. Philip Q. Roche, *The Criminal Mind* (1958), 191–192.
87. Laura Reider, "Toward a New Test for the Insanity Defense: Incorporating the Discoveries of Neuroscience into Moral and Legal Theories," 46 *U.C.L.A. Law Review* 289, 325 (1998).
88. See, for example, People v. Yukl, 83 Misc.2d 364, 372 N.Y.S.2d 313 (1975).
89. This was one of the arguments made in Hinckley's case. See Alan Stone, *Law, Psychiatry and Morality* (1984), 86 (discussing a CT scan that showed a "widening" of sulci in Hinckley's brain).
90. See, for example, United States v. Alexander and Murdock, 71 F.2d 923 (D.C. Cir. 1972).
91. Caspi Avshalom et al., "Role of Genotype in the Cycle of Violence in Maltreated Children," 297 *Science* 851 (2002).
92. A large body of evidence suggests that, compared to the general population, individuals suffering from schizophrenia are from 4 to 8 times more likely to commit homicide. Taina Laajasaol & Helena Hakkanen, "Offence and Offender Characteristics Among Two Groups of Finnish Homicide Offenders with Schizophrenia: Comparison of Early- and Late-Start Offenders," 16 *Journal of Forensic Psychiatry and Psychology* 41 (2005) (summarizing research). But among offenders, schizophrenia is not a major predictor of crime. See James Bonta et al., "The Prediction of Criminal and Violent Recidivism Among Mentally Disordered Offenders: A Meta Analysis," 123 *Psychological Bulletin* 123 (1998); Marnie E. Rice and Grant T. Harris, "A Comparison of Criminal Recidivism Among Schizophrenic and Nonschizophrenic Offenders," 15 *International Journal of Law & Psychiatry* 397 (1992) (finding that subjects with schizophrenia were less likely to commit offenses upon release than their nonschizophrenic counterparts).
93. DSM-IV, 649–650 (describing criteria for antisocial personality disorder to include "failure to conform to social norms with respect to lawful behaviors as indicated by repeatedly performing acts that are grounds for arrest," "irritability and aggressiveness, as indicated by repeated physical fights or assaults," "reckless disregard for safety of self or others," and "evidence of conduct disorder with onset before age 15 years").
94. Michael Moore, "Causation and the Excuses," 73 *California Law Review* 1091, 1130 (1985).
95. Moore, *Law and Psychiatry*, 33.
96. Ibid., 13–25, 190–245. For a more detailed summary of Moore's reasoning in this regard, see Christopher Slobogin, "A Rational Approach to Responsibility," 83 *Michigan Law Review* 820, 822–827 (1985).

97. Morse's arguments appear in several fora. His most elaborate exegesis on the point in the text is "Culpability and Control," 142 *University of Pennsylvania Law Review* 1587 (1994), but this brief summary will come from several of his works.

98. Ibid., 1590–1605, 1616–1619.

99. Morse, "Immaturity and Responsibility," 30.

100. Stephen J. Morse, "Crazy Behavior, Morals and Science: An Analysis of Mental Health Law," 51 *Southern California Law Review* 527, 584 (1978).

101. Morse, "Immaturity and Responsibility," 30.

102. Stephen Morse, "Causation, Compulsion and Involuntariness," 22 *Bulletin of the American Academy of Psychiatry and Law* 159, 179 (1994); Morse, "Immaturity and Irresponsibility," 29–30. Other advocates of the irrationality test make similar arguments. See Herbert Fingarette, *The Meaning of Criminal Insanity* (1972), 160, 172; Schopp, *Psychology of Criminal Responsibility,* 202.

103. 18 U.S.C. §20 (1984).

104. Goldstein, *The Insanity Defense,* 49–53.

105. Robert D. Hare, *Without Conscience: The Disturbing World of the Psychopaths among Us* (1993), 34, 44.

106. Model Penal Code §4.01(2).

107. See DSM-IV, 650 (indicating that the criteria for antisocial personality disorder can include "impulsivity and failure to plan ahead," "consistent irresponsibility," and "lack of remorse," any one of which may be lacking in some recidivists).

108. See DSM-IV, 40 (definition of retardation).

109. C. Benjamin Crisman and Rockne J. Chickinell, "The Mentally Retarded Offender in Omaha-Douglas County," 8 *Creighton Law Review* 622, 646 (1975). See also James Ellis, "Mentally Retarded Criminal Defendants," 53 *George Washington Law Review* 414, 441 (1985).

110. See American Association for the Mentally Retarded, "Position Statement on Criminal Justice," available at www.aamr.org/Policies ("People with mental retardation must be exempt from the death penalty but not from other appropriate punishment, on a case-by-case basis").

111. Atkins v. Virginia, 536 U.S. 304 (2002).

112. Union County Indictment no. 632079 (Sup.Ct. N.J. Crim. Div. 1981).

113. Ibid.

114. Richard J. Bonnie, "Why 'Appreciation of Wrongfulness' Is the Morally Preferable Standard for the Insanity Defense," presentation at Conference on the Affirmative Defense of Insanity, Austin, Texas, February 7, 2003, available at

www.txpsych.org (Insanity Conference), 54. Bonnie's comments at the conference cross-reference his earlier paper, "The Moral Basis of the Insanity Defense," 69 *American Bar Association Journal* 194 (1984), which proposed that the definition of mental disease or defect for purposes of the insanity defense be as follows: "those severely abnormal mental conditions that grossly and demonstrably impair a person's perception or understanding of reality and that are not attributable primarily to the voluntary ingestion of alcohol or other psychoactive substances." Ibid., 197.

115. See Henry J. Steadman et al., "Violence by People Discharged from Acute Psychiatric Inpatient Facilities and by Others in the Same Neighborhoods," 55 *Archives General Psychiatry* 393 (1998); Paul S. Appelbaum et al., "Violence and Delusions: Data from the MacArthur Violence Risk Study," 157 *American Journal of Psychiatry* 566 (2000) (reporting data that suggest delusions do not increase the overall risk of violence in persons with mental illness).

116. See generally, Peter McGuffin and Anita Thapar, "Genetics and Antisocial Personality Disorder," in *Psychopathy: Antisocial, Criminal and Violent Behavior,* ed. Theodore Millon et al. (1998), 215–230; Larry J. Siever, "Neurobiology in Psychopathy," in *Psychopathy,* 231–246.

117. Compare O. Kernberg, "The Psychotherapeutic Management of Psychopathic, Narcissistic, and Paranoid Transferences," in *Psychopathy,* 372, 377 (the prognosis for effectively treating psychopathy "is practically zero") to Reisner et al., *Law and the Mental Health System,* 38 (reporting response rates of people with psychosis to antipsychotic medication of approximately 75 percent).

118. Reid Meloy, "Psychopathy," paper presented at Mental Health Law in the Twenty-first Century, San Diego, Calif., March 23, 2000. See also Henry Richards, "Evil Intent: Violence and Disorders of the Will," in *Psychopathy,* 71–72 (describing research in which psychopaths "inappropriately substituted attributions of happiness or indifference for appropriate guilt," failed to make distinctions between "aggressive transgression and transgressions of moral convention," demonstrated both "abnormal processing of emotional stimuli . . . using startle reflex modulation" and "model of fear image processing," and showed a "pattern of deficits and dissociated affective processing").

119. People v. Charles Manson et al., 61 Cal.App. 3d 102, 124 (2d Dist. 1976).

120. Brian Melley, "Charles Manson Denied Parole for a 10th Time," April 24, 2002, available at www.sfsu.edu ("psychiatric reports show he is a violent schizophrenic").

121. Vincent Bugliosi, with Curt Gentry, *Helter Skelter: The True Story of the Manson Murders* (1974), 328–332.

122. Manson fired his first attorney after the attorney requested a psychiatric evaluation. Ibid., 370, 532.

123. See William Finnegan, "Defending the Unabomber," *New Yorker*, March 16, 1998, 52.

124. William Glaberson, "Lawyers for Kaczynski Agree He Is Competent to Stand Trial," *New York Times*, January 21, 1998, A1.

125. See William Glaberson, "Kaczynski Can't Drop Lawyers or Block a Mental Illness Defense," *New York Times*, January 8, 1998, A1.

126. Stephen J. Dubner, "I Don't Want to Live Long. I Would Rather Get the Death Penalty than Spend the Rest of My Life in Prison," *Time Magazine*, October 18, 1999, 44, 46 (Kaczynski "says he pleaded guilty last year only to stop his lawyers from arguing he was a paranoid schizophrenic").

127. Steven A. Egger, *The Killers among Us* (2002), 8–12.

128. See generally, DSM-IV-TR, 527–528 (noting that pedophiles often explain their activities "with excuses or rationalizations that they have 'educational value' for the child, that the child derives 'sexual pleasure' from them, or that the child was 'sexually provocative'").

129. Moore, *Law and Psychiatry*, 100–108.

130. Ibid., 244–245. Moore repeats this explanation in his later book, *Placing Blame: A General Theory of the Criminal Law* (1997), 608–609.

131. Morse, "Immaturity and Irresponsibility," 30.

132. Moore also equates a lack of responsibility with the inability to engage in practical reasoning; see Moore, *Law and Psychiatry*, 198–210. But he defines this inability in terms of irrationality, Ibid., 105, and thus the tautology stands. Robert Schopp makes the same initial move, but explains defective practical reasoning more in terms of thought process than content. Schopp, *The Psychology of Criminal Responsibility*, 190.

133. Moore, *Placing Blame*, 609.

134. Morse puts this point another way in another work: "There is simply no scientific or clinical evidence that 'abnormal' desires are necessarily stronger than 'normal' desires and thus that abnormal desires uniquely threaten unbearable dysphoria and produce a consequently harder choice." Morse, *Culpability and Control*, 1631.

135. Schopp, *The Psychology of Criminal Responsibility*, 185–187.

136. Ibid., 160–162.

137. Ibid., 186–187.

138. Ibid., 197–198.

139. H. L. A. Hart, *Punishment and Responsibility: Essays in the Philosophy of Law* (1968), 151. See also Thomas Szasz, *Ideology and Insanity* (1987), 271–272

(suggesting that the "command from God" cases are not different, in terms of "intentionality," from the everyday occurrence of being asked to close a door by someone).

140. See DSM-IV, 668–669 (describing the symptoms of dependent personality disorder, including going "to excessive lengths to obtain nurturance and support from others, to the point of volunteering to do things that are unpleasant").

141. Compare *MPC Commentaries* to §2.09 cmt. 3, 376 ("It is obvious that even homicide may sometimes be the product of coercion that is truly irresistible . . . This section is framed on [this] assumption.") with LaFave, *Criminal Law,* 434 ("the case law . . . has generally held that duress cannot justify murder").

142. Mary would probably have to show, *inter alia,* that she felt the homicide was the only way to avoid being killed by the bad people. This is similar in type to the showing that women relying on the battered woman syndrome try to make in an attempt to justify killing their batterer despite what might seem, to the objective observer, less violent options. See, for example, State v. Kelly, 97 N.J. 178, 478 A.2d 364 (1984).

143. This individual was interviewed by the author under a promise of confidentiality, so the name and other identifying facts have been changed.

144. Drew Ross, *Looking into the Eyes of a Killer: A Psychiatrist's Journey through the Murderer's World* (1998), 87. Ross also states that patients with mental illness "usually . . . have a good heart underlying their loss of reality." Ibid. But most of his examples seem to belie this point when the patients are murderers. See 83–87 (reporting the case of Mark, who killed out of delusional jealousy); 91–93 (reporting the case of Ned, who killed during a burglary in part out of anger at his mother); 129–132 (reporting the case of Maria, who killed a hated uncle); 201–204 (reporting the case of Ernest, who stabbed a young girl, perhaps to prevent detection or due to envy of her youth).

145. Richard Rogers, "APA's Position on the Insanity Defense: Empiricism versus Emotionalism," 42 *American Psychologist* 840, 842 (1987) (citing Goodwin et al., "Clinical Significance of Hallucinations in Psychiatric Disorders: A Study of 116 Hallucinatory Patients," 24 *Archives of General Psychiatry* 76 [1971], for the proposition that "most schizophrenics are able to ignore or otherwise control their hallucinatory activity").

146. See, for example, Freddo v. State, 127 Tenn. 376, 155 S.W. 170 (Tenn. 1913), involving the case of an orphan defendant, particularly sensitive to insults to womanhood, who killed after being called a "son of a bitch"; Bedder v. Director of Public Prosecutions, 1 W.L.R. 1119 (.L. 1954), involving a sexually im-

potent and emotionally distressed defendant who killed after being taunted for his inability to have intercourse.

147. Morse e-mail to author, February 7, 2000, suggesting that some addicts and pedophiles "cannot access the good reasons not to behave badly"; Morse, *Culpability and Control,* 1636 (wondering whether psychopaths should be excused on irrationality grounds); 1649 (suggesting that "crimes of 'passion,' committed in heightened emotional states, such as fear and rage, . . . may seal off access to the ordinary desires, beliefs, and intentions that permit volitions to resolve the inevitable conflict by being properly responsive to . . . background factors").

148. Although modern cases provide few examples of this phenomenon, Sir Isaac Ray reported several cases "in which the desire to destroy life is prompted by no motive whatever, but solely by an irresistible impulse, without any appreciable disorder of mind or body." Ray, *A Treatise on Insanity,* 149–168. But even in these cases the individual was usually aware of when the "irresistible impulse" was upon them and asked to be restrained in some manner or clearly intended the crime. Ibid.

149. Morse, *Culpability and Control,* 1595–1605.

150. See generally LaFave, *Criminal Law,* 249–252.

151. Hall, "Negligent Behavior," 643.

152. See Model Penal Code §210.4.

153. Ibid., §2.02(2)(d). Both courts and commentators have endorsed a similar standard. See, for example, Trujillo v. People, 133 Colo. 186, 292 P.2d 980 (1956); Low, "The Model Penal Code," 556.

154. Model Penal Code §3.02(2). See also People v. Decina, 2 N.Y.2d 133, 157 N.Y.S.2d 558, 138 N.E.2d 799 (1956).

155. See generally Paul H. Robinson, "Causing the Conditions of One's Own Defense: A Study in the Limits of Theory in Criminal Law Doctrine," 71 *Virginia Law Review* 1 (1985).

156. Norman J. Finkel and Christopher Slobogin, "Insanity, Justification, and Culpability: Toward a Unifying Schema," 19 *Law and Human Behavior* 447, 460 (1995). See also David Wexler, "Inducing Therapeutic Compliance through the Criminal Law," 14 *Law and Psychology Review* 43 (1999).

157. Associated Press, "Yates Claimed She Killed Kids to Keep Them from Going to Hell," March 1, 2002, available at www.courttv.com/trials/yates/. Even Park Dietz, the prosecution's witness, admitted Yates told him that if she did not kill her children, "they would be tormented by Satan." Timothy Roche, "Andrea Yates: More to the Story," *Time Magazine,* March 18, 2002.

158. This account is taken from a presentation of Park Dietz (an expert witness for the prosecution in the Yates case), Meeting of American Association of Psychiatry and Law, Newport Beach, Calif., October 24, 2002. See also Associated Press, "Yates Suffered Mental Illness," March 8, 2002, available at www.courttv.com/trials/yates (describing hiding of symptoms and refusal to take medication); Forensic Files, "Court TV: Texas Mom Drowns Kids (Case Background)," at www.courttv.com/trials/yates (reporting that Yates told a psychiatrist two years before the killings: "I had a fear I would hurt somebody. . . . I thought it better to end my own life and prevent it. There was a voice, then an image of the knife. I had a vision in my mind, get a knife, get a knife. . . . I had a vision of this person getting stabbed, and the after-effects.").

159. Even here, however, Yates would not be convicted of murder under an Integrationist approach, but only of some lesser degree of homicide, consonant with her culpability. See Model Penal Code §3.02(2) (barring conviction for a crime requiring purpose or knowledge when the defendant recklessly or negligently causes condition of his or her defense).

160. This example is based on an interview with an individual with mental retardation who asked whether it was "okay" to kill someone who called him "retarded."

161. John Austin, *Lectures on Jurisprudence*, 3d ed. (1869), 498–499.

162. Jerome Hall, *General Principles of Criminal Law*, 2d ed. (1960), 380–383.

163. The person upon which this hypothetical is based asked whether such an action was justifiable, suggesting at the least an uncertainty on the issue.

164. Paul Magnarella, "Justice in a Culturally Pluralistic Society: The Cultural Defense on Trial," 19 *Journal of Ethnic Studies* 65 (1991) (noting that courts do not formally recognize a "cultural defense" and recounting only one case, People v. Kimura, No. A-091133, L.A. Super. Ct. [1985], in which specific ignorance of the law due to culture may have played a role in mitigating punishment; even there the defendant was convicted on lesser charges).

165. Bonnie, "Appreciation of Wrongfulness," 59.

166. See Dale E. McNiel, "The Relationship between Aggressive Attributional Style and Violence by Psychiatric Patients," 71 *Journal of Consulting and Clinical Psychology* 404, 405 (2003) (reporting a literature review that found that mentally ill individuals "are more likely to behave violently when they (a) perceive that someone intends to do them harm, (b) believe they have been personally targeted for harm, (c) perceive the intended harm as a misdeed committed by the perpetrator, (d) believe that they are in imminent danger, (e) believe that physical force is the best means of protection or retaliation against the perpetrator, and (f) attribute blame to the perpetrator based on his or her dispositional qualities, e.g., 'he wishes to harm me because he is evil'").

167. Bonnie, "Appreciation of Wrongfulness," 59–60.

168. Several scholars have endorsed this approach. See, for example, Abraham Goldstein and Jay Katz, "Abolish the Insanity Defense—Why Not?" 72 *Yale Law Journal* 853 (1963); Norval Morris, *Madness and the Criminal Law* (1982), 53–70; American Medical Association, "Insanity Defense in Criminal Trials and Limitations of Psychiatric Testimony: Report of the Board of Trustees," 251 *Journal of the American Medical Association* 2967 (1984).

169. State v. Korrell, 213 Mont. 316, 334, 690 P.2d 992, 1002 (1984); State v. Searcy, 118 Idaho 632, 798 P.2d 914 (1990); State v. Herrera, 895 P.2d (Utah 1995). But see Finger v. State, 117 Nev. 548, 27 P.3d 66 (2001).

170. In particular, Leland v. Oregon, 343 U.S. 790, 799 (1952), held that the due process clause does not prohibit forcing a defendant to prove insanity beyond a reasonable doubt. See also Rivera v. Delaware, 429 U.S. 877 (1976).

171. 518 U.S. 37 (1996).

172. Ibid. at 51.

173. Ibid.

174. It should also be noted that, in a jurisdiction that subjectifies defenses such as self-defense, provocation, and duress, the mens rea alternative to the insanity defense is grossly unfair, because it limits the relevance of mental disability to mens rea. We can hardly deny a defense to those with mental illness that we freely grant to others.

175. David Bazelon, "The Dilemma of Criminal Responsibility," 72 *Kentucky Law Journal* 263, 277 (1982–1983). See also Perlin, *Jurisprudence of Insanity Defense*, 13 ("[t]he public's outrage over a jurisprudential system that could allow a defendant who shot an American president on national television to plead 'not guilty' (for *any* reason) became a 'river of fury' after the jury's verdict was announced").

176. Perlin, *Insanity Defense*, 14–30 (also recounting, inter alia, the statement of Edward Meese, another U.S. attorney general, that eliminating the insanity defense would "rid . . . the streets of some of the most dangerous people that are out there, that are committing a disproportionate number of crimes").

177. Michael Perlin, "On 'Sanism,'" 46 *Southern Methodist University Law Review* 373, 394 (1992) (defining sanism as "an irrational prejudice of the same quality and character of other irrational prejudices such as racism, sexism, heterosexism and ethnic bigotry").

178. See Judi Chamberlin, *On Our Own* (1978), 202 ("[A]n 'ex-mental patient' is a code word for a violent, dangerous, unpredictable individual").

179. See Amerigo Farina et al., "Role of Stigma and Set in Interpersonal Interaction," 71 *Journal of Abnormal Psychology* 421 (1966).

180. Deborah C. Scott et al., "Monitoring Insanity Acquittees: Connecticut's Psychiatric Security Review Board," 41 *Hospital and Community Psychiatry* 980, 982 (1990) (insanity acquittees are the "most despised" and "morally repugnant" group of individuals in society).

181. See Robert Fein, "How the Insanity Acquittal Retards Treatment," in *Therapeutic Jurisprudence: The Law as a Therapeutic Agency* (1990), 49–54 (1990); Ross, *Eyes of a Killer,* 168 ("appreciation, both cognitively and emotionally, of the wrongfulness of the act . . . is harder to achieve for those acquitted by reason of insanity"). See also Joshua Dressler, "Reflections of Excusing Wrongdoers: Moral Theory, New Excuses and the Model Penal Code," 19 *Rutgers Law Review* 671, 689 (1988) ("[I]t is often psychologically desirable and, in any case, morally right, for a wrongdoer to feel guilty").

182. Bruce Winick, "Ambiguities in the Legal Meaning and Significance of Mental Illness," 1 *Psychology, Public Policy and Law* 534, 603 (1995).

183. See Richard Bonnie and Norval Morris, "Should the Insanity Defense Be Abolished? A Debate," 1 *Journal of Law and Health* 113, 119 (1986–1987) (in which Morris states, "the special defense of insanity . . . distracts from . . . the organization and allocation of such psychiatric resources as we are prepared to bring to bear on the very serious and practical problems of the relationship between mental illness and crime").

184. State v. Jones, 50 N.H. 369, 387 (1871).

185. See T. Howard Stone, "Therapeutic Implications of Incarceration for Persons with Severe Mental Disorders: Searching for Rational Health Policy," 24 *American Criminal Law Review* 283, 285 (1997) (estimating 87,000 people with *severe* mental disorder in prison).

186. Compare Jennifer S. Bard, "Re-arranging Deck Chairs on the Titanic: Why the Incarceration of Individuals with Serious Mental Illness Violates Public Health, Ethical, and Constitutional Principles and Therefore Cannot Be Made Right by Piecemeal Changes to the Insanity Defense," 5 *Houston Journal of Health Law and Policy* 1 (2005).

3.   Mental Disability and the Death Penalty

1. See generally Gary Melton et al., *Psychological Evaluations for the Courts: A Handbook for Mental Health Professionals and Lawyers* 2d ed. (1997), 253 (in indeterminate sentencing, "[t]he criteria to be used in individualizing are typically unspecified and could be related to the offenders' culpability, treatability, or dangerousness, as well as less legitimate factors").

2. For example, Arizona formally recognizes the following circumstance as a

mitigator, which can reduce sentence by up to 50 percent : "The defendant's capacity to appreciate the wrongfulness of the defendant's conduct or to conform the defendant's conduct to the requirements of law was significantly impaired, but not so impaired as to constitute a defense to prosecution." Ariz. Stat. §13–702(A)(D).

3. See Michael L. Perlin and Keri K. Gould, "Rashomon and the Criminal Law: Mental Disability and the Federal Sentencing Guidelines," 22 *American Journal of Criminal Law* 431, 448–449 (1995) (noting that downward departures on grounds of mental disability are usually "summarily rejected").

4. See, for example, United States v. Booker, 125 S.Ct. 738 (2005) (striking down the provision in the federal sentencing guidelines that makes them mandatory).

5. See Part 2 of this chapter.

6. 477 U.S. 399 (1986).

7. See National Mental Health Association, "Death Penalty and People with Mental Illness" (March 10, 2001), available at www.nmha.org/position/deathpenalty (describing estimates ranging from 5 to 10 percent); Mark D. Cunningham and Mark P. Vigen, "Death Row Inmate Characteristics, Adjustment, and Confinement: A Critical Review of the Literature," 20 *Behavioral Science and Law* 191, 193, 200 (2002) (noting that incidence of schizophrenia on death row is at least 5 percent and perhaps higher). A widely cited statement by one commentator, to the effect that in 1981, 70 percent of those on death row had been diagnosed with schizophrenia, seems highly inflated, however. Amnesty International, *United States of America: The Death Penalty* (1986), 108–109 (citing R. Johnson, *Condemned to Die: Life Under Sentence of Death* [1981]).

8. 536 U.S. 304 (2002).

9. 125 S.Ct. 1183 (2005).

10. 356 U.S. 86 (1958).

11. Ibid., 100–101.

12. See Harmelin v. Michigan, 501 U.S. 957, 1000 (1991); Penry v. Lynaugh, 492 U.S. 302, 331 (1989).

13. 536 U.S. at 313–315.

14. Ibid., 316 ("[I]t appears that even among those States that regularly execute offenders and that have no prohibition with regard to the mentally retarded, only five have executed offenders possessing a known IQ less than 70 since we decided *Penry*"); Ibid., n. 21 (listing national and international organizations).

15. See, for example, Coker v. Georgia, 433 U.S. 584 (1977) (finding only one state permitted the death penalty for rape); Solem v. Helm, 463 U.S. 277 (1983)

(stating only one state permitted a life sentence without parole for the types of crimes at issue); Ford v. Wainwright, 477 U.S. 399 (1986) (noting no state authorized execution of those who are incompetent to be executed); Enmund v. Florida, 458 U.S. 782 (1982) (finding only eight out of thirty-six death penalty states permitted the death penalty for a robbery in which an accomplice took a life).

16. 536 U.S. at 343 (emphasis added). Scalia noted that the Court had upheld the death penalty for major participation in a felony with reckless indifference to life when only eleven of thirty-seven death penalty states (30 percent) prohibited such punishment—Tison v. Arizona, 481 U.S. 137 (1987)—and for people who commit murder at age sixteen when fifteen of thirty-six (42 percent) death penalty states prohibited capital punishment for such offenders. Stanford v. Kentucky, 492 U.S. 361 (1989). Of course, the latter case has been reversed by *Simmons*, by which time eighteen death penalty states had prohibited execution of those under age eighteen. 125 S.Ct., 1192.

17. 536 U.S. at 346 (Scalia, J., dissenting) (reporting, inter alia, a source that indicated that 10 percent of those on death row suffer from mental retardation). Other reports estimate up to 30 percent of those on death row have mental retardation. See, for example, Clive A. Stafford-Smith and Remy Voisin Starns, "Folly by Fiat: Pretending That Death Row Inmates Can Represent Themselves in Post-Conviction Proceedings," 45 *Loyola Law Review* 55, 70 n. 92 (1999).

18. Penry v. Lynaugh, 492 U.S. 302 (1989).

19. 536 U.S., 347 (Scalia, J., dissenting).

20. Ibid.

21. Ibid., 321–326 (Rehnquist, C. J., dissenting).

22. Ibid., 312.

23. 433 U.S. 584, 597 (1977).

24. In *Coker* itself, for instance, the Court made the quoted statement after noting that the national legislative consensus was clearly against imposing the death penalty for rape. Ibid.

25. See Stanford v. Kentucky, 492 U.S. 361, 379 (1989).

26. 536 U.S. at 321.

27. Ibid., 349 (Scalia, J., dissenting).

28. Gregg v. Georgia, 428 U.S. 153, 183 (1976). See also Enmund v. Florida, 458 U.S. 782, 792 (1982) ("Unless the death penalty . . . contributes to one or both of these goals it 'is nothing more than the purposeless and needless imposition of pain and suffering,' and hence an unconstitutional punishment").

29. 536 U.S. at 313.

30. Ibid., 318.

31. 536 U.S. at 319.

32. Ibid. The Court also asserted that people with mental retardation are more likely to confess falsely and are less able to assist counsel at trial, so that "in the aggregate [they] face a special risk of wrongful execution." Ibid., 320. I do not focus on this issue because it amounts to an attack on all criminal prosecutions of people with retardation, not just their execution.

33. 125 S.Ct., 1197 ("Once the diminished culpability of juveniles is recognized, it is evident that the penological justifications for the death penalty apply to them with lesser force than to adults").

34. Compare *Penry*, 492 U.S. at 334.

35. 477 U.S. 399, 408 (1986).

36. Conn. Gen. Stat. §53a–46a(h).

37. 473 U.S. 432 (1985).

38. Ibid., 442–447.

39. FCC v. Beach Communications, Inc., 508 U.S. 307, 313 (1993).

40. *Beach Communications*, 508 U.S. at 315.

41. Lehnhausen v. Lake Shore Auto Parts Co., 410 U.S. 356, 364 (1973).

42. New Orleans v. Dukes, 427 U.S. 297, 303 (1976) (per curiam).

43. 473 U.S. at 450.

44. Ibid., 448.

45. Ibid., 437.

46. James W. Ellis and Ruth A. Luckasson, "Mentally Retarded Criminal Defendants," 53 *George Washington Law Review* 414, 426 (1985) ("The best modern evidence suggests that the incidence of criminal behavior among people with mental retardation does not greatly exceed the incidence of criminal behavior among the population as a whole"); Craig Smith et al., "Prison Adjustment of Youthful Inmates with Mental Retardation," 28 *Mental Retardation* 177, 179 (June 1990) (finding that a group of offenders with mental retardation had twice as many disciplinary reports involving assault than a matched group without retardation).

47. See, for example, *Kentucky Practice: Methods of Practice,* vol. 3A, §25.5, 3d ed. (1990) ("land use and zoning regulations may be employed to prevent danger and congestion in the circulation of people").

48. See, for example, Gayle Lynn Pettinga, "Rational Basis with Bite: Intermediate Scrutiny by Any Other Name," 62 *Indiana Law Journal* 779, 793–799 (1987); William B. Lockhart et al., *Constitutional Law: Cases-Comments-Questions,* 8th ed. (1996), 1161–1162. See also 473 U.S. at 458 (Marshall, J., concurring)

("however labeled, the rational basis test invoked today is most assuredly not the rational-basis test [applied in earlier cases]").

49. 509 U.S. 312 (1993).

50. Ibid., 322.

51. Addington v. Texas, 441 U.S. 418 (1978). The Court also asserted that commitment visits more serious consequences on people with mental illness, in the guise of powerful antipsychotic medication. *Heller,* 509 U.S. at 324–325. The dissent argued to the contrary, noting that many people with retardation receive medication and that they often spend their whole life in an institution, while people with mental illness are often released within a short period of time. *Heller,* 341–342 (Souter, J., dissenting). While the dissent's contentions are worth considering, "treatment" of people with mental illness is much more likely to involve use of invasive medications and, under constitutionally correct procedures, prolonged detention must be periodically reviewed. See Fasulo v. Arafeh, 378 A.2d 553 (Conn. 1977); Matter of Harhut, 385 N.W.2d 305 (Minn. 1986). Thus, the consequence of any given commitment is not exceedingly different for the two groups.

52. See Leonard E. Heller, Sec'y, Ky. Cabinet for Human Res., Petitioner v. Samuel Doe, by His Mother and Next Friend, Mary Doe, et al., Respondents, No. 92–351, October Term, 1992, February 23, 1993, Reply Brief for Petitioner.

53. *Heller,* 509 U.S. at 348 (Souter, J., dissenting).

54. 531 U.S. 356 (2001).

55. Ibid., 360.

56. Ibid., 367.

57. Ibid., 375 (Kennedy, J., concurring).

58. Ibid. at 381–382 (Breyer, J., dissenting) (arguing that the ADA's prohibition of discrimination based on mental disability implements the Court's holding in *Cleburne*).

59. Mark C. Weber, "Disability Harassment in the Public Schools," 43 *William and Mary Law Review* 1079, 1128 (2002).

60. 504 U.S. 71, 86 (1992). The plurality found that the Equal Protection Clause was violated by continued confinement, on dangerousness grounds, of an insanity acquittee who was no longer mentally ill when other persons who committed criminal acts could not be confined on those grounds. Ibid., 84–86. Justice O'Connor wrote a separate opinion in *Foucha,* stating, "Although I think it unnecessary to reach equal protection issues on the facts before us, the permissibility of holding an acquittee who is not mentally ill longer than a person convicted of the same crimes could be imprisoned is open to serious question." Ibid., 88 (O'Connor, J., concurring in part and concurring in judgment).

61. DSM-IV-TR, 274, 285.

62. Robert Schopp, *Automatism, Insanity, and the Psychology of Criminal Responsibility: A Philosophical Inquiry* (1991), 185–187 (describing these and other symptoms).

63. See generally Melton et al., *Psychological Evaluations,* 204–208 (describing and distinguishing these defenses). Statutory language regarding the relevance of mental disability to capital sentencing is discussed in Part 2 of this chapter.

64. Henry J. Steadman et al., "Factors Associated with a Successful Insanity Plea," 140 *American Journal of Psychiatry* 401, 402–403 (1983).

65. Ralph Reisner, Christopher Slobogin and Arti Rai, *Law and the Mental Health System: Civil and Criminal Aspects,* 4th ed. (2004), 573–575 (noting that only half of the states recognize the diminished capacity defense and no state has adopted a diminished responsibility defense based *explicitly* on mental abnormality); Wayne LaFave, *Criminal Law,* 3d ed. (2000), 711 (noting that in many states a provocation defense based on "special mental qualities" is not recognized).

66. See, for example, Bigby v. Dretke, 2005 WL 540048 (reversing death sentence imposed on a person with severe schizophrenia); Illinois v. Haynes, 737 N.E.2d 169, 193–196 (Ill. 2000) (Harrison, C. J., dissenting) (noting five of six experts found the defendant to be delusional at the time of trial and well before it); Walton v. Angelone, 2002 U.S. Dist. LEXIS 5240, 20–24, 45–49, 62–63, 76 (W.D. Va. 2002) (upholding the death sentence despite very strong evidence of schizophrenia at the time of offense and at the trial); Feguer v. United States, 302 F.2d 214, 228–236 (8th Cir. 1962) (same outcome); People v. Rittger, 355 P.2d 645 (Cal. 1960) (same outcome); People v. Crews, 522 N.E.2d 1167 (Ill. 1988) (upholding the death sentence for a defendant found guilty but mentally ill, with mental illness defined as "a substantial disorder of thought, mood, or behavior which afflicted a person at the time of the commission of the offense and which impaired that person's judgment"); Illinois v. Scott, 594 N.E.2d 217 (Ill. 1992) (same outcome); State v. Wilson, 413 S.E.2d 19 (S.C. 1992) (same outcome); Colburn v. Texas, 966 S.W.2d 511, 512 (Tex. Crim. App. 1998) (rejecting the argument that an "extensive history of paranoid schizophrenia" prevents the imposition of the death penalty); Hernandez v. Johnson, 248 F.3d 344 (5th Cir. 2001) (upholding the death sentence despite an admission from a prosecution witness that schizophrenia was the "primary" diagnosis and despite jury instructions that did not call attention to mental illness as a mitigating factor but rather merely told the jury to consider all the evidence and determine whether the defendant "deliberately" killed and was dangerous); State v. Berry, 686 N.E.2d 1097, 1103–1104 (Ohio 1997) (up-

holding the death sentence of an offender who was diagnosed with schizophrenia and psychosis prior to the offense and who "confessed" on condition
that the state would execute him); Corcoran v. Indiana, 774 N.E2d 495, 503
(Ind. Sup. Ct. 2002) (upholding the death sentence over a dissent that cited
Atkins in concluding that "because Corcoran is obviously severely mentally ill,
he should be sentenced to life without the possibility of parole, not death").
See generally Phyllis L. Crocker, "Concepts of Culpability and Deathworthi-
ness: Differentiating between Guilt and Punishment in Death Penalty Cases,"
66 *Fordham Law Review* 21, 27, 66–78, nn. 218, 231 (1997) (stating that "courts
frequently employ the guilt-phase insanity test as the standard by which to
judge a defendant's punishment-phase mitigating evidence of mental illness"
and citing and describing cases).

67. See DSM-IV-TR, 39 (noting that mental retardation is measured in part
through an assessment of "general intellectual functioning," which is defined
by the intelligence quotient, which in turn is obtained by use of "one or more
of the standardized, individually administered intelligence tests").

68. Field studies of interrater reliability on specific diagnoses of serious mental
illness indicate a relatively low rate of agreement. See, for example, Paul
Lieberman and Frances Baker, "The Reliability of Psychiatric Diagnosis in the
Emergency Room," 36 *Hospital and Community Psychiatry* 291 (1985) (finding
41 percent agreement on schizophrenia, 50 percent agreement on mood disorders; and 37 percent agreement on organic disorders).

69. DSM-IV-TR, 275.

70. People with nonpsychotic personality disorders and depression are routinely
committed under civil commitment statutes. Mary L. Durham, "Civil Commitment of the Mentally Ill: Research, Policy and Practice," in *Mental Health
and Law: Research, Policy and Services,* ed. Bruce Sales and Saleem Shah (1996),
19. See also Matter of D.C., 679 A.2d 634 (N.J. 1996) (upholding constitutionality of amended New Jersey commitment statute clarifying that "mental illness" does not require that a person be psychotic).

71. The low ratios for interrater reliability described earlier came from emergency
room settings, which are quite different from the considered evaluation
process that would occur in death penalty contexts. Research on the diagnosis
of schizophrenia in more sedate environs has found agreement rates above 80
percent. See Reisner, Slobogin, and Rai, *Law and the Mental Health System,*
429–430. See also Kenneth K. Fukunaga et al., "Insanity Plea: Inter-Examiner
Agreement and Concordance of Psychiatric Opinion and Court Verdict," 5 *Law
and Human Behavior* 325 (1981) (finding 92 percent interrater agreement on

gross impairment); Michael R. Phillips et al., "Psychiatry and the Criminal Justice System: Testing the Myths," 145 *American Journal of Psychiatry* 605 (1988) (finding 76 percent agreement on psychosis).

72. See Michael Perlin, *The Jurisprudence of the Insanity Defense* (1994), 238–241. Perlin states that "there is virtually no evidence that feigned insanity has ever been a remotely significant problem of criminal procedure" (Ibid., 238), that advances in detection of malingering can discern faking in more than 90 percent of the cases in which it does occur (Ibid., 240), and that seriously mentally disabled criminal defendants will often feign sanity in an effort to avoid stigmatization as mentally ill, even where such evidence might serve as powerful mitigating evidence in death penalty cases (Ibid., 240–241, noting that "juveniles imprisoned on death row were quick to tell Dr. Dorothy Lewis and her associates, 'I'm not crazy,' or 'I'm not a retard'").

73. DSM-IV-TR, 39.

74. David L. Rumley, "A License to Kill: The Categorical Exemption of the Mentally Retarded from the Death Penalty," 24 *St. Mary's Law Journal* 1299, 1329–1340 (1993) (discussing the unreliability of IQ tests and stating that, as a result, "the obtained score is only one of a number of possible scores that may be achieved with different sample questions or with the same questions at different times"); Jonathan L. Bing, "Protecting the Mentally Retarded from Capital Punishment: State Efforts Since *Penry* and Recommendations for the Future," 22 *New York University Law and Social Change* 59, 67–70 (1996) (discussing debates about whether the cut-off score should be 70 or as high as 85); 73–74 (discussing how tests may be biased against minorities or by examiner behavior).

75. DSM-IV-TR, 39–40.

76. See Douglas Mossman, "Atkins v. Virginia: A Psychiatric Can of Worms," 33 *New Mexico Law Review* 255, 265–269 (2003). See also Bing, "Protecting the Mentally Retarded," 70 (discussing the various definitions of "adaptive functioning").

77. See Murphy v. State, 54 P.3d 556, 568 (Okla. Crim. App. 2002).

78. It is possible that the Supreme Court will eventually decide that, in implementing *Atkins*, the state must prove nonretardation beyond a reasonable doubt to a jury. Compare Ring v. Arizona, 536 U.S. 584, 609 (2003) (holding invalid under the Sixth Amendment a death penalty statute that provided that the sentencing judge, sitting alone, may determine the aggravating factors required for imposition of the death penalty when those factors "operate as 'the functional equivalent of an element of a greater offense'"). If so, the standard

of proof with respect to people alleging mental illness obviously could not be any higher. However, legislatures could still place a heavier burden of *production* on members of the latter group, requiring them to make a stronger prima facie case before the issue goes to the jury. See Christopher Slobogin, "Mental Disorder as an Exemption from the Death Penalty: The ABA Task Force Recommendations," 54 *Catholic University Law Review* 1133, 1138–1139 (2005).

79. DSM-IV-TR, 282.

80. See Erwin Chemerinsky, *Constitutional Law: Principles and Policies* (2002), 518–519.

81. DSM-IV-TR, 282.

82. Ibid., 275–276.

83. See generally Herbert Y. Meltzer and S. Hossein Fatemi, "Treatment of Schizophrenia," in *Essentials of Clinical Pharmacology,* ed. Alan F. Schatzberg and Charles B. Nemeroff (2001), 406.

84. *Textbook of Psychiatry,* ed. John A. Talbott et al. (1988), 710–711 (discussing the need for "long-term" programs for those with mental retardation).

85. DSM-IV-TR, 279 ("Lack of insight is common and may be one of the best predictors of poor outcome, perhaps because it predisposes the individual to noncompliance with treatment.")

86. See Patricia L. Gilbert et al., "Neuroleptic Withdrawal in Schizophrenia Patients: A Review of the Literature," 52 *Archives General Psychiatry* 173, 182 (1995); Ebrahim M. Gul, "Patient Response to Clozapine in a Forensic Psychiatric Hospital," 45 *Hospital and Community Psychiatry* 271 (1994).

87. Robert Pear, "Few Seek to Treat Mental Disorders Common, U.S. Says; Many Not Treated," *New York Times,* December 13, 1999, A1.

88. Ellis and Luckasson, "Mentally Retarded Criminal Defendants," 439.

89. 536 U.S., 350 (Scalia, J., dissenting).

90. See Part 2, B of Chapter 2.

91. James Bonta et al., "The Prediction of Criminal and Violent Recidivism among Mentally Disordered Offenders: A Meta Analysis," 123 *Psychological Bulletin* 123 (1998); Marnie E. Rice and Grant T. Harris, "A Comparison of Criminal Recidivism among Schizophrenic and Nonschizophrenic Offenders," 15 *International Journal of Law and Psychiatry* 397 (1992) (finding that subjects with schizophrenia were less likely to commit offenses upon release than their nonschizophrenic counterparts).

92. Compare the data describing recidivism among offenders with mental illness in the previous note with Health Evidence Bulletins, hebw.uwcm.ac.uk/ learningdisabilities, December 31, 1999 (concluding that "[s]tudies [of offend-

ers with intellectual disability] have found re-offending rates of untreated of-fenders of between 40 and 70% [and] re-offending rates following treatment to be between 20 and 55% depending on the type of treatment and the of-fence").

93. 536 U.S., 305.

94. See Ronald Tabak, "Overview of Task Force Proposal on Mental Disability and the Death Penalty," 54 *Catholic Law Review* 1123, 1125 (2005).

95. Morse, "Culpability and Control," 1626 ("[I]t is difficult to envision a case in which the defendant was suffering from a severe mental disorder with marked 'coercive' features, but was substantially rational"); Richard Bonnie, "The Moral Basis of Insanity Defense," 69 *American Bar Association Journal* 194, 196–197 (1983).

96. As a member of the American Bar Association's Task Force on Mental Disor-der and the Death Penalty, I helped draft this resolution, but was unsuccessful in having the word "severe" removed. Many members of the task force were worried that its deletion would hurt the resolution's chances for passage by the ABA House of Delegates and other deliberative bodies.

97. See Peter Arenella, "Convicting the Morally Blameless: Reassessing the Rela-tionship between Legal and Moral Accountability," 39 *U.C.L.A. Law Review* 1511 (1992).

98. Compare Paul Robinson, "Causing the Conditions of One's Own Defense: A Study in the Limits of Theory in Criminal Law Doctrine," 71 *Virginia Law Re-view* 1, 31 (1985) (arguing that one who "causes" his defense should be denied it only when, "at the time that the actor engages in his initial conduct he has a culpable state of mind as to causing the conduct constituting the offense" [e.g., the mens rea for first degree murder]).

99. See, for example, Woodson v. North Carolina, 428 U.S. 280, 303 (1976).

100. *Atkins,* 536 U.S. at 350–351.

101. Ibid., 350.

102. Donald N. Bersoff, "Some Contrarian Concerns about Law, Psychology, and Public Policy," 26 *Law and Human Behavior* 565, 568–569 (2002).

103. See, for example, Godfrey v. Georgia, 446 U.S. 420, 433 (1980) (setting aside a death sentence because the crime did not reflect "a consciousness materi-ally more 'depraved' than that of any person guilty of murder"). See generally Zant v. Stephens, 462 U.S. 862, 876–877 (1983).

104. Respondent's Brief at 2, Penry v. Johnson, 532 U.S. 782 (2001) (No. 00–6677).

105. These facts are taken from *Atkins,* 536 U.S. at 338 (Scalia, J., dissenting).

106. People v. Wolff, 394 P.2d 959, 975 (1964) (emphasis omitted).

107. DSM-IV-TR, 43. See also Penry v. Lynaugh, 492 U.S. 302, 345 (1989) (Brennan, J., concurring in part and dissenting in part) (quoting a brief of the American Association on Mental Retardation) (citations omitted).

108. An account of Penry's first two death sentences, both of which were overturned by the Supreme Court, is found at Penry v. Johnson, 261 F.3d 541 (5th Cir. 2001). Penry was retried and resentenced to death a third time, prior to *Atkins.* Penry v. Coker, No. 15918–04, 2003 WL 21401978, at *1 (Tex. Crim. App. June 18, 2000).

109. Thomas Grisso and Paul Appelbaum, "Abilities of Patients to Consent to Psychiatric and Medical Treatments," 19 *Law and Human Behavior* 149, 171 (1995) (finding that nearly half of the schizophrenia group performed in the "adequate" range across all decision-making measures, and that a significant portion performed at or above the mean for persons without mental illness); Melton et al., *Psychological Evaluations for the Courts,* 144 (reporting research finding that many people with mental retardation are competent to stand trial, whether measured psychometrically or judicially).

110. See, for example, Uniform Probate Code §5–101 (amended 1982 and 1989), which permits an incompetency finding for a person with mental disability only if he "lacks sufficient understanding or capacity to make or communicate responsible decisions concerning his person."

111. See, for example, Bruce Link and Ann Stueve, "New Evidence on the Violence Risk Posed by People with Mental Illness," 55 *Archives General Psychiatry* 403 (1998); Gregory Leong et al., "Dangerous Mentally Disordered Criminals: Unresolvable Societal Fear?" 36 *Journal of Forensic Science* 210, 215 (1991); Linda Teplin, "The Criminality of the Mentally Ill: A Dangerous Misconception," 142 *American Journal of Psychiatry* 593, 597–598 (1985); John Monahan, "Mental Disorder and Violent Behavior: Perceptions and Evidence," 47 *American Psychologist* 511, 511 (1992) (discussing, inter alia, how public fears about the purported link between mental illness and dangerousness "drive the formal laws and policies governing mental disability jurisprudence"); Bernice A. Pescosolido et al., "The Public's View of the Competence, Dangerousness, and Need for Legal Coercion of Persons with Mental Health Problems," 89 *American Journal of Public Health* 1339, 1341 (1999) (reporting that while 17 percent of a random sample of citizens felt that a "troubled person" was "very likely" or "somewhat likely" to be violent, 33.3 percent said the same of the depressed person, and 60 percent said the same of a person with schizophrenia).

112. For a description of the Capital Jury Sentencing Project, see William J. Bowers, "The Capital Jury Project: Rationale, Design, and Preview of Early Findings," 70 *Indiana Law Journal* 1043 (1995).

113. Steven P. Garvey, "The Emotional Economy of Capital Sentencing," 75 *New York University Law Review* 26, 59–61 (2000) (tables 8, 9).

114. Ibid., 56 (table 7).

115. As Connecticut has demonstrated, legislative action is possible. Similarly, state governors, through implementation of executive clemency, can recognize the mitigating effects of mental illness. See, for example, Elizabeth Rapaport, "Straight Is the Gate: Capital Clemency in the United States from *Gregg* to *Atkins*, 33 *New Mexico Law Review* 349 (2003) (describing Governor James Gilmore's 1999 commutation of the death sentence of Calvin Eugene Swann, who allegedly suffered from schizophrenia at time of his offense—see Swann v. Virginia, 441 S.E.2d 195, 203 [Va. 1994]—and clearly did at time of commutation).

116. John E. Nowak and Ronald D. Rotunda, *Constitutional Law,* 5th ed. (1995), 511.

117. See Ellen Fels Berkman, "Mental Illness as an Aggravating Circumstance in Capital Sentencing," 89 *Columbia Law Review* 291, 296–298 (1989).

118. 438 U.S. 586 (1978).

119. Ibid., 604 (emphasis in original). See also Eddings v. Oklahoma, 455 U.S. 104 (1982) (holding that the trial court's refusal to consider an offender's emotional problems violated the Eighth and Fourteenth Amendments).

120. Berkman, "Mental Illness as an Aggravating Factor," 298.

121. American Law Institute, Model Penal Code §210.6(4).

122. Compare with Model Penal Code §210.3(1)(b).

123. Compare with Model Penal Code §4.01(1).

124. Gary Goodpaster, "The Trial for Life: Effective Assistance of Counsel in Death Penalty Cases," 58 *New York University Law Review* 299, 332 (1983).

125. C. J. Judson et al., "A Study of the California Penalty Jury in First-Degree-Murder Cases," 21 *Stanford Law Review* 1297 (1969).

126. David Baldus et al., *Equal Justice and the Death Penalty* (1990), 644–645 (two tables, each looking at fifteen factors but using different statistical models, showing that assertion of a defense of "insanity or delusional compulsion" correlated with a death sentence at an extremely high level of statistical significance, that is, $p \geq .0000$). See also Ibid., 640–641.

127. David Baldus et al., "Racial Discrimination and the Death Penalty in the Post-*Furman* Era: An Empirical and Legal Overview, with Recent Findings from Philadelphia," 83 *Cornell Law Review* 1638, 1688–1689 (1998) (table 6).

128. Ibid., 1689. The factor was significant at the .10 level; social science convention is to accord statistical significance only to factors that reach the .05 level. See John Monahan and Laurens Walker, *Social Science in Law* 78 (1994).

129. Julie Goetz and Gordon P. Waldo, "Why Jurors in Florida Vote for Life or Death: The Florida Component of the Capital Jury Project," presented at the conference on Life over Death XV, Fort Lauderdale, Fla., September 27, 1996, 34.

130. Lawrence T. White, "Juror Decision Making in the Capital Penalty Trial: An Analysis of Crimes and Defense Strategies," 11 *Law and Human Behavior* 113, 125 (1987).

131. Wainright v. Witt, 469 U.S. 412 (1985).

132. Phoebe C. Ellsworth et al., "The Death-Qualified Jury and the Defense of Insanity," 8 *Law and Human Behavior* 81 (1984).

133. Ibid., 90.

134. Several researchers have observed that dangerousness is the paramount concern of most capital sentencing jurors, regardless of their jurisdiction's law on the matter. See, for example, Austin Sarat, "Violence, Representation, and Responsibility in Capital Trials: The View from the Jury," 70 *Indiana Law Journal* 1103, 1131–1133 (1995); Joseph L. Hoffmann, "Where's the Buck?—Juror Misperception of Sentencing Responsibility in Death Penalty Cases," 70 *Indiana Law Journal* 1137, 1153 (1995); Stephen P. Garvey, "Aggravation and Mitigation in Capital Cases: What Do Jurors Think?," 98 *Columbia Law Review* 1538, 1559 (1998). In addition, see Aletha Claussen-Schulz et al., "Dangerousness Risk Assessment, and Capital Sentencing," 10 *Psychology, Public Policy & Law* 471, 480 (2004) (finding, in a study using mock jurors, that concerns about future violent conduct accounted for more variance in the sentencing decision than did other aggravating circumstances); Sally Costanzo and Mark Costanzo, "Life or Death Decisions: An Analysis of Capital Jury Decision Making Under the Special Issues Sentencing Framework," 18 *Law and Human Behavior* 151 (1994) (finding, based on interviews of capital sentencing jurors, that jurors tended to spend most of their deliberation time deciding whether the defendant would be violent if not executed); John H. Blume et al., "Future Dangerousness in Capital Cases: Always 'At Issue,'" 86 *Cornell Law Review* 397, 398 (2001) (same).

135. Compare Lawrence T. White, "The Mental Illness Defense in the Capital Penalty Hearing," 5 *Behavioral Science and Law* 411, 419 (1987).

136. 462 U.S. 862 (1983).

137. Ibid., 885 (emphasis added).

138. See James S. Liebman and Michael J. Shepard, "Guiding Capital Sentencing Discretion Beyond the 'Boiler Plate': Mental Disorder as a Mitigating Factor," 66 *Georgetown Law Journal* 757, 791–806 (1978) (describing the prevalent mitigating role that mental disorder has played in the law of capital punishment).

139. 343 So. 2d 29 (Fla. Sup. Ct. 1977).
140. Ibid., 34.
141. 373 So. 2d 882 (Fla. Sup. Ct. 1979).
142. Ibid., 885.
143. See Randy Hertz and Robert Weisberg, "In Mitigation of the Penalty of Death: *Lockett v. Ohio* and the Capital Defendant's Right to Consideration of Mitigating Circumstances," 69 *California Law Review* 317, 333, 340–341 (1981).
144. Webster's New Collegiate Dictionary (1998).
145. Compare Penry v. Lynaugh, 492 U.S. 302, 323–324 (1989); State v. Gretzler, 659 P.2d 1 (Ariz. Sup. Ct. 1983).
146. Christopher Slobogin, "Should Juries and the Death Penalty Mix? A Prediction about the Supreme Court's Answer," 70 *Indiana Law Journal* 1249, 1264 n. 56 (1995).
147. For instance, a recent study concludes that psychological evidence, especially of schizophrenia and retardation, "can have significant effects on sentencing outcomes in death penalty litigation." Michelle E. Barnett et al., "When Mitigation Evidence Makes a Difference: Effects of Psychological Mitigating Evidence on Sentencing Decisions in Capital Trials," 22 *Behavioral Science and Law* 751, 766 (2004). It should be noted, however, that this study relied on undergraduate responses to vignettes, and simulated only the sentencing stage of the capital process, meaning that it cannot be known whether the subjects might have also found the individuals insane at trial.
148. See McCleskey v. Kemp, 481 U.S. 279 (1987).
149. Tennard v. Dretke, 124 S.Ct. 2562, 2573 (2004) (expressing concern that the prosecutor, during closing argument, stated "that Tennard's low IQ was irrelevant in mitigation, but relevant to the question whether he posed a future danger"); Atkins v. Virginia, 537 U.S. 304, 321 (2003) ("reliance on mental retardation as a mitigating factor can be a two-edged sword that may enhance the likelihood that the aggravating factor of future dangerousness will be found by the jury"); Penry v. Lynaugh, 492 U.S., 302, 323–325 (1989) (same).
150. E. Coke, *Institutes,* vol. 3, 6th ed. (1680), 6.
151. 477 U.S. 399, po. 406–411.
152. Ibid., 410.
153. Ibid., 422 (Powell, J., concurring).
154. See, for example, Geoffrey C. Hazard Jr. and David W. Louisell, "Death, the State, and the Insane: Stay of Execution," 9 *UCLA Law Review* 381 (1962); Barbara A. Ward, "Competency for Execution: Problems in Law and Psychiatry," 14 *Florida State University Law Review* 35, 48–57 (1986).

155. Craig J. Albert, "Challenging Deterrence: New Insights on Capital Punishment Derived from Panel Data," 60 *University of Pittsburgh Law Review* 321, 323 (1999).

156. See Hazard and Louisell, "Stay of Execution," 387; Ward, "Competency for Execution," 56. See also Michael Radelet and George Barnard, "Ethics and the Psychiatric Determination of Competency to Be Executed," 14 *Bulletin American Academy of Psychiatry and Law* 37, 39 (1986) ("the exemption [of the incompetent] can be understood if . . . the primary goal of capital punishment is retribution").

157. Musselwhite v. State, 60 So. 2d 807, 809 (Miss. Sup. Ct. 1952).

158. Ward, "Competency for Execution," 68.

159. Bob Egelko, "Federal Court Blocks Killer's Execution: New Hearing Ordered on Right to Appeal," *Orange County Press,* June 10, 1998, A-4 (Marin County Superior Court jury approved Kelly's execution on a 9–3 vote, finding that he was aware he was about to be executed and why).

160. Victoria Slind-Flor, "Is Convict Sane Enough to Execute?" *National Law Journal,* April 20, 1998, A8 (col. 1). See also "Death Row Inmate Horace Kelly Gets Go-Ahead for New Hearing," *San Francisco Chronicle,* June 27, 1998, A24.

161. See Walton v. Angelone, 321 F.3d 422, 456 (4th Cir. 2003) (finding an offender competent despite his belief that death would bring him back to earth "in a new and better form"); Billiot v. State, 655 So.2d 1, 6 (Miss. 1995) (finding competent an offender who believed that he was an angel, that he had received absolution for his crime, and that the state would not be able to execute him); Garrett v. Collins, 951 F.2d 57, 59 (5th Cir. 1992) (finding competent an offender who believed his dead aunt would protect him from the effects of the drugs administered to execute him); State v. Harris, III, 789 P.2d 60, 67 (Wash. 1990) (finding competent an offender who had a "delusional hope" he would not be executed).

162. 498 U.S. 1075 (1991).

163. 494 U.S. 210 (1990).

164. State v. Perry, 610 So. 2d 746 (La. Sup. Ct. 1992).

165. Ibid., 761.

166. 539 U.S. 136 (2003).

167. This was the holding in Singleton v. Norris, 319 F.3d 1018 (8th Cir. 2003).

168. Ibid., 751. See also David L. Katz, "Perry v. Louisiana: Medical Ethics on Death Row—Is Judicial Intervention Warranted?" 4 *Georgetown Journal of Legal Ethics* 707 (1991).

169. This maxim comes from the Hippocratic Oath, which has been called "the

most important rule in practice" from the perspective of the doctor-patient relationship. V. Tähkä, *The Patient-Doctor Relationship* 38 (1984).

170. The American Medical Association (AMA) has stated that a "physician . . . should not be a participant in a legally authorized execution." AMA, "Proceedings of the House of Delegates," *Capital Punishment* (1980), 85–86. The American Psychiatric Association (APA) has similarly stated that "[a] psychiatrist should not be a participant in a legally authorized execution." APA, "The Principles of Medical Ethics," 1985, §1(4) (applicable to all members of the APA). The National Medical Association Section on Psychiatry and Behavioral Sciences (NMA) takes the position that doctors should treat condemned mentally ill people, but "under no circumstances directly or indirectly assist in an execution of a 'death row' inmate." NMA, *Position Statement on the Role of the Psychiatrist in Evaluating and Treating Death Row Inmates*, 5. See also Kirk Heilbrun et al., "The Debate on Treating Individuals Incompetent for Execution," 149 *American Journal of Psychiatry* 596, 604 (1992) (carefully canvassing ethical arguments and concluding that "[i]t appears unethical to administer against the prisoner's wishes treatment that is highly relevant to competency, such as antipsychotic medication for psychotic disorders").

171. Richard J. Bonnie, "Dilemmas in Administering the Death Penalty: Conscientious Abstention, Professional Ethics, and the Needs of the Legal System," 14 *Law and Human Behavior* 67, 81–82 (1990).

172. Maryland commutes the incompetent person's death sentence to a life sentence without parole—see Md. Ann. Code art. 27, §75A(d)(3)—although it is unclear whether a person who can be restored to competency is considered incompetent under the statute. See *Perry*, 610 So. 2d at 770–771. Compare Michael L. Radelet and George W. Barnard, "Treating Those Found Incompetent for Execution: Ethical Chaos with Only One Solution," 16 *Bulletin of the American Academy of Psychiatry and Law* 297 (1988) (recounting professionals' ethical difficulties in dealing with the treatment issue and concluding that commutation is the only solution).

173. Compare Perlin and Gould, "Mental Disability and the Federal Sentencing Guidelines," 448–449 (noting that courts often refuse to grant downward departures for depression, manic psychosis, severe emotional stress, and psychosis).

174. See Stephen J. Morse, "Diminished Rationality, Diminished Responsibility," 1 *Ohio State Journal of Criminal Law* 289, 290, 300 (2003) (arguing that "a generic partial responsibility excuse is a moral imperative for a just criminal law that attempts never to punish defendants more than they deserve" and

proposing that mitigation be recognized when "the defendant suffered from substantially diminished rationality for which the defendant was not responsible and which substantially affected the defendant's criminal conduct").

175. Alaska, Delaware, Georgia, Kentucky, Illinois, Indiana, Michigan, Nevada, New Mexico, Pennsylvania, South Carolina, South Dakota, and Utah currently have GBMI laws.

176. The text describes the Michigan statute, which has been the model for other states. Mich. Comp. Laws §768.36.

177. National Center for State Courts, *The "Guilty but Mentally Ill" Plea and Verdict: An Empirical Study* (1985). This report is composed of three sections: a final report, descriptive data, and a telephone survey. Much of the data included in the report is summarized in Ingo Keilitz, "Researching and Reforming the Insanity Defense," 39 *Rutgers Law Review* 289 (1987).

178. For an in-depth analysis of the claims made by GBMI supporters, see Christopher Slobogin, "The Guilty but Mentally Ill Verdict: An Idea Whose Time Should Not Have Come," 53 *George Washington Law Review* 494 (1985).

179. See, for example, Ga. Code Ann. §17–7–131(g); Ind. Code §35–36–2–5(a); S.D. Codified Laws Ann. §23A–27–38.

180. For instance, those found guilty but mentally ill in Georgia received an average sentence of 11.76 years, compared to an average sentence of just over 9 years for all Georgia offenders. NCSC, *The "Guilty but Mentally Ill" Plea,* 27. See also, Keilitz, "Reforming the Insanity Defense," 318–319; Lisa Callahan et al., "Measuring the Effects of the Guilty but Mentally Ill (GBMI) Verdict," 16 *Law and Human Behavior* 447, 460 (1992).

181. Leone v. State, 797 N.E.2d 743 (Ind. 2003); State v. Crews, 522 N.E.2d 1167 (Ill. 1988).

182. See, for example, Alaska §12.47.040(b); Ky Rev. Stat. §504.130(1)(b); 18 Pa. Cons. Stat. §314(a).

183. See, for example, Ga. Code Ann. §17–7–131(g); Ind. Code §35–36–2–5(b) (1981); 42 Pa. Cons. Stat. §9727(b).

184. *NCSC, The "Guilty but Mentally Ill" Plea,* 37. See also, statement of Bill Meyer, Director, Forensic Psychiatry Center, State of Michigan, at State Mental Health Directors Third Annual Conference (September 29, 1982) (75 percent of those found guilty but mentally ill are sent to prison because they do not need treatment); memorandum by Juliette Spence, Governor's Fellow, Indiana Department of Mental Health 3 (September 24, 1984) (of the forty-three defendants found guilty but mentally ill in Indiana during a twenty-one-month period, only two were transferred to mental hospitals and the two guilty-but-mentally-ill transferees represented only 6 percent of all offenders transferred); Statement

of Terry Brelje, coordinator for the Forensic Psychiatry Program at Chester Mental Health Center, Illinois, at Mental Health Forensic Directors Third Annual conference (September 29, 1982) (of the 45 defendants found guilty but mentally ill in Illinois during a thirteen-month period, all were incarcerated in the Department of Corrections). In many states, offenders who are found guilty but mentally ill receive postconviction evaluation more often than do other offenders; therefore, their treatment needs are more likely to be identified. See, for example, Ga. Code Ann. §17-7-131(g); 42 Pa. Cons. Stat. §9727(b). But all offenders should receive a thorough postconviction evaluation. Obviously the GBMI verdict is not the most efficient way to accomplish the goal.

185. See Robert J. Favole, "Mental Disability in the American Criminal Process: A Four Issue Survey," in *Mentally Disordered Offenders,* 281–295.

186. Ralph Slovenko, "The Insanity Defense in the Wake of the Hinckley Trial," 14 *Rutgers Law Journal,* 373, 393 (1983).

4.   A Jurisprudence of Dangerousness

1. For a description of the many contexts in which dangerousness determinations play a role in the criminal process, see Christopher Slobogin, "Dangerousness as a Criterion in the Criminal Process," in *Law, Mental Health and Mental Disorder,* ed. Bruce Sales and Daniel Shuman (1996), 360–363.

2. Kansas v. Hendricks, 521 U.S. 346, 355 (1997).

3. The Garry David case is described in C. Robert Williams, "Psychopathy, Mental Illness and Preventive Detention: Issues Arising from the David Case," 16 *Monash University Law Review* 161, 162, 170–178 (1990).

4. Vivienne Walt, "French Investigator Tackles Terrorism's 'Cancer,'" *USA Today,* November 8, 2001, 11A.

5. Moussaoui was charged with conspiracy in connection with the September 11 hijackings, but "direct contact" between the hijackers and Moussaoui "was never alleged" and at one time it was thought that the government would have to try him on other charges. Viveca Novak, "How the Moussaoui Case Crumbled," *Time,* October 27, 2003, 33, 35. In 2005, however, Moussaoui pleaded guilty to the conspiracy charge. Neil A. Lewis, "Moussaoui Tells Court He's Guilty of a Terror Plot," *New York Times,* April 23, 2005, A1. Whether he *was* involved remains unclear. David Johnston and Neil A. Lewis, "Officials Say There Is No Evidence to Back Moussaoui's Story," *New York Times,* April 27, 2004, A14.

6. See Foucha v. Louisiana, 504 U.S. 71, 83 (1992) (White, J., writing for a plurality of the Court) (emphasis added); see also "Developments in the Law, Civil

Commitment of the Mentally Ill," 87 *Harvard Law Review* 1201, 1229–1233 (1974).

7. Matter of Care and Treatment of Hendricks, 912 P.2d 129, 138 (Kan. 1996).

8. See Williams, "Issues Arising from the David Case," 172–174 (describing the "amendment" of the Victorian Mental Health Act's definition of "mental illness" to include antisocial personality disorder and thus ensure David's detention).

9. 521 U.S. 346, 350 (1997).

10. Ibid., 356–358.

11. 434 U.S. 407, 411–413 (2002).

12. 521 U.S., 371.

13. In Hamdi v. Rumsfeld, 124 S.Ct. 2633 (2004), five members of the Court held that if a terrorist such as Moussaoui can be classified as an enemy combatant, he may be preventively detained. More is said about this issue later in the chapter.

14. Although *Hendricks* did not directly address this issue, it implicitly endorsed commitments based on such predictions. See 521 U.S., 357–358, 371. Other Supreme Court decisions have made clear that dangerousness predictions, whether made by experts or laypeople, may form the basis for deprivations of liberty. See, for example, Jurek v. Texas, 428 U.S. 262, 275 (1976); Schall v. Martin, 467 U.S. 253, 278 (1984).

15. I address elsewhere the equally important questions of whether we can prove dangerousness with the requisite level of certainty—see Slobogin, "Dangerousness as a Legal Criterion, 372–379—and how we might do so. See Christopher Slobogin, "Dangerousness and Expertise," 133 *University of Pennsylvania Law Review* 97 (1984).

16. Michael J. Corrado, "Punishment and the Wild Beast of Prey: The Problem of Preventive Detention," 86 *Journal of Criminal Law and Criminology* 778, 793 (1996).

17. Ibid., 794.

18. See, for example, Paul Robinson and John Darley, *Justice, Liability and Blame: Community Views and the Criminal Law* (1995), 226 (noting that in 20 percent of the scenarios that subjects were asked to rate in terms of culpability, the standard deviation on culpability ratings exceeded 3.50, a number suggesting extremely low agreement); Norman J. Finkel, *Commonsense Justice: Jurors' Notions of the Law* (1995), 134, 166, 248 (table 13.1), 252 (table 13.2) (finding significant disagreement among study subjects on scenarios involving mens rea, felony murder, and self-defense); Harry Kalven and Hans Zeisel, *The American Jury* (1971), 56 and table 11 (finding disagreement between judges and juries sitting on the same criminal case in 24.6 percent of the cases studied).

19. See Mark Fondacaro, "Toward an Ecological Jurisprudence Rooted in Concepts of Justice and Empirical Research," 69 *UMKC Law Review* 179, 187 (2000). Even staunch advocates of retributivism recognize this point. Jeffrie Murphy, "Moral Epistemology, the Retributive Emotions, and the 'Clumsy Moral Philosophy' of Jesus Christ," in *The Passions of Law,* ed. Susan Bandes (1999), 157 (noting that it is hard to know another's mind, much less whether they acted from a "hardened, abandoned and malignant heart"). I have tried to explicate why accurate information about past mental states is so difficult to come by in Christopher Slobogin, "Doubts about *Daubert:* Psychiatric Anecdata as a Case Study," 57 *Washington and Lee Law Review* 919, 927–932 (2000).

20. 365 A.2d 64, 87 (D.C. 1976).

21. 428 U.S. 262, 275 (1976).

22. Zant v. Stephens, 462 U.S. 862, 876 (1982).

23. *Jurek,* 428 U.S., 275–276.

24. 463 U.S. 880 (1983).

25. Ibid., 901.

26. See generally Michael L. Perlin, "The Supreme Court, the Mentally Disabled Criminal Defendant, Psychiatric Testimony in Death Penalty Cases, and the Power of Symbolism: Dulling the *Ake* in *Barefoot's* Achilles Heel," 3 *New York Law School Journal of Human Rights* 91, 108–121 (1985).

27. The difficulties include obtaining complete information about the extent of antisocial activity after predictions are made, and the associated fact that a prediction of dangerousness virtually always results in incapacitation, treatment, or both, making follow-up data about recidivism ambiguous. See generally John Monahan, *The Clinical Prediction of Violent Behavior* (1981), 52–60.

28. See, for example, John Monahan, *Rethinking Risk Assessment: The MacArthur Study of Violence and Disorder* (2001), 127 (describing a technique "[u]sing only risk factors commonly available in hospital records or capable of being routinely assessed in clinical practice" that placed individuals into "five risk classes for which the prevalence of violence during the first 20 weeks following discharge into the community varied between 1% and 76%"); Vernon L. Quinsey et al., *Violent Offenders: Appraising and Managing Risk* (1988), 148–151 and fig. 8.1 (discussing the ability of the Violence Risk Appraisal Guide [VRAG] to identify groups of offenders with a 55 percent, 75 percent, and 95 percent likelihood of recidivism); Grant T. Harris et al., "Prospective Replication of the Violence Risk Appraisal Guide in Predicting Violent Recidivism among Forensic Patients," 26 *Law and Human Behavior* 377 (2002) (a prospective study using the VRAG that accurately identified clusters of pa-

tients with a 71 percent and 100 percent recidivism rate); William Gardner et al., "A Comparison of Actuarial Methods for Identifying Repetitively Violent Patients with Mental Illness," 20 *Law and Human Behavior* 35, 41–42 (1996) (describing a "regression tree" that identified a small group of patients—3 percent of the sample population—who committed violent acts at the rate of 2.75 incidents per month); Marnie E. Rice et al., "An Evaluation of a Maximum Security Therapeutic Community for Psychopaths and Other Mentally Disordered Offenders," 16 *Law and Human Behavior* 399 (1992) (reporting that 77 percent of those who scored higher than 25 on the Psychopathy Checklist-Revised committed a violent offense despite treatment); Jay Apperson et al., "Short-Term Clinical Prediction of Assaultive Behavior: Artifacts of Research Methods," 150 *American Journal of Psychiatry* 1374 (1993) (reporting a 25 percent false positive rate); Thomas Litwack and Louis Schlesinger, "Assessing and Predicting Violence: Research, Law, and Applications," in *Handbook of Forensic Psychology*, ed. Irving Weiner and G. Hess (1987), 205, 224 (asserting that "clear and convincing evidence" of future violence exists if there is (1) a recent history of repeated violence; (2) a more distant history of violence together with evidence that the complex of traits that led to violence still exist and the circumstances that led to past violence will reoccur; or (3) an unequivocal threat or other like evidence of serious intentions to commit violence).

29. A number of different predictive techniques have yielded false positive rates between 30 and 50 percent. See, for example, Charles Lidz et al., "The Accuracy of Predictions of Violence to Others," 269 *JAMA* 1007 (1993) (47 percent false positive rate); Deidre Klassen and William O'Connor, "A Prospective Study of Predictors of Violence in Adult Male Mental Health Admissions," 12 *Law and Human Behavior* 143 (1988) (40 percent false positive rate); Diana Sepejak et al., "Clinical Predictions of Dangerousness Two-Year Follow-Up of 408 Pre-Trial Forensic Cases," 11 *Bulletin of American Academy of Psychiatry and Law* 171 (1983) (44 percent false positive rate).

30. The single most important advance in this regard might be a requirement that courts consider actuarial information in combination with "structured" clinical risk assessment. See, for example, Gary Melton et al., *Psychological Evaluations for the Courts: A Handbook for Mental Health Professionals and Lawyers* 290–292, 2d ed. (1997); Kevin S. Douglas et al., "Evaluation of a Model of Violence Risk Assessment among Forensic Psychiatric Patients," 54 *Psychiatric Services* 1372 (2003).

31. I have argued that, given its relatively weak probative value and its prejudicial nature, clinical prediction testimony should not be admissible on behalf of the state unless the defendant decides to rely on it as well. Slobogin, *Dangerousness*

and Expertise, 148–149. Many authors have made other suggestions, ranging from the manner in which prediction evaluations should be conducted to the way in which prediction information is communicated to the fact finder. See generally R. Karl Hanson, "What Do We Know about Sex Offender Risk Assessment?" 4 *Psychology, Public Policy and Law* 50, 67 (1998); Donald G. MacGregor et al., "Violence Risk Assessment and Risk Communication: The Effects of Using Actual Cases, Providing Instruction, and Employing Probability Versus Frequency Formats," 24 *Law and Human Behavior* 271 (2000).

32. 478 U.S. 364 (1986).
33. Ibid., 370.
34. 521 U.S., 369.
35. Compare Markey v. Wachtel, 264 S.E.2d 437 (W. Va. 1979) (no right to jury at civil commitment hearing); Ted McGraw et al., "Civil Commitment in New York City: An Analysis of Practice," 5 *Pace Law Review* 259, 290–291 (1985) (commitment courts routinely allow hearsay testimony that would probably be prohibited in a criminal case on right-to-confrontation grounds).
36. 478 U.S., 380 (Stevens, J., dissenting).
37. Ibid.
38. W. Lawrence Fitch and Debra A. Hammen, "The New Generation of Sex Offender Commitment Laws: Which States Have Them and How Do They Work?" in *Protecting Society from Sexually Dangerous Offenders,* ed. Bruce J. Winick and John Q. LaFond (2003), 33 (table showing that, while approximately ten states passed sexual predator laws between 1997 and 1999, no state has done so since then).
39. Ibid., 32 (as of fall 2001, in the nine states whose post-*Hendricks* sexual predator laws had gone into effect, including California and Florida, only 473 individuals had been committed, with the average commitment rate per state amounting to roughly fifteen to twenty annually); see also John Q. LaFond, "The Costs of Enacting a Sexual Predator Law," 4 *Psychology, Public Policy and Law* 468, 492 (1998) ("Though it is too early to tell with certainty, it is likely that in the not-too-distant future, these sexual predator laws will be used less frequently," given the higher sentences being meted out to sex offenders).
40. Two journals have devoted entire issues to the subject. See Symposium, "The Civil-Criminal Distinction," 7 *Journal of Contemporary Legal Issues, No. 1* (1996); Symposium, "The Intersection of Tort and Criminal Law," 76 *Boston University Law Review* 1 (1996) (in both issues nos. 1 and 2).
41. Paul H. Robinson, "Punishing Dangerousness: Cloaking Preventive Detention as Criminal Justice," 114 *Harvard Law Review* 1429, 1432 (2001) ("[I]t is impossible to 'punish dangerousness.' . . . [P]unishment can only exist in relation

to a past wrong"); see also Christopher Slobogin and Mark Fondacaro, "Rethinking Deprivations of Liberty: Possible Contributions from Therapeutic and Ecological Jurisprudence," 18 *Behavioral Science and Law* 499, 504 n. 24 (2000) ("Punishment is a reaction to a past act, not an attempt to prevent a future one").

42. See generally Michael Perlin, *Mental Disability Law: Civil and Criminal,* 2d. ed. (1998), 322–341, 353–358.

43. 406 U.S. 715 (1972).

44. Ibid., 738.

45. Ibid.

46. Youngberg v. Romeo, 457 U.S. 307, 319 (1982).

47. Seling v. Young, 531 U.S. 250, 265 (2001) (rejecting the claim that the sexual predator statute as applied to the petitioner was not "civil," but recognizing that a *Jackson* due process claim might lie if conditions of confinement do not bear a reasonable relationship to the reasons for confinement, and noting that the statute provided for confinement and treatment).

48. As my coauthors and I argue elsewhere, the language in *Youngberg* quoted in the text "could easily be parlayed into a robust right to treatment necessary to reduce prolonged confinement." Christopher Slobogin et al., "A Prevention Model of Juvenile Justice: The Promise of Kansas v. Hendricks for Children," 1999 *Wisconsin Law Review* 185, 213; see also Eric S. Janus and Wayne A. Logan, "Substantive Due Process and the Involuntary Confinement of Sexually Violent Predators," 35 *Connecticut Law Review* 319, 358–359 (2003) (arguing that *Youngberg* "embodies . . . the police power right to treatment" and also arguing that "a strong right to treatment can be derived from the *Jackson* principle that the duration of confinement must be reasonably related to the purposes of confinement"); Note, "The Supreme Court: 1981 Term," 96 *Harvard Law Review* 62, 84 (1982) ("[T]he Court's reasoning [in *Youngberg*] implies the existence of expansive rights that protect the patient's principal liberty interest—the interest in release from involuntary confinement. . . . [T]he majority's liberty-based rationale suggests that mental patients have a constitutional right to habilitative rather than merely protective treatment"). For supportive cases, see Wyatt v. Rogers, 985 F. Supp. 1356 (M.D. Ala. 1997) (holding that state was continuing to violate due process by treating patients in overly restrictive conditions); Cameron v. Tomes, 783 F. Supp. 1511, 1526 (D. Mass. 1992) (holding that *Youngberg* requires the state to ensure professional assessment of sex offender's access to community programs); Clark v. Cohen, 613 F. Supp. 684 (E.D. Pa. 1985), aff'd, 794 F.2d 79 (3d Cir.) (finding *Youngberg* and

substantive due process were violated when patient was deprived of training in community living despite professional judgment that she should be released from the institution).

49. *Hendricks,* 366.

50. The point is probably moot in any event, because even the most incorrigible offenders are in some sense "treatable." See *Psychopathy: Antisocial, Criminal, and Violent Behavior,* eds. Theodore Millon et al. (1998), 359–462 (containing six articles from different authors relying on different therapeutic perspectives that acknowledge the difficulty of treating psychopathy and other "untreatable" patients, but nonetheless indicate that it can be done).

51. 504 U.S. 71, 88 (1992) (O'Connor, J., concurring). I discuss this issue more fully in Slobogin, "Dangerousness as a Legal Criterion," 369–370.

52. See, for example, Jeffrey Rogers et al., "After Oregon's Insanity Defense: A Comparison of Conditional Release and Hospitalization," 5 *International Journal of Law and Psychiatry* 391 (1982) (describing a post-insanity acquittal commitment system that relies on a multi-disciplinary board to implement treatment plans using conditional release and close monitoring, and reporting a recidivism rate of only 6 percent); W. L. Marshall et al., "A Three-Tiered Approach to the Rehabilitation of Incarcerated Sex Offenders," 11 *Behavioral Science and Law* 441 (1993) (describing a model criminal justice-based program that could easily be implemented as preventive detention).

53. For instance, at least forty-seven states require that involuntary patients be committed to treatment in the least restrictive setting. Ingo Keilitz et al., "Least Restrictive Treatment of Involuntary Patients: Translating Concepts into Practice," 29 *St. Louis University Law Journal* 691, 709 (1985).

54. See Janus and Logan, "Involuntary Confinement."

55. Dan M. Kahan, "What Do Alternative Sanctions Mean?" 63 *University of Chicago Law Review* 591, 652 (1996).

56. *Hendricks* emphasized this aspect of the sexual predator statute in finding that it was not punishment. 521 U.S., 363–364 (1997). Similarly, in Connecticut Department of Public Safety v. Doe, 123 U.S. 1160, 1164 (2003), the Court strongly suggested that, when dangerousness is the basis for a state deprivation of liberty, a hearing is required to prove "current dangerousness."

57. In Jones v. United States, the Court appeared to hold that, in post-insanity acquittal commitment hearings, the state may impose the burden of proof on the acquittee, because commitment follows "only if the acquittee himself advances insanity as a defense and proves that his criminal act was a product of his mental illness." 463 U.S. 354, 367 (1983).

58. See, for example, Addington v. Texas, 441 U.S. 418 (1979).

59. See Hanson, "Sex Offender Risk Assessment," 51 (noting that "there is much more evidence to justify committing offenders than there is for releasing them," because there is much more empirical information about "static" risk factors, such as past offenses, than "dynamic" risk factors, such as compliance with treatment and alcoholism).

60. John Q. LaFond, "Washington's Sexually Violent Predator Law: A Deliberate Misuse of the Therapeutic State for Social Control," 15 *University of Puget Sound Law Review* 655, 696 (1992).

61. For a description of the inadequacies of community treatment even during a period when society was much more committed to it than it is today, see Lawrence Scull, "A New Trade in Lunacy: The Recommodification of the Mental Patient," 8 *American Behavioral Scientist* 741 (1981).

62. See, for example, Rogers et al., "Conditional Release and Hospitalization."

63. The usual proposed alternative to preventive detention is a recidivist statute that enhances sentences based on the number of crimes committed, an approach that has been described as "irrational, internally inconsistent, and racially discriminatory." Markus Dirk Dubber, "Recidivist Statutes as Arational Punishment," 43 *Buffalo Law Review* 689, 719 (1995); compare Lockyer v. Andrade, 538 U.S. 63 (2003) (upholding two consecutive terms of twenty-five years to life for theft of tapes worth about $150 and prior convictions for nonviolent offenses). See also Seymour Halleck, *The Mentally Disordered Offender* (1987), 199 ("[I]ndeterminate programs have usually released offenders earlier than determinate programs, and they have almost always provided greater numbers of offenders with greater opportunities for freedom").

64. Halleck, *The Mentally Disordered Offender,* 202 (the preventive approach "is less discriminatory, imposes less pain on offenders as a group, and is especially merciful toward selected offenders who can be released when they are judged to be nondangerous to society").

65. Herbert Packer, *The Limits of the Criminal Sanction* (1968), 79–80.

66. John Calvin Jeffries Jr., "Legality, Vagueness, and the Construction of Penal Statutes," 71 *Virginia Law Review* 189, 196 (1985).

67. Ibid., 212.

68. In Connally v. General Construction Co., 269 U.S. 385, 391 (1926), the Court stated that "a statute which either forbids or requires the doing of an act in terms so vague that men of common intelligence must necessarily guess at its meaning and differ as to its application, violates the first essential of due process of law."

69. See, for example, Chicago v. Morales, 527 U.S. 41 (1999); Kolender v. Lawson, 461 U.S. 352 (1983); Papachristou v. City of Jacksonville, 405 U.S. 156 (1972).

70. State v. Musser, 223 P.2d 193 (Utah 1950); State v. Bowling, 427 P.2d 928 (Ariz. Ct. App. 1967).

71. See, for example, Ala. Code §22–52–10.4(a) (permitting commitment of those who are mentally ill and present a "real and present threat of substantial harm to self and/or others").

72. State v. Williams, 451 N.W.2d 886 (Minn. Ct. App. 1990); Marchand v. Superior Court, 246 Cal. Rptr. 531, 545 (Cal. Ct. App. 1988).

73. Iowa is one of the few states that explicitly permits civil commitment for "serious emotional injury." That criterion is defined as "[i]njury which does not necessarily exhibit any physical characteristics, but which can be recognized and diagnosed by a licensed physician or other qualified mental health professional and which can be causally connected with the act or omission of a person who is, or is alleged to be, mentally ill." Iowa Code §229.1(14) (2003). That definition makes dangerousness dependent on the subjective, ever-changing, and inconsistent diagnostic preferences of the mental health professions. See In Interest of J.P., 574 N.W.2d 340 (Iowa 1998) (rejecting commitment based on "emotional trauma").

74. See Kramer v. Price, 712 F.2d 174 (5th Cir. 1983) (invalidating statute that punished as harassment any communication that "annoys or alarms the recipient," largely because of the lack of a sufficiently restrictive definition of these terms).

75. See Alan Dershowitz, "Dangerousness as a Criterion for Confinement," 2 *Bulletin of the American Academy of Psychiatry and Law* 172, 176 (1974).

76. U.K. Stat. 1998, ch. 37, pt. 1, c I §§1 (2004).

77. See Lynn O'Donnell, "Britain Acts to Curb Actions Judged Antisocial Behavior," *San Francisco Chronicle,* February 27, 2005, A4.

78. See, for example, Mass. Gen. Laws ch. 123, §1 (2003); Fla. Stat. Ann. §394.467(2) (2002).

79. For instance, to be eligible for commitment under the Kansas statute at issue in *Hendricks,* a person must have been convicted of an offense, acquitted of an offense on mental defense grounds, or found incompetent to stand trial. Kan. Stat. Ann. §59–29a03(a) (2002).

80. Ralph Reisner et al., *Law and the Mental Health System: Civil and Criminal Aspects,* 4th ed. (2004), 710.

81. Model Penal Code §211.2.

82. Ibid., §1.13(5).

83. See, for example, Miller v. State, 449 N.E.2d 1119 (Ind. Ct. App. 1983); People v. Lucchetti, 305 N.Y.S.2d 259 (1969); State v. Hanson, 256 N.W.2d 364 (N.D. 1977).

84. Under the Model Penal Code, recklessness requires proof that the person "consciously" disregards a substantial and unjustifiable risk. Model Penal Code §2.02(2)(c).

85. In Montana, one of the few states with a negligent endangerment statute—see Mont. Code Ann. §45–5–208—negligence is defined as either conscious disregard of a risk or disregard of a risk "of which the person should be aware." Ibid., §45–2–101 (42).

86. All these factors correlate to some extent with violence. Monahan, *Clinical Prediction,* 69–76 (examining correlations with respect to first five factors); R. J. Sampson et al., "Neighborhoods and Violent Crime: A Multilevel Study of Collective Efficacy," 277 *Science* 918 (1997) (showing a significant correlation between concentrated poverty and crime).

87. 355 U.S. 225 (1957).

88. Ibid., 229.

89. Jeffries, "Legality," 211.

90. Ibid., 211–212.

91. In the movie *Gattaca* (Columbia/Tristar Studios 1997), the government is able to predict, simply through DNA analysis, a person's propensities.

92. The latter two characteristics are clearly correlated with violence. See, for example, Eric Silver et al., "Assessing Violence Risk among Discharged Psychiatric Patients: Toward an Ecological Approach," 23 *Law and Human Behavior* 237, 245 (1999).

93. Packer, *Limits of Criminal Sanction,* 74.

94. Ibid. Although Packer's comments would seem to apply to any exercise of state power, he made them while analyzing the scope of the criminal law, "that most coercive of legal instruments." Ibid. The Supreme Court seems to have made the same distinction in Robinson v. California, 370 U.S. 660 (1962). There it held that conviction of a person for being an addict is cruel and unusual punishment, the same as punishing a person for the " 'crime' of having a common cold." Ibid., 667. Yet the Court also suggested that, if necessary to promote "the general health and welfare," the state could impose "compulsory treatment, involving quarantine, confinement, or sequestration" on addicts, people with mental illness, or those afflicted with leprosy or venereal disease even, apparently, in the absence of any specific conduct. Ibid., 666. The Court's distinction makes sense as a matter of Eighth Amendment jurisprudence—because pre-

ventive treatment is not punishment and therefore cannot violate that amendment's prohibition—but it cannot stand in the face of legality concerns, for the reasons discussed in the text.

95. Stephen J. Morse, "Blame and Danger: An Essay on Preventive Detention," 76 *Boston University Law Review* 113, 152 (1996); cf. Corrado, "Punishment and the Wild Beast of Prey," 806–811.

96. See, for example, Ferdinand D. Schoeman, "On Incapacitating the Dangerous," 16 *American Philosophical Quarterly* 27, 34 (1979) ("If there is something worse about civil preventive detention . . . than there is about quarantine, not only have we failed to locate it, but whatever it is that makes the distinction is nowhere to be found in the literature."); Corrado, "Punishment and the Wild Beast of Prey," 811–815.

97. Compare Harris v. State, 879 So2d 1223 (Fl. Dist. Ct. App. 2002).

98. Compare Bryan v. United States, 524 U.S. 184, 189–190 (1998). In a similar context, the Supreme Court has held that when an offender is or should be aware that the prosecution can appeal his sentence under a special offender law, he has no legitimate expectation in the finality of the sentence. United States v. DiFrancesco, 449 U.S. 117, 137–139 (1980).

99. See, for example, George Dix, "Acute Psychiatric Hospitalization of the Mentally Ill in the Metropolis: An Empirical Study," 1968 *Washington University Law Quarterly* 485, 504–557. Dix describes forty-five commitment cases, several of which illustrate the point in the text. For instance, illustration 5 involved a patient who believed he was an FBI agent, carried at least one weapon, and accused his wife of being a "spy" and his mother-in-law of poisoning him. Contrast that case to illustration 29, where the patient had reportedly threatened members of the family and, on the morning of the hearing, had thrown a cup of coffee on her sister.

100. 392 U.S. 1 (1968).

101. Ibid., 22.

102. Conspiracy requires an agreement among two or more individuals to carry out a crime. See LaFave, *Criminal Law* 622. Although the agreement can be tacit and proven by inference from subsequent course of conduct (Ibid., 622–623), mere proof that a communication took place is unlikely to be sufficient. Had Moussaoui's case gone to trial, this element of conspiracy would have been very difficult to prove. See Sadiq Reza, "Unpatriotic Acts: An Introduction," 48 *New York Law Review* 3, 11 n. 17 (2003) (noting that, as a sanction for the government's failure to produce a potentially exculpatory witness, the trial court in Moussaoui's case prohibited the introduction of evidence

about 9/11, and that "[t]he government has . . . long since given up its theory that Mr. Moussaoui was the '20th hijacker' . . .").

103. See editorial, "Terror and the Constitution," *Christian Science Monitor*, August 4, 2003, 8 (describing confinement of Yaser Esam Hamdi, Jose Padilla, and six Yemeni men from Buffalo, all American citizens, the first two labeled "unlawful enemy combatants" and held incommunicado with no lawyers and no specific charge, the Yemeni convicted after pleading guilty because they "were petrified they would be declared unlawful enemy combatants and sent to a military jail").

104. On the agreement requirement, see LaFave, *Criminal Law*, 623–623. The actus reus for attempt, variously defined as conduct that puts the actor in dangerous proximity to committing the crime, conduct that unequivocally indicates criminal intent, or a "substantial step" toward committing the crime, must generally go beyond "mere preparation" to meet the act requirement for attempt. Ibid., 588–593.

105. See Hamdi v. Rumsfeld, 124 S.Ct. 2633 (2004) (holding that an American citizen held as an enemy combatant is entitled to notice of the factual basis of that assertion, and a hearing in front of a neutral decision maker to determine its accuracy).

106. Packer, *Limits of the Criminal Sanction*, 75.

107. Morse, "Blame and Danger," 151; Jean E. Floud and Warren Young, *Dangerousness and Criminal Justice* (1981), 44; R. A. Duff, "Penal Communications: Recent Work in the Philosophy of Punishment," 20 *Crime and Justice* 1, 11 (1996).

108. Schoeman, "On Incapacitating the Dangerous," 34.

109. On the mere preparation doctrine, see LaFave, *Criminal Law*, 588–593 (describing why mere preparation is insufficient basis for attempt liability). On the abandonment defense, see Model Penal Code §5.01(4) (recognizing a defense to attempt "under circumstances manifesting a complete and voluntary renunciation of . . . criminal purpose").

110. G. W. F. Hegel, *Elements of the Philosophy of Right*, ed. Allen W. Wood, trans. H. B. Nisbet, 1991 (1821), 126 (emphasis deleted).

111. Ibid. (emphasis deleted).

112. Ibid.

113. For instance, Kant believed that punishment is designed to serve the individual's ends, namely recognition of and respect for the individual's humanity. See Immanuel Kant, *The Metaphysical Elements of Justice*, trans. John Ladd, 1965 (1797), 100–102. See generally Leo Katz et al., *Foundations of Criminal*

Law (1999), 83–96 (including excerpts from Herbert Morris and Michael Moore and concluding that "retributivists like Kant, Morris, and Moore . . . believe that criminals have a right to be punished").

114. After reviewing a large number of studies on motivation, Bruce Winick concluded: "People who believe they lack the capacity to control their harmful conduct because of an internal deficit that seems unchangeable predictably develop expectations of failure. As a result, they may not even attempt to exercise self-control, or may do so without any serious commitment to succeed. . . . Labeling sex offenders as 'violent sexual predators' therefore may reinforce their antisocial sexual behavior." Bruce J. Winick, "Sex Offender Laws in the 1990s: A Therapeutic Jurisprudence Analysis," 4 *Psychology, Public Policy and Law* 534, 539 (1998).

115. See Vernon L. Quinsey, "Review of the Washington State Special Commitment Center Program for Sexually Violent Predators," 15 *University of Puget Sound Law Review* 704, 705–707 (1992) (reporting that residents of sexual predator programs "perceive the law to be arbitrary and excessive," and have more disciplinary violations than they did in prison because of, inter alia, "[r]esident bitterness concerning the indeterminate nature of their confinement and its imposition at the end of their sentence").

116. See Tom Tyler, *Why People Obey the Law* (1990), 63–68 (summarizing research findings to the effect that compliance with law is based as much on perceived legitimacy as on deterrence and other factors); Edward Zamble and Frank Porporino, "Coping, Imprisonment, and Rehabilitation," 17 *Criminal Justice and Behavior* 53, 59 (1990) (finding correlation between little respect for system and recidivism).

117. Kyron Huigens, "The Dead End of Deterrence, and Beyond," 41 *William and Mary Law Review* 943, 1029 (2000). Huigens is the most prolific recent adherent of this approach.

118. Ibid.; see also Kyron Huigens, "Virtue and Inculpation," 108 *Harvard Law Review* 1423, 1447–1448 (1995) (describing the Aristoleian view that people are responsible for their character).

119. 481 U.S. 739 (1987).

120. Ibid., 747–748.

121. See, for example, H. L. A. Hart, *The Morality of the Criminal Law* (1964), 31–32; H. L. A. Hart, *Punishment and Responsibility* (1968), 88, 182–183, 231–235.

122. Kyron Huigens, "Solving the Apprendi Puzzle," 90 *Georgetown Law Journal* 387, 392, 441 (2002).

123. Norval Morris was one of the first to make such a suggestion. See Norval Morris, "Predicting Violence with Statistics," 34 *Stanford Law Review* 249, 253 (1981).

124. Indeterminate sentences were quite popular in this country and in Great Britain until the mid-1970s. See generally David Garland, *The Culture of Control* (2001), 34, 53.

125. For instance, under the old version of the sexual predator laws—the "mentally disordered sex offender" statutes that were popular until the 1970s—commitment substituted for punishment. See George E. Dix, "Special Dispositional Alternatives for Abnormal Offenders," in *Mentally Disordered Offenders: Perspectives from Law and Social Science,* ed. John Monahan and Henry J. Steadman (1983), 142–144.

126. Kan. Stat. Ann. § 59–29a02(a) (2002).

127. Kansas v. Hendricks, 521 U.S. 346, 362 (1997).

128. Ibid., 358.

129. Ibid., 358, 364.

130. Ibid., 360.

131. 534 U.S. 407 (2002).

132. Ibid., 413.

133. Ibid., 415.

134. For a sampling of the commentary in this vein, see Stephen Morse, "Uncontrollable Urges and Irrational People," 88 *Virginia Law Review* 1025, 1026–1027 (2002) (arguing that sexual predator commitment should be limited to those who are "nonresponsible"); Robert F. Schopp, *Competence, Condemnation, and Commitment* (2001), 149–150, 165–166 (arguing that police power commitment is permissible only for those who lack "retributive competence" and comparing the latter concept to insanity); Eric Janus, "Hendricks and the Moral Terrain of Police Power Civil Commitment," 4 *Psychology, Public Policy and Law* 297, 298 (1998) ("Properly understood, the *Hendricks* decision will limit civil commitment to those who are 'too sick to deserve punishment.'" [quoting Millard v. Harris, 406 F.2d 964, 969 (D.C. Cir. 1968)]).

135. 521 U.S. 346, 358 (1997).

136. See Melton et al., *Psychological Evaluations for the Courts,* 203–204.

137. The Model Penal Code defines involuntary acts to include reflexes and convulsions, bodily movement during sleep, conduct during hypnosis, and other "bodily movement that otherwise is not a product of the effort or determination of the actor, either conscious or habitual." Model Penal Code §2.01(2).

138. See Stephen Morse, Culpability and Control, 142 *University of Pennsylvania Law Review* 1587, 1619–1634 (1994); Robert Schopp, *Automatism, Insanity, and the Psychology of Criminal Responsibility: A Philosophical Inquiry* (1991), 165–174.

139. See Herbert Fingarette, *The Meaning of Criminal Insanity* (1972), 162 (noting that regardless of how impaired a person is, it is still "the person himself who initiates and carries out the deed, it is his desire, his mood, his passion, his belief which is at issue, and it is he who acts to satisfy this desire, or to express this mood, emotion, or belief of his"); Schopp, *The Psychology of Criminal Responsibility*, 181 ("[A]ccepting the proposition that individuals cannot control . . . intrusive urges and fantasies . . . does not entail that they cannot refrain from acting on these mental events"); E. Michael Coles, "Impulsivity in Major Mental Disorders," in *Impulsivity: Theory, Assessment and Treatment*, ed. Christopher D. Webster and Margaret A. Jackson (1997), 189 ("With the obvious exceptions of delirious and comatose individuals . . . the expression of a socially unacceptable impulse invariably reflects some control"); Morse, "Culpability and Control," 1605 (concluding that "out of control agents should sometimes be excused, but not because they do not choose to do what they do").

140. Ibid., 1624 ("[F]or many people affected by the so-called paraphilias, some impulse disorders, and drug dependence, satisfying the desire produces positive pleasure as well as the avoidance of pain").

141. Michael Moore, "Responsibility and the Unconscious," 53 *Southern California Law Review* 1563, 1665 (1980).

142. See Kansas v. Crane, 534 U.S. 407, 412 (2002).

143. The recidivism rate for burglary (31.9 percent) is four times higher than that for rape (7.7 percent). David P. Bryden and Roger C. Park, " 'Other Crimes' Evidence in Sex Offense Cases," 78 *Minnesota Law Review* 529, 572 (1994).

144. Morse, "Culpability and Control," 1631.

145. Robert Plutchik and Herman M. van Praag, "The Nature of Impulsivity: Definitions, Ontology, Genetics, and Relations to Aggression," in *Impulsivity and Aggression*, ed. Eric Hollander and Dan J. Stein (1995), 7–8; see also Coles, "Impulsivity," 187 (speaking of "the status of impulsivity as a primary, if not universal, criterion of every mental disorder that is clearly anti-social and/or irrational").

146. One of the reasons this area of inquiry is so difficult is that we do not know how to distinguish which of these two possibilities, if either, is in operation during "impulsive" action. See generally P. S. Greenspan, "Genes, Electro-

transmitters, and Free Will," in *Genetics and Criminal Behavior*, ed. David Wasserman and Robert Wachbroit (2001), 248.

147. One review of the methods used to measure impulsivity concluded that "researchers need to be very cautious when selecting impulsivity measures," because the different measures "appear to be assessing very different constructs," even when they use the same methodology. James D. A. Parker and R. Michael Bagby, "Impulsivity in Adults: A Critical Review of Measurement Approaches," in *Impulsivity*, 154–155; see also Judy Zaparniuk and Steven Taylor, "Impulsivity in Children and Adolescents," in *Impulsivity*, 174; Mairead Dolan and Rachel Fullam, "Behavioural and Psychometric Measures of Impulsivity in a Personality Disordered Population," 15 *Journal of Forensic Psychiatry and Psychology* 426 (2004) (finding that "behavioural measures did not correlate well with psychometric measures of impulsivity and these measures appear to assess different constructs").

148. Zaparniuk and Taylor, "Impulsivity in Adults," 154.

149. See American Psychiatric Association, *Statement on the Insanity Defense* (December 1982), 11.

150. A number of those who have advocated this position are noted at the beginning of Part 2 of this chapter. At one time, I endorsed this approach as well—see Slobogin, "Dangerousness as a Legal Criterion," 364–366—although this chapter refines that position.

151. See Chapter 2.

152. See APA, *Statement on the Insanity Defense*, 11 ("Many psychiatrists . . . believe that psychiatric information relevant to determining whether a defendant understood the nature of his act, and whether he appreciated its wrongfulness, is more reliable and has a stronger scientific basis than, for example, does psychiatric information relevant to whether a defendant was able to control his behavior").

153. In addition to the difficulty of assessing volitional impairment, another reason for this position may be that "the exculpation of pyromaniacs [and others with so-called impulse disorders] would be out of touch with commonly shared moral intuitions." Richard J. Bonnie, "The Moral Basis of the Insanity Defense," 69 *American Bar Association Journal* 194, 197 (1983).

154. Morse, "Culpability and Control," 1626.

155. Additionally, Hendricks stated that "he hoped he would not sexually molest children again." Kansas v. Hendricks, 521 U.S., 555.

156. See Morse, "Uncontrollable Urges and Irrational People," 1036.

157. Morse, "Culpability and Control," 1632.

158. For instance, according to Ronald Blackburn, "labels implying 'compulsion' are . . . applied when neither the perpetrator nor an observer can account for the behaviour in terms of motives which are current, popular, or culturally sanctioned." Ronald Blackburn, *The Psychology of Criminal Conduct: Theory, Research, and Practice* (1993), 74. He continued: "[Impulse control disorders are] explanatory fictions introduced when people are unable to attribute their repeated deviant acts to an 'acceptable' or 'rational' cause. . . . While there is a case for subdividing particular forms of repetitive deviant behaviour according to categories of motive (or reinforcer), a classification which effectively rests on arbitrary distinctions between 'rational' and 'irrational' has no scientific utility." Ibid. See also Robert Menzies, "A Sociological Perspective on Impulsivity: Some Cautionary Comments on the Genesis of a Clinical Construct," in *Impulsivity*, 54. Morse himself seems to recognize this problem when he states that "[a]lthough I am sympathetic to claims that the rationality of desires or ends is difficult to assess, I am finally convinced, by malignantly circular reasoning perhaps, that it must be irrational to want to produce unjustified harm so intensely that failure to satisfy that desire will create sufficient dysphoria to warrant an excuse." Morse, "Culpability and Control," 1634.

159. As noted in Chapter 2, Morse contemplates that all these people might behave irrationally, although he thinks such cases will be very rare. Morse, "Uncontrollable Urges and Irrational People," 1074 ("[A] small number of sexual predators may have a rationality defect that extends generally over the domain of sexual behavior. . . . Leroy Hendricks may have presented precisely this case"); Stephen J. Morse, "Rationality and Responsibility," 74 *Southern California Law Review* 251, 263 (2000) (stating that "'addictions,' so-called 'pathological' or 'compulsive' gambling, 'deviant' sexual desires, and the like" do not involve problems of compulsion "but in some cases the desire may be so intense that it undermines the capacity for rationality"); Morse, "Culpability and Control," 1649 (suggesting that "crimes of 'passion,' committed in heightened emotional states, such as fear and rage . . . may seal off access to the ordinary desires, beliefs, and intentions that permit volitions to resolve the inevitable conflict by being properly responsive to . . . background factors"); Ibid., 1636 (wondering whether some psychopaths should be excused on irrationality grounds).

160. 534 U.S., 420 (Scalia, J., dissenting) (emphasis in original).

161. Cf. Model Penal Code §2.01(2).

162. See Deborah W. Denno, "Crime and Consciousness: Science and Involuntary Acts," 87 *Minnesota Law Review* 269, 285 (2002).

163. For a description of this test, see United States v. Kunak, 17 C.M.R. 346, 357–358 (C.M.A. 1954).

164. See case of Seth Hedges, in Melton et al., *Psychological Evaluations,* 563–567.

165. See In re Kunshier, No. C7–95–1490, 1995 Minn. App. LEXIS 1422 (Minn. Ct. App. November 21, 1995), reported in Alan Held, "The Civil Commitment of Sexual Predators—Experience under Minnesota's Law," in *The Sexual Predator: Law, Policy, Evaluation and Treatment,* ed. Anita Schlank and Fred Cohen (1999), 2–19.

166. See In re Crocker, No. C0–95–2500, 1996 Minn. App. LEXIS 495 (Minn. Ct. App. April 23, 1996), aff'd (Minn. January 21, 1997), reported in Held, "The Civil Commitment of Sexual Predators," 2–19. It is not clear from the facts reported by the Court whether Hendricks would meet the recklessly undeterrable test, although it appears that several of his crimes were committed under circumstances in which detection was a foregone conclusion. See *Hendricks,* 521 U.S., 354 (recounting that Hendricks was convicted for molesting two young boys while working at a carnival, was paroled after two years, re-arrested for molesting a seven-year-old girl, spent five years in prison, and then "shortly thereafter" molested two more children).

167. See Tom Kuntz, "From Thought to Deed: In the Mind of a Killer Who Says He Served God," *New York Times,* September 24, 1995, 7 (recounting the case of Michael Griffin, who argued a combination of temporary insanity/necessity defense, but was convicted of shooting physicians outside abortion clinics in Florida).

168. See Mark C. Alexander, "Religiously Motivated Murder: The Rabin Assassination and Abortion Clinic Killings," 39 *Arizona Law Review* 1161, 1161–1663 (1997) (recounting the case of Yigal Amir, who killed Israeli Prime Minister Yitzhak Rabin and argued at trial that the killing was necessary to save Israeli Jews from Rabin and his peace plan).

169. Consider, for example, the events of September 11, 2001.

170. See, for example, State v. Dorsey, 395 A.2d 855 (N.H. 1978) (defendants charged with trespass at a nuclear power plant asserted that the danger posed by the plant warranted a "choice of evils" defense).

171. Gibeaut, "Prosecuting Moussaoui," 38.

172. Philip Shenon, "Man Charged in Sept. 11 Attacks Demands that Qaeda Leaders Testify," *New York Times,* March 22, 2003, B12.

173. Ex parte Quirin, 317 U.S. 1 (1942); Hamdi v. Rumsfeld, 124 S.Ct. 2686 (2004).

174. When an "undeterrable" individual violates a misdemeanor law, preventive detention would usually be impermissible, for reasons explored in Part 4.

175. See Andrew von Hirsch, *Censure and Sanctions* (1993), 36–46 (proposing a five-year maximum for homicide and a three-year maximum for all other crimes).

176. This is the language used by the student authors of the *Harvard Law Review* note that remains one of the best treatments of the state's authority to commit its citizens. "Developments in the Law," 1233.

177. 534 U.S., 414.

178. Stephen J. Schulhofer, "Two Systems of Social Protection: Comments on the Civil-Criminal Distinction, with Particular Reference to Sexually Violent Predator Laws," 7 *Journal of Contemporary Legal Issues,* 69 (1996); see also Eric S. Janus, "Preventing Sexual Violence: Setting Principled Constitutional Boundaries on Sex Offender Commitments," 72 *Indiana Law Journal* 157, 160 (1996).

179. Schulhofer, "Two Systems of Social Protection," 87.

180. Ibid., 96.

181. Ibid., 94–96 (arguing against commitment of sexual predators who are not seriously mentally ill). Schulhofer also makes clear that he would impose a second limitation on preventive detention, beyond the gap-filler rationale: it should be applied only to those wrongdoers who are not autonomous. Ibid., 90–91. But then the gap-filler rationale becomes a redundancy and should not be advanced at all, given its above-described potential for abuse.

182. See generally Melton et al., *Psychological Evaluations for the Courts,* 307.

183. Ibid., 307–308.

184. Alexander D. Brooks, "The Constitutionality and Morality of Civilly Committing Violent Sexual Predators," 15 *University of Puget Sound Law Review* 709, 753 (1992).

185. LaFond, "Sexually Violent Predator Law," 698–699.

186. See Monahan, *Clinical Prediction of Violent Behavior,* 115 (indicating that dangerousness evaluation must consider sources of future stress, whether contexts in which violence occurred in the past will reoccur, the likely victims of violence and their availability, and the means the person possesses to commit violence).

187. For instance, persons in the Illinois sex offender program are housed in a wing of the maximum-security prison complex. See Allen v. Illinois, 478 U.S. 364, 372 (1986).

188. In Minnesota, which has had a statute similar to Kansas's since 1939, "[n]ot one person committed since 1975 has been discharged from a final sex offender commitment," although one was provisionally discharged and five

others were put in state nursing homes. Eric S. Janus, "Preventing Sexual Violence: Setting Principled Constitutional Boundaries on Sex Offender Commitments," 72 *Indiana Law Journal* 157, 206 (1996). As noted earlier, preventive detention governed by *Jackson* would not function this way. Nonetheless, even under a well-run preventive regime some sexual offenders would stay incarcerated for a very long period unless other limitations, such as those discussed herein, are imposed.

189. Under the federal Speedy Trial Act, for instance, trial need not start until one hundred days after arrest—18 U.S.C. §§3161(b), (c)(1) (2000)—and delays are quite common. Compare 18 U.S.C. §3161(h)(1)–(9) (2000) (listing exemptions to the speedy trial requirement).

190. The average length of stay for acutely ill patients is probably less than two weeks, although "chronic" patients may spend months or years in the hospital. See *State Profile Highlights: Length of Stay in State Psychiatric Hospitals No. 0206* (July 2002, at www.nri.rdmc.org/Profiles) (22.7 percent of patients were discharged within seven days, and 61.5 percent of patients were discharged within thirty days).

191. See United States v. Sharpe, 470 U.S. 675 (1985).

192. See, for example, Kan. Stat. Ann. §59–29a07(a) (2002).

193. See, for example, Federal Bail Reform Act of 1984, 18 U.S.C. §3142(e) (2000).

194. Addington v. Texas, 441 U.S. 418 (1979).

195. Actually, most states do not specify a standard of proof in these circumstances. See Reisner, Slobogin, and Rai, *Law and the Mental Health System*, 772. But see Cal. Welf. and Inst. Code §5150 (West 2003) (emergency detention requires a finding of probable cause that a person is mentally disordered and, as a result, dangerous to others).

196. Terry v. Ohio, 392 U.S. 1, 27 (1968).

197. Compare McNeil v. Dir., Patuxent Inst., 407 U.S. 245, 249–250 (1972) (substantive and procedural limitations on commitment increase as the length of commitment increases).

198. Compare Alaska Stat. § 47.30.705 (2002) ("likely to cause serious harm to . . . others"); 405 Ill. Com Stat. 5/1–119 (1999) ("reasonably expected to inflict serious physical harm upon . . . another in the near future"); Mass. Ann. Laws ch. 123, §1 (Law. Co-op 1989) ("a substantial risk of physical harm to other persons").

199. This observation was first made in John Monahan and David Wexler, "A Definite Maybe: Proof and Probability in Civil Commitment," 2 *Law and Human Behavior* 37 (1978).

200. See, for example, John Monahan, "Violence Risk Assessment: Scientific Validity and Evidentiary Admissibility," 57 *Washington and Lee Law Review* 901, 910 (2000). Legal scholars have accepted the same reasoning. See Corrado, "The Problem of Preventive Detention," 792 (arguing that even when risk is low, if the detained person belongs to the designated risk group, "there is a one hundred percent chance that person presents a risk of harm").

201. For instance, some psychoses are particularly resistant to treatment. DSM-IV-TR, 298–299.

202. Judith V. Becker and William D. Murphy, "What We Know and Do Not Know about Assessing and Treating Sex Offenders," 4 *Psychology, Public Policy and Law* 116, 127–131 (1998) (discussing biological and cognitive therapies and their efficacy).

203. My coauthors and I have made a similar suggestion in the context of juvenile justice. See Slobogin et al., "A Prevention Model of Juvenile Justice," 210. There we suggested that a durational limit has three other advantages: "First, of course, it minimizes the harm caused by an erroneous prediction. Second, a time limit known to the offender avoids the demoralization that can occur in an indeterminate regime. Third, such a limit can have a positive therapeutic effect because it gives the [individual] a specific behavioral goal to achieve (that is, no antisocial activity within the specified period in order to obtain release)." Ibid.

204. Franklin E. Zimring and Gordon Hawkins, *Incapacitation: Penal Confinement and the Restraint of Crime* (1995), 3–14.

205. At least five states make dangerousness an aggravating factor in capital cases. Idaho Sess. Laws ch. 19, §§ 515(9)(h), (g)(8); Okla. Stat. tit. 21, §701.12(7); Tex. Crim. Proc. Code Ann. §37.071(b)(2); Va. Code Ann. §19.2–264.4C; Wash. Rev. Code Ann. §10.95.070.

206. Of course, dangerousness can play a role in defining result crimes as well. Compare Paul H. Robinson, "The Role of Harm and Evil in Criminal Law: A Study in Legislative Deception?" 5 *Journal of Contemporary Legal Issues* 299 (1994). Given the complicated and ambiguous role of dangerousness in connection with completed crimes, this chapter focuses solely on those crimes where the dangerousness requirement is more explicit.

207. See Richard J. Bonnie et al., *Criminal Law* (1997), 225–229.

208. LaFave, *Criminal Law*, 574–579.

209. Ibid., 540 (attempt); Ibid., 567 (conspiracy).

210. A retributivist might say that these actions are criminalized solely on the ground that the actor's decision to engage in antisocial or risky conduct

demonstrates sufficient blameworthiness. See, for example, Larry Alexander and Kimberly D. Kessler, "Mens Rea and Inchoate Crimes," 87 *Journal Criminal Law and Criminology* 1138, 1170 (1997). Even so, the backward-looking retributive judgment cannot be made without an assessment of the harm or risk occasioned by the decision, either from an objective standpoint or as perceived by the actor.

211. See Kolender v. Lawson, 461 U.S. 352, 353 n. 1 (1983); Chicago v. Morales, 527 U.S. 41 (1999).

212. Ibid.

213. See Debra Livingston, "Police Discretion and the Quality of Life in Public Places: Courts, Communities, and the New Policing," 97 *Columbia Law Review* 551, 622–624 (1997).

214. See Garland, *The Culture of Control,* 181 (although "no one in particular is harmed by the conduct in question, this does not prevent the invocation of a collective victim—'the community' and its 'quality of life'—that is deemed to suffer the ill-effects that must always flow from prohibited behaviour, however trivial").

215. See Livingston, "Police Discretion," 622 n. 337.

216. Model Penal Code §211.2 (1976).

217. Compare Payne v. State, 7 S.W.3d 25, 28 (Tenn. 1999) (noting that the Model Penal Code's formulation of reckless endangerment "supports a broad interpretation" that a "mere possibility" of danger is sufficient for conviction).

218. See, for example, Fla. Stat. Ann. §316.193.

219. See Cal. Penal Code § 466 (defining crowbars and screwdrivers as burglars' tools); see also Dotson v. State, 260 So.2d 839 (Miss. 1972) (conviction for possession of screwdriver and a large bolt); People v. Diaz, 244 N.E.2d 878 (N.Y. 1969) (screwdriver wrapped in newspaper).

220. Markus Dubber, "Policing Possession: The War on Crime and the End of Criminal Law," 91 *Journal of Criminal Law and Criminology* 829, 859 (2001) (describing the mens rea element of possession offenses and concluding that "many possession statutes, particularly in the drug area . . . are so-called strict liability crimes").

221. Ibid., 860.

222. Ibid., 926.

223. Recent television advertisements suggest that drug possession crimes harm those who are killed and assaulted by the cartels that grow and distribute the drugs. Of course, the cartels would not exist if drug use were legal or regulated differently. In any event, the causative link between possession of a small amount of marijuana and a killing in Colombia is tenuous at best.

224. The typical vagrancy statute is a misdemeanor and usually results simply in removal from the area, sometimes via a night in jail. Under the Model Penal Code, for instance, loitering is a "violation"—Model Penal Code §250.6—that "does not constitute a crime," may not result in incarceration, and "shall not give rise to any disability or legal disadvantage based on conviction of a criminal charge." Ibid., §1.04(5).

225. See, for example, Fla. Stat. Ann. § 316.193 (providing for imprisonment of not more than six months after the first drunken driving offense); Model Penal Code §§211.2; 1.04(3), (4) (providing that reckless endangerment is a misdemeanor, which generally can result in imprisonment of up to one year).

226. Alexander Brooks proposed that dangerousness be broken down into "four component elements: (1) magnitude of harm; (2) probability that harm will occur; (3) frequency with which the harm will occur; and (4) imminence of harm." Alexander D. Brooks, *Law, Psychiatry and the Mental Health System* (1974), 680–682. He then noted: "A person can be characterized as 'dangerous' or not, depending on a balancing of these four components. For example a harm which is not likely to occur, but which is very serious, may add up to 'dangerousness.' By the same token, a relatively trivial harm which is highly likely to occur with great frequency might also add up to dangerousness. On the other hand, a trivial harm, even though it is likely to occur, might not add up to dangerousness." Ibid., 680.

227. Dubber, "Policing Possession," 859 ("New York boasts no fewer than 115 felony possession offenses, all of which require a minimum of one year in prison; eleven of them provide for a maximum sentence of life imprisonment").

228. The typical endangerment statute requires that the danger be real, not merely perceived. See, for example, Tenn. Code Ann. §39–13–103 (1997); Conn. Gen. Stat. §53a–63 (2001).

229. 441 U.S. 418 (1979).

230. Ibid., 432–433.

231. Ibid., 427.

232. To the same effect are arguments that society's attempts to commit dangerous individuals are analogous to an individual's attempts to protect himself or herself against danger. Larry Alexander, "A Unified Excuse of Preemptive Self-Protection," 74 *Notre Dame Law Review* 1475, 1477 (1999) ("Self-defense, therefore, is preemptive action . . . analogous to civil commitment of the dangerous, gun control, 'no contact' orders, preemptive military strikes, and other practices in which the future dangerousness of others, not their past transgressions, is taken to justify depriving them of life, liberty, or property");

Randy Barnett, "Getting Even: Restitution, Preventive Detention, and the Tort/Crime Distinction," 76 *Boston University Law Review* 157, 160–161 (1996). Because we require a high degree of danger for self-defense (that is, imminent threat of serious physical harm), we should do the same for those situations in which the state engages in self-defense, whether it is through anticipatory crimes or civil commitment.

233. For two articles that make similar arguments, see William Stuntz, "The Pathological Politics of the Criminal Law," 100 *Michigan Law Review* 505, 591–596 (2001), and Dubber, "Policing Possession," 994–995.

5.   The Civilization of the Criminal Law

1. Barbara Wootton, *Crime and the Criminal Law* (1963), chs. 2–3.
2. Sheldon Glueck, *Law and Psychiatry* (1963), ch. 4.
3. Karl Menninger, *The Crime of Punishment* (1966), ch. 8. For perhaps the earliest work advocating this approach, see Enrico Ferri, *Criminal Sociology* (1917). See also G. H. Mead, "The Psychology of Punitive Justice," 23 *American Journal of Sociology* 577 (1918).
4. Barbara Wootton, "Book Review of A. Goldstein, *The Insanity Defense*," 77 Yale Law Journal 1019, 1030 (1968).
5. See generally Kirk Heilbrun, "Prediction versus Management Models Relevant to Risk Assessment: The Importance of Legal Decision-Making Context," 21 *Law and Human Behavior* 347, 351–353 (1997).
6. For a current treatment of risk assessment, see John Monahan, *Rethinking Risk Assessment* (2001), chs. 3–6 (discussing "criminological" risk factors, "clinical" risk factors, and methods of customizing risk assessment).
7. Heilbrun, "Prediction versus Management Models," 352–353.
8. 521 U.S., 368–369.
9. M. F. Plattner, "The Rehabilitation of Punishment," 44 *The Public Interest* 104 (1976).
10. As noted in Chapter 3, the Supreme Court's recent decisions in Blakely v. Washington, 542 U.S. 296 (2004), and *United States v. Booker*, 125 S. Ct 728 (2005) may call for substantial revision of the procedures associated with determinate sentencing regimes, but are unlikely to lead to their disappearance. See Stephanos Bibas, "Blakely's Federal Aftermath," 16 *Federal Sentencing Reporter* 331 (2004).
11. Kevin R. Reitz, *Model Penal Code: Sentencing, Plan for Revision* (2002), 16–28.
12. Michael S. Moore, *Law and Psychiatry: Rethinking the Relationship* (1984), 238–239.

13. Paul H. Robinson, "Punishing Dangerousness," Cloaking Preventive Detention as Criminal Justice," 114 *Harvard Law Review* 1429, 1432 (2001).

14. *Hendricks,* 521 U.S., 354–355.

15. See generally Michael S. Moore, "The Moral Worth of Retribution," in *Responsibility, Character and Emotions,* ed. Ferdinand Schoeman (1987), 214 (arguing that feelings of guilt "engender the judgment that we deserve punishment . . . that we *ought* to be punished").

16. Herbert Morris, *On Guilt and Innocence* (1976), 46.

17. Jean Hampton, "Forgiveness, Resentment and Hatred," in Jeffrie G. Murphy and Jean Hampton, *Forgiveness and Mercy* (1988), 125.

18. For a description of one very effective risk management program that uses these types of methods (called multisystemic therapy), see Curt R. Bartol, *Criminal Behavior: A Psychosocial Approach* (1999), 400–401. This type of therapy is described in more detail later in the chapter.

19. Consider this standard statement about treatment, in connection with sex offenders: "We have now recognized that as with other kinds of craving disorders (e.g., alcoholism, substance abuse, and compulsive gambling), it is not a person's fault that he or she suffers from the problem. It is that person's responsibility, however, to seek help, and one way to begin that process is with the person's admission of a lack of adequate self-control and a need for proper assistance." Fred S. Berlin, "The Etiology and Treatment of Sexual Offending," in *The Science, Treatment, and Prevention of Antisocial Behaviors: Application to the Criminal Justice System,* ed. Diane H. Fishbein (2000), 21–28.

20. Gabrielle Maxwell and Allison Morrris, "The Role of Shame, Guilt, and Remorse in Restorative Justice Processes for Young People," in *Restorative Justice: Theoretical Foundations,* ed. Elmar G. M. Weitekamp and Hans-Jurgen Kerner (2002), 279.

21. Ibid., 280. It should also be noted that the notion that punishment is necessary to bring emotional closure for the victim is suspect at best. See Deborah Morris, *Forgiving the Dead Man Walking* (2000) (describing a victim's search for solace after the execution of her assailant, and concluding "justice did nothing for me, forgiveness did").

22. As two researchers concluded after a study of violence amount people with disorder, it is "a mistake . . . to conceptualize violence as a characteristic of a person without giving equal attention to the underlying or concurrent interpersonal and clinical processes and contexts." Sue E. Estroff and Catherine Zimmer, "Social Networks, Social Support, and Violence among Persons with Severe, Persistent Mental Illness," in *Violence and Mental Disorder:*

Developments in Risk Assessment, ed. John Monahan and Henry Steadman (1994), 259.

23. See generally Urie Bronfenbrenner, *The Ecology of Human Development: Experiments by Nature and Design* (1979), 3–42.

24. Robinson, "Punishing Dangerousness," 1434 ("[T]he use of the criminal justice system as the primary mechanism for preventing future crimes seriously perverts the goals of our institutions of justice").

25. Ibid., 1444; see also Paul Robinson and John Darley, "The Utility of Desert," 91 *Northwestern University Law Review* 451, 457 (1997).

26. On the popularity of legislation regarding sexual predators, see Chapter 4. A good illustration of the public's reaction to three-time loser laws comes from California, where public outrage over the legislature's failure to pass such a statute resulted in Proposition 184, "one of the fastest qualifying propositions in state history," which passed with 72 percent of the vote. Nathan H. Seltzer, "When the Tail Wags the Dog: The Collision Course between Recidivism Statutes and the Double Jeopardy Clause," 83 *Boston University Law Review* 921, 922 (2003).

27. Even citizens in countries with lower crimes rates share this obsession. See generally *Making Punishments Work: Report of a Review of the Sentencing Framework for England and Wales,* www.homeoffice.gov.uk/docs/halliday, App. 5 (July 2001), 107 ("The general public are very clear about what they want sentencing to achieve: a reduction in crime").

28. Michael Perlin, *The Jurisprudence of the Insanity Defense* (1994), 13.

29. Paul H. Robinson and John M. Darley, *Justice Liability and Blame: Community Views and the Criminal Law* (1995), 169–181 (study finding subjects willing to impose a murder conviction on a person who negligently kills during a felony); Ibid., 84–96 (study finding subjects willing to impose punishment for negligent actions outside the homicide context).

30. See Wootton, "Book Review," 1029.

31. Paul Robinson, "Rules of Conduct and Principles of Adjudication," 57 *University of Chicago Law Review* 729 (1990).

32. Ibid., 731, 743. Robinson notes at another point: "Wide dissemination of the principles of adjudication is not necessary either to condemn violation of or to gain compliance with the rules of conduct." Ibid., 770.

33. Here are examples of conduct rules that Robinson proposes: "No person shall engage in conduct that creates a risk of death to another person"; "No person shall engage in intercourse or make sexual contact with or expose his genitals to another person without such other person's consent"; "No person shall take,

exercise control over, or transfer property of another without consent of the owner." Ibid., 760.

34. Wayne R. LaFave et al., *Criminal Procedure,* 2d ed. (1999), 102–103 (noting that the proportion of pretrial diversions to rehabilitation programs may "come close to equaling the number convicted of the crime" and that diversion of those charged with felonies can range from 5 to 20 percent, depending on the jurisdiction); Ibid., 145 (noting that as a result of parole and good time credits, prisoners serve only between 40 and 60 percent of the mean maximum sentence).

35. See the discussion in Part 2 of Chapter 2.

36. See, for example, John M. Darley et al., "Incapacitation and Just Deserts as Motives for Punishment," 24 *Law and Human Behavior* 659, 676 (2000).

37. Francis T. Cullen et al., "Public Opinion about Punishment and Corrections," 27 *Crime and Justice* 1, 34 (2000) (reporting research finding that while "offense seriousness explained the largest amount of variation in sentencing preferences" exhibited by those surveyed, "when respondents were asked in a separate question what was the purpose of the sentence they assigned to the offender in the vignette, the goal of just deserts ranked fourth behind special deterrence, boundary setting, and rehabilitation as a 'very important' reason for choosing the sentence"); J. V. Roberts, "Public Opinion, Criminal Record, and the Sentencing Process," 39 *American Behavioral Scientist* 488 (1996) (finding that, for mildly or moderately serious crimes, people are willing to abandon the retributive principle that punishment should be proportional to the gravity of the crime).

38. See Gary Watson, "Two Faces of Responsibility," 24 *Philosophical Topics* 227 (1996) (noting that we tend to condemn most severely conduct that is seen as characteristic, that is, conduct committed by the dangerous person); Robinson and Darley, "The Utility of Desert," 14–28 (1995) (finding that laypeople treat offenders who show remorse more leniently, which could be due to an assessment that such offenders are less blameworthy or to the conclusion that they are less dangerous).

39. Retributivists recognize this problem. See, for example, Moore, *Law and Psychiatry,* 212–213 (trying to distinguish rage at wrongdoers from the more "virtuous" emotion of guilt feelings as a basis for establishing the moral worth of retribution); Joshua Dressler, "Hating Criminals: How Can Something That Feels So Good Be Wrong?" 88 *Michigan Law Review* 1448, 1451–1453 (1990) (expressing discomfort with the "hate the criminal" justification for retributivism).

40. See Mark R. Fondacaro, "Toward an Ecological Jurisprudence Rooted in Concepts of Justice and Empirical Research," 69 *UMKC Law Review* 179, 192 (2001).

41. Research has established that most of us routinely attribute to individual choice actions that are more likely the result of situational variables, a heuristic known as fundamental attribution error. See Lee Ross et al., "Social Roles, Social Control, and Biases in Social-Perception Processes," 35 *Journal Personality Social Psychology* 485 (1977) (summarizing studies that find observers significantly exaggerate the causal power of personality). A system that deemphasizes the importance of individual choice would tend to counteract this type of error, which is less prevalent in societies with less punitive criminal regimes. See Neal Feigensen, *Legal Blame: How Jurors Think and Talk about Accidents* (2000), 58 n. 15.

42. Neil Vidmar, "Retribution and Revenge," in *Handbook of Justice Research in Law,* ed. Joseph Sanders and V. Lee Hamilton (2002), 54 (hypothesizing that "punishment of the offender might actually increase anger and cognitions of harm [by validating] the perception of harm or remov[ing] any ambiguity about the motivation or character of the offender," although noting there is no research on this issue).

43. See F. De Waal, *Good Natured: The Origins of Right and Wrong in Humans and Other Animals* (1996), 210 (theorizing, based on research with chimpanzees, that "many of the sentiments and cognitive abilities underlying human morality antedate the appearance of our species on this planet," and suggesting that assignments of blame may be a consequence of genetically predisposed rage reactions).

44. Henry M. Hart Jr., "The Aims of the Criminal Law," 23 *Law and Contemporary Problems* 401, 407–408 (1958).

45. Ibid., 408.

46. See Dan M. Kahan, "Ignorance of Law Is an Excuse—but Only for the Virtuous," 96 *Michigan Law Review* 127, 137–141 (1997) (discussing "prudent obfuscation" and vague terminology as a means of fostering law-abiding behavior). Note also that all well-informed putative criminals will know that excuse defenses no longer exist under a preventive regime.

47. Michael Vitiello, "Book Review of *Punishment and Democracy: A Hard Look at Three Strikes' Overblown Promises*," 90 *California Law Review* 257, 268–270 (2002) (discussing the possible deterrent effect of such laws and reporting that one district attorney who teaches inmates about three strikes stated, "There is no other topic of conversation within the institutions other than the impact of [three strikes]").

48. David Garland, *The Culture of Control* (2001), 106–107.

49. Neil Kumar Katyal, "Deterrence's Difficulty," 95 *Michigan Law Review* 2385, 2475 (1997) (showing how criminal penalties may actually increase certain types of crime due to substitution, norming, and other effects, and suggesting that, if the difficulty of determining whether and when deterrence works is borne out, "other nondeterrent-based approaches to criminal punishment should be explored"); Dan M. Kahan, "The Secret Ambition of Deterrence," 113 *Harvard Law Review* 413, 427 (1999) ("Deterrence, in short, presupposes a consequentialist theory of value. Yet nothing intrinsic to the deterrence theory supplies one").

50. Tyler, *Why People Obey the Law*, 168–169.

51. See, for example, Steven D. Levitt, "Why Do Increased Arrest Rates Appear to Reduce Crime?: Deterrence, Incapacitation or Measurement Error?" 36 *Economic Inquiry* 353 (1998); Peter W. Greenwood, "Controlling the Crime Rate through Imprisonment," in *Crime and Policy*, ed. James Q. Wilson (1984); Paul H. Robinson and John M. Darley, "Does Criminal Law Deter?: A Behavioural Science Investigation," *Oxford Journal of Legal Studies* 173 (2004) (finding that potential offenders commonly do not know the legal rules; that even if they do, they usually perceive the likelihood of punishment to be minimal or distant; and that even if they do not, social, situational, and chemical influences lead them to ignore their best interests).

52. David A. Anderson, "The Deterrence Hypothesis and Picking Pockets at the Pickpocket's Hanging," 4 *American Law and Economics Review* 1, 20–21 (fall 2002).

53. Although note that even people whom we would regard as relatively "rational" do not seem to be deterred by criminal sanctions. See Sally S. Simpson, *Corporate Crime, Law, and Social Control* (2002)(describing a study concluding that on balance deterrence does not work for corporations or their managers).

54. Andrew Ashworth, *Sentencing and Criminal Justice* (1995), 60.

55. Hart, "The Aims of the Criminal Law," 410.

56. In addition to Huigens, whose work is described below, Dan Kahan's expressive theory of punishment might fit in this category, although only tenuously so. See Kyron Huigens, "The Dead End of Deterrence, and Beyond," 41 *William and Mary Law Review* 943, 944 (2000) (arguing that virtue ethics "picks up where Kahan's work leaves off").

57. The example appears in Ibid., 968 n. 116.

58. See, for example, Paul H. Robinson, *Criminal Law Defenses* (1984), vol. I, §62(c)(2), 253 and n. 23 (listing and criticizing reasonable mistake provisions).

59. Huigens, "The Dead End of Deterrence," 968 n. 116.

60. Kyron Huigens, "Rethinking the Penalty Phase," 32 *Arizona State Law Journal* 1195, 1237–1238 n. 150 (2000).

61. See, for example, Raymond Paternoster and Lee Ann Iovanni, "The Deterrent Effect of Perceived Severity: A Reexamination," 64 *Social Forces* 751, 769 (1986); Robert Meir and Weldon Johnson, "Deterrence as Social Control: The Legal and Extralegal Production of Conformity," 42 *American Sociology Review* 292, 302 (1977); Tyler, *Why People Obey the Law,* 23–24.

62. See Denise Park, "Acts of Will?" 54 *American Psychologist* 461 (1999) (summarizing four research articles as suggesting "that we perceive ourselves to have far more control over our everyday behavior than we actually do," and that "the source of behavioral control comes not from active awareness but from subtle cues in the environment and from thought processes and information not readily accessible to consciousness").

63. Barefoot v. Estelle, 463 U.S. 880, 901 n. 7 (citing John Monahan, *The Clinical Prediction of Violent Behavior* (1981), 47–49).

64. John Monahan, "The Prediction of Violent Behavior: Toward a Second Generation of Theory and Policy," 141 *American Journal of Psychiatry* 10, 11 (1984).

65. Ibid. See also Christopher Slobogin, "Dangerousness and Expertise," 133 *University of Pennsylvania Law Review* 97, 114–117 (1984) (recounting methodological problems with the studies).

66. John Monahan, *Rethinking Risk Assessment* (2001), ch. 5.

67. Marnie E. Rice et al., "An Evaluation of a Maximum Security Therapeutic Community for Psychopaths and Other Mentally Disordered Offenders," 16 *Law and Human Behavior* 399 (1992).

68. The relevant research is reported in Chapter 4, Part 1, especially notes 28–29.

69. See, for example, David Crump and Susan Waite Crump, "In Defense of the Felony Murder Doctrine," 8 *Harvard Journal of Law and Public Policy* 359, 361–363 (1985) (describing arguments for and against imposition of murder liability for accidental and negligent deaths caused during a felony); J. F. Stephen, *A History of the Criminal Law of England* (1883), 94 (arguing that sudden, "wanton" killing ought to be considered as culpable as killing committed with "malice aforethought"). Debate flourishes in virtually every arena, however, not just with respect to homicide. See, for example, Glanville Williams, *Criminal Law: The General Part* (2d ed. 1961), 122–124 (describing retributive and deterrence arguments for and against liability on negligence grounds); Robert Weisberg, "Reappraising Complicity," 4 *Buffalo Criminal Law Review* 217, 236 (2000) ("[f]or decades, the American courts and legislatures have de-

bated whether knowledge or 'true purpose' should be the required mens rea for accomplice liability").

70. See Kenneth W. Simons, "Should the Model Penal Code's Mens Rea Provisions Be Amended?" 1 *Ohio State Journal of Criminal Law* 179, 204 (2003) (noting that even though the Model Penal Code's mens rea provisions are "a dramatic improvement over prior law . . . courts have encountered difficulty with numerous concepts [in the code,] including mistake of law, recklessness, willful blindness and extreme indifference").

71. See generally Christopher Slobogin, "Doubts About Daubert: Psychiatric Anecdata as a Case Study," 57 *Washington and Lee Law Review* 919, 924–930 (2000) (describing the difficulty of producing scientific information about past mental states).

72. David A. Dolinko, "Three Mistakes of Retributivism," 39 *UCLA Law Review* 1623, 1640 (1992) (stating that most retributivists are unconcerned about the possible unjustness of their culpability judgments and that others who have tried to be more principled "fail to provide any method for determining the amount of punishment that a particular crime or criminal deserves"); Ezzat A. Fattah, "From Philosophical Abstraction to Restorative Action, from Senseless Retribution to Meaningful Restitution: Just Deserts and Restorative Justice Revisited," in *Restorative Justice: Theoretical Foundations,* 315 ("It is possible to grade various criminal offences according to their objective and/or perceived seriousness [but] to come up with a prison term equivalent to theft or robbery, to assault or rape, is inevitably arbitrary, capricious and despotic."); Katyal, "Deterrence's Difficulty," 2389 (discussing "the complexity of the deterrence question" and stating that "a simple and elegant answer to the deterrence question has not yet been found").

73. Michael H. Marcus, "Comments on the Model Penal Code: Sentencing Preliminary Draft No. 1," 30 *American Journal of Criminal Law* 135, 146 n. 44 (2003) ("It makes no sense to deride the [prediction required by dangerous offender statutes] when the default we defend is overwhelmingly less informed, less careful, less analytical, and routinely productive of astoundingly high recidivism rates").

74. Martin Wright, *Restoring Respect for Justice* (1999), chs. 5–6.

75. Dan M. Kahan, "Between Economics and Sociology: The New Path of Deterrence," 95 *Michigan Law Review* 2477, 2494 (1997).

76. Edward Rubin has recently made this point at length. Edward Rubin, "Just Say No to Retribution," 7 *Buffalo Criminal Law Review* 17, 28 (2004).

77. See Conn. Dep't of Public Safety v. Doe, 538 U.S. 1, 7–8 (2003) (strongly sug-

gesting that a hearing is required when dangerousness is relevant under the pertinent statute); Kansas v. Hendricks, 521 U.S. 346, 363–364 (1997) (emphasizing that Kansas law required periodic review).

78. Consider this assessment by the authors of several studies that evaluate risk assessment and risk management challenges posed by dangerous offenders: "Almost all of the treatments suggested for use with offenders and mentally disordered offenders could be provided in the community. In fact some of the treatments (for example, social skills training, life skills training, relapse prevention programs) actually might be more successful in a community setting. With the exception of high scorers on Management Problems and Aggression (toward self as well as other) and Active Psychotic Symptoms scales . . . it is difficult to argue that institutionalization is necessary, or even desirable, for treatment. Rather, in most cases the only reason for institutionalization is to protect the public. . . . For low-risk individuals treatment for criminogenic ends could be provided under modest supervision in the community. For higher risk clients, treatment for criminogenic factors could occur within the institution, or at least begin in the institution, and continue under aggressive community supervision." Vernon L. Quinsey et al., *Violent Offenders: Appraising and Managing Risk* (1998), 214–215.

Research also suggests that imprisonment is criminogenic. See, for example, Jeffrey Fagan et al., "Be Careful What You Wish for: The Comparative Impacts of Juvenile versus Criminal Court Sanctions on Recidivism among Adolescent Felony Offenders" (December 2003), available at Columbia Law School, Pub. Law Res. Paper No. 03–61 www.ssrn.com/abstract=491202 (reporting a study finding that nonindividualized harsh treatment of juveniles in juvenile court increases recidivism and is "ineffective at specific deterrence of serious crime").

79. Lawrence T. Burick, "An Analysis of the Illinois Sexually Dangerous Persons Act," 59 *Journal of Criminal Law, Criminology and Police Science* 254, 261 n. 73 (1968) (discussing release data from sex psychopath programs from 1938 to 1952 indicating that up to 50 percent were released within a relatively short time frame). Even these programs, however, were not really prevention-oriented. See Estelle Freedman, "Uncontrolled Desires: The Response to the Sexual Psychopath," 1920–1960, 74 *Journal of American History* 83 (1987).

80. Michael C. Dorf and Charles F. Sabel, "Drug Treatment Courts and Emergent Experimentalist Government," 53 *Vanderbilt Law Review* 831, 834, 839 (2000).

81. Chapter 4 also proposed adoption of a consistency principle, which mandates

that the degree of danger required to criminalize inchoate and anticipatory conduct be consonant with the degree of danger required for commitment (that is, clear and convincing evidence), a position that could lead to a significant degree of decriminalization.

82. Francis A. Allen, *The Decline of the Rehabilitative Ideal: Penal Policy and Social Purpose* (1981), 49, 52, 57, 72–73.

83. See generally Santiago Redondo et al., "The Influence of Treatment Programs on the Recidivism of Juveniles and Adult Offenders: An European Meta-Analytic Review," 5 *Psychology, Crime, and Law* 251 (1999); D. A. Andrews et al., "Does Treatment Work? A Clinically Relevant and Psychologically Informed Meta-analysis," 28 *Criminology* 369 (1990).

84. Grant T. Harris and Marnie E. Rice, "Mentally Disordered Offenders: What Research Says about Effective Service," in *Impulsivity: Theory Assessment and Treatment* 361, 374 (1997). See also David A. Andrews, "The Psychology of Criminal Conduct and Effective Treatment," in *What Works: Reducing Reoffending*, ed. James McGuire (1998), 35.

85. Scott W. Henggeler et al., "Family Preservation Using Multisystemic Treatment: Long-Term Followup to a Clinical Trial with Serious Juvenile Offenders," 2 *Child and Family Studies* 283 (1993).

86. Paul Gendreau et al., "Intensive Rehabilitation Supervision, The Next Generation in Community Corrections?" in *Contemporary Corrections: Probation, Parole and Intermediate Sanctions*, ed. Joan Petersilia (1997), 252.

87. See, for example, D. Banks and D. Gottfredson, "The Effects of Drug Treatment and Supervision on Time to Rearrest among Drug Treatment Court Participants," 33 *Journal of Drug Issues* 385, 397 (2003) (finding 40 percent recidivism rate among drug court offenders and 80 percent rate among control group); Daniel Eisman, "Drug Courts: Changing People's Lives," 46 *Advocate* 16, 17–18 (2003) (finding a reduction from 42 percent to 18 percent for drug-related offenses and from 63 percent to 38 percent for all offenses).

88. M. Alexander, "Sex Offender Treatment: Does It Work?" cited in Leroy L. Kondo, "The Tangled Web—Complexities, Fallacies and Misconceptions Regarding the Decision to Release Treated Sexual Offenders from Civil Commitment into Society," 23 *Northern Illinois Law Review* 195, 199 n. 14 (2003) (finding a 10 percent difference—14.4 percent versus 25.8 percent—between treated and untreated child molesters); W. L. Marshall and H. E. Barbaree, "Long Term Evaluation of the Behavioral Treatment Program for Child Molesters," 26 *Behavioral Research and Therapy* 499, 508 (1988) (finding a 25 per-

cent difference—32 percent versus 57 percent—in recidivism between treated and untreated sex offenders).

89. M. W. Lipsey and D. B. Wilson, "The Efficacy of Psychological, Education, and Behavioral Treatment," 48 *American Psychologist* 1181 (1993).

90. The phrase derives from Robert Martinson, "What Works?—Questions and Answers about Prison Reform," 35 *The Public Interest* 22 (1974), in which Martinson concluded "[w]ith few and isolated exceptions, the rehabilitative efforts that have been reported so far have had no appreciable effect on recidivism." Ibid., 25. The article had an "immediate and widespread impact." Allen, *The Decline of the Rehabilitative Ideal,* 57.

91. Robert Martinson, "New Findings, New Views: A Note of Caution Regarding Sentencing Reform," 7 *Hofstra Law Review* 243, 254 (1979).

92. See generally Dan M. Kahan, "Social Influence, Social Meaning, and Deterrence," 83 *Virginia Law Review* 349, 352–361 (1997).

93. Darryl K. Brown, "Street, Crime, Corporate Crime, and the Contingency of Criminal Liability," 149 *University of Pennsylvania Law Review* 1295 (2001).

94. Ibid., 1311–1316, 1345, 1351–1357.

95. See also Darryl K. Brown, "Cost-Benefit Analysis in Criminal Law," 92 *California Law Review* 323 (2003) (arguing that a true assessment of the costs of the punitive approach might lead to adoption of more "problem-solving" and "community" courts).

96. See Bordenkircher v. Hayes, 434 U.S. 357 (1978) (upholding mandatory life sentence imposed on an offender who was prosecuted as an habitual offender after turning down a plea offer pursuant to which the prosecutor would have recommended a five-year sentence); Tate v. State, 864 So.2d 44, 49 (Fl. Ct. App. 2003) (involving a life sentence imposed on twelve-year-old prosecuted as an adult after he turned down a plea offer of three years in juvenile detention and ten years probation).

97. See, for example, Norman Abrams, "Prosecution: Prosecutorial Discretion," in 3 *Encyclopedia of Crime and Justice,* ed. Sanford H. Kadish (1983), 1275 ("[T]he American prosecutor has complete discretion with respect to the selection of the charge").

98. The classic statement on this score comes from Andrew von Hirsch, *Doing Justice: The Choice of Punishments* (1976), 49–55.

99. Consider these remarks: "It is neither fair nor equitable to give those found guilty of identical or similar crimes identical prison sentences. The same prison term does not entail the same amount of pain and suffering, does not involve identical deprivations, and does not carry with it the same conse-

quences to different offenders. The pains and consequences of imprisonment are far different even when offenders are kept in the same institution, in similar conditions, for the same length of time." Fattah, "From Philosophical Abstraction to Restorative Action," 316.

100. Michael Tonry, "Mandatory Minimum Penalties and the U.S. Sentencing Commission's 'Mandatory Guidelines,'" 4 *Federal Sentencing Reporter* 129, 132, 133 n. 12 (1991) (citing the Report of the Federal Courts Study Committee [1990], 37–38, that describes a survey finding that a common complaint of district court judges about the Federal Sentencing Guidelines was the elimination of judicial discretion).

101. Plattner, "The Rehabilitation of Punishment," 110.

102. For instance, "staged" treatment is an well-accepted modality even for sex offenders. See, for example, W. L. Marshall et al., "A Three-Tiered Approach to the Rehabilitation of Incarcerated Sex Offenders," 11 *Behavioral Science and Law* 441 (1993).

103. Research suggests that setting an achievable treatment goal, one agreed on by the offender, may be indispensable to change, and fosters motivation and effective functioning. Albert Bandura, *Social Foundations of Thought and Action: A Social Cognitive Theory* (1986), 338, 467–479; Edward L. Deci, *The Psychology of Self-Determination* (1980), 208–210.

104. Allen, *The Decline of the Rehabilitative Ideal,* 54–55.

105. John Q. LaFond, "The Costs of Enacting A Sexual Predator Law," 4 *Psychology, Public Policy and Law* 468, 500 (1998).

106. See Christopher Slobogin et al, "A Prevention Model of Juvenile Justice: The Promise of Kansas v. Hendricks for Children, 1999 *Wisconsin Law Review* 185, 224 n. 122 (citing study). See also S. Aos et al., "The Comparative Costs and Benefits to Reduce Crime: A Review of National Research Findings" (1999) (Washington State Institute for Public Policy) (indicating that the cost of multisystemic therapy was one-fifth that of institutionalization, and estimating costs savings of $30,000 to $131,000 per juvenile based on prevention of subsequent incidents, or $8.38 for every dollar spent on multisystemic therapy).

107. See, for example, Jeff Tauber and C. West Huddleston, *Rentry Drug Courts* (1999), 19 (reporting an Oregon study estimating more than $10 million in savings, or $10 saved for every $1 spent on drug court).

108. Kristin Parsons Winokur et al., "What Works in Juvenile Justice Outcome Measurement—A Comparison of Predicted Success to Observed Performance," 66 *Federal Probation* 50, 53 (2002) (using a sophisticated methodology to evaluate a range of treatment programs, finding that "community-based ap-

proach offers not only the greatest effectiveness when controlling for youths' individual risk factors, but also does it at minimal cost").

109. See generally Nkechi Taifa, "'Three-Strikes-and-You're-out'—Mandatory Life Imprisonment for Third Time Felons," 20 *University of Dayton Law Review* 717, 722 (1995) (describing costs).

110. For instance, roughly 5 to 8 percent of chronic offenders commit more than 50 percent of juvenile crime. David P. Farrington et al., *Understanding and Controlling Crime* (1986), 50–51; Michael Schumacher and Gwen A. Kurz, *The 8% Solution: Preventing Serious, Repeat Juvenile Crime* (2001), 4–5 (reporting a study finding that 8 percent of juvenile offenders committed 55 percent of repeat offenses, and that more than half of these offenders continued crime as an adult).

111. Randy J. Nelson et al., "Behavioral Abnormalities in Male Mice Lacking Neuronal Nitric Oxide Synthase," 378 *Nature* 383 (1995): F. Saudou, "Enhanced Aggressive Behavior in Mice Lacking 5-HT1b Receptor," 265 *Science* 1875 (1994).

112. Hill Goldsmith and Irving I. Gottesman, "Heritable Variability and Variable Heritability in Developmental Psychopathology," in *Frontiers in Developmental Psychopathology*, ed. M. Lenzenweger and J. Haugaard (1996), 5; Remi J. Cadoret et al., "Genetic-Environmental Interaction in the Genesis of Aggressivity and Conduct Disorders," 52 *Archives of General Psychiatry* 916 (1995).

113. Evan Balaban et al., "Mean Genes and the Biology of Human Aggression: A Critical Review of Recent Animal and Human Research," 11 *Journal of Neurogenetics* 1 (1996) (noting that more than fifty studies have shown a relationship between serotonin and antisocial behavior, but criticizing their methodology and conclusions); Jonathan H. Pincus, "Aggression, Criminality, and the Frontal Lobes," in the *Human Frontal Lobes: Functions and Disorders* 547, eds., Bruce L. Miller and Jeffrey L. Cummings (1999) (discussing impairments resulting from frontal lobe dysfunction). See generally Peter McGuffin and Anita Thapar, "Genetics and Antisocial Personality Disorder," in *Psychopathy: Antisocial, Criminal and Violent Behavior*, eds. Theodore Millon et al. (1998), 215.

114. Caspi Avshalom et al., "Role of Genotype in the Cycle of Violence in Maltreated Children," 297 *Science* 851 (2002). Also of interest is research correlating psychopathy with abnormal neurological symptoms. See generally, Bartol, *Criminal Behavior*, 92–105 (summarizing EEG research on psychopathy).

115. See, for example, Katherine I. Morley and Wayne D. Hall, "Is There a Genetic Susceptibility to Engage in Criminal Acts?" *Trends and Issues in Crime and Criminal Justice* (October 2003).

116. See generally John A. Bargh and Tanya L. Chartrand, "The Unbearable Automacity of Being," 54 *American Psychologist* 462 (1999); Irving Kirsch and Steven J. Lynn, "Automaticity in Clinical Psychology," 54 *American Psychologist* 504 (1999).

117. On the effect of personality on information processing, see Brendan P. Bradley et al., "Selective Processing of Negative Information: Effects of Clinical Anxiety, Concurrent Depression, and Awareness," 104 *Journal of Abnormal Psychology* 532 (1995), and Karin Mogg et al., "Subliminal Processing of Emotional Information in Anxiety and Depression," 102 *Journal of Abnormal Psychology* 304 (1993). On the development of neural pathways that control access to stimuli, see Joseph LeDoux, *The Emotional Brain: The Mysterious Underpinnings of Emotional Life* (1996). On the effects of heuristic thinking, see Daniel Kahneman and Amos Tversky, "On the Reality of Cognitive Illusions," 103 *Psychological Review* 582 (1996) (responding to suggestions that heuristic thinking usually results in accurate judgments).

118. See Amost Tversky and Daniel Kahneman, "Judgment Under Uncertainty: Heuristics and Biases," 185 *Science* 1124, 1125 (1974).

119. Richard E. Nisbett and T. D. Wilson, "Telling More Than We Can Know: Verbal Reports on Mental Processes," 84 *Psychological Review* 231 (1977).

120. See I. Keller and H. Heckhausen, "Readiness Potentials Preceding Spontaneous Motor Acts: Voluntary v. Involuntary Control," 76 *Electroencephalography and Clinical Neurophysiology* 351 (1990).

121. See, for example, Richard Lowell Nygaard, "Free Will, Determinism, Penology and the Human Genome: Where's a New Leibniz, When We Really Need Him?" 3 *University of Chicago Scholar Roundtable* 17, 421–422, 430 (1996); Steven I. Friedland, "The Criminal Law Implications of the Human Genome Project: Reimagining a Genetically Oriented Criminal Justice System," 86 *Kentucky Law Journal* 303, 333 (1998).

122. See, for example, Dan W. Brock and Allen E. Buchanan, "The Genetics of Behavior and Concepts of Free Will and Determinism," in *Genetics and Criminality*, ed. J. R. Botkin et al. (1999), 67.

123. This is a well-documented aspect of human development. See Jean Piaget, *The Moral Judgment of the Child*, trans. Marjorie Gabain (1965); Lawrence Kohlberg, *The Philosophy of Moral Development: Moral Stages and the Idea of Justice* (1981) (arguing, based on research, that ideas of moral obligation originate in early childhood but evolve as youths mature into adulthood). As to the development of a "criminal" character, see Terrie Moffit, "Adolescence-Limited and Life-Course-Persistent Antisocial Behavior: A Development Tax-

onomy," 100 *Psychological Review* 674, 679 (1993) (describing life-course persistent offenders who "exhibit changing manifestations of antisocial behavior:
biting and hitting at age four, shoplifting and truancy at age ten, selling drugs
and stealing cars at age sixteen, robbery and rape at age twenty-two, and fraud
and child abuse at age thirty").

124. Compare Hilary Bok, *Freedom and Responsibility* (1998) (compatibilist account) and John Martin Fischer and Mark Ravizza, *Responsibility and Control:
A Theory of Moral Responsibility* (1998) (same) with Derk Pereboom, *Living
without Free Will* (2001) (hard determinist account) and Saul Smilansky, *Free
Will and Illusion* (2000) (same).

125. See Part 2 of Chapter 1.

126. For a description of the scientific basis of a number of other defenses of this
sort (including epilepsy, hypoglycemic syndrome, dissociative states, post-
traumatic stress disorder, and genetic aberrations), see Gary P. Melton et al.,
*Psychological Evaluations for the Courts: A Handbook for Mental Health Profes-
sionals and Lawyers* (2d ed. 1997), 218–225.

127. Consider these comments from David Dolinko: "[T]he retributivist mind-set
encourages legal actors to brush aside qualms about whether the wretched
economic, social, and psychological background of many criminals somehow
undercuts our right to inflict condign punishment. For if to credit such
qualms is to question the criminal's status as a fully responsible individual,
then respect for the criminal's very personhood counsels us to reject those
qualms and to affirm our deep respect for the offender by refusing to mitigate
his punishment no matter how 'deprived' his background" (Dolinko, "Three
Mistakes of Retributivism," 1647).

128. See Perlin, *The Jurisprudence of the Insanity Defense,* 120–128.

129. See Wayne LaFave, *Criminal Law* (3d ed. 2000), 434 (noting the courts' "un-
critical acceptance of the general statement that the mistake must be reasonable");
Ibid., 493–494 (noting the law generally requires that the defendant's belief in
the necessity of force to prevent harm to himself be a reasonable one").

130. Richard J. Bonnie et al., *Criminal Law* (1997), 360.

131. These various aspects of the Model Penal Code were described in Part 1 of
Chapter 2.

132. The commentary to the Code notes that, in this provision, "[t]he term 'situation' . . . is designedly ambiguous and is plainly flexible enough to allow the
law to grow in the direction of taking account of mental abnormalities that
have been recognized in the developing law of diminished responsibility."
Model Penal Code and Commentaries 72. However, the commentary later

states, "[l]ike temperament or unusual excitability . . . there are surely other forms of abnormality that should not be taken into account for this purpose." Ibid., 73.

133. Ibid., 375 (equating definition of situation in connection with duress with the definition of situation in appraising recklessness and negligence).

134. Ibid., 242 and n. 27 (indicating that these factors "would not be held material in judging negligence" and then stating the recklessness provision "requires the same discriminations demanded by the standard of negligence").

135. Model Penal Code § 2.02(3).

136. Perhaps the most blatant example of this type of reasoning is found in the Montana Supreme Court's decision in State v. Korrell, 213 Mont. 316, 331, 690 P.2d 992, 1000 (1984), which upheld a legislative decision to abolish the insanity defense because evidence of mental disorder could still be heard at sentencing.

137. This is still true after the Supreme Court's decision in Blakley v. Washington, 542 U.S. 296 (2004), which requires only factors in *aggravation* to be decided by juries.

138. Stephen J. Morse, "Diminished Rationality, Diminished Responsibility," 1 *Ohio State Journal of Criminal Law* 289, 294–298 (2003).

139. Ibid., 302, 300 (emphasis deleted), 304.

140. Morse does countenance one variation on his generic guilty-but-partially-responsible defense. The discount for diminished responsibility could vary inversely with the seriousness of the crime, he states, because defendants who commit more serious crimes are "more dangerous" and thus should be confined for longer periods. Ibid., 303. Leaving aside the fact that those who commit serious crimes are not necessarily more dangerous than those who commit less serious ones, this concession to public safety raises the question this entire chapter has addressed: Why should dangerousness not *replace* blame as the core consideration of the criminal law?

141. 521 U.S., 358.

142. 342 U.S. 246, 250 (1952). The Court also noted Blackstone's statement in the eighteenth century that crime requires a "vicious will." Ibid., 251.

143. U.S. Constitution, Sixth Amendment. This language has been construed to require jury trials for any crime that can lead to "punishment" of six months or longer—Baldwin v. New York, 399 U.S. 66 (1970)—so, as a technical matter, a preventive regime relying on periodic review every six months might elude the Sixth Amendment's jury trial constraints (although the due process clause would still apply).

144. The Court's language in *Morrissette* was dictum and, in any event, was merely in aid of interpreting a federal statute, not framed as a constitutional requirement. In earlier cases, the Court had stated that "in the prohibition or punishment of particular acts, the State may in the maintenance of a public policy provide 'that he who shall do them shall do them at his peril and will not be heard to plead in defense good faith or ignorance.'" United States v. Balint, 258 U.S. 250, 252 (1922) (quoting Shevlin-Carpenter Co. v. Minnesota, 218 U.S. 57, 70 [1910]). More recently, in Egelhoff v. Montana, 518 U.S. 37 (1996), the Court held that Montana's elimination of the intoxication defense did not violate due process, in large part because the defense is "of recent vintage." Most other mens rea concepts are relatively recent developments as well. See Martin R. Gardner, "The Mens Rea Enigma: Observations on the Role of Motive in the Criminal Past and Present," 1993 *Utah Law Review* 635, 664 (suggesting that, before the nineteenth century, the law posited that "the accused acts intentionally unless she can show that commission of the actus reus was accidental [or] unless she raises one of the recognized defenses," that is, self-defense—defined in terms of reasonableness—and infancy and insanity—defined narrowly); Paul H. Robinson, "A Brief History of Distinctions in Criminal Culpability," 31 *Hastings Law Journal* 815, 844–845 (1989) (noting that even into the nineteenth century, English courts did not often conduct serious investigations of subjective mental state). Finally, there is the interesting statement in Powell v. Texas, 392 U.S. 514 (1968) (plurality opinion): "The doctrines of actus reus, mens rea, insanity, mistake, justification, and duress have historically provided the tools for a constantly shifting adjustment of the tension between the evolving aims of the criminal law and changing religious, moral, philosophical, and medical views of the nature of man. This process of adjustment has always been thought to be the province of the States." Ibid., 535–536.

145. C. S. Lewis objected that a preventive regime could "be criticized only by fellow experts on technical grounds, never by men as men and on grounds of justice." C. S. Lewis, "The Humanitarian Theory of Punishment," *Res Judicatae* 224, 229 VI (June 1953).

146. See Christopher Slobogin, "The 'Ultimate Issue' Issue," 7 *Behavioral Science and Law* 259, 260–261 (1989) (arguing against permitting experts to address ultimate issues such as culpability and whether intervention may occur based on dangerousness, because "[m]ental health professionals are not trained, as are judges, nor institutionally qualified, as are juries, to reach legal or moral conclusions").

147. 434 U.S. 407, 411–413 (2002).

148. For an argument that *Hendricks* not only does not prohibit, but also might actually bolster, the case for a separate, preventively-oriented juvenile court, see Slobogin et al. "A Prevention Model of Juvenile Justice, 185.

149. Paul H. Robinson, "The Criminal-Civil Distinction and the Utility of Desert," 76 *Boston Univeristy Law Review* 201, 207 (1996) (arguing that the reason the distinction between civil and criminal systems persists is that "the human desire to make moral judgements is universal").

150. This notion was discussed at length in Chapter 4. See generally Herbert Packer, *The Limits of the Criminal Sanction* (1968), 75 ("The idea of free will in relation to conduct is not, in the legal system, a statement of fact, but rather a value preference having very little to do with the metaphysics of determinism and free will").

151. In finding that commitment under the sexual predator statute at issue in *Hendricks* was not punishment, the Court emphasized both the absence of a requirement that the offender be found criminally responsible for the act and the lack of a "scienter requirement." 521 U.S., 362–363. Conversely, if both are required, post-conviction disposition would probably be considered sufficiently punitive to satisfy due process. This conclusion is also supported by the Court's decision in Penn. ex rel. Sullivan v. Ash, 302 U.S. 51, 61 (1937) ("[The state] may inflict a deserved penalty merely to vindicate the law or to deter or to reform the offender or for all of these purposes . . . [The offender's] past may be taken to indicate his present purposes and tendencies and significantly to suggest the period of restraint and the kind of discipline that ought to be imposed upon him").

6.   Competency in the Criminal Process

1. See Hawaii v. Standard Oil Co., 405 U.S. 251, 257–260 (1972) (describing the parens patriae power).

2. See Sell v. United States, 539 U.S. 166 (2003) (recognizing the state's authority to forcibly medicate defendants who are incompetent to stand trial and dangerous to others, incompetent to make treatment decisions, and/or charged with a serious offense). Although this chapter discusses limitations on forced restoration of competency, discussion of *Sell* and its ramifications is reserved for Chapter 7.

3. See William Glaberson, "Death Penalty Issue Is Raised as Unabomber Jury Selection Begins," *New York Times*, November 13, 1997, A25.

4. See, for example, "Expert Consensus: Intelligence Sets This Loner Apart," *Boston Globe*, April 5, 1996, 12.

5. See William Glaberson, "Lawyers for Kaczynski Agree He Is Competent to Stand Trial," *New York Times*, Jan. 21, 1998, A1 (noting that the court-appointed expert, Dr. Sally Johnson, diagnosed Kaczynski as suffering from "schizophrenia, paranoid type," "the same diagnosis the defense team . . . suggested applie[d] to Mr. Kaczynski").

6. See David S. Jackson, "At His Own Request," *Time*, January 12, 1998, 40.

7. See William Glaberson, "Kaczynski Can't Drop Lawyers or Block a Mental Illness Defense," *New York Times*, Jan. 8, 1998, A1.

8. A necessity, or "choice of evils," defense is recognized if the harm caused by the crime is necessary to prevent a greater harm. See Wayne R. LaFave, *Criminal Law* (3d ed., 2000), 476.

9. This statement is conjecture, based on Kaczynski's willingness at one point to be represented by Tony Serra, knowing that Serra's strategy might be a necessity defense. See Unabomber, *Transcript of Kaczynski Case*, January 5, 1998 (visited March 8, 2000), www.unabombertrial.com/transcripts.

10. *Transcript of Kaczynski Case*.

11. See David van Biema, "A Fool for a Client," *Time*, February 6, 1995, 66; Glaberson, "Lawyers for Kaczynski Agree," A1.

12. According to Glaberson, Ibid., the trial judge had indicated, prior to Kaczynski's plea, that he would probably allow the lawyers to raise such a defense over Kaczynski's objection, using nonexpert testimony during the guilt phase and expert testimony during the penalty phase.

13. The government's agreement to forego a trial and capital punishment was also prompted by Kaczynski's willingness to waive his Fourth Amendment claim concerning the search of his cabin. See William Glaberson, "Kaczynski Avoids a Death Sentence with Guilty Plea," *New York Times*, January 23, 1998, A1.

14. Ibid.

15. See American Bar Association, *Model Rules of Professional Conduct* (1999), Rule 1.2(a) and comment; *Model Code of Professional Responsibility* (1980), Ethical Consideration 7–7.

16. 509 U.S. 389 (1993).

17. 478 F.2d 211, 214 (9th Cir. 1973).

18. 362 U.S. 402 (1960).

19. 478 F.2d 214 (citations omitted).

20. Ibid., 215 (quoting Schoeller v. Dunbar, 423 F.2d 1183, 1194 [9th Cir. 1970]).

21. Ibid., 214–215.

22. Moran v. Godinez, 972 F.2d 263, 266 (9th Cir. 1992).

23. 478 F.2d, 215.

24. Ibid., 214–215.

25. See Note, "Competence to Plead Guilty: A New Standard," 1974 *Duke Law Journal* 149, 155.

26. State v. Heral, 342 N.E.2d 34, 37 (Ill. 1976) (quoting Note, "Competence to Plead Guilty," 170).

27. 509 U.S., 398.

28. Ibid., 399 (emphasis omitted).

29. 422 U.S. 806 (1975).

30. Ibid., 836.

31. Ibid., 834.

32. 509 U.S. 400 (emphasis in original).

33. Ibid., 400–401.

34. Ibid., 401 n. 12 (citation and emphasis omitted).

35. See Gary B. Melton et al., *Psychological Evaluations for the Courts: A Handbook for Mental Health Professionals and Lawyers* (2d ed. 1997), 121–124.

36. 509 U.S., 399. The concurring opinion of Justice Kennedy, which Justice Scalia joined, is even more adamant on this point. See Ibid., 404 (Kennedy, J., concurring in part and concurring in the judgment) ("If a defendant elects to stand trial and to take the foolish course of acting as his own counsel, the law does not for that reason require any added degree of competence").

37. See, for example, Dunn v. Johnson, 162 F.3d 302, 307–308 (5th Cir. 1998); United States v. Schmidt, 105 F.3d 82, 88 (2d. Cir. 1997); United States v. Day, 998 F.2d 622, 627 (8th Cir. 1993). But see Wilkins v. Bowersox, 145 F.3d 1006, 1011–1012 (8th Cir. 1998) (conducting a much more sensitive inquiry).

38. 509 U.S., 413 (Blackmun, J., dissenting).

39. Courts routinely appoint "standby counsel" to assist the pro se defendant, but such counsel are to intervene only at the defendant's request. See, for example, McKaskle v. Wiggins, 465 U.S. 168, 183 (1984).

40. 509 U.S., 416 (Blackmun, J., dissenting).

41. See Faretta v. California, 422 U.S. 806, 834 (1975). *Faretta* also emphasized the "inestimable worth of free choice." Ibid., 833–834.

42. Ibid., 835 (quoting Adams v. United States ex rel. McCann, 317 U.S. 269, 279 (1969)).

43. See United States v. Patterson, 140 F.3d 767, 775 (8th Cir. 1998).

44. At least one court has expressly recognized this fact. Brooks v. McCaughtry, 380 F.3d 1009, 1011–1012 (7th Cir. 2004) ("there is a difference between mental functioning, which is the ability to process information, and the informa-

tion itself; more information may be required for an effective waiver of the right to counsel than for being able to follow the goings-on at one's trial").

45. 509 U.S. 396 (citing Dusky v. United States, 362 U.S. 402, 402 [1960]).

46. 509 U.S. 392.

47. Ibid., 409–411 (Blackmun, J., dissenting).

48. Ibid., 402. It should be noted, however, that *Godinez* was a habeas case, a procedural posture that may have reduced the Court's willingness to explicate its holding.

49. See Richard J. Bonnie, "The Competence of Criminal Defendants: Beyond *Dusky* and *Drope*," 47 *University of Miami Law Review* 539, 589–591 (1993). See also Richard J. Bonnie, "The Competence of Criminal Defendants: A Theoretical Reformulation," 10 *Behavioral Science and Law* 291, 293 (1992) (calling for "theoretical attention to the concept of competence in relation to criminal defense").

50. See Bonnie, "Beyond *Dusky* and *Drope*," 554–560.

51. Ibid., 551.

52. Ibid., 552.

53. Ibid., 553.

54. See Paul Appelbaum and Thomas Grisso, "Assessing Patients' Capacities to Consent to Treatment," 319 *New England Journal of Medicine* 1635 (1988).

55. Bonnie, "Beyond *Dusky* and *Drope*," 571–576.

56. Most prominent in the criminal context is Bruce Winick, "Incompetency to Stand Trial: An Assessment of Costs and Benefits, and a Proposal for Reform," 39 *Rutgers Law Review* 243 (1987). See also Loren Roth et al., "Tests of Competency to Consent to Treatment," 134 *American Journal of Psychiatry* 279, 283 (1977).

57. See Bonnie, "Beyond *Dusky* and *Drope*," 577–578.

58. See Ibid., 579.

59. See Winick, "Incompetency to Stand Trial," 251–258.

60. See Melton et al., *Psychological Evaluations*, 128–129; Thomas Grisso et al., "The Organization of Pretrial Forensic Evaluation Services: A National Profile," 18 *Law and Human Behavior* 377, 382–388 (1994).

61. In virtually every jurisdiction, time spent in jail because of denial of bond is credited toward one's sentence. See, for example, Federal Sentencing Guidelines, 28 *Code of Federal Regulations* §2.10(a); Fla. Stat. Ann. § 907.041(4)(j). Those incompetent defendants who have been denied bond should also generally receive credit for any time spent hospitalized, and often do. See 38 Ill. Com Stat. Ann. §104–26(5); Ohio Rev. Code Ann. §5120.17(F) (Anderson

1998). In the jurisdictions where such credit is explicitly denied, an extremely strong equal protection argument could be made. See ABA *Criminal Justice Mental Health Standards* (1989), commentary to Standard 7–4.15.

62. Acquittal by reason of insanity normally results in hospitalization for as long as the acquittee remains mentally ill and dangerous. See Jones v. United States, 463 U.S. 354, 370 (1983). However, if either the mental illness or dangerousness is successfully treated, release should occur. See Foucha v. Louisiana, 504 U.S. 71, 77 (1992).

63. See generally John Monahan et al., "Prisoners Transferred to Mental Hospitals," in *Mentally Disordered Offenders,* eds. John Monahan and Henry Steadman (1983), 233 (providing data on the frequency of such transfers).

64. See Michael McConville and Chester L. Mirsky, "The Skeleton of Plea Bargaining," *New Law Journal,* Oct. 9, 1992, 1374 ("in the American plea bargaining system, the defense attorney's concern is no longer with the sufficiency of the State's evidence but with admonishing the defendant not to be foolhardy and insist upon a trial.").

65. Bonnie, Beyond *Dusky* and *Drope,* 579. Ultimately, as a "simplifying proposal" Bonnie suggests that the reasoned choice test should govern whenever "the defendant waives counsel, or insists on acting contrary to counsel's advice in a manner that raises doubts about the client's rationality." Ibid., 586.

66. See, for example, Elyn R. Saks, "Competency to Refuse Treatment," 69 *North Carolina Law Review* 945, 948–961 (1991).

67. Ibid., 950.

68. Elyn R. Saks and Stephen H. Behnke, "Competency to Decide on Treatment and Research: MacArthur and Beyond," 10 *Journal of Contemporary Legal Issues* 103, 115 (1999).

69. Bonnie, "Beyond *Dusky* and *Drope,*" 575.

70. Duncan Kennedy, "Distributive and Paternalist Motives in Contract and Tort Law, With Special Reference to Compulsory Terms and Unequal Bargaining Power," 41 *Maryland Law Review* 563, 644 (1982). Under Bonnie's definition of reasoned choice, a person who fails one of the other tests can still, in theory, meet the reasoned choice test; an irrational person can often make logical connections between (delusional) premises and conclusions. However, as the text asserts, in practice evaluating the quality of thought "process" very often, and perhaps inevitably, requires consideration of thought content.

71. See, for example, American Psychiatric Association, *Diagnostic and Statistical Manual of Mental Disorders–Text Revised* (4th ed. 2000), 297 ("[A] common characteristic of individuals with Delusional Disorder is the apparent normal-

ity of their behavior and appearance when their delusional ideas are not being discussed or acted on.").

72. See Saks, "Competency to Refuse Treatment," 992–998.

73. See Jackson, "At His Own Request," 40.

74. See Pre-Trial Transcript of In Camera Discussion (Redacted), Kaczynski, No. CR-S-96–259GEB, 1997 WL 812617 (E.D. Cal. Dec. 24, 1997); Order, United States v. Kaczynski, No. CR-S-96–259GEB, 1997 WL 797428F, at * 1 (E.D. Cal. Dec. 22, 1997); see also Order, Kaczynski, No. CR-S-96–259GEB, 1998 WL 226796, at *2, *7 (E.D. Cal. May 4, 1998) (describing the December 22 agreement).

75. Pre-Trial Transcript Proceedings, Kaczynski, No. CR-S-96–259GEB, 1998 WL 10757, at *5 (E.D. Cal. Jan. 7, 1998).

76. Official Trial Transcript, Kaczynski, No. CR-S-96–259GEB, 1998 WL 4657, at *10 (E.D. Cal. Jan. 8, 1998).

77. See Theodore Kaczynski, *Manifesto,* www.uk.dir.yahoo.com/government/ Law/Cases/Theodore_Kaczynski_Case (visited Mar. 8, 2004), para.168 ("To many of us, freedom and dignity are more important than a long life or avoidance of physical pain."). Kaczynski repeated similar sentiments to Time magazine. See Stephen J. Dubner, "I Don't Want to Live Long. I Would Rather Get the Death Penalty than Spend the Rest of My Life in Prison," *Time,* Oct. 18, 1999, 46 ("[H]e will not tolerate being called, as he put it, 'a nut,' or 'a lunatic' or 'a sicko.' He says he pleaded guilty last year only to stop his lawyers from arguing he was a paranoid schizophrenic. . . .").

78. See Deborah C. Scott et al., "Monitoring Insanity Acquittees: Connecticut's Psychiatric Security Review Board," 41 *Hospital and Community Psychiatry* 980, 982 (1990) (stating that insanity acquittees are the "most despised" group of individuals in society).

79. Lack of insight is one of the most common "symptoms" considered diagnostic of mental illness and of incompetency. See Grant H. Morris, "Judging Judgment: Assessing the Competence of Mental Patients to Refuse Treatment," 32 *San Diego Law Review* 343, 432 (1995).

80. Field research indicates that reliability even for major diagnoses such as schizophrenia (41 percent), mood disorders (50 percent), and organic disorder (37 percent) is low. See Paul B. Lieberman and Frances F. Baker, "The Reliability of Psychiatric Diagnosis in the Emergency Room," 36 *Hospital and Community Psychiatry* 291, 292 (1985). As Chapter 3 noted, more leisurely evaluation produces better results, but disagreement occurs even then.

81. See Stephen J. Morse, "Crazy Behavior, Morals and Science: An Analysis of Mental Health Law," 51 *Southern California Law Review* 527, 605–606 (1978).

82. See Ibid., 607. Interestingly, Kaczynski made similar points in his Manifesto. See Kaczynski, *Manifesto,* para. 119 ("The concept of 'mental health' in our society is defined largely by the extent to which an individual behaves in accord with the needs of the system and does so without showing signs of stress"), para. 155 ("Our society tends to regard as a 'sickness' any mode of thought or behavior that is inconvenient for the system, and this is plausible because when an individual doesn't fit into the system it causes pain to the individual as well as problems for the system.").

83. It is possible that the beliefs underlying Kaczynski's necessity argument were delusional. For instance, he may have believed that the world will explode in 40 years if all technological advancements are not completely eliminated. However, nothing in his written works suggests his beliefs were irrational in this sense. See generally Dubner, "I Don't Want to Live Long," 49 ("In the Unabomber's mind, society was in desperate need of a brave and brazen savior who wouldn't let murder stand in his way. . . . What Kaczynski wants is a true movement, 'people who are reasonably rational and self controlled and are seriously dedicated to getting rid of the technological system.'").

84. 509 U.S. 389 (1993).

85. 670 N.Y.S.2d 327 (App. Div. 1998).

86. See Moran v. Godinez, 972 F.2d 263, 264–268 (9th Cir. 1992).

87. See *Godinez,* 509 U.S., 392–393; *Godinez,* 972 F.2d, 268.

88. The caveat stems from the belief that waiver of counsel requires comprehension of the various roles an attorney carries out in the course of trial and sentencing. The answers Moran gave in this regard were "monosyllabic" and thus the amount of evidence on this point is less than ideal. See *Godinez,* 509 U.S. at 411 (Blackmun, J., dissenting). On the other hand, Moran was of average intelligence and the Ninth Circuit subsequently characterized the trial judge's questions about Moran's understanding of the consequences of waiving counsel as "probing and thorough." Moran v. Godinez, 40 F.3d 1567, 1575 (9th Cir. 1994), amended by 57 F.3d 690 (9th Cir. 1995) (upholding Moran's death sentences).

89. See *Godinez,* 509 U.S., 409–410 (Blackmun, J., dissenting) (describing doctors' conclusions that Moran was "very depressed" and that his purpose was to prevent all presentation of mitigating evidence at sentencing).

90. Ibid., 410–411.

91. See *Godinez,* 972 F.2d, 265.

92. See generally John H. Blume, "Killing the Willing: 'Volunteers,' Suicide and Competency, 103 *Michigan Law Review* 939, 963 (2005) (finding in a group of 106 "volunteers" that roughly 20% suffered from clinical depression or bipolar

disorder and that 39 percent chose to waive appeals out of a sense of "hope-lessness").

93. See Van Biema, "A Fool for a Client," 66.

94. See John T. McQuiston, "Adviser Says L.I.R.R. Suspect Prefers Conviction to Insanity Finding," *New York Times*, Feb. 10, 1995, B5.

95. See Van Biema, "A Fool for a Client," 66.

96. See Robin Topping, "Weighing Competence vs. Sanity," *Newsday*, Feb. 5, 1995, A6 (Nassau and Suffolk ed).

97. See Ibid.

98. For a description of these facts, see Michael L. Perlin, "'Dignity was the First to Leave'": Godinez v. Moran, Colin Ferguson, and the Trial of Mentally Disabled Criminal Defendants," 14 *Behavioral Science and Law* 61, 73 (1996).

99. Although *Godinez* only established the federal standard, it was handed down before *Ferguson* commenced and the state court in that case applied a test "to-tally consistent" with that ruling. Ibid., 72.

100. Topping, "Weighing Competence vs. Sanity."

101. ABA, *Model Code*, Ethical Consideration 7–12.

102. ABA, *Model Rules*, Rule 1.14.

103. See ABA, *Mental Health Standards*, Standard 7–4.2(c).

104. See John M. Burkoff, *Criminal Defense Ethics* (1991), § 6.3(b).

105. See Paul A. Chernoff and William G. Schaffer, "Defending the Mentally Ill: Ethical Quicksand," 10 *American Criminal Law Review* 505, 520–521 (1972); Rodney J. Uphoff, "The Role of the Criminal Defense Lawyer in Representing the Mentally Impaired Defendant: Zealous Advocate or Officer of the Court?," 1988 *Wisconsin Law Review* 65, 106, 108 n. 175 (suggesting, however, that such situations should be "rare"); Bruce J. Winick, "Reforming Competency to Stand Trial and Plead Guilty: A Restated Proposal and a Response to Professor Bonnie," 85 *Journal of Criminal Law and Criminology*, 571, 580–581 (1995); see also Josephine Ross, "Autonomy Versus a Client's Best Interests: The De-fense Lawyer's Dilemma When Mentally Ill Clients Seek to Control Their De-fense," 35 *American Criminal Law Review* 1343, 1372–1381 (1998) (discussing how an "ethic of care" might call for disregarding incompetency concerns).

106. See generally Henry J. Steadman et al., *The Mentally Ill in Jail: Planning for Es-sential Services* (1989). Many jails lack even routine mental health screening services. See Linda A. Teplin and James Swartz, "Screening for Severe Mental Disorder in Jails," 13 *Law and Human Behavior* 1, 2 (1989).

107. See Uphoff, "Role of Criminal Defense Lawyer," 101 n.151 (noting that men-tally ill defendants "fare poorly on probation").

108. See Ross, "Autonomy Versus a Client's Best Interests," 1370 n.106 (1998) (describing analogous "continuance[s] without a finding," which result in incarceration if probation is violated).

109. Cf. Roesch and Golding, *Competency to Stand Trial,* 197.

110. In Florida, for instance, persons charged with misdemeanors may not be evaluated or treated in a forensic hospital, but must be evaluated and treated either on an outpatient basis or in a civil hospital. See Onwu v. State, 692 So. 2d 881, 882–883 (Fla. 1997).

111. See Jackson v. Indiana, 406 U.S. 715, 738–739 (1972).

112. See Alan Stone, *Mental Health and the Law: A System in Transition* (1976), 212–213 (1976) (stating that virtually all defendants can be restored or declared unrestorable within six months). In 1979, one study found that in the jurisdictions studied the average time spent in the hospital for evaluation was only about seventeen days. See Ronald Roesch, "Determining Competency to Stand Trial: An Examination of Evaluation Procedures in an Institutional Setting," 47 *Journal of Consulting and Clinical Psychology* 542, 548 (1979). If anything, that average has gone down appreciably in the past twenty years.

113. See Grant H. Morris and J. Reid Meloy, "Out of Mind? Out of Sight: The Uncivil Commitment of Permanently Incompetent Criminal Defendants," 27 *University of California Davis Law Review* 1, 77–78 (1993) (stating that, as of 1993, a majority of jurisdictions ignore or circumvent *Jackson*).

114. Clinicians who work at state treatment facilities, if honest, must concede that restoration should take no longer than six months, an expert opinion that should be extremely helpful evidence to a defense attorney seeking release of an inappropriately detained client. In my conversations with state hospital employees in Florida over the past twenty years, however, I have been told repeatedly that defense attorneys tend to forget about clients who have been hospitalized, and that these attorneys, as well as prosecutors and courts, often ignore reports from hospital staff to the effect that the defendant is restored, especially in serious cases.

115. See generally *Treating the Homeless: Urban Psychiatry's Challenge,* ed. Billy E. Jones (1986).

116. See Uphoff, "The Role of the Defense Attorney," 108 n. 175.

117. Ibid., 88, 91–92.

118. Ibid., 101.

119. See Samuel Jan Brakel et al., *The Mentally Disabled and the Law* (1985), tbl. 12.6, col. 8 (1985) (reporting that, as of 1985, the federal government, the District of Columbia and over twenty states enforce such a ban). In Estelle v.

Smith, 451 U.S. 454 (1981), the Supreme Court strongly suggested that if such protection is not provided, state evaluators must afford those subjected to competency to stand trial evaluations a right to remain silent, which is hardly conducive to a useful evaluation. Ibid., 467–469.

120. Winick, "Reforming Competency to Stand Trial," 581–582.

121. At certain points in his original article on the topic, Winick seemed willing to endorse a competency test akin to the preference standard. See Winick, "Incompetency to Stand Trial," 271. But in later work he reiterated that he would require defendants to meet a test similar to the basic rationality standard. See Winick, "Reforming Competency to Stand Trial," 597.

122. Defense attorneys raise the competency issue far too often, although perhaps unnecessary motions are fewer in number today than a few decades ago. Steven K. Hoge et al., "Attorney-Client Decisionmaking in Criminal Cases: Client Competence and Participation as Perceived by Their Attorneys," 10 *Behavioral Science and Law* 385, 392 (1992). Some of these referrals are "unnecessary" only in the sense that the attorneys are applying a too rigorous competency standard, for which they can hardly be faulted, given the confusion over the correct standard. But many referrals occur for entirely inappropriate reasons. See Melton et al., *Psychological Evaluations for the Courts,* 70–71.

123. See ABA, *Model Rules,* Rules 3.1 (Meritorious Claims and Contentions) and 3.3 (Candor Toward the Tribunal).

124. See Winick, "Reforming Competency to Stand Trial," 615–618.

125. Note that the attorney still could raise the competency issue in these two situations out of a desire to determine whether the client's competency is restorable or because the client vehemently disagrees with the attorney and the attorney feels compelled to let the court know about the disagreement.

126. For discussion of these two approaches, see David A. Binder et al., *Lawyers as Counselors: A Client-Centered Approach* (1991), 16–19.

127. 463 U.S. 745 (1983).

128. Ibid., 751.

129. Ibid., 743 n.6 ("With the exception of these specified fundamental decisions, an attorney's duty is to take professional responsibility for the conduct of the case, after consulting with his client.").

130. 466 U.S. 668 (1984).

131. Ibid., 691.

132. Ibid., 690.

133. 422 U.S. 806 (1975).

134. Ibid., 834.

135. Ibid., 820.

136. Ibid., 820–821.

137. ABA, *Model Code*, Disciplinary Rule 7–101(B)(1).

138. ABA, *Model Rules*, Rule 1.2 comment [1].

139. ABA, *Standards for Criminal Justice* (1992), Standard 4–5.2. See also *Restatement (Third) of the Law Governing Lawyers* § 33 (Proposed Final Draft No. 1, Mar. 29, 1996) (reserving to the client the decisions on pleading, waiving jury trial, testifying, and appeal). Unlike the ABA Standards, the Restatement allows the client to cede the authority to control these decisions to counsel. Ibid., § 32(1).

140. See Rodney J. Uphoff and Peter B. Wood, "The Allocation of Decisionmaking Between Defense Counsel and Criminal Defendant: An Empirical Study of Attorney-Client Decisionmaking," 47 *University of Kansas Law Review* 1, 39 table 5 (1998).

141. Ibid.

142. See David S. Cohn, "Offensive Use of the Insanity Defense: Imposing the Insanity Defense Over the Defendant's Objection," 15 *Hastings Constitutional Law Quarterly* 295, 299–301 and n.31 (1988). Most recent cases considering the issue—in the context of whether the client has a Sixth Amendment ineffective assistance claim when counsel overrides a decision about the insanity defense—have held that the client controls the decision. See Jacobs v. Commonwealth, 870 S.W.2d 412, 418 (Ky. 1994); Treece v. State, 547 A.2d 1054, 1062 (Md. 1988). But see Robert D. Miller et al., "Forcing the Insanity Defense on Unwilling Defendants: Best Interests and the Dignity of the Law," 24 *Journal of Psychology and Law* 487, 504 (1996) (reporting, based on a survey of state attorneys general, that the insanity defense can be raised over the defendant's objection or without the defendant's knowledge in seventeen states).

143. See State v. Jones, 811 P.2d 757, 773 (Cal. 1991); State v. Samuel, 838 P.2d 1374, 1382 (Haw. 1992).

144. See William Booth, "Kaczynski Is Competent For Trial, Lawyers Agree," *Washington Post*, Jan. 21, 1998, at A1 ("Burrell has stated in court that Kaczynski's attorneys are 'in control' of his mental health defense. . . .").

145. See State v. Frierson, 705 P.2d 396, 403–404 (Cal. 1985).

146. Compare Zagorski v. State, 983 S.W.2d 654, 658 (Tenn. 1998) and People v. Hattery, 488 N.E.2d 513, 519 (Ill. 1985), with People v. Deere, 710 P.2d 925, 931 (Cal. 1985) and State v. Hightower, 518 A.2d 482, 483 (N.J. Super. Ct. App. Div. 1986). See generally Richard J. Bonnie, "The Dignity of the Condemned," 74 *Virginia Law Review* 1363, 1380–1389 (1988).

147. See Uphoff and Wood, "An Empirical Study of Attorney-Client Decisionmaking," 39 table 5.

148. Richard Bonnie et al., "Decision-Making in Criminal Defense: An Empirical Study of Insanity Pleas and the Impact of Doubted Client Competence," 87 *Journal Criminal Law and Criminology* 48, 57 (1996). Most of the defendants in this study were "non-objecting;" nonetheless, the results indicate attorney willingness to neglect client desires. See also Justine A. Dunlap, "What's Competence Got to Do With It?: The Right Not to Be Acquitted by Reason of Insanity," 50 *Oklahoma Law Review* 495, 523–527 (1997) (describing cases in which defendants were acquitted by reason of insanity while incompetent to proceed).

149. 346 F.2d 812 (D.C. Cir.), cert. denied, 382 U.S. 862 (1965).

150. Id. at 818 (Bazelon, J., dissenting). Judge Bazelon later suggested a reconsideration of *Whalem,* see United States v. Robertson, 507 F.2d 1148, 1161 (D.C. Cir. 1974), but subsequently strongly affirmed it. See United States v. Wright, 627 F.2d 1300, 1311–1312 (D.C. Cir. 1980).

151. In Lynch v. Overholser, 369 U.S. 705 (1962), the Supreme Court held that when the insanity defense is judicially imposed the state may not criminally commit the defendant. See Ibid., 711–712. But *Lynch* still permits civil commitment, and in any event rested solely on a construction of the relevant statutes. Ibid.

152. See Frendak v. United States, 408 A.2d 364, 376–378 (D.C. Cir. 1979). See generally Cohn, "Offensive Use of the Insanity Defense," 312–313 (reviewing possible motivations for rejecting an insanity defense).

153. See *Wright,* 627 F.2d, 1310 and nn. 72–73. This latter scenario is to be distinguished from the situation in which a defendant claims innocence but wants to plead guilty for strategic reasons (i.e., fear of a longer sentence if convicted at trial). See, for example, North Carolina v. Alford, 400 U.S. 25, 37 (1970).

154. *Wright,* 627 F.2d, 1310.

155. See Cohn, "Offense Use of the Insanity Defense," 311–312.

156. Only a few states have abolished the insanity defense. See Chapter 2.

157. See Andrew E. Taslitz, "A Feminist Approach to Social Scientific Evidence: Foundations," 5 *Michigan Journal of Gender and the Law* 1, 12–27 (1998).

158. Nationwide, the defense is successful in only one-quarter of the cases in which it is raised, and over 70 percent of these "successful" acquittals represent cases in which the prosecution agreed that the defendant was so "crazy" there was no need to prosecute. See Melton et al., *Psychological Evaluation for the Courts,* 188 (summarizing studies). One study indicates: "the only defendant who will

likely be found universally insane is the totally mad individual who acts impulsively in response to a glaring psychotic process that is itself tied thematically to a criminal action . . . *Even with respect to such a prototypically insane person,* however, the concept of guilt still has appeal to the lay public." Caton F. Roberts et al., "Implicit Theories of Criminal Responsibility: Decision Making and the Insanity Defense," 11 *Law and Human Behavior* 207, 226 (1987) (emphasis added).

159. See Woodson v. North Carolina, 428 U.S. 280 (1976); Lockett v. Ohio, 438 U.S. 586, 604 (1978).

160. See Ralph Reisner et al., *Law and the Mental Health System: Civil and Criminal Aspects* 573 (4th ed. 2004); Bethea v. United States, 365 A.2d 64, 85–86 (D.C. App. 1976).

161. See, e.g., Model Penal Code (1962), § 4.02 cmt. 2 ("If states of mind [such as deliberation or premeditation] are accorded legal significance, psychiatric evidence should be admissible when relevant to prove or disprove their existence to the same extent as any other relevant evidence."); ABA, *Mental Health Standards,* Standard 7–6.2 comment (finding such a rule required by "logical relevance").

162. For instance, as Chapter 2 noted, in virtually all cases in which the jury finds the defendant was insane, the defendant intended to commit the criminal act.

163. See People v. Wetmore, 583 P.2d 1308, 1310 (Cal. 1978). The California Supreme Court stated that if a diminished capacity defense results in acquittal because there is no lesser included offense "the state's remedy is to institute civil commitment proceedings." Ibid.

164. Still another reason is that mental state defenses explicitly admit that the defendant committed the crime, thus "increasing the likelihood of conviction if unsuccessful." Anne C. Singer, "The Imposition of the Insanity Defense on an Unwilling Defendant," 41 *Ohio State Law Journal* 637, 668 (1980).

165. See Peter Arenella, "Rethinking the Functions of Criminal Procedure: The Warren and Burger Courts' Competing Ideologies," 72 *Georgetown Law Journal* 185, 197–202 (1983).

166. See Nancy Jean King, "Priceless Process: Negotiable Features of Criminal Litigation," 47 *UCLA Law Review* 113, 170 (1999).

167. See Illinois v. Allen, 397 U.S. 337, 343 (1970) (holding that the right to be present in courtroom may be forfeited if, after being warned, the defendant continues to act "in a manner so disorderly, disruptive, and disrespectful of the court that his trial cannot be carried on with him in the courtroom.").

168. See Chandler v. Florida, 449 U.S. 560, 575 (1981) (holding that the news media may be removed from the courtroom if its presence "compromised the ability of the particular jury . . . to adjudicate fairly"); Richmond Newspapers, Inc. v. Virginia, 448 U.S. 555, 581 (1980) (holding that the right of the public to attend trials may be curtailed by "overriding" interests, such as the need to assure quiet and orderly trials).

169. The Court has repeatedly stated that "death is different" with respect to society's need to ensure reliable determinations. See California v. Ramos, 463 U.S. 992, 998–999 (1983).

170. Bonnie argues for the same position, in part because, even if precluded from directing the defense, the "recalcitrant defendant could still effectively preclude the development and presentation of evidence essential to a 'reliable' decision regarding the suitability of a death sentence." Bonnie, "Death with Dignity," 1387. This type of defendant has in fact autonomously chosen the death penalty, or at least chosen to forego trial on the issue. I am not sure, however, that Moran fit this category. Contrary to the assumption in the text, I think he probably would not have tried to help *or* hurt his defense. Compare him to the defendant in People v. Bloom, 774 P.2d 698 (Cal. 1989): "Defendant stated that he did not want to put on a defense, that it would be 'counterproductive' to do so because he did not 'intend spending the rest of [his] natural life in some institution,' and that if granted self-representation he would help the prosecution obtain a death verdict and would address the jury and 'seek the death penalty.'" Ibid., 709–710.

171. For discussion of the issues, see Melton et al., *Psychological Evaluations for the Courts,* 130–133.

172. 406 U.S. 715 (1972).

173. See Ibid., 723–730.

174. Ibid., 738.

175. See Morris and Meloy, "Out of Mind? Out of Sight," 9–10.

176. See Robert Burt and Norval Morris, "A Proposal for the Abolition of the Incompetency Plea," 40 *University of Chicago Law Review* 66, 76 (1972); see also ABA, *Mental Health Standards,* Standard 7–4.13 (providing that incompetent defendants charged with minor crimes be released or civilly committed, and that those charged with serious felonies be tried and, if convicted, committed under provisions identical to those used for insanity acquittees).

177. 521 U.S. 346 (1997).

178. Thomas R. Litwack, "The Competency of Criminal Defendants to Refuse, for Delusional Reasons, a Viable Insanity Defense Recommended by Counsel," 21 *Behavioral Science and Law* 135, 154 (2003).

179. One means of providing a check on the lawyer in this situation would be to require the lawyer to confer with another attorney, analogous to the "second opinion" requirement in medical practice. See Bonnie, Beyond *Dusky* and *Drope*, 584.

7.   Treatment Decision Making

1. Even when no particular treatment is contemplated, deprivation of liberty may be necessary for effective treatment. See generally Browning Hoffman and Lawrence Foust, "Least Restrictive Treatment of the Mentally Ill: A Doctrine in Search of Its Senses," 14 *San Diego Law Review* 1100, 1141 (1977).

2. For one of the most comprehensive works on this subject, see Bruce Winick, *The Right to Refuse Mental Health Treatment* (1997).

3. For a comparison of the two generations of drugs and a discussion of the possible legal consequences of recent advances in psychiatric medicine, see Douglas Mossman, "Unbuckling the 'Chemical Straitjacket': The Legal Significance of Recent Advances in the Pharmacological Treatment of Psychosis," 39 *San Diego Law Review* 1033 (2002).

4. See, for example, Khiem v. United States, 612 A.2d 160, 168 (D.C. Ct.App. 1992) ("most of the courts which have been asked to do so have upheld the involuntary administration of psychotropic drugs to restore or maintain a defendant's competency to stand trial"). See also United States v. Charters, 863 F.2d 302, 304–306 (4th Cir. 1988).

5. 539 U.S. 166 (2003).

6. See, for example, Rogers v. Commissioner, 390 Mass. 489, 458 N.E.2d 308 (1983).

7. See, for example, Rennie v. Klein, 653 F.2d 836 (3d Cir. 1981).

8. 494 U.S. 210 (1990).

9. Ibid., 226.

10. 406 U.S. 715 (1972).

11. 494 U.S., 248 n. 16 (Stevens, J., dissenting). The doctor's report went on to suggest that the medication may have "exacerbated" the psychosis. Ibid.

12. Ibid., 240.

13. Ibid., 239.

14. Ibid., 248 ("Harper's own record reveals that administrative segregation and standard disciplinary sanctions were frequently imposed on him over and above forced medication").

15. Ibid., 249.

16. 504 U.S. 127 (1992).

17. Ibid., 135.

18. Ibid., 138.

19. Some writers and courts have expressed concern that juries are less likely to consider an insanity claim credible if the defendant is medicated and thus exudes "sanity." See, for example, State v. Hayes, 118 N.H. 458, 389 A.2d 1379 (1978). Of course, if left unmedicated in order to simulate the alleged mental state at the time of the offense, the defendant will be unable to communicate with counsel at trial and there is no guarantee that the simulation will even approximate the individual's mental state at the time of the offense. Juries are presumably capable of understanding and incorporating into their decision expert testimony that the defendant's present mental state has been altered by treatment. A videotape of the defendant in an unmedicated state would also be admissible and, if made shortly after the offense, would be much less misleading than the demeanor of an unmedicated defendant at trial.

20. Robert Miller et al., "The Right to Refuse Treatment in a Forensic Patient Population: Six-Month Review," 17 *Bulletin of American Academy of Psychiatry and Law* 107 (1989).

21. 539 U.S., 180.

22. Ibid.

23. Ibid.

24. Ibid., 181–182.

25. Ibid., 184–185.

26. See, for example, John Petrila et al., "Preliminary Observations from an Evaluation of the Broward County Florida Mental Health Court," 37 *Court Review* 14 (2001) (describing the creation of mental health courts in twenty-five jurisdictions, designed to divert people with mental illness out of the criminal justice system into mental health treatment).

27. 539 U.S., 180.

28. See Grant H. Morris and J. Reid Meloy, "Out of Mind? Out of Sight: The Uncivil Commitment of Permanently Incompetent Criminal Defendants," 27 *University of California, Davis Law Review* 1, 77–78 (1993).

29. T. Howard Stone, "Therapeutic Implications of Incarceration for Persons with Severe Mental Disorders: Searching for Rational Health Policy," 24 *American Journal of Criminal Law* 283, 292–293 (1997) ("many persons with mental disorders are charged with misdemeanors or other minor offenses just to get them off the streets and as a means of obtaining mental health treatment that is not available in a civil, as opposed to a criminal, setting").

30. United States v. Weston, 255 F.3d 873, 882 (D.C. Cir. 2001).

31. 593 U.S., 182–183.

32. 494 U.S., 215 n. 3.

33. See in particular Joel Feinberg, *Harm to Self* (1986). I have defended the so-called predicted deterioration standard for civil commitment, assuming the state can show the person's history demonstrates a failure to conform to a specified treatment regiment when left unsupervised and that the absence of treatment results in violent behavior, and assuming further that people so committed are eligible for automatic release after a certain time period (unless their dangerousness becomes imminent while they are committed). See Christopher Slobogin, "Involuntary Community Treatment of People Who Are Violent and Mentally Ill: A Legal Analysis," 45 *Hospital and Community Psychiatry* 685, 687 (1994).

34. 422 U.S. 563, 575 (1975).

35. Ibid., 583 (Burger, C. J., concurring).

36. 441 U.S. 418, 426 (1979).

37. 539 U.S., 183.

38. Ralph Reisner, Christopher Slobogin, and Arti Rai, *Law and the Mental Health System: Civil and Criminal Aspects* (4th ed. 2004), 742.

39. Kenneth Kress, "Is Competency Competent?" paper presented at conference on Competency to Consent to Treatment and/or Research: Legal and Psychiatric Dimensions, University of Southern California Law School, April 17, 2004.

40. See Grant H. Morris, "Judging Judgment: Assessing the Competence of Mental Patients to Refuse Treatment," 32 *San Diego Law Review* 343 (1995) (finding that during treatment competence hearings "[m]ost psychiatrists equated incompetence with either their finding of mental disorder or the patient's unwillingness to acknowledge mental disorder" and that "[w]hen psychiatrists made a professional judgment that a medication was medically appropriate to treat the patient's disorder, they often viewed any patient objections as irrational").

41. Elyn R. Saks, "Competency to Refuse Treatment," 69 *North Carolina Law Review* 945, 988–992 (1991).

42. Ibid., 990–991.

43. Ibid., 988. See also Elyn R. Saks, *Refusing Care: Forced Treatment and the Rights of the Mentally Ill* (2002), 190–191.

44. See, for example, Conservatorship of Waltz, 227 Cal. Rptr. 436 (Ct. App. 1986); Lillian F. v. Superior Court. 206 Cal. Rptr. 603 (Ct. App. 1984).

45. See, for example, Loren Roth et al., "Tests of Competency to Consent to Treatment," 134 *American Journal of Psychiatry* 279, 283 (1977); Bruce Winick,

"Competency to Consent to Voluntary Hospitalization: A Therapeutic Jurisprudence Analysis of Zinermon v. Burch," 14 *International Journal of Law and Psychiatry* 168, 191–198 (1991). Although Saks at one time espoused a one-competency standard regime similar to the one proposed here, she has since concluded that for "extremely consequential or risky decisions," an easier-to-meet "impairment" standard is warranted. Saks, *Refusing Care*, 197–200.

46. Robert Farr, "A Mental Health Program for the Mentally Ill in the Los Angeles Skid Row Area," in *Treating the Homeless: Urban Psychiatry's Challenge*, ed. Billy E. Jones (1986), 71 (describing research finding the vast majority of homeless people in Los Angeles "would rather live in filth and be subjected to beatings and violence than to be institutionalized even in our finest mental hospitals").

47. Harold I. Kaplan and Benjamin J. Sadock, *Synopsis of Psychiatry*, 8th ed. (1996), 2520 (reporting studies showing that modern "stereotactic" psychosurgery procedures bring benefits for 25 to 70 percent of those treated—generally people with depression and anxiety disorders—with about 25 percent showing "outstanding improvement").

48. Cf. Aden v. Younger, 57 Cal.App. 3d 6622, 129 Cal. Rptr. 535 (4th Dist. 1976) (discussing and generally approving legislation that requires a panel of doctors must find that the patient has the capacity to consent to psychosurgery and electroconvulsive therapy).

49. See Benedict Carey, "Study Finds Little Advantage in New Schizophrenia Drugs," *New York Times*, Sept. 20, 2005, F1 ("A landmark government-financed study that compared drugs used to treat schizophrenia has confirmed what many psychiatrists long suspected: newer drugs that are highly promoted and widely prescribed offer few—if any—benefits over older medicines that sell for a fraction of the cost"); Sheldon Gelman, "Looking Backward: The Twentieth Century Revolutions in Psychiatry, Law, and Public Mental Health," 29 *Ohio Northern University Law Review* 531, 541–544 (2003) (arguing that larger studies show "the newer drugs do not appear more effective than older drugs overall," and that the lesser side effects of the newer drugs might be mostly attributable to the fact that they are administered in more moderate dosages).

50. Roth et al., "Tests of Competency," 279.

51. The part of the study relevant here is found primarily in Paul S. Appelbaum and Thomas Grisso, "The MacArthur Treatment Competence Study, I: Mental Illness and Competence to Consent to Treatment," 19 *Law and Human Behavior* 105, 113 (1995), and Thomas Grisso et al., "The MacArthur Treatment Competence Study, II: Measures of Abilities Related to Competence to Con-

sent to Treatment," 19 *Law and Human Behavior* 127, 130–131 (1995). Also an important source on the group's approach to treatment competency is Thomas Grisso and Paul S. Appelbaum. "A Comparison of Standards for Assessing Patients Capacities to Make Treatment Decisions," 152 *American Journal of Psychiatry* 1033 (1995).

52. Grisso et al., "Competence Study II," 133.

53. For instance, the instrument the MacArthur group has devised to evaluate competency to stand trial seems to adopt an approach close to the basic rationality test advocated here. See S. Kenneth Hoge et al., "The MacArthur Adjudicative Competence Study: Development and Validation of a Research Instrument," 21 *Law and Human Behavior* 141 (1997).

54. Paul S. Appelbaum and Thomas Grisso, *Manual for Perceptions of Disorder* (1992), 6–7.

55. Saks, *Refusing Care*, 191.

56. Even laboratory research, using the refined criteria of the DSM-IV, was able to obtain a reliability rate of only 81 percent for schizophrenia; field studies produced a reliability rate of 41 percent. See, for example, Paul Lieberman and Frances M. Baker, "The Reliability of Psychiatric Diagnosis in the Emergency Room," 36 *Hospital and Community Psychiatry* 291 (1985).

57. See generally Judi Chamberlin, "The Ex-Patient's Movement," 11 *Journal of Mind and Behavior* 324 (1990); Michael Perlin, "On Sanism," 46 *Southern Methodist Law Review* 373 (1992).

58. For instance, one study found that doctors' answers ranged from .20 to .80 when asked to give a numerical probability equivalent for the term "moderate," from .30 to .95 for the term "probably," and from .10 to .80 for the term "sometimes." G. D. Bryant and G. R. Norman, "Expressions of Probability: Words and Numbers," 302 *New England Journal of Medicine* 411 (1980). As an aside, even if the BPRS can be reliably administered, a score of 40, the cutoff that defines severe symptoms under the NOD, may be too low as an "objective" measure. The BPRS has eighteen items, like those noted in the text, which are rated on a scale of 1 to 7 (1 = not present, 4 = moderate, and 7 = extremely severe). To obtain a score of 40 would require a rating of only 4 (that is, moderate) on eight of these items and a "not present" rating on the other ten (for a total of 42), which hardly seems indicative of severe symptomatology under any regime.

59. Cf. Loren Roth and Paul Appelbaum et al., "The Dilemma of Denial in the Assessment of Competency to Refuse Treatment," 139 *American Journal of Psychiatry* 910 (1982).

60. Appelbaum & Grisso, Manual for Perceptions of Disorder, 14.

61. See Xavier F. Amador and Andrew A. Shiva, "Insight into Schizophrenia: Anosognosia, Competency, and Civil Liberties," 11 *George Mason Civil Rights Law Journal* 25, 26–39 (2000).

62. Grisso et al., "Competence Study II," 133 (table 1).

63. Maya Bar-Hillel, "Base-Rate Fallacy in Probability Judgments," 44 *Acta Psychologica* 211 (1980); Eugene Borgida and Nancy Brekke, "The Base-Rate Fallacy in Attribution and Prediction," in *New Directions in Attribution Research,* ed. John H. Harvey et al. (1981), 63.

64. Sarah Lichtenstein et al., "Judged Frequency of Lethal Events," 4 *Journal of Experimental Psychology: Human Learning and Memory* 551 (1978).

65. W. C. Thompson, "Psychological Issues in Informed Consent," in *Making Health Care Decisions,* vol. 3 (1982), 85.

66. *POD Manual,* 50–53.

67. The survey involved fifty-three law students (none of whom had taken a mental health law course) on the first day of a social science in law course. Twenty-six students were given a hypothetical involving an angina patient who refused medication after being told it had a 90 percent success rate, and twenty-seven were given the same hypothetical for a person with schizophrenia. Each group was then asked which, if any, of the eight reasons listed in the text would be indicative of incompetency. A significant majority of students in both groups found the patient "competent" regardless of the reason given (although the patient with schizophrenia was more likely to be found incompetent than the patient with angina). For the twenty-seven students given the mentally ill person condition, the number of incompetency findings associated with the eight reasons listed in the text (in the same order) were as follows: 0, 4, 7, 6, 9, 10, 4, and 2. For the twenty-six students given the angina patient condition, the analogous results were 0, 2, 5, 1, 5, 4, 0, 1.

68. Grisso et al., "Competence Study II," 132.

69. Although the interviewer is instructed to ask the patient whether he or she is worried about side effects, *POD Manual,* 43, the answer to this question "do[es] not contribute to any POD subscale." Ibid., 58.

70. This observation comes from Grant Morris. As he puts it, "even if a patient does not objectively affirm the symptoms of his or her disorder, continued questioning is warranted to assure that the patient's statements demonstrate an inability to recognize symptoms, rather than a conscious refusal to do so." Letter from Grant Morris to Christopher Slobogin (March 20, 1996).

71. Morris, "Judging Judgment," 408–422 (table 8).

72. Compare Bruce J. Winick, "The Right to Refuse Mental Health Treatment: A First Amendment Perspective," 44 *University of Miami Law Review* 1, 72 (1996), with Darold Treffert, "The Practical Limits of Patients' Rights," 5 *Psychiatric Annals* 4 (1975).

73. Margie Patlak, "Schizophrenia: Real Lives, Imaginary Terror," 31(6) *FDA Consumer* 23 (1997). See generally Gelman, "Looking Backward," 534 (stating that "little evidence indicates that medicated patients—even the majority who respond favorably—enjoy better lifetime outcomes than patients experienced before drugs, or that medicated patients' quality of life has improved").

74. See Richard Rogers and Christopher Webster, "Assessing Treatability in Mentally Disordered Offenders," 13 *Law and Human Behavior* 19, 20–21 (1989) (finding that involuntary patients have a poorer prognosis than cooperative patients); Bruce Winick, "Coercion and Mental Health Treatment," 74 *Denver Law Review* 1145, 1159–1166 (1997).

75. For this reason, Saks has proposed that the state should be able to forcibly treat a competent individual after the first "break," so that the individual has more information about the effects of the treatment. Saks, *Refusing Care*, 56–68. I can tentatively subscribe to this proposal because, consistent with Millsian philosophy, it provides people with information about feelings, thoughts, and behavior about being medicated that they could not otherwise have, and thus should improve their subsequent decision making. But, aside from this "first bite at the apple" exception, the comments in the text stand.

76. Robert Rosenheck et al., "A Comparison of Clozapine and Haloperidol in Hospitalized Patients with Refractory Schizophrenia," 337 *New England Journal of Medicine* 809, 812 (1997) (in a study conducted at Veterans Administration facilities, the per capita pharmacy cost of clozapine was $3,199 a year).

77. See Mary Durham and John Q. LaFond. "The Empirical Consequences and Policy Implications of Broadening the Statutory Criteria for Civil Commitment," 3 *Yale Law and Policy Review* 395, 401 (1985).

78. See Alexander Brooks, "The Right to Refuse Antipsychotic Medication: Law and Policy," 39 *Rutgers Law Review* 339 (1987).

79. See John Monahan et al., "From Coercion to Contract: Reframing the Debate on Mandated Community Treatment for People with Mental Disorders," 29 *Law and Human Behavior* 485, 488–489 (2005).

80. Ibid.

81. John Stuart Mill, *On Liberty* (1859), ed. Elizabeth Rapaport (1978), 101. See also Michael Sandel, *Liberalism and the Limits of Justice* (1982), 175–183.

82. Philip Cushman, *Constructing the Self, Constructing America* (1995), 26–33 (arguing that different social conditions generate different forms of "mental illness").

83. J. L. Hill, "The Five Faces of Freedom in American Political and Constitutional Thought," 45 *Boston College Law Review* 499, 549 (2004).

84. It is well established in criminal law that consent is not a defense to serious crime, outside of the athletic context and the charge of rape. See, for example, Model Penal Code §2.11(2).

85. See David Shapiro, "Courts, Legislatures, and Paternalism," 74 *Virginia Law Review* 519, 519–520 (1988).

8.   Rethinking Legally Relevant Mental Disorder

1. Children under the age of seven have an infancy defense. See Wayne R. LaFave, *Criminal Law* (3d ed. 2000), 424, 467, 474. The duress defense is available to nonmentally ill adults but is based on external threats rather than "internal" volitional impairment. Ibid., 467.

2. Foucha v. Louisiana, 504 U.S. 71, 83 (1992) (White, J., plurality opinion).

3. See Gary B. Melton et al., *Psychological Evaluations for the Court: A Handbook for Mental Health Professionals and Lawyers* (2d ed. 1997), 340–341 ("Many state [guardianship] statutes . . . require findings of a threshold status [for example, mental illness, idiocy, and senility]").

4. Kansas v. Hendricks, 521 U.S. 346, 359 (1997).

5. *DMS-IV-TR*, xxiii.

6. Donald H. J. Hermann, *The Insanity Defense: Philosophical, Historical and Legal Perspectives* (1983), 129.

7. Model Penal Code §4.01(1) (1962).

8. LaFave, *Criminal Law*, 331.

9. Model Penal Code §4.01(2) (1962).

10. LaFave, *Criminal Law*, 351 (stating that "most" ALI states include this paragraph).

11. See, for example, Me. Rev. Stat. Ann. tit. 17, § 39; see also Conn. Gen. Stat. Ann. § 53a-13.

12. 18 U.S.C. §17. The legislative history states the word was used to exclude "nonpsychotic behavior disorders or neuroses such as an 'inadequate personality,' 'immature personality,' or a pattern of 'antisocial tendencies.'" S. Rep. No. 98-225, at 229 (1983).

13. United States v. Lyons, 731 F.2d 243, 247 (5th Cir. 1984) (stating that drug addiction is not a mental disease unless it causes "actual drug-induced or drug-

aggravated psychosis, or physical damage to the brain or nervous system"); Thompson v. Commonwealth, 70 S.E.2d 284, 292 (Va. 1952) ("Frenzy arising solely from the passion of anger and jealousy, regardless of how furious, is not insanity").

14. Mich. Com Laws Ann. §330.1400(g).

15. See, for example, DSM-IV-TR, 634 (stating that people with paranoid personality disorder "often feel that they have been deeply and irreversibly injured by another person or persons even when there is no objective evidence for this"); Ibid., 645 (describing symptoms of "schizotypal personality disorder" to include "odd beliefs or magical thinking," and "unusual perceptual experiences, including bodily illusions"); Ibid., 651 (noting that "[d]uring periods of extreme stress," people with borderline personality disorder can experience "transient paranoid ideation or dissociative symptoms").

16. People v. Doan, 366 N.W.2d 593, 597–598 (Mich. Ct. App. 1984) (interpreting the language of the Michigan insanity statute to permit a defense based on nonpsychotic disorder and stating that "mental impairment due to any cause, physical or purely psychological, may form the basis for a finding of mental illness").

17. See Michigan State Bar Standing Comm. on Standard Jury Instructions, *Michigan Criminal Jury Instructions* §7.12, 2d ed. (2003 Supp.) (definition of guilty but mentally ill).

18. See Mich. Com Laws Ann. §768.36(3) (stating that a person found guilty but mentally ill shall be sentenced to "any sentence that could be imposed by law upon a defendant who is convicted of the same offense").

19. See Melton et al., *Psychological Evaluations*, 307.

20. Ibid.

21. See Addington v. Texas, 441 U.S. 418, 426 (1979).

22. 521 U.S. 346 (1997).

23. Ibid., 358.

24. See DSM-IV-TR, 646. People with antisocial personality disorder tend to make decisions "on the spur of the moment, without forethought, and without consideration for the consequences to self or others," display "a pattern of impulsivity" and "a reckless disregard to the safety of themselves or others," and also tend to be "consistently and extremely irresponsible." Ibid.

25. Kansas v. Crane, 534 U.S. 407, 413 (2002); *Hendricks*, 521 U.S., 358.

26. The Supreme Court itself recognized this fact in *Crane*, 534 U.S., 412, where it stated that the dangerous-beyond-control "distinction is necessary lest 'civil commitment' become a 'mechanism for retribution or general deterrence'—

functions properly those of criminal law, not civil commitment," and then cited Reid Moran, "The Epidemiology of Antisocial Personality Disorder," 34 *Social Psychiatry and Psychiatric Epidemiology* (1999), 234, for the proposition that 40 to 60 percent of the male prison population is diagnosable with antisocial personality disorder.

27. See Janine DeFao, "Jerry Brown's About-Face on Criminal Sentencing," *San Francisco Chronicle*, February 18, 2003, A1 ("[S]eventy-one percent of California's inmates land back in prison within eighteen months").

28. A Westlaw search, conducted in March 2005, of cases that include the terms "definition" and "mental" produced more than eight hundred decisions, more than two-thirds of which deal with the definition of mental abnormality in sex offender commitment cases.

29. Converse v. Dep't of Children and Families, 823 So. 2d at 295, 297 (Fla. Ct. App. 2002); In re Civil Commitment of Ramey, 648 N.W.2d 260, 266–267 (Minn. Ct. App. 2002); Thomas v. State, 74 S.W.3d 789, 790 (Mo. 2002).

30. People v. Wollschlager, 122 Cal. Rptr. 2d 171, 174 (Ct. App. 2002); In re Luckabaugh, 568 S.E.2d 338, 348 (S.C. 2002); In re Laxton, 647 N.W.2d 784, 793–795 (Wisc. 2002).

31. See, e.g., Cal. Penal Code §§ 2960–2981 (permitting commitment of people who have a severe mental disorder that is not in remission and cannot be kept in remission without treatment and who represent a substantial danger of physical harm to others).

32. See generally Melton et al., *Psychological Evaluations*, 309–310.

33. See Robert Schopp, *Competence, Condemnation, and Commitment* (2001), 82; Note, "Developments in the Law—Civil Commitment of the Mentally Ill," 87 *Harvard Law Review* 1190, 1212–1217 (1974).

34. Addington v. Texas, 441 U.S. 418, 426 (1979).

35. DSM-IV-TR, 243.

36. Ibid., 416–417 (characterized by persistent fear of one or more social situations).

37. See Robert Farr, "A Mental Health Program for the Mentally Ill in the Los Angeles Skid Row Area," in *Treating the Homeless: Urban Psychiatry's Challenge*, Billy E. Jones ed. (1986), 71.

38. Thomas Grisso and Paul Appelbaum, "Abilities of Patients to Consent to Psychiatric and Medical Treatments," 19 *Law and Human Behavior* 149, 171 (1995) (reporting research that found that, regardless of how competency is defined, only 52 percent of patients with schizophrenia showed impairment).

39. See, for example, Cal. Welf. and Inst. Code §5008(h)(1) (defining gravely disabled as "[a] condition in which a person, as a result of a mental disorder, is

unable to provide for his or her basic personal needs for food, clothing, or shelter"). Interestingly, Michigan has pretty much the same commitment criterion. See Mich. Laws Ann. §330.1401.

40. 362 U.S. 402 (1960).

41. See, for example, Fla. Stat. Ann. §916.12(2).

42. See Mont. Code Ann. §46–14–201(2).

43. See Durham v. United States, 214 F.2d 862 (D.C. Cir. 1954).

44. Stephen J. Morse, "A Preference for Liberty: The Case Against Involuntary Commitment of the Mentally Disordered," 70 *California Law Review* 54, 60 (1982).

45. See Cal. Penal Code §§ 2960–2981.

46. See Darold A. Treffert, "The Obviously Ill Patient in Need of Treatment: A Fourth Standard for Civil Commitment," 36 *Hospital and Community Psychiatry* 259 (1985).

47. Thomas Szasz, *Insanity: The Idea and Its Consequences* (1987), 249–250.

48. See Grant H. Morris, "Judging Judgment: Assessing the Competence of Mental Patients to Refuse Treatment," 32 *San Diego Law Review* 343, 432 (1995) (finding in a study of competency determinations that "[m]ost psychiatrists equated incompetence with either their finding of mental disorder or the patient's unwillingness to acknowledge mental disorder," and that psychiatrists "often viewed any patient objections [to proposed treatment] as irrational").

49. 509 U.S. 389 (1993).

50. Michael Moore, *Law and Psychiatry: Rethinking the Relationship* (1984), 100–108; Schopp, *Competence, Condemnation, and Commitment*, 165–166.

51. See, for example, Thomas Grisso et al., "The MacArthur Treatment Competence Study. II: Measures of Abilities Related to Competence to Consent to Treatment," 19 *Law and Human Behavior* 127, 134–136 (1995) (discussing a competency instrument that seeks to measure reasoning capacity by examining ability to seek information, generate and weigh consequences, and engage in consequential, comparative, complex, transitive, and probabilistic thinking).

52. Chapter 2 described the volitional tests for insanity, and Chapter 4 described the Supreme Court's "dangerous beyond control" predicate for civil commitment. The notion that incompetency is a form of volitional impairment is described in Ralph Reisner, Christopher Slobogin, and Arti Rai, *Law and the Mental Health System: Civil and Criminal Aspects* (4th ed. 2004), 895.

53. See, for example, Peter Arenella, "Convicting the Morally Blameless: Reassessing the Relationship Between Legal and Moral Accountability," 39 *U.C.L.A. Law Review* 1511, 1524 (1992).

54. See Karl Menninger, *The Crime of Punishment* (1968), 253–268. The product test for insanity announced in Durham v. United States, 214 F.2d 862, 875 (D.C. Cir. 1954), discussed in Chapter 2, is the best formal legal example of this approach.

55. See, for example, In re Boyer, 636 P.2d 1085, 1088–1089 (Utah 1981).

56. See generally Deborah Denno, "Crime and Consciousness: Science and Involuntary Acts," 87 *Minnesota Law Review* 269, 344–351 (2002).

57. Compare Pollard v. United States, 282 F.2d 450 (6th Cir. 1960) (reversing conviction of a police officer whose experts asserted he was insane because he was driven to commit a series of robberies by his unconscious desire to be punished for not protecting his wife and child, who were brutally murdered when he was not at home).

58. Consider these comments from Arenella, who argues for a character-based assessment of culpability but recognizes possible problems with this approach: "[S]houldn't we view moral agency on a continuum rather than as a bipolar 'all or nothing' determination? And, if we do, should not serious deficiencies in the actor's ability to exercise these moral capacities support a full excuse? If so, then evil could . . . turn out to be its own exemption." Arenella, "Convicting the Morally Blameless," 1613.

59. Moore, *Law and Psychiatry*, 100–108.

60. Melton et al., *Psychological Evaluations*, 196.

61. See, for example, DSM-IV-TR, 287 (stating that delusions in people with paranoid schizophrenia "may be multiple, but are usually organized around a coherent theme"); Ibid., 297 ("[A] common characteristic of individuals with Delusional Disorder is the apparent normality of their behavior and appearance when their delusional ideas are not being discussed or acted on").

62. See Morris, "Judging Judgment," 405–407 (documenting that patients whom psychiatrists thought were seriously disordered often refused medication because of side effects, and noting that such a reason "may be a rational basis to support a medication refusal").

63. Bruce J. Winick, "Reforming Competency to Stand Trial and Plead Guilty: A Restated Proposal and a Response to Professor Bonnie," 85 *Criminal Law and Criminology* 571, 581–582 (1995).

64. See Melton et al., *Psychological Evaluations*, 188–189 (reporting studies indicating that most people acquitted by reason of insanity spend as long or longer in the hospital than felons convicted of the same offense).

65. Grisso et al., "The MacArthur Treatment Competence Study," 139, 144 (indicating lower interrater reliability for the TRAT (Thinking Rationally about

Treatment) instrument than for the UTD (Understanding Treatment Disclosures), and concluding that, while "most subtests" in these two instruments and the POD (Perception of Disorder) instrument "can be scored reliably by nonprofessionals," certain TRAT subtests "may require special care and consideration"); see also Thomas Grisso and Paul Appelbaum, *Manual for Thinking Rationally About Treatment* (1993), 19 (reporting relatively low kappa correlations when TRAT was not scored by "master scorer").

66. Melton et al., *Psychological Evaluations* 44 (discussing potential for malingering in forensic assessments).

67. See Elyn Saks, *Refusing Care: Forced Treatment and the Rights of the Mentally Ill* (2002), 187 ("[M]any patients decide to accept treatment on the basis of an unconscious fantasy that their doctor is omnipotent and will protect them from all harm").

68. See Carol Christian, "New Witness Challenges Yates' Sanity," *Houston Chronicle*, March 6, 2002, available at www.Chron.com/cs.

69. Dep't Human Servs. v. Northern, 563 S.W.2d 197, 210 (Tenn. Ct. App. 1978).

70. See generally Bruce J. Winick, "Sex Offender Laws in the 1990s: A Therapeutic Jurisprudence Analysis," 4 *Psychology, Public Policy and Law* 505, 547 (1998) (discussing stigmatizing effects of "mentally ill" and "mentally abnormal" labels).

Index

Addington v. Texas, 149, 232

Allen, Francis, 167, 169, 170

Allen v. Illinois, 111–112

American Bar Association: resolution concerning capital cases, 64, 81–82, 88; rules regarding lawyer control over decision making, 205, 210–211; rules regarding commitment of unrestorable defendant, 362n176

American Psychiatric Association: resolution concerning capital cases, 64, 81–82; insanity test, 266–267; treatment of incompetent to be executed, 307n170. *See also* Diagnostic and Statistical Manual of Mental Disorders

American Psychological Association: resolution concerning capital cases, 64, 81–82

Anderson, David,161–162

Anti-psychotic medication: reasons not taken, 78–79; use in capital cases, 95; atypical medications, 223, 235; side effects, 225–226; authority to forcibly administer, 224–244; use in treating those who are a danger to others, 224–227; use in treating incompetent defendants, 227–230; use in treating those who are a danger to self, 231–233; competency to refuse, 233–244

Appelbaum, Paul, 236

Atkins v. Virginia: description, 64–68; criticism, 65–66, 83–87; implementation, 76; destigmatizing effect, 86–87

Attorneys, defense: decision to present mitigating evidence, 91; role in cases involving clients of questionable competency, 183–185, 205–219

Automatism defense, 135–136, 278n13

Barefoot v. Estelle, 111

Battered woman syndrome, 37, 288n142

Bazelon, David: insanity defense, 31, 36; authority to impose insanity defense, 212–213, 214

Bentham, Jeremy: rationale for deprivation of liberty, 10

Bersoff, Donald: criticism of *Atkins,* 84–86

Bethea v. United States, 110

Blackmun, Harry J.: opinion in *Godinez,* 189

Bonnie, Richard: insanity defense, 44, 56–57; coerced treatment in capital cases, 96; competency theory, 191–195, 198, 199, 220, 234; offender's control over capital sentencing, 362n170

Breyer, Stephen: opinion in *Sell,* 228, 230, 232

Brown, Darryl, 169

Burger, Warren, 232

City of Cleburne v. Cleburne Living Center, 68–70

Commitment, civil: for emotional harm, 116–117; police power commitment, 141, 253–254; definition of mental disorder, 253–254; incapacity as basis for, 254–255; parens patriae commitment, 254–255. *See also* Preventive detention

Competency to be executed: rationale, 92–95; restoration of competency, 95–97